taste of home.
MOST
requested
RECIPES

RECIPES READERS LOVE MOST!

Taste of Home editors receive countless letters from readers who sing the praises of their all-time favorite recipes. Online, the accolades continue among the TasteofHome.com web community where hundreds of popular dishes are highlighted.

With all this sharing, it seemed only natural to offer readers a one-stop-shop for all their tried-and-true, can't-live-without recipes. So we sifted through the dozens of letters and online comments to collect those treasured standbys readers can't seem to stop talking about and placed them into this brand-new cookbook, **Taste of Home Most Requested Recipes.**

We've packed 437 of these best-loved dishes into 10 scrumptious chapters, including Snacks & Appetizers, Breakfast & Brunch; Soups & Sandwiches; Sides, Salads & Breads; Main Dishes; Quick & Easy; and Desserts. Just one taste and you'll soon realize why Buffalo Chicken Dip (p. 48), Hamburger Noodle Casserole (p. 9), Seafood Lasagna (p. 20) and Chocolate Malted Cookies (p. 22) became reliable staples with families just like yours.

You'll also find unique chapters such as Editors' Favorites that showcase the recipes readers have written about or requested most often, as well as a few very special selections taken directly from our editors' personal recipe boxes. Guilt-Free Fare proves you can still eat healthy while enjoying comforting favorites such as Southwest Pasta Bake (p. 150) and luscious Frosted Mocha Cake (p. 147). Seasonal Selections features the very best dishes created especially for a specific season or holiday. Look for specialties such as Easter Bunny Bread (p. 184), Colossal Caramel Apple Trifle (p. 192) and Herbed Standing Rib Roast (p. 187).

Aside from hundreds of can't-fail recipes, you'll also find handy kitchen tips, convenient prep and cook times and helpful comments from TasteofHome.com community members. These "Readers' Raves" explain why a recipe is so popular, and offer tasty alterations these home cooks use to "personalize" the dish.

With everyday ingredients, easy-to-follow instructions and enticing full-color photos, Most Requested Recipes is sure to become the most-used cookbook in your kitchen.

tasteofhome. MOST requested RECIPES

Taste of Home is a registered trademark of The Reader's Digest Association, Inc.

© 2010 Reiman Media Group, Inc.
5400 S. 60th St., Greendale WI 53129
All rights reserved.

Editor in Chief	Catherine Cassidy
Vice President, Executive Editor/Books	Heidi Reuter Lloyd
Creative Director	Ardyth Cope
Food Director	Diane Werner RD
Senior Editor/Books	Mark Hagen
Editor	Sara Lancaster
Art Director	Rudy Krochalk
Content Production Supervisor	Julie Wagner
Project Design Layout Artist	Heather Meinen
Proofreader	Linne Bruskewitz
Recipe Asset System Manager	Coleen Martin
Premedia Supervisor	Scott Berger
Recipe Testing & Editing	Taste of Home Test Kitchen
Food Photography	Taste of Home Photo Studio
Administrative Assistant	Barb Czysz

North American Chief Marketing Officer	Lisa Karpinski
Vice President/Books Marketing	Dan Fink
Creative Director/Creative Marketing	Jim Palmen

THE READER'S DIGEST ASSOCIATION, INC.

President and Chief Executive Officer	Robert E. Guth
Executive Vice President, RDA, and President, North America	Dan Lagani

International Standard Book Number (10): 0-89821-769-5
International Standard Book Number (13): 978-0-89821-769-8
Library of Congress Control Number: 2009935067

For other Taste of Home books and products, visit ShopTasteofHome.com

For more Reader's Digest products and information, visit rd.com (in the United States) or see rd.ca (in Canada).

COVER PHOTOGRAPHY
Photographers   Lori Foy, Grace Natoli-Sheldon
Food Stylists   Jennifer Janz, Kaitlyn Besasie
Set Stylists   Stephanie Marchese, Grace Natoli-Sheldon

Pictured on front cover: Donna Lasagna (p. 118), Pear Chicken Salad with Maple Vinaigrette (p. 91), Turkey Potpies (p. 117), Cappuccino Torte (p. 225) and Roasted Vegetable Medley (p. 93)

Pictured on back cover: Spicy Chicken Wings (p. 30)

Printed in China
5 7 9 10 8 6 4

TABLE OF CONTENTS

49   160   12

editors' favorites

Our editors read, test and taste hundreds of recipes. Here they've gathered their top picks—from crowd-pleasing appetizers and sides, to must-have main dishes and desserts and every course in between. They're the recipes they've been asked about time and again...and they think you will, too.

HAMBURGER NOODLE CASSEROLE / PAGE 9

KELLY WILLIAMS, MORGANVILLE, NEW JERSEY

I can't go anywhere without taking along these appetizer puffs. They are pretty enough for a wedding reception but also make a hearty snack while watching the big game on TV. A platter of these bites stuffed with a corned beef filling will disappear quickly even with a small group.

rye party puffs

PREP: 30 MINUTES / **BAKE:** 20 MINUTES + COOLING

1	cup water
1/2	cup butter, cubed
1/2	cup all-purpose flour
1/2	cup rye flour
2	teaspoons dried parsley flakes
1/2	teaspoon garlic powder
1/4	teaspoon salt
4	eggs

Caraway seeds

CORNED BEEF FILLING:

2	packages (8 ounces *each*) cream cheese, softened
2	packages (2 ounces *each*) thinly sliced deli corned beef, chopped
1/2	cup mayonnaise
1/4	cup sour cream
2	tablespoons minced chives
2	tablespoons diced onion
1	teaspoon spicy brown *or* horseradish mustard
1/8	teaspoon garlic powder
10	small pimiento-stuffed olives, chopped

In a large saucepan over medium heat, bring water and butter to a boil. Add flours, parsley, garlic powder and salt all at once; stir until a smooth balls forms. Remove from the heat; let stand for 5 minutes. Beat in eggs, one at a time. Beat until smooth.

Drop batter by rounded teaspoonfuls 2 in. apart onto greased baking sheets. Sprinkle with caraway seeds. Bake at 400° for 18-20 minutes or until golden. Remove to wire racks. Immediately cut a slit in each puff to allow steam to escape; cool. In a large bowl, combine the first eight filling ingredients. Stir in olives. Split puffs; add filling. Refrigerate. **YIELD: 4-1/2 dozen.**

BETSY SAMS, JAMESVIILLE, NEW YORK
When planning your next fiesta, look no further than this robust and colorful salsa. Seasoned with coriander, cumin, garlic and cilantro, it's always a can't-fail, crowd-pleasing favorite.

salsa for a crowd

PREP/TOTAL TIME: 30 MINUTES

4	cans (14-1/2 ounces *each*) diced tomatoes
4	large tomatoes, chopped
2	cups frozen corn, thawed
1	can (15 ounces) black beans, rinsed and drained
1	medium sweet onion, finely chopped
1/3	cup lime juice
1/4	cup minced fresh cilantro
2	tablespoons cider vinegar
2	tablespoons hot pepper sauce
1	garlic clove, minced
1	tablespoon coriander seeds, crushed
1	tablespoon ground cumin
1	teaspoon salt
1	teaspoon coarsely ground pepper

Chopped jalapeno pepper, optional

Corn chips *or* tortilla chips

Place two undrained cans of tomatoes in a large bowl; drain the two remaining cans and add tomatoes to the bowl. Stir in the chopped fresh tomatoes, corn, beans, onion, lime juice, cilantro, vinegar, hot pepper sauce, garlic and seasonings. Stir in jalapeno if desired. Cover and refrigerate salsa until serving. Serve with corn chips or tortilla chips. **YIELD: 56 servings (1/4 cup each).**

EDITOR'S NOTE: When cutting hot peppers, disposable gloves are recommended. Avoid touching your face.

CATHIE VALENTINE, GRANITEVILLE, SOUTH CAROLINA
It takes 10 minutes to assemble this cool and tasty treat that tastes and looks as though you spent hours of effort creating it.

ice cream sandwich dessert

PREP: 10 MINUTES + FREEZING

17	miniature ice cream sandwiches, *divided*
1	jar (12 ounces) caramel ice cream topping
1	carton (12 ounces) frozen whipped topping, thawed
1/4	cup chocolate syrup
1	Symphony candy bar (7 ounces), chopped

Arrange 14 ice cream sandwiches in an ungreased 13-in. x 9-in. dish. Cut remaining sandwiches in half lengthwise; fill in the spaces in the dish. Spread with caramel and whipped toppings. Drizzle with chocolate syrup. Sprinkle with chopped candy bar. Cover and freeze for at least 45 minutes. Cut into squares. **YIELD: 15-18 servings.**

AMY SAUSER, OMAHA, NEBRASKA

I came across this recipe in a local fund-raiser cookbook. I've made some slight adjustments to it over time, but it is still a trusted standby when grilling. You might even say it's the perfect summertime meal.

pacific rim salmon

PREP: 15 MINUTES + MARINATING / **GRILL:** 15 MINUTES

- 1/2 cup unsweetened pineapple juice
- 1/4 cup soy sauce
- 2 tablespoons prepared horseradish
- 2 tablespoons minced fresh parsley
- 5 teaspoons sesame oil, *divided*
- 2 teaspoons honey
- 1/2 teaspoon coarsely ground pepper
- 8 salmon fillets (6 ounces *each*)
- 5 green onions, coarsely chopped

In a small bowl, combine the pineapple juice, soy sauce, horseradish, parsley, 3 teaspoons sesame oil, honey and pepper. Pour 2/3 cup marinade into a large resealable plastic bag; add the salmon and green onions. Seal bag and turn to coat; refrigerate for 1 to 1-1/2 hours, turning occasionally. Add remaining sesame oil to remaining marinade. Cover and refrigerate for basting.

Coat grill rack with cooking spray before starting the grill. Drain and discard marinade. Grill salmon, covered, over medium heat or broil 4-6 in. from the heat for 8-12 minutes or until fish flakes easily with a fork, basting frequently with reserved marinade. **YIELD: 8 servings.**

BRENDA JOHNSON, DAVISON, MICHIGAN

While it looks complicated, this attractive Southwestern-flavored, meatball-filled ring is really very easy to assemble. My family loves tacos, and we find that the crescent roll dough is a nice change from the usual tortilla shells or chips.

taco meatball ring

PREP: 30 MINUTES / **BAKE:** 15 MINUTES

- 2 cups (8 ounces) shredded cheddar cheese, *divided*
- 2 tablespoons water
- 2 to 4 tablespoons taco seasoning
- 1/2 pound ground beef
- 2 tubes (8 ounces *each*) refrigerated crescent rolls
- 1/2 medium head iceberg lettuce, shredded
- 1 medium tomato, chopped
- 4 green onions, sliced
- 1/2 cup sliced ripe olives
- 2 jalapeno peppers, sliced

Sour cream and salsa, optional

In a large bowl, combine 1 cup cheese, water and taco seasoning. Crumble beef over mixture and mix well. Shape into 16 balls.

Place meatballs on a greased rack in a shallow baking pan. Bake, uncovered, at 400° for 12 minutes or until meat is no longer pink. Drain meatballs on paper towels. Reduce heat to 375°.

Arrange crescent rolls on a greased 15-in. pizza pan, forming a ring with pointed ends facing the outer edge of the pan and wide ends overlapping.

Place a meatball on each roll; fold point over meatball and tuck under wide end of roll (meatball will be visible). Repeat. Bake for 15-20 minutes or until rolls are golden brown.

Transfer to a serving platter. Fill the center of the ring with lettuce, tomato, onions, olives, jalapenos, remaining cheese, and sour cream and salsa if desired. **YIELD: 16 servings.**

EDITOR'S NOTE: When cutting hot peppers, disposable gloves are recommended. Avoid touching your face.

SHIRLEY JOAN HELFENBEIN, LAPEER, MICHIGAN

When I was growing up, we couldn't afford to have meat very often, so it was a special evening when we had these tender chops. The apples, raisins and apple cider give this dish a sweet touch and a pretty appearance.

apple-raisin pork chops

PREP: 25 MINUTES / COOK: 25 MINUTES

8	bone-in pork loin chops (3/4 inch thick and 8 ounces *each*)
1	tablespoon canola oil
1/2	teaspoon salt
1/4	teaspoon pepper
2	cups apple cider *or* juice
3	tablespoons spicy brown mustard
3	medium red apples, sliced
1/2	cup sliced green onions
1/4	cup raisins
1/4	cup dried currants
2	tablespoons cornstarch
1/4	cup cold water

In a large skillet, brown pork chops in oil in batches on both sides. Sprinkle the chops with salt and pepper. Return all chops to the skillet.

Combine the cider and mustard; pour over meat. Bring to a boil; reduce heat. Cover and simmer for 13-18 minutes or until a meat thermometer reads 160°. Remove chops to a serving platter; keep warm.

Add the apples, onions, raisins and currants to the skillet. Cover and cook over medium heat for 5-6 minutes or until apples are tender. Combine cornstarch and water until smooth; stir into apple mixture. Bring to a boil; cook and stir for 2 minutes or until thickened. Serve with pork chops. **YIELD: 8 servings.**

MARIAN LEVIN, LOS ALTOS, CALIFORNIA

This classic dessert is always well received at any celebration—large or small. For variety, I like to use assorted fresh fruit as toppings. Try strawberries, kiwi, raspberries, blueberries or whatever happens to be your favorite.

old-fashioned cheesecake

PREP: 20 MINUTES / BAKE: 50 MINUTES + CHILLING

1-1/3	cups whole almonds, toasted and ground
3/4	cup crushed vanilla wafers
1/3	cup butter, melted
3	packages (8 ounces *each*) cream cheese, softened
1	cup sugar
3	eggs, lightly beaten
2	teaspoons vanilla extract
3/4	teaspoon grated lemon peel

TOPPING:

2	cups (16 ounces) sour cream
3	tablespoons sugar
1	teaspoon vanilla extract

Assorted fresh fruit

In a bowl, combine almonds and wafer crumbs; stir in butter. Press crumb mixture onto the bottom and 2 in. up the sides of an ungreased 9-in. springform pan. Bake at 350° for 5 minutes. Cool crust on a wire rack.

In a large bowl, beat cream cheese and sugar until smooth. Add eggs; beat on low speed just until combined. Beat in vanilla and lemon peel just until blended. Pour into crust. Place pan on a baking sheet. Bake at 350° for 40-45 minutes or until center is almost set.

Combine the sour cream, sugar and vanilla; carefully spread over filling. Bake 10 minutes longer or until edges appear dry. Cool on a wire rack for 10 minutes. Carefully run a knife around edge of pan to loosen; cool 1 hour longer. Cover and chill overnight. Remove sides of pan. Top with fresh fruit. Refrigerate leftovers. **YIELD: 12 servings.**

ANN MARIE MOCH, KINTYRE, NORTH DAKOTA

Of all the mouthwatering holiday side dishes, this recipe is by far one of the most delicious surprises I've ever come across. The flaky, rustic-looking pastry shells hold a sweet and spicy pecan layer under the tender squash slices.

rustic squash tarts

PREP: 30 MINUTES / **BAKE:** 35 MINUTES

1	medium butternut squash, peeled, seeded and cut into 1/8-inch slices
1	medium acorn squash, peeled, seeded and cut into 1/8-inch slices
2	tablespoons water
1/4	cup olive oil
1	tablespoon minced fresh thyme
1	tablespoon minced fresh parsley
1/2	teaspoon salt
1/4	teaspoon pepper
1/2	cup all-purpose flour
1/2	cup ground pecans
6	tablespoons sugar
1/2	teaspoon ground nutmeg
1/2	teaspoon ground cinnamon
1	package (17.3 ounces) frozen puff pastry, thawed
1	egg, lightly beaten
2	tablespoons butter

In a large microwave-safe bowl, combine squash and water. Cover and cook on high for 5 minutes or until crisp-tender. Drain; transfer to a large resealable plastic bag. Add the oil, thyme, parsley, salt and pepper; seal bag and shake to coat. Set aside. In a small bowl, combine the flour, pecans, sugar, nutmeg and cinnamon; set aside.

Unfold pastry sheets on a lightly floured surface. Roll each pastry to 1/8-in. thickness; transfer each to an ungreased baking sheet. Sprinkle with pecan mixture. Arrange the squash slices to within 1-1/2 in. of the edges, alternating slices of butternut and acorn squash.

Fold up edges of pastry over filling, leaving centers uncovered. Brush pastry with egg. Dot squash with butter. Bake at 375° for 35-40 minutes or until crust is golden brown. **YIELD: 2 tarts (8 servings each).**

EDITOR'S NOTE: This recipe was tested in a 1,100-watt microwave.

MARTHA HENSON, WINNSBORO, TEXAS

People have a hard time believing this homey and hearty noodle casserole uses lighter ingredients. The taste is so rich and creamy! It makes a great weeknight family entree!

hamburger noodle casserole

PREP: 30 MINUTES / **BAKE:** 35 MINUTES

5	cups uncooked egg noodles
1-1/2	pounds lean ground beef (90% lean)
2	garlic cloves, minced
3	cans (8 ounces *each*) tomato sauce
1/2	teaspoon sugar
1/2	teaspoon salt
1/8	teaspoon pepper
1	package (8 ounces) reduced-fat cream cheese
1	cup reduced-fat ricotta cheese
1/4	cup reduced-fat sour cream
3	green onions, thinly sliced, *divided*
2/3	cup shredded reduced-fat cheddar cheese

Cook noodles according to package directions. Meanwhile, in a large nonstick skillet over medium heat, cook beef and garlic until meat is no longer pink; drain. Stir in the tomato sauce, sugar, salt and pepper; heat through. Drain noodles; stir into beef mixture.

In a small bowl, beat the cream cheese, ricotta cheese and sour cream until blended. Stir in half of the onions.

Spoon half of the noodle mixture into a 13-in. x 9-in. baking dish coated with cooking spray. Top with the cheese mixture and remaining noodle mixture.

Cover and bake at 350° for 30 minutes. Uncover; sprinkle with cheese. Bake 5-10 minutes longer or until heated through and the cheese is melted. Sprinkle with the remaining onions. **YIELD: 10 servings.**

GLORIA CASTRO, SANTA ROSE, CALIFORNIA

You'll love the smell in your kitchen—and the smiles on every-body's faces—when you make this scrumptious pie that is drizzled with a heavenly caramel sauce. It takes me back home to my childhood in Virginia and being at my granny's table.

caramel-pecan apple pie

PREP: 45 MINUTES / **BAKE:** 55 MINUTES + COOLING

7	cups sliced peeled tart apples
1	teaspoon lemon juice
1	teaspoon vanilla extract
3/4	cup chopped pecans
1/3	cup packed brown sugar
3	tablespoons sugar
4-1/2	teaspoons ground cinnamon
1	tablespoon cornstarch
1/4	cup caramel ice cream topping, room temperature
1	unbaked pastry shell (9 inches)
3	tablespoons butter, melted

STREUSEL TOPPING:

3/4	cup all-purpose flour
2/3	cup chopped pecans
1/4	cup sugar
6	tablespoons cold butter
1/4	cup caramel ice cream topping, room temperature

In a large bowl, toss apples with lemon juice and vanilla. Combine the pecans, sugars, cinnamon and cornstarch; add to apple mixture and toss to coat. Pour caramel topping over bottom of pastry shell; top with apple mixture (shell will be full). Drizzle with butter.

In a small bowl, combine the flour, pecans and sugar. Cut in the butter until mixture resembles coarse crumbs. Sprinkle over filling.

Bake at 350° for 55-65 minutes or until filling is bubbly and topping is browned. Immediately drizzle with caramel topping. Cool on a wire rack. **YIELD: 8 servings.**

BECKY GOLDSMITH, EDEN PRAIRIE, MINNESOTA

Our guests always comment on how moist and flavorful this elegant entree is. Rubbed with garden-fresh herbs, this golden turkey has such a wonderful aroma when it's roasting that it lures everyone into the kitchen!

herb-roasted turkey

PREP: 10 MINUTES / **BAKE:** 4 HOURS

1	turkey (14 pounds)
1	tablespoon salt
1	teaspoon pepper
18	sprigs fresh thyme, *divided*
4	medium onions, sliced
4	celery ribs, sliced
2	medium carrots, sliced
3	bay leaves
1	tablespoon peppercorns
1/2	cup butter, melted
1	teaspoon minced fresh sage *or* 1/2 teaspoon rubbed sage
1	teaspoon minced fresh thyme *or* 1/2 teaspoon dried thyme
1	teaspoon minced chives

Rub the surface of the turkey and sprinkle cavity with salt and pepper. Place 12 sprigs of thyme in cavity. In a large heavy roasting pan, place onions, celery, carrots, bay leaves, peppercorns and remaining thyme sprigs. Place the turkey, breast side up, over vegetables. Drizzle butter over turkey and sprinkle with minced herbs.

Cover loosely with foil. Bake at 325° for 2-1/2 hours. Remove foil; bake 1-1/2 to 2 hours longer or until a meat thermometer reads 180°, basting every 20 minutes.

Cover and let stand for 20 minutes before carving. Discard bay leaves and peppercorns; thicken the pan drippings for gravy if desired. **YIELD: 12-14 servings.**

MARIE HATTRUP, THE DALLES, OREGON

After tasting this terrific salad my daughter made, I was eager to get the recipe and try it myself. The dressing, which includes hard-cooked egg yolks, is easy to mix up in the blender.

romaine caesar salad

PREP: 10 MINUTES + CHILLING

2	hard-cooked eggs
1/4	cup lemon juice
2	tablespoons balsamic vinegar
1	anchovy fillet
1	tablespoon Dijon mustard
2	garlic cloves, peeled
1	teaspoon Worcestershire sauce
1	teaspoon pepper
3/4	teaspoon salt
1/2	cup olive oil
1	bunch romaine, torn
1	cup (4 ounces) shredded Parmesan cheese
1	cup Caesar salad croutons

Slice eggs in half; remove yolks. Refrigerate whites for another use. In a blender or food processor, combine the lemon juice, vinegar, anchovy, mustard, garlic, Worcestershire sauce, pepper, salt and egg yolks; cover and process until blended. While processing, gradually add oil in a steady stream. Cover and refrigerate for 1 hour.

In a salad bowl, combine the romaine, Parmesan cheese and croutons. Drizzle with dressing; toss to coat. Serve immediately. **YIELD: 8 servings.**

LYLA LEHENBAUER, NEW LONDON, MISSOURI

There's more to pumpkin than pie as proven with this impressive trifle. It looks so elegant with alternating layers of gingerbread cake and pumpkin-butterscotch pudding. Try making it ahead of time for a fuss-free dessert when you're planning to entertain a lot of guests.

pumpkin trifle

PREP: 1 HOUR + COOLING

1	package (14-1/2 ounces) gingerbread cake mix
1-1/4	cups water
1	egg
4	cups cold fat-free milk
4	packages (1 ounce *each*) sugar-free instant butterscotch pudding mix
1	can (15 ounces) solid-pack pumpkin
1	teaspoon ground cinnamon
1/4	teaspoon *each* ground ginger, nutmeg and allspice
1	carton (12 ounces) frozen reduced-fat whipped topping, thawed

In a large bowl, combine the cake mix, water and egg, beat on low speed for 30 seconds. Beat on medium for 2 minutes. Pour into an ungreased 8-in. square baking pan.

Bake at 350° for 35-40 minutes or until a toothpick inserted near the center comes out clean. Cool for 10 minutes before removing from pan to a wire rack. When completely cooled, crumble the cake. Set aside 1/4 cup crumbs for garnish.

In a large bowl, whisk milk and pudding mixes for 2 minutes or until slightly thickened. Let stand for 2 minutes or until soft-set. Stir in pumpkin and spices until well blended.

In a trifle bowl or 3-1/2-qt. glass serving bowl, layer a fourth of the cake crumbs, half of the pumpkin mixture, a fourth of the cake crumbs and half of the whipped topping. Repeat layers. Garnish with reserved cake crumbs. Serve immediately or refrigerate until serving. **YIELD: 18 servings.**

BETHANY ELEDGE, CLEVELAND, TENNESSEE

The inspiration for this clever cake came from one of my favorite flowers, the sunflower. Yellow peeps make petals.

peeps sunflower cake

PREP: 15 MINUTES / **BAKE:** 30 MINUTES + COOLING

1	package (18-1/4 ounces) yellow cake mix
2	cans (16 ounces *each*) chocolate frosting
19	yellow chick Peeps candies
1-1/2	cups semisweet chocolate chips

Prepare and bake cake according to package directions, using two greased and waxed paper-lined 9-in. round baking pans. Cool for 10 minutes before removing from pans to wire racks to cool completely; carefully remove waxed paper.

Level tops of cakes. Spread chocolate frosting between layers and over the top and sides of cake.

Without separating Peeps and curving slightly to fit, arrange chicks around the edge of the cake for sunflower petals. For sunflower seeds, arrange chocolate chips in the center of the cake. **YIELD: 12 servings.**

SUE GRONHOLZ, BEAVER DAM, WISCONSIN

In my search for the perfect mocha cheesecake, I ended up combining a few of my favorite recipes to create this delicious version. It's as much a feast for the eyes as for the palate!

layered mocha cheesecake

PREP: 30 MINUTES / **BAKE:** 55 MINUTES + CHILLING

1-1/2 cups cream-filled chocolate sandwich cookie crumbs

1/4 cup butter, melted

FILLING:

2 tablespoons plus 1-1/2 teaspoons instant coffee granules

1 tablespoon boiling water

1/4 teaspoon ground cinnamon

4 packages (8 ounces *each*) cream cheese, softened

1-1/2 cups sugar

1/4 cup all-purpose flour

4 eggs, lightly beaten

2 teaspoons vanilla extract

2 cups (12 ounces) semisweet chocolate chips, melted and cooled

GLAZE:

1/2 cup semisweet chocolate chips

3 tablespoons butter

Chocolate-covered coffee beans, optional

Combine cookie crumbs and butter; press onto the bottom of a greased 9-in. springform pan. In a small bowl, combine the coffee granules, water and cinnamon; set aside.

In a large bowl, beat the cream cheese, sugar and flour until smooth. Add eggs; beat on low speed just until combined. Stir in vanilla. Divide batter in half. Stir melted chocolate into one portion; pour over crust. Stir coffee mixture into the remaining batter; spoon over chocolate layer.

Place pan on a double thickness of heavy-duty foil (about 16 in. square). Securely wrap foil around pan. Place in a large baking pan; add 1 in. of hot water to larger pan.

Bake at 325° for 55-65 minutes or until center is just set and top appears dull. Remove springform pan from water bath. Cool on a wire rack for 10 minutes. Carefully run a knife around edge of pan to loosen; cool 1 hour longer. Refrigerate overnight.

In a microwave-safe bowl, melt chocolate chips and butter; stir until smooth. Spread over cheesecake. Remove sides of pan. Garnish with coffee beans if desired. Refrigerate leftovers. **YIELD: 16 servings.**

JANE MONTGOMERY, HILLIARD, OHIO

A party guest brought this attractive appetizer to our home, and we fell in love with it immediately. Now I often make it myself whenever we have company.

raspberry cheese spread

PREP: 10 MINUTES + CHILLING

4 ounces cream cheese, softened

1 cup mayonnaise

2 cups (8 ounces) shredded part-skim mozzarella cheese

2 cups (8 ounces) shredded cheddar cheese

3 green onions, finely chopped

1 cup chopped pecans

1/4 cup seedless raspberry preserves

Assorted crackers

In a small bowl, beat cream cheese and mayonnaise until smooth. Beat in cheeses and onions. Stir in pecans. Spread into a plastic wrap-lined 9-in. round dish. Refrigerate until set, about 1 hour.

Invert onto a serving plate; spread with preserves. Serve with crackers. **YIELD: about 3-1/2 cups.**

PAT STEVENS, GRANBURY, TEXAS

With a ready-made crust, this pizza can be on a serving tray in half an hour. The triple-cheese blend will make these slices go fast.

three-cheese pesto pizza

PREP/TOTAL TIME: 30 MINUTES

1/2	cup finely chopped red onion
1/2	cup finely chopped sweet red pepper
1	tablespoon olive oil
1	prebaked 12-inch pizza crust
1/2	cup prepared pesto
1	cup (4 ounces) crumbled feta cheese
1	cup (4 ounces) shredded part-skim mozzarella cheese
1	cup (4 ounces) shredded Parmesan cheese
1	can (4-1/4 ounces) chopped ripe olives
1	medium tomato, thinly sliced

In a small skillet, saute onion and red pepper in oil until tender. Remove from the heat; set aside.

Place crust on an ungreased 14-in. pizza pan. Spread pesto to within 1/2 in. of edges. Layer with the cheeses, onion mixture, olives and tomato. Bake at 400° for 15-18 minutes or until cheese is melted. **YIELD: 16 slices.**

TAWANA FLOWERS, EL MACERO, CALIFORNIA

This light, airy and refreshing dessert is a heavenly choice when you want an alternative to heavier chocolate options. People always comment on the delicate lemon flavor.

ladyfinger lemon dessert

PREP: 15 MINUTES + CHILLING

1	can (12 ounces) evaporated milk
1	package (3 ounces) ladyfingers, split
1	package (3 ounces) lemon gelatin
1	cup boiling orange juice
1/2	cup sugar
1/3	cup lemon juice
2	teaspoons grated lemon peel
1	cup reduced-fat whipped topping

Pour milk into a small metal bowl; place mixer beaters in the bowl. Cover and refrigerate for at least 2 hours or overnight. Line the sides of a 9-in. springform pan with ladyfingers; set aside.

In a large bowl, dissolve gelatin in orange juice. Stir in the sugar, lemon juice and peel; cool to room temperature.

Beat chilled milk until soft peaks form; fold into gelatin mixture. Pour into prepared pan. Refrigerate for at least 3 hours or until firm. Spread with whipped topping. Remove sides of pan. Refrigerate leftovers. **YIELD: 10 servings.**

SUSAN EMERY, EVERETT, WASHINGTON
There's nothing like fresh salmon, and my mom bakes it just right so it nearly melts in your mouth. The sour cream sauce is subtly seasoned with dill and horseradish so that it doesn't overpower the delicate salmon flavor.

salmon with creamy dill sauce

PREP/TOTAL TIME: 30 MINUTES

1	salmon fillet (about 2 pounds)
1	to 1-1/2 teaspoons lemon-pepper seasoning
1	teaspoon onion salt
1	small onion, sliced and separated into rings
6	lemon slices
1/4	cup butter

DILL SAUCE:

1/3	cup sour cream
1/3	cup mayonnaise
1	tablespoon finely chopped onion
1	teaspoon lemon juice
1	teaspoon prepared horseradish
3/4	teaspoon dill weed
1/4	teaspoon garlic salt

Pepper to taste

Line a 15-in. x 10-in. baking pan with heavy-duty foil; grease lightly. Place salmon skin side down on foil. Sprinkle with lemon-pepper and onion salt. Top with onion and lemon slices. Dot with butter. Fold foil around salmon; seal tightly,

Bake at 350° for 20 minutes. Open foil. Broil 4-6 in. from the heat for 8-12 minutes or until the fish flakes easily with a fork.

Combine the sauce ingredients until smooth. Serve with salmon. **YIELD: 6 servings.**

JEAN PARSONS, SARVER, PENNSYLVANIA
We have four very productive apple trees in our backyard, so I make a lot of recipes that call for apples. This apple dessert is one of my family's favorites. If you're serving a larger group, I've found that it goes a little further when cut into squares.

apple pastry squares

PREP: 30 MINUTES / **BAKE:** 40 MINUTES

FILLING:

1/4	cup packed brown sugar
2	tablespoons cornstarch
1	cup water
5	cups thinly sliced peeled apples
1/2	teaspoon ground cinnamon
1/4	teaspoon ground nutmeg
1	tablespoon lemon juice

PASTRY:

2	cups all-purpose flour
1/2	teaspoon salt
2/3	cup cold shortening
2	egg yolks, beaten
1/4	cup cold water
1	tablespoon lemon juice

GLAZE:

1/2	cup confectioners' sugar
1	tablespoon milk
1	tablespoon butter, melted
1/2	teaspoon vanilla extract

For filling, combine sugar, cornstarch and water in a saucepan. Mix until well blended. Add apples; heat to boiling, stirring constantly. Reduce heat and simmer 5 minutes, stirring occasionally. Remove from the heat. Stir in spices and lemon juice; set aside.

For pastry, combine flour and salt. Cut in shortening until mixture is crumbly. Combine egg yolks, water and lemon juice; blend into flour. Mixture will form a ball. Divided in half.

On a lightly floured surface, roll the dough between two pieces of waxed paper to fit the bottom and halfway up the sides of a 13-in. x 9-in. baking pan. Spread filling over pastry. Roll remaining pastry to fit pan exactly; place on top of filling. Fold bottom pastry over the top and press to seal. Cut a few small slits in the top crust.

Bake at 400° for about 40 minutes or until lightly browned. For glaze, combine all ingredients and drizzle over the warm pastry. **YIELD: 24 servings.**

AMBER KIMMICH, POWHATAN, VIRGINIA
My guests are so disappointed if these savory bites aren't on the appetizer buffet. They're made quite easily thanks to hassle-free refrigerated crescent rolls and a flavorful chicken and cream-cheese filling.

champion chicken puffs

PREP/TOTAL TIME: 30 MINUTES

4	ounces cream cheese, softened
1/2	teaspoon garlic powder
1/2	cup shredded cooked chicken
2	tubes (8 ounces *each*) refrigerated crescent rolls

In a small bowl, beat cream cheese and garlic powder until smooth. Stir in chicken.

Unroll crescent dough; separate into 16 triangles. Cut each triangle in half lengthwise, forming two triangles. Place 1 teaspoon of chicken mixture in the center of each. Fold short side over the filling; press sides to seal and roll up.

Place 1 in. apart on greased baking sheets. Bake at 375° for 12-14 minutes or until golden brown. Serve the puffs warm. **YIELD: 32 appetizers.**

NICOLE MARCOTTE, SMITHERS, BRITISH COLUMBIA
My friends threaten not to come to parties unless this dip is on the menu! The rich spread bakes right in the bread bowl and goes well with almost any dipper. Plus, cleanup is a breeze.

warm bacon cheese spread

PREP: 15 MINUTES / BAKE: 1 HOUR

1	round loaf (1 pound) sourdough bread
1	package (8 ounces) cream cheese, softened
1-1/2	cups (12 ounces) sour cream
2	cups (8 ounces) shredded cheddar cheese
1-1/2	teaspoons Worcestershire sauce
3/4	pound sliced bacon, cooked and crumbled
1/2	cup chopped green onions

Assorted crackers

Cut the top fourth off the loaf of bread; carefully hollow out the bottom, leaving a 1-in. shell. Cut the removed bread and top of loaf into cubes; set aside.

In a large bowl, beat the cream cheese until fluffy. Add the sour cream, cheddar cheese and Worcestershire sauce until blended; stir in bacon and onions.

Spoon cheese mixture into bread shell. Wrap in a piece of heavy-duty foil (about 24 in. x 17 in.). Bake at 325° for 1 hour or until heated through. Serve spread with crackers and reserved bread cubes. **YIELD: 4 cups.**

KIMARIE MAASSEN, AVOCA, IOWA
It was just last year when we stopped for a snack while Christmas shopping that I was inspired to make these cookie cups. I changed a few things when I got home, and my fudgy creation became a favorite with my husband and family.

fudge puddles

PREP: 25 MINUTES / BAKE: 20 MINUTES/BATCH

1/2	cup butter, softened
1/2	cup creamy peanut butter
1/2	cup sugar
1/2	cup packed light brown sugar
1	egg
1/2	teaspoon vanilla extract
1-1/4	cups all-purpose flour
3/4	teaspoon baking soda
1/2	teaspoon salt

FUDGE FILLING:

1	cup milk chocolate chips
1	cup (6 ounces) semisweet chocolate chips
1	can (14 ounces) sweetened condensed milk
1	teaspoon vanilla extract

Chopped peanuts

In a large bowl, cream the butter, peanut butter and sugars. Beat in egg and vanilla. Combine the flour, baking soda and salt. Gradually add to creamed mixture. Chill for 1 hour.

Shape into 48 balls, 1 in. each. Place balls in lightly greased mini-muffin tins. Bake at 325° for 14-16 minutes or until lightly browned. Using the end of a wooden spoon handle, make a 3/8- to 1/2-in.-deep indentation in the center of each ball. Cool in pans for 5 minutes, before removing to wire racks to cool completely.

For filling, in a microwave or small saucepan, melt chocolate chips. Stir in the milk and vanilla until smooth. Fill each shell with chocolate filling. Sprinkle with chopped peanuts. (Leftover chocolate filling can be stored in the refrigerator and served warm over ice cream.) **YIELD: 4 dozen.**

TASTE OF HOME TEST KITCHEN

Cherry tomato quarters form the wings of these adorable little ladybug bites dreamed up by our home economists. The delightful creatures are perched on crunchy crackers spread with a seasoned cream cheese mixture.

ladybug appetizers

PREP/TOTAL TIME: 30 MINUTES

2	ounces cream cheese, softened
2	tablespoons sour cream

Black paste food coloring

1/2	teaspoon minced chives
1/8	teaspoon garlic salt
1/8	teaspoon minced fresh parsley
36	butter-flavored crackers
18	cherry tomatoes, quartered
18	large pitted ripe olives
72	fresh chive pieces (about 1-1/2 inches long)

In a small bowl, beat the cream cheese and the sour cream until smooth. Remove 1 tablespoon to a small bowl and tint black. Place the tinted cream cheese mixture in a small plastic bag; set aside.

Add the chives, garlic salt and parsley to the remaining cream cheese mixture. Spread over crackers. Arrange two tomato quarters on each for the ladybug wings.

For heads, halve the ripe olives widthwise; place one half on each cracker. Insert two chives into olives for antennae. Use the tinted cream cheese mixture to pipe spots onto the wings. **YIELD: 3 dozen.**

AMY MITCHELL, SABETHA, KANSAS

One of my mother's friends used to bring this sweet delight over at the holidays—it never lasted long. With the tangy raspberry filling, tender cake and crunchy topping, it has become a favorite at our house year-round.

raspberry streusel coffee cake

PREP: 25 MINUTES + COOLING / **BAKE:** 40 MINUTES

3-1/2	cups unsweetened raspberries
1	cup water
2	tablespoons lemon juice
1-1/4	cups sugar
1/3	cup cornstarch

BATTER:

3	cups all-purpose flour
1	cup sugar
1	teaspoon baking powder
1	teaspoon baking soda
1	cup cold butter, cubed
2	eggs, lightly beaten
1	cup (8 ounces) sour cream
1	teaspoon vanilla extract

TOPPING:

1/2	cup all-purpose flour
1/2	cup sugar
1/4	cup butter, softened
1/2	cup chopped pecans

GLAZE:

1/2	cup confectioners' sugar
2	teaspoons milk
1/2	teaspoon vanilla extract

In a large saucepan, cook raspberries and water over medium heat for 5 minutes. Add lemon juice. Combine sugar and cornstarch; stir into fruit mixture. Bring to a boil; cook and stir for 2 minutes or until thickened. Cool.

In a large bowl, combine the flour, sugar, baking powder and baking soda. Cut in butter until mixture resembles coarse crumbs. Stir in eggs, sour cream and vanilla (batter will be stiff).

Spread half into a greased 13-in. x 9-in. baking dish. Spread raspberry filling over batter; spoon remaining batter over filling. Combine topping ingredients; sprinkle over top.

Bake at 350° for 40-45 minutes or until topping is golden brown. Combine the glaze ingredients; drizzle the glaze over warm cake. **YIELD: 12-16 servings.**

KELLY TURNBULL, JUPITER, FLORIDA
Here's a great weeknight supper that's budget-friendly, healthy and liked by children of all ages. And with such a thick, cheesy topping, who'd ever guess that it's relatively light?

skillet pasta florentine

PREP: 20 MINUTES / **COOK:** 30 MINUTES

3	cups uncooked spiral pasta
1	egg, beaten
2	cups (16 ounces) 2% cottage cheese
1-1/2	cups reduced-fat ricotta cheese
1	package (10 ounces) frozen chopped spinach, thawed and squeezed dry
1	cup (4 ounces) shredded part-skim mozzarella cheese, *divided*
1	teaspoon *each* dried parsley flakes, oregano and basil
1	jar (14 ounces) meatless spaghetti sauce
2	tablespoons grated Parmesan cheese

Cook pasta according to package directions. Meanwhile, in a large bowl, combine the egg, cottage cheese, ricotta cheese, spinach, 1/2 cup mozzarella cheese and herbs.

Drain pasta. Place half of sauce in a large skillet; layer with pasta and remaining sauce. Top with cheese mixture.

Bring to a boil. Reduce heat; cover and cook for 25-30 minutes or until a thermometer reads 160°. Sprinkle with Parmesan cheese and remaining mozzarella cheese; cover and cook 5 minutes longer or until the cheese is melted. Let stand for 5 minutes before serving. **YIELD: 6 servings.**

READERS' RAVES

> We really liked Skillet Pasta Florentine, and the recipe was very easy to follow. It is much like an inside-out stuffed shell. Because I love garlic, I think I will add a clove or three to kick up the flavor the next time I make it.
>
> —MissMelissa from TasteofHome.com

KAREN JOHNSON, BAKERSFIELD , CALIFORNIA
Chock-full of chicken, potatoes, peas and corn, the recipe for this autumn standby makes two golden pies, so you can serve one at supper and save the other for a busy night. Hearty, savory and homemade, they're perfect for company or family.

chicken potpie

PREP: 40 MINUTES / **BAKE:** 35 MINUTES + STANDING

2	cups diced peeled potatoes
1-3/4	cups sliced carrots
2/3	cup chopped onion
1	cup butter, cubed
1	cup all-purpose flour
1-3/4	teaspoons salt
1	teaspoon dried thyme
3/4	teaspoon pepper
3	cups chicken broth
1-1/2	cups milk
4	cups cubed cooked chicken
1	cup frozen peas
1	cup frozen corn

Pastry for two double-crust pies (9 inches)

Place potatoes and carrots in a large saucepan; cover with water. Bring to a boil. Reduce heat; cover and simmer for 8-10 minutes or until crisp-tender. Drain and set aside.

In a large skillet, saute onion in butter until tender. Stir in the flour, salt, thyme and pepper until blended. Gradually stir in broth and milk. Bring to a boil; cook and stir for 2 minutes or until thickened. Add the chicken, peas, corn, potatoes and carrots; remove from the heat.

Line two 9-in. pie plates with bottom pastry; trim pastry even with edge. Fill pastry shells with chicken mixture. Roll out remaining pastry to fit top of pies. Cut slits or decorative cutouts in pastry. Place over filling; trim, seal and flute edges.

Bake one potpie at 425° for 35-40 minutes or until crust is lightly browned. Let stand for 15 minutes before cutting. Cover and freeze remaining potpie for up to 3 months. **YIELD: 2 potpies (6-8 servings each).**

TO USE FROZEN POT PIE: Shield frozen pie crust edges with foil; place on a baking sheet. Bake at 425° for 30 minutes. Reduce heat to 350°; bake 70-80 minutes longer or until crust is golden brown.

MARILYN MCSWEEN, MENTOR, OHIO
These palate-pleasing little nibbles almost taste like dessert. With their savory-sweet filling, they tend to steal the spotlight at all my gatherings.

brie cherry pastry cups

PREP/TOTAL TIME: 30 MINUTES

1	sheet frozen puff pastry, thawed
1/2	cup cherry preserves
4	ounces Brie cheese, cut into 1/2-inch cubes
1/4	cup chopped pecans *or* walnuts
2	tablespoons minced chives

Unfold puff pastry; cut into 36 squares. Gently press squares onto the bottoms of 36 greased miniature muffin cups. Bake at 375° for 10 minutes. Using the end of a wooden spoon handle, make a 1/2-in.-deep indentation in the center of each. Bake 6-8 minutes longer or until golden brown. With spoon handle, press the squares down again.

Spoon a rounded 1/2 teaspoonful of preserves into each cup. Top with cheese; sprinkle with nuts and chives. Bake for 3-5 minutes or until cheese is melted. **YIELD: 3 dozen.**

RUTHANN GREGG, PRESCOTT VALLEY, ARIZONA
Got a minute? Then you've got a fun, fast dessert with these dressed up, store-bought ice cream sandwiches. It will make everyone scream for ice cream.

banana split delight

PREP/TOTAL TIME: 10 MINUTES

1	small banana, sliced
1/8	teaspoon lemon juice
2	Neapolitan ice cream sandwiches
1	cup whipped topping
1	tablespoon caramel ice cream topping
1	tablespoon chocolate ice cream topping
1	tablespoon chopped pecans

Gently toss banana with lemon juice; set aside. Line the bottom and sides of a 5-3/4-in. x 3-in. loaf pan with plastic wrap.

Layer one ice cream sandwich, half of the banana and 1/2 cup whipped topping in pan. Top with second ice cream sandwich, reversing direction of ice cream flavors.

Layer with remaining banana and whipped topping. Top with caramel and chocolate toppings; sprinkle with pecans. Cover and freeze for 4-6 hours or until firm.

Remove from the freezer 5 minutes before serving. Using plastic wrap, lift dessert out of pan. Discard plastic wrap; cut dessert in half. **YIELD: 2 servings.**

JEAN ECOS, HARTLAND, WISCONSIN

All of my favorite Southwestern ingredients are combined in this delectable appetizer cheesecake. Served with assorted crackers, It's one starter that tastes as fantastic as it looks!

santa fe cheesecake

PREP: 25 MINUTES / **BAKE:** 30 MINUTES + CHILLING

1	cup crushed tortilla chips
3	tablespoons butter, melted
2	packages (8 ounces *each*) cream cheese, softened
2	eggs, lightly beaten
2	cups (8 ounces) shredded Monterey Jack cheese
1	can (4 ounces) chopped green chilies, drained
1	cup (8 ounces) sour cream
1	cup chopped sweet yellow pepper
1/2	cup chopped green onions
1/3	cup chopped tomato

In a small bowl, combine tortilla chips and butter; press onto the bottom of a greased 9-in. springform pan. Place on a baking sheet. Bake at 325° for 15 minutes or until lightly browned.

In a large bowl, beat the cream cheese and eggs on low speed just until combined. Stir in the shredded Monterey Jack cheese and green chilies; pour over crust. Bake for 30-35 minutes or until the center is almost set.

Place pan on a wire rack. Spread sour cream over cheesecake. Carefully run a knife around edge of pan to loosen; cool for 1 hour. Refrigerate overnight.

Remove sides of pan just before serving. Garnish cheesecake with yellow pepper, onions and tomato. Refrigerate leftovers. **Yield: 16-20 servings.**

MARY BILYEU, ANN ARBOR, MICHIGAN

Topped with a fluffy frosting and fun chocolate sprinkles, these extra-rich, extra-delicious cupcakes smell so wonderful while baking and taste even better!

special mocha cupcakes

PREP: 25 MINUTES / **BAKE:** 20 MINUTES + COOLING

2	eggs
1/2	cup cold brewed coffee
1/2	cup canola oil
3	teaspoons cider vinegar
3	teaspoons vanilla extract
1-1/2	cups all-purpose flour
1	cup sugar
1/3	cup baking cocoa
1	teaspoon baking soda
1/2	teaspoon salt

MOCHA FROSTING:

3	tablespoons milk chocolate chips
3	tablespoons semisweet chocolate chips
1/3	cup butter, softened
2	cups confectioners' sugar
1	to 2 tablespoons brewed coffee
1/2	cup chocolate sprinkles

In a large bowl, beat the eggs, coffee, oil, vinegar and vanilla until well blended. In a small bowl, combine the flour, sugar, cocoa, baking soda and salt; gradually beat into coffee mixture until blended.

Fill paper-lined muffin cups three-fourths full. Bake at 350° for 20-25 minutes or until a toothpick comes out clean. Cool for 10 minutes before removing from pan to a wire rack to cool.

For frosting, in a microwave, melt chips and butter; stir until smooth. Transfer chocolate mixture to a large bowl. Gradually beat in confectioners' sugar and coffee until smooth. Pipe frosting onto cupcakes. Top with sprinkles. **YIELD: 1 dozen.**

ELENA HANSEN, RUIDOSO, NEW MEXICO

This rich and satisfying dish, adapted from a recipe given to me by a friend, is my husband's favorite. It's loaded with scallops, shrimp and crab and smothered in a creamy sauce. I consider this the "crown jewel" in my repertoire of recipes.

seafood lasagna

PREP: 35 MINUTES / **BAKE:** 35 MINUTES + STANDING

1	green onion, finely chopped
2	tablespoons canola oil
2	tablespoons plus 1/2 cup butter, *divided*
1/2	cup chicken broth
1	bottle (8 ounces) clam juice
1	pound bay scallops
1	pound uncooked small shrimp, peeled and deveined
1	package (8 ounces) imitation crabmeat, chopped
1/4	teaspoon white pepper, *divided*
1/2	cup all-purpose flour
1-1/2	cups milk
1/2	teaspoon salt
1	cup heavy whipping cream
1/2	cup shredded Parmesan cheese, *divided*
9	lasagna noodles, cooked and drained

In a large skillet, saute onion in oil and 2 tablespoons butter until tender. Stir in broth and clam juice; bring to a boil. Add scallops, shrimp, crab and 1/8 teaspoon pepper; return to a boil. Reduce heat; simmer, uncovered, for 4-5 minutes or until shrimp turn pink and scallops are firm and opaque, stirring gently. Drain, reserving cooking liquid; set seafood mixture aside.

In a large saucepan, melt the remaining butter; stir in flour until smooth. Combine milk and reserved cooking liquid; gradually add to the saucepan. Add salt and remaining pepper. Bring to a boil; cook and stir for 2 minutes or until thickened. Remove from the heat; stir in cream and 1/4 cup Parmesan cheese. Stir 3/4 cup white sauce into the seafood mixture.

Spread 1/2 cup white sauce in a greased 13-in. x 9-in. baking dish. Top with three noodles; spread with half of the seafood mixture and 1-1/4 cups sauce. Repeat layers. Top with remaining noodles, sauce and Parmesan.

Bake, uncovered, at 350° for 35-40 minutes or until golden brown. Let lasagna stand for 15 minutes before cutting. **YIELD: 12 servings.**

KRISTA FRANK, RHODODENDRON, OREGON

I wanted to make my youngest son an ice cream cake one year for his summer birthday, as he prefers ice cream to cake. He picked the flavors, and I decided to try my favorite brownie recipe as a crust. It worked with lip-smacking results!

summer celebration ice cream cake

PREP: 15 MINUTES / **BAKE:** 20 MINUTES + FREEZING

1	cup sugar
3	tablespoons butter, melted
3	tablespoons orange yogurt
1	egg
1	teaspoon grated orange peel
1	teaspoon vanilla extract
3/4	cup all-purpose flour
1/3	cup baking cocoa
1	cup (6 ounces) semisweet chocolate chips
1-3/4	quarts vanilla ice cream, softened
4	to 6 ounces semisweet chocolate, chopped
1	tablespoon shortening

Mixed fresh berries

Line an 8-in. square baking dish with foil and grease the foil; set aside. In a large bowl, combine the sugar, butter, yogurt, egg, orange peel and vanilla until blended. Combine flour and cocoa; stir into sugar mixture. Add chocolate chips.

Spread into prepared dish. Bake at 325° for 20-25 minutes or until a toothpick inserted near the center comes out with moist crumbs. Cool on a wire rack. Spread ice cream over cake. Cover and freeze for 3 hours or until firm.

Remove the ice cream cake from the freezer 10 minutes before serving. In a microwave-safe bowl, melt chocolate and shortening; stir until smooth. Using foil, lift dessert out of dish; gently peel off foil. Cut into squares. Garnish with berries and drizzle with chocolate. **YIELD: 9 servings.**

DAWN SCHUTTE, SHEBOYGAN, WISCONSIN
At work, we always have a holiday feast at which everyone brings a dish to pass. A co-worker made this delightfully different cracker dip, which went over so well that I decided to adopt it as my own.

sesame chicken dip

PREP: 35 MINUTES + CHILLING

2	tablespoons soy sauce
4	teaspoons sesame oil
2	garlic cloves, minced
4	cups shredded cooked chicken breast
3	packages (8 ounces *each*) reduced-fat cream cheese
8	green onions, thinly sliced
1/2	cup chopped salted peanuts
2	cups chopped fresh baby spinach
1	jar (10 ounces) sweet-and-sour sauce

Sesame rice crackers

In a large resealable plastic bag, combine the soy sauce, sesame oil and garlic; add the chicken. Seal bag and turn to coat; refrigerate for at least 1 hour.

Spread cream cheese onto a large serving platter; top with the chicken mixture. Sprinkle with green onions, peanuts and spinach. Drizzle with sweet-and-sour sauce. Cover and refrigerate for at least 2 hours. Serve the dip with sesame rice crackers. **YIELD: 36 servings (1/4 cup each).**

FRANCES VANFOSSAN, WARREN, MICHIGAN
For a taste of absolute paradise, try this light and creamy confection. It's low in fat, sugar and fuss. Dessert doesn't get any easier than this refreshing finale!

fluffy key lime pie

PREP: 20 MINUTES + CHILLING

1	package (.3 ounce) sugar-free lime gelatin
1/4	cup boiling water
2	cartons (6 ounces *each*) key lime yogurt
1	carton (8 ounces) frozen fat-free whipped topping, thawed
1	reduced-fat graham cracker crust (8 inches)

In a large bowl, dissolve gelatin in boiling water. Whisk in yogurt. Fold in whipped topping. Pour into crust. Cover and refrigerate for at least 2 hours or until set. **YIELD: 8 servings.**

BECKY AYLOR, SISTERS, OREGON

Here's a delightful spin on the traditional Asian-inspired egg roll. Packed with plenty of Southwestern flair and served with a creamy, guacamole-like dip, these crispy wraps are sure to be a hit with party goers.

southwest egg rolls & cool avocado dip

PREP: 35 MINUTES / **COOK:** 5 MINUTES/BATCH

2-1/2	cups shredded cooked chicken
1-1/2	cups (6 ounces) shredded Mexican cheese blend
2/3	cup frozen corn, thawed
2/3	cup canned black beans, rinsed and drained
5	green onions, chopped
1/4	cup minced fresh cilantro
1	teaspoon salt
1	teaspoon ground cumin
1	teaspoon grated lime peel
1/4	teaspoon cayenne pepper
20	egg roll wrappers

Oil for frying

DIP:

1	cup ranch salad dressing
1	medium ripe avocado, peeled and mashed
1	tablespoon minced fresh cilantro
1	teaspoon grated lime peel

In a large bowl, combine the first 10 ingredients. Place 1/4 cup of chicken mixture in the center of one egg roll wrapper. (Keep remaining wrappers covered with a damp paper towel until ready to use.) Fold bottom corner over filling. Fold sides toward center over filling. Moisten remaining corner with water; roll up tightly to seal. Repeat.

In an electric skillet or deep-fat fryer, heat oil to 375°. Fry egg rolls, a few at a time, for 2 minutes on each side or until golden brown. Drain on paper towels.

Meanwhile, combine the dip ingredients. Serve with egg rolls. **YIELD: 20 egg rolls (1-1/2 cups sauce).**

TERI RASEY-BOLF, CADILLAC, MICHIGAN

These cookies are the next best thing to a good old-fashioned malted milk. Made with malted milk powder, chocolate syrup plus chocolate chips and chunks, these are the best cookies I have ever tasted.

chocolate malted cookies

PREP/TOTAL TIME: 30 MINUTES

1	cup butter-flavored shortening
1-1/4	cups packed brown sugar
1/2	cup malted milk powder
2	tablespoons chocolate syrup
1	tablespoon vanilla extract
1	egg
2	cups all-purpose flour
1	teaspoon baking soda
1/2	teaspoon salt
1-1/2	cups semisweet chocolate chunks
1	cup milk chocolate chips

In a large bowl, beat the shortening, brown sugar, malted milk powder, chocolate syrup and vanilla for 2 minutes. Add egg.

Combine the flour, baking soda and salt; gradually add to creamed mixture, mixing well after each addition. Stir in the chocolate chunks and chips.

Shape dough into 2-in. balls; place 3 in. apart on ungreased baking sheets. Bake at 375° for 12-14 minutes or until golden brown. Cool for 2 minutes before removing to a wire rack. **YIELD: about 1-1/2 dozen.**

DIANNE BETTIN, TRUMAN, MINNESOTA
My favorite entree for Christmas and other special occasions is this crown roast that's surprisingly easy to prepare. Both its elegant appearance and excellent flavor are sure to impress your family.

crown roast of pork

PREP: 15 MINUTES / **BAKE:** 3 HOURS + STANDING

1	tablespoon dried parsley flakes
1	tablespoon canola oil
1	teaspoon salt
1/2	teaspoon pepper
1	pork crown roast (14 ribs and about 8 pounds)

Foil *or* **paper frills for rib ends**

In a small bowl, combine the parsley, oil, salt and pepper; rub over roast. Place on a rack in a large shallow roasting pan. Cover rib ends with pieces of foil. Bake at 350° for 3 to 3-1/2 hours or until a meat thermometer reads 160°.

Transfer roast to a serving platter. Let stand for 10-15 minutes. Remove foil pieces. Garnish rib ends with foil or paper frills. Cut between ribs to serve. **YIELD: 14 servings.**

PAM SJOLUND, COLUMBIA, SOUTH CAROLINA
This is one of my favorite cakes. It's moist, light and satisfying. I've been tweaking it for years, and now this luscious dessert is almost guilt-free.

pineapple orange cake

PREP: 15 MINUTES / **BAKE:** 25 MINUTES + CHILLING

1	package (18-1/4 ounces) yellow cake mix
1	can (11 ounces) mandarin oranges, undrained
4	egg whites
1/2	cup unsweetened applesauce

TOPPING:

1	can (20 ounces) crushed pineapple, undrained
1	package (1 ounce) sugar-free instant vanilla pudding mix
1	carton (8 ounces) reduced-fat whipped topping

In a large bowl, beat the cake mix, oranges, egg whites and applesauce on low speed for 2 minutes. Pour into a 13-in. x 9-in. baking dish coated with cooking spray.

Bake at 350° for 25-30 minutes or until a toothpick inserted near the center comes out clean. Cool on a wire rack.

In a bowl, combine the pineapple and pudding mix. Fold in whipped topping just until blended. Spread over cake. Refrigerate for at least 1 hour before serving. **YIELD: 15 servings.**

READERS' RAVES

"This Pineapple Orange Cake is the best low-calorie, low-sugar dessert I have ever made! It is easy to fix, and I get rave reviews when I serve it to friends. I LOVE this recipe.

—Cjmyers from TasteofHome.com

I used cheesecake pudding instead of vanilla—DELICIOUS! Try adding a little orange extract to the batter next time, too.

—Wolfpiano from TasteofHome.com"

MARY ANNE FIELDS, GREENEVILLE, TENNESSEE
These irresistible nibbles can be served hot or at room temperature. I have experimented often with the ingredients and have found the recipe lends itself to a variety of tastes.

spicy sausage wonton stars

PREP: 35 MINUTES / **BAKE:** 15 MINUTES

1	pound bulk spicy pork sausage
2	medium carrots, finely shredded
1	medium onion, finely chopped
1/2	cup finely chopped sweet red pepper
1/2	cup finely chopped green pepper
1	cup (4 ounces) finely shredded pepper Jack cheese
1	cup (4 ounces) finely shredded cheddar cheese
1/2	cup sour cream
2	garlic cloves, minced
1	teaspoon lemon-pepper seasoning
36	wonton wrappers
1	tablespoon butter, melted
1/8	teaspoon garlic powder

Sliced cherry tomatoes, optional

In a large skillet, cook sausage over medium heat until no longer pink; drain. In a large bowl, combine the sausage, carrots, onion, peppers, cheeses, sour cream, garlic and lemon-pepper.

Press wonton wrappers into miniature muffin cups coated with cooking spray. In a small bowl, combine the butter and garlic powder; brush over edges. Bake at 350° for 8-9 minutes or until lightly browned.

Spoon sausage mixture into cups. Bake 5-7 minutes longer or until heated through. Garnish cups with tomatoes if desired. **YIELD: 3 dozen.**

RENAE MONCUR, BURLEY, IDAHO
This crispy and creamy dessert is perfect for a Fourth of July or other patriotic celebration! With red, white and blue colors and a light, fluffy filling, this summery delight will be the "star" of your get-together.

star-spangled fruit tart

PREP: 25 MINUTES / **BAKE:** 10 MINUTES + COOLING

1	tube (18 ounces) refrigerated sugar cookie dough, softened
1	package (8 ounces) cream cheese, softened
1/4	cup sugar
1/2	teaspoon almond extract
1	cup fresh blueberries
1	cup fresh raspberries
1	cup halved fresh strawberries

Press cookie dough onto an ungreased 12-in. pizza pan. Bake at 350° for 10-15 minutes or until golden brown. Cool cookie crust on a wire rack.

In a small bowl, beat the cream cheese, sugar and extract until smooth. Spread over crust. In center of tart, arrange berries in the shape of a star; add a berry border. Refrigerate until serving. **YIELD: 16 servings.**

READERS' RAVES

> I didn't have a pizza pan. Instead I used a muffin pan and made individual tarts. Unfortunately, that meant I couldn't make this design, so instead I chopped up the strawberries into pieces the size of the blueberries and just sprinkled the tops of each individual tart. They were a huge hit!
>
> —Christina72684
> from TasteofHome.com

BECKY RUFF, MONONA, IOWA
One of my high school friends brought this fuss-free appetizer to a party, and the rest of us couldn't get enough of it. I've since made it for family parties and potlucks, where the bowl is quickly emptied.

hot cheddar-mushroom spread

PREP/TOTAL TIME: 25 MINUTES

2	cups mayonnaise
2	cups (8 ounces) shredded cheddar cheese
2/3	cup grated Parmesan cheese
4	cans (4-1/2 ounces *each*) sliced mushrooms, drained
1	envelope ranch salad dressing mix

Minced fresh parsley

Assorted crackers

In a large bowl, combine the mayonnaise, cheeses, mushrooms and dressing mix. Spread into a greased 9-in. pie plate. Bake, uncovered, at 350° for 20-25 minutes or until cheese is melted. Sprinkle with parsley. Serve with crackers. **YIELD: 3 cups.**

EDITOR'S NOTE: Reduced-fat or fat-free mayonnaise is not recommended for this recipe.

SANDRA SEAMAN, GREENSBURG, PENNSYLVANIA
Kids' eyes light up when they see these cute jungle goodies. They never fail to make my grandkids smile, and they're always a hit at bake sales.

monkey cupcakes

PREP: 30 MINUTES / **BAKE:** 20 MINUTES + COOLING

1	package (18-1/4 ounces) chocolate cake mix
1	can (16 ounces) chocolate frosting
24	vanilla wafers

Black and red decorating gel

48	pastel blue *and/or* green milk chocolate M&M's
12	peanut butter cream-filled sandwich cookies

Prepare and bake cake according to package directions for cupcakes. Cool completely on wire racks.

Set aside 1/4 cup frosting. Frost cupcakes with remaining frosting. With a serrated knife, cut off and discard a fourth from each vanilla wafer. Place a wafer on each cupcake, with the rounded edge of wafer near edge of cupcake, for face. Add dots of black gel for nostrils. With red gel, pipe a mouth on each.

Place M&M's above wafers for eyes; add dots of black gel for pupils. Using reserved frosting and a #16 star tip, pipe hair. Carefully separate sandwich cookies; cut each in half. Position one on each side of cupcakes for ears. **YIELD: 2 dozen.**

PEN PEREZ, BERKELEY, CALIFORNIA

My friend asked me to make her son's 5th birthday cake, and when I asked her what he wanted on it, she said, "Oh, just put on gobs and gobs of candy." Instead of piling on sweet treats haphazardly, I thought it should look like the Candy Land board game. The birthday boy loved it!

candy land cake

PREP: 2 HOURS / **BAKE:** 30 MINUTES + COOLING

> 2   packages (18-1/4 ounces *each*) cake mix of your choice
>
> Vanilla and chocolate frosting
>
> Green mist food color spray, optional
>
> Assorted decorations: Starburst candies, red Fruit Roll-Up, red coarse sugar, Dots, regular and miniature peanut butter cups, chocolate jimmies, large and small gumdrops, Dum Dum Pops, miniature candy canes, clear and blue rock candy, cake and waffle ice cream cones, multicolored sprinkles, green colored sugar, miniature marshmallows, round peppermints and conversation hearts

Line two 13-in. x 9-in. baking pans with waxed paper and grease the paper. Prepare cake batter; pour into prepared pans. Bake according to package directions. Cool for 15 minutes before removing from pans to wire racks to cool completely; remove waxed paper. Level tops of cakes; place side by side on a covered board. Frost the top and sides of cake with vanilla frosting; mist with food color spray if desired.

With Candy Land game board as your guide, form a path using Starburst candies. With vanilla frosting, pipe "Happy Birthday" on candies. With chocolate frosting, make an arrow. Pipe the word "Start" on the arrow with the vanilla frosting.

For the Mountain/Gumdrop pass, use a red Fruit Roll-Up, red coarse sugar and Dots. For forests, add peanut butter cups topped with piped chocolate frosting, chocolate jimmies, gumdrops, Dum Dum Pops, candy canes and rock candy. For castle, pipe vanilla frosting into ice cream cones. Garnish with Dots and sprinkles.

Between the pathways, add green colored sugar, sprinkles, miniature marshmallows, peppermints and conversation hearts. Pipe additional frosting to fill in spaces; top with sprinkles. Pipe the vanilla frosting around the base of cake; place the peppermints around top edge of cake. **YIELD: 30-40 servings.**

EDITOR'S NOTE: This cake is best eaten the day it's prepared. Do not refrigerate.

DIANNE BETTIN, TRUMAN, MINNESOTA

I make this recipe for almost every holiday and often take it to potlucks. Usually, I make the pilaf ahead to allow the flavors to blend and then reheat it in the microwave before serving.

wild rice pilaf

PREP: 1 HOUR / **BAKE:** 25 MINUTES

2	cans (14-1/2 ounces *each*) chicken broth
3/4	cup uncooked wild rice
1	cup uncooked long grain rice
1	large onion, chopped
2	medium carrots, halved lengthwise and sliced
1	garlic clove, minced
1/2	teaspoon dried rosemary, crushed
1/2	cup butter, cubed
3	cups fresh broccoli florets
1/4	teaspoon pepper

In a large saucepan, bring broth to a boil. Add wild rice; reduce heat. Cover and cook for 30 minutes. Add long grain rice; cook 20-25 minutes longer or until liquid is absorbed and rice is tender.

Meanwhile, in a large skillet, saute the onion, carrots, garlic and rosemary in butter until vegetables are tender. Stir in the rice, broccoli and pepper.

Transfer to a greased shallow 2 qt. baking dish. Cover and bake at 350° for 25-30 minutes or until broccoli is crisp-tender. Fluff rice with a fork before serving. **YIELD: 10 servings.**

LYN RENWICK, CHARLOTTE, NORTH CAROLINA

Baked in miniature muffin cups, wonton wrappers make perfect choice for these crunchy Southwestern bites. In addition to two different cheeses, green chilies and chives, the zippy appetizers are also seasoned with a hint of cumin.

chili-cheese wonton cups

PREP/TOTAL TIME: 30 MINUTES

24	wonton wrappers

Refrigerated butter-flavored spray

1	cup (4 ounces) shredded reduced-fat cheddar cheese
1/2	cup reduced-fat ricotta cheese
1	can (4 ounces) chopped green chilies, well drained
1	tablespoon minced chives
1/4	teaspoon salt
1/4	teaspoon ground cumin
3	tablespoons sliced ripe olives

Press the wonton wrappers into miniature muffin cups coated with cooking spray, forming a cup. Spritz with butter-flavored spray. Bake at 350° for 8-9 minutes or until edges are golden.

In a small bowl, combine the cheeses, chilies, chives, salt and cumin. Spoon into cups. Top with olives. Bake for 10 minutes longer or until filling is golden brown and bubbly. Serve warm. **YIELD: 2 dozen.**

snacks & appetizers

Need to calm a craving? Kids hungry before dinner? Looking for something to bring to Saturday's party? Whatever the situation, this chapter offers you plenty of munchable snacks and crowd-pleasing party starters that readers have been raving about.

ANTIPASTO KABOBS / PAGE 32

MARGARET SCHISSLER, MILWAUKEE, WISCONSIN

Great for a game-day party, this hearty appetizer will bring your guests back for more. If you prefer, the cheesy, Italian-inspired dip can be made with Italian sausage instead of ground beef. Add a little more pizza sauce if the mixture seems too thick.

pizza fondue

PREP/TOTAL TIME: 25 MINUTES

1/2	pound ground beef
1	cup chopped fresh mushrooms
1	medium onion, chopped
1	garlic clove, minced
1	tablespoon cornstarch
1-1/2	teaspoons fennel seed
1-1/2	teaspoons dried oregano
1/4	teaspoon garlic powder

2	cans (15 ounces *each*) pizza sauce
2-1/2	cups (10 ounces) shredded cheddar cheese
1	cup (4 ounces) shredded part-skim mozzarella cheese
2	tablespoons chopped ripe olives

Breadsticks, bagel chips, baked pita chips *and/or* tortilla chips

In a large skillet, cook the beef, mushrooms, onion and garlic over medium heat until meat is no longer pink; drain. Stir in the cornstarch, fennel, oregano and garlic powder until blended. Stir in pizza sauce. Bring to a boil; cook and stir for 1-2 minutes or until thickened. Gradually stir in cheeses until melted. Stir in olives.

Transfer mixture to a fondue pot or warmer and keep warm. Serve the fondue with breadsticks, bagel chips, baked pita chips and/or tortilla chips. **YIELD:** 5-1/2 cups.

GAY AVERY, MASSENA, NEW YORK
If you like your snacks to have a little kick, you won't want to pass up a tray of these zesty wings. A saucy mix of soy sauce, hot pepper sauce, ginger and garlic blends together for just the right amount of heat in every bite.

spicy chicken wings

PREP: 50 MINUTES / **BAKE:** 45 MINUTES

32	pounds chicken wingettes and drumettes
3/4	cup cornstarch
8	cups soy sauce
2	cups water
1/2	to 2 cups hot pepper sauce
8	teaspoons ground ginger
2	garlic cloves, minced
2	cups canola oil

Place the wings in greased large baking pans. Bake at 375° for 40-50 minutes or until juices run clear.

Meanwhile, in a Dutch oven, combine the cornstarch, soy sauce and water until smooth. Stir in the pepper sauce, ginger and garlic. Bring to a boil; cook and stir for 2 minutes or until thickened. Remove from the heat; whisk in oil.

Drain wings; transfer to large roasting pans. Top with sauce and stir to coat. Bake for 45-55 minutes, stirring occasionally, until lightly glazed and heated through. **YIELD: about 24 dozen.**

LORRAINE CHEVALIER, MERRIMAC, MASSACHUSETTS
I borrowed this recipe from a friend, whose husband is diabetic, and have been making these colorful cheesecake bites ever since. Topped with slices of kiwifruit and mandarin oranges, they are a delicious, guilt-free treat.

cheesecake phyllo cups

PREP/TOTAL TIME: 25 MINUTES

4	ounces reduced-fat cream cheese
1/2	cup reduced-fat sour cream

Sugar substitute equivalent to 2 tablespoons sugar

1	teaspoon vanilla extract
2	packages (2.1 ounces *each*) frozen miniature phyllo shells, thawed
1	can (11 ounces) mandarin oranges slices, drained
1	kiwifruit, peeled, sliced and cut into quarters

In a bowl, whisk together the cream cheese, sour cream, sugar substitute and vanilla until smooth. Pipe or spoon into phyllo shells. Top each with an orange segment and kiwi piece. Refrigerate until serving. **YIELD: 2-1/2 dozen.**

EDITOR'S NOTE: This recipe was tested with Splenda sugar blend.

RHONDA BIANCARDI, BLAINE, MINNESOTA
This quick dip is a must for our family parties. In fact, this recipe has been made more times than I can count! It catches the eye on the buffet...for the short time while it lasts!

taco dip

PREP/TOTAL TIME: 10 MINUTES

- 1 package (8 ounces) cream cheese, softened
- 1 cup (8 ounces) sour cream
- 1 carton (8 ounces) French onion dip
- 1 envelope taco seasoning
- 4 cups shredded lettuce
- 2 cups (8 ounces) shredded cheddar cheese
- 1-1/2 cups chopped tomatoes
- Tortilla chips

In a small bowl, beat the cream cheese, sour cream, onion dip and taco seasoning until blended. Spread onto a 12-in. round serving platter. Top with lettuce, cheese and tomatoes. Serve with tortilla chips. **YIELD: 10-12 servings.**

TERI RASEY-BOLF, CADILLAC, MICHIGAN
I appreciate recipes like this one that are easy to assemble. The rich, creamy dip is a fun appetizer for holiday gatherings and casual get-togethers alike.

hot crab dip

PREP: 5 MINUTES / **COOK:** 3 HOURS

- 1/2 cup milk
- 1/3 cup salsa
- 3 packages (8 ounces *each*) cream cheese, cubed
- 2 packages (8 ounces *each*) imitation crabmeat, flaked
- 1 cup thinly sliced green onions
- 1 can (4 ounces) chopped green chilies
- Assorted crackers

In a small bowl, combine milk and salsa. Transfer salsa mixture to a greased 3-qt. slow cooker. Stir in cream cheese, crab, onions and chilies. Cover and cook on low for 3-4 hours, stirring every 30 minutes. Serve with crackers. **YIELD: about 5 cups.**

ANITA CURTIS, CAMARILLO, CALIFORNIA
If you're looking for a great make-ahead nibble, try these snackable squares. They're nice to have in the freezer for lunch with soup or a salad, too. My family loves to nosh on them anytime.

cheese squares

PREP/TOTAL TIME: 30 MINUTES

- 1 cup butter, softened
- 2 jars (5 ounces *each*) sharp American cheese spread, softened
- 1 egg
- 1 can (4 ounces) chopped green chilies, drained
- 1/4 cup salsa
- 2 cups (8 ounces) shredded cheddar cheese
- 2 loaves (1-1/2 pounds *each*) thinly sliced sandwich bread, crusts removed

In a bowl, cream butter, cheese spread and egg until smooth. Stir in chilies, salsa and cheddar cheese. Spread about 1 tablespoon cheese mixture on each slice of one loaf of bread.

Top with remaining bread; spread with more cheese mixture. Cut each sandwich into four squares; place on a greased baking sheet. Bake at 350° for 10 to 15 minutes.

To freeze, place squares in a single layer on a baking sheet. Freeze for 1 hour. Remove from the baking sheet and store in an airtight container in the freezer until needed.

To bake frozen cheese squares, place squares on a greased baking sheet. Bake at 350° for 15-20 minutes or until bubbly and browned. **YIELD: 8 dozen.**

LEE ANN LOWE, GRAY, MAINE
For holiday parties and summer picnics alike, I stuff handheld wonton cups with a zesty south-of-the-border chicken filling. You can make them ahead of time and freeze them, too. Simply reheat the savory bites after thawing.

chicken taco cups

PREP: 20 MINUTES / **BAKE:** 20 MINUTES

- 1   pound boneless skinless chicken breasts, cut into 1-inch pieces
- 1   envelope reduced-sodium taco seasoning
- 1   small onion, chopped
- 1   jar (16 ounces) salsa, *divided*
- 2   cups (8 ounces) shredded reduced-fat cheddar cheese, *divided*
- 36   wonton wrappers

Sour cream, chopped green onions and chopped ripe olives, optional

Sprinkle chicken with taco seasoning. In a large skillet coated with cooking spray, cook and stir the chicken over medium heat for 5 minutes or until juices run clear. Transfer chicken to a food processor; cover and process until chopped. In a large bowl, combine the chicken, onion, half of the salsa and 1 cup cheese.

Press wonton wrappers into miniature muffin cups coated with cooking spray. Bake at 375° for 5 minutes or until lightly browned.

Spoon rounded tablespoonfuls of chicken mixture into cups; top with remaining salsa and cheese. Bake 15 minutes longer or until heated through. Serve taco cups warm. Garnish with sour cream, green onions and olives if desired. **YIELD: 3 dozen.**

DENISE HAZEN, CINCINNATI, OHIO
My husband and I met while taking a cooking class and have loved creating menus and entertaining ever since. These do-ahead appetizers are always a hit.

antipasto kabobs

PREP: 35 MINUTES + MARINATING

- 1   package (9 ounces) refrigerated cheese tortellini
- 40   pimiento-stuffed olives
- 40   large pitted ripe olives
- 3/4   cup Italian salad dressing
- 40   thin slices pepperoni
- 20   thin slices hard salami, halved

Fresh parsley sprigs, optional

Cook tortellini according to package directions; drain and rinse in cold water. In a large resealable plastic bag, combine the tortellini, olives and salad dressing. Seal bag and turn to coat; refrigerate for 4 hours or overnight.

Drain and discard marinade. For each appetizer, thread a stuffed olive, folded pepperoni slice, tortellini, folded salami piece, ripe olive and parsley sprig if desired on a toothpick or short skewer. **YIELD: 40 appetizers.**

READERS' RAVES

> I have done these so many times and they are delicious. I prefer to use the shorter kabob skewers and make them into a centerpiece.
>
> —Jawilkin from TasteofHome.com

> Easy, make-ahead recipe when you have to bring hors d'oeuvres somewhere. You can change the ingredients to whatever antipasto items you like.
>
> —SMLing from TasteofHome.com

SHIRLEY GAWLIK, OAKFIELD, NEW YORK
This hot party dip delivers the great flavor of the chicken wings we love to snack on without any bones!

no-bones chicken wing dip

PREP: 15 MINUTES / **BAKE:** 25 MINUTES

1	package (8 ounces) cream cheese, softened
2	cups (16 ounces) sour cream
1	cup blue cheese salad dressing
1/2	cup buffalo wing sauce
2-1/2	cups shredded cooked chicken
1	block (8 ounces) provolone cheese, shredded

Baby carrots, celery ribs and crackers

In a large bowl, beat the cream cheese, sour cream, salad dressing and buffalo wing sauce until blended. Stir in chicken and provolone cheese.

Transfer mixture to a greased 2-qt. baking dish. Cover and bake at 350° for 25-30 minutes or until hot and bubbly. Serve dip warm with baby carrots, celery and crackers. **YIELD: 6-1/2 cups.**

TAMRA KRIEDEMAN, ENDERLIN, NORTH DAKOTA
These light, crispy onion rings are sliced thin and spiced just right with a blend of garlic powder, cayenne pepper, chili powder and cumin. My family likes them alongside grilled burgers. They're even good as leftovers.

southwestern onion rings

PREP: 10 MINUTES + SOAKING / **COOK:** 10 MINUTES

2	large sweet onions
2-1/2	cups buttermilk
2	eggs
3	tablespoons water
1-3/4	cups all-purpose flour
2	teaspoons salt
2	teaspoons chili powder
1	to 2 teaspoons cayenne pepper
1	teaspoon sugar
1	teaspoon garlic powder
1	teaspoon ground cumin

Oil for deep-fat frying

Cut onions into 1/4-in. slices; separate into rings. Place in a large bowl; cover with buttermilk and soak for 30 minutes, stirring twice.

In a shallow dish, beat eggs and water. In another shallow bowl, combine the flour, salt, chili powder, cayenne, sugar, garlic powder and cumin. Drain onion rings; dip in egg mixture, then roll in flour mixture.

In an electric skillet or deep-fat fryer, heat 1 in. of oil to 375°. Fry onion rings, a few at a time, for 1 to 1-1/2 minutes on each side or until golden brown. Drain on paper towels. **YIELD: 8 servings.**

MELODY MELLINGER, MYERSTOWN, PENNSYLVANIA
When we host Sunday dinner, I frequently serve these tangy meatballs. Everyone loves the distinctive sauce—they're often surprised to learn it is made with gingersnaps.

sweet 'n' sour meatballs

PREP: 30 MINUTES / **BAKE:** 40 MINUTES

3	eggs
1	medium onion, chopped
1-1/2	cups dry bread crumbs
1	teaspoon salt
2	pounds ground beef
2	tablespoons canola oil

SAUCE:

3-1/2	cups tomato juice
1	cup packed brown sugar
10	gingersnaps, finely crushed
1/4	cup white vinegar
1	teaspoon onion salt

In a bowl, combine the eggs, onion, bread crumbs and salt. Crumble beef over mixture and mix well. Shape into 1-1/2-in. balls. In a large skillet, brown meatballs in batches in oil. Transfer to a greased 13-in. x 9-in. baking dish.

In a saucepan, combine the sauce ingredients. Bring to a boil over medium heat, stirring until cookie crumbs are dissolved. Pour over meatballs.

Bake, uncovered, at 350° for 40-45 minutes or until meat is no longer pink. **YIELD: 8 servings.**

CAMILLE WISNIEWSKI, JACKSON, NEW JERSEY
When my children have friends over, I enjoy helping them with the cooking, and this dip is always one they request. Cashew nuts give this creamy, snackable mixture a nice crunch.

warm asparagus-crab spread

PREP/TOTAL TIME: 30 MINUTES

1	medium sweet red pepper, chopped
3	green onions, sliced
2	medium jalapeno peppers, seeded and finely chopped
2	teaspoons canola oil
1	can (15 ounces) asparagus spears, drained and chopped
2	cans (6 ounces *each*) crabmeat, drained, flaked and cartilage removed
1	cup mayonnaise
1/2	cup grated *or* shredded Parmesan cheese
1/2	cup chopped cashews

Assorted crackers

In a large skillet, saute the red pepper, onions and jalapenos in oil until tender. Add the asparagus, crab, mayonnaise and Parmesan cheese; mix well.

Transfer to a greased 1-qt. baking dish. Sprinkle with cashews. Bake, uncovered, at 375° for 20-25 minutes or until bubbly. Serve with crackers. **YIELD: 3 cups.**

EDITOR'S NOTE: When cutting hot peppers, disposable gloves are recommended. Avoid touching your face. Reduced-fat or fat-free mayonnaise is not recommended for this recipe.

LINDA THOMPSON, SOUTHAMPTON, ONTARIO

I always try to have a supply of these on hand in the freezer. If guests drop in, I just pull out and reheat some. You can serve them as a snack, for brunch or along with a lighter lunch.

almond cheddar appetizers

PREP/TOTAL TIME: 25 MINUTES

- 1 cup mayonnaise
- 2 teaspoons Worcestershire sauce
- 1 cup (4 ounces) shredded sharp cheddar cheese
- 1 medium onion, chopped
- 3/4 cup slivered almonds, chopped
- 6 bacon strips, cooked and crumbled
- 1 loaf (1 pound) French bread

In a bowl, combine the mayonnaise and Worcestershire sauce; stir in cheese, onion, almonds and bacon.

Cut bread into 1/2-in. slices; spread with cheese mixture. Cut slices in half; place on a greased baking sheet. Bake at 400° for 8-10 minutes or until bubbly. **YIELD: about 4 dozen.**

EDITOR'S NOTE: Unbaked appetizers may be frozen. To freeze, place in a single layer on a baking sheet; freeze for 1 hour. Remove the appetizers from the baking sheet and store in an airtight container for up to 2 months. When ready to use, place unthawed appetizers on a greased baking sheet. Bake at 400° for 10 minutes or until bubbly.

CHARLIE CLUTTS, NEW TAZEWELL, TENNESSEE

These pretty pinwheel appetizers are fun to nibble with their yummy ranch-flavored cream cheese filling that's layered with ham. One is never enough.

ranch ham roll-ups

PREP: 15 MINUTES + CHILLING

- 2 packages (8 ounces *each*) cream cheese, softened
- 1 envelope ranch salad dressing mix

- 3 green onions, chopped
- 11 flour tortillas (8 inches)
- 22 thin slices deli ham

In a small bowl, beat cream cheese and salad dressing mix until smooth. Stir in onions. Spread about 3 tablespoons over each tortilla; top each with two ham slices.

Roll up tightly and wrap in plastic wrap. Refrigerate until firm. Unwrap and cut into 3/4-in. slices. **YIELD: about 7-1/2 dozen.**

JESSE & ANNE FOUST, BLUEFIELD, WEST VIRGINIA

In our opinion, these deviled eggs are tops. With the perfect blend of seasonings, they've become a bit of a party staple in our family.

best deviled eggs

PREP/TOTAL TIME: 15 MINUTES

- 12 hard-cooked eggs
- 1/2 cup mayonnaise
- 1 teaspoon dried parsley flakes
- 1/2 teaspoon minced chives
- 1/2 teaspoon ground mustard
- 1/2 teaspoon dill weed
- 1/4 teaspoon salt
- 1/4 teaspoon paprika
- 1/8 teaspoon pepper
- 1/8 teaspoon garlic powder
- 2 tablespoons milk

Fresh parsley

Additional paprika

Slice eggs in half lengthwise; remove yolks and set whites aside. In a small bowl, mash yolks. Add the next 10 ingredients; mix well. Evenly fill the whites. Garnish with parsley and paprika. **YIELD: 2 dozen.**

CONNIE MILINOVICH, CUDAHY, WISCONSIN

Loaded with popular pizza ingredients, this cheesy concoction is wonderful on crackers, bagel chips, pita chips or slices of crusty Italian bread. You can even vary the ingredients to suit your family's tastes. The possibilities are endless!

pepperoni pizza spread

PREP: 10 MINUTES / **BAKE:** 25 MINUTES

2	cups (8 ounces) shredded part-skim mozzarella cheese
2	cups (8 ounces) shredded cheddar cheese
1	cup mayonnaise
1	cup chopped pimiento-stuffed olives
1	cup chopped pepperoni
1	can (6 ounces) ripe olives, drained and chopped
1	can (4 ounces) mushroom stems and pieces, drained and chopped
1/2	cup chopped onion
1/2	cup chopped green pepper

Crackers, breadsticks *and/or* French bread

In a large bowl, combine the first nine ingredients. Transfer mixture to an 11-in. x 7-in. baking dish. Bake, uncovered, at 350° for 25-30 minutes or until edges are bubbly and lightly browned. Serve spread with crackers, breadsticks and/or French bread. **YIELD: 6 cups.**

EDITOR'S NOTE: Reduced-fat or fat-free mayonnaise is not recommended for this recipe.

KELLIE REMMEN, DETROIT LAKES, MINNESOTA

These quick hors d'oeuvres may be mini, but their bacon-and-tomato flavor is full size. I serve the fresh-tasting nibbles at parties, brunches and picnics or whenever I need an easy and portable snack. If you're a fan of the classic sandwich, you'll love these!

blt bites

PREP: 25 MINUTES + CHILLING

16	to 20 cherry tomatoes
1	pound sliced bacon, cooked and crumbled
1/2	cup mayonnaise
1/3	cup chopped green onions
3	tablespoons grated Parmesan cheese
2	tablespoons snipped fresh parsley

Cut a thin slice off of each tomato top. Scoop out and discard pulp. Invert the tomatoes on a paper towel to drain. In a small bowl, combine all remaining ingredients. Spoon mixture into tomatoes. Refrigerate for several hours. **YIELD: 16-20 appetizer servings.**

KAY DALY, RALEIGH, NORTH CAROLINA

It's impossible to stop munching on warm pieces of this cheesy, oniony bread. The sliced loaf fans out for a fun presentation and perfect start to any festivity. It's also very portable, making it an ideal option for bring-a-dish event.

savory party bread

PREP/TOTAL TIME: 30 MINUTES

- 1 unsliced round loaf (1 pound) sourdough bread
- 1 pound Monterey Jack cheese, sliced
- 1/2 cup butter, melted
- 1/2 cup chopped green onions
- 2 to 3 teaspoons poppy seeds

Cut the bread lengthwise and widthwise without cutting through the bottom crust. Insert cheese between cuts. Combine butter, onions and poppy seeds; drizzle over the bread. Wrap bread in foil; place on a baking sheet. Bake at 350° for 15 minutes. Unwrap; bake 10 minutes longer or until the cheese is melted. **YIELD: 6-8 servings.**

KIMBERLY LEDON, ST. MARYS, GEORGIA

On-the-go families will love these handheld pizzas. They're made in a wink with convenient refrigerated biscuits and a jar of prepared spaghetti sauce.

beefy biscuit cups

PREP/TOTAL TIME: 30 MINUTES

- 1 pound ground beef
- 1 jar (14 ounces) spaghetti sauce
- 2 tubes (8 ounces *each*) large refrigerated biscuits
- 1 cup (4 ounces) shredded cheddar cheese

In a large skillet, cook beef over medium heat until no longer pink; drain. Stir in the spaghetti sauce; cook over medium heat for 5-10 minutes or until heated through.

Press biscuits onto the bottom and up the sides of greased muffin cups. Spoon 2 tablespoons beef mixture into the center of each cup.

Bake at 375° for 15-17 minutes or until golden brown. Sprinkle with cheese; bake 3 minutes longer or until cheese is melted. **YIELD: 8 servings.**

BARBARA MCCALLEY, ALLISON PARK, PENNSYLVANIA

This is one of the appetizers my friends request most. The tomato mixture is fresh and delicious. The red pepper flakes and chopped basil create a pleasant kick and change of pace to your usual bruschetta recipe.

tomato basil bruschetta

PREP/TOTAL TIME: 30 MINUTES

- 3 tablespoons olive oil, *divided*
- 1 loaf (1 pound) Italian bread, cut into 1/2-inch slices
- 1-1/2 cups chopped seeded plum tomatoes
- 1 jar (4 ounces) diced pimientos, rinsed and drained
- 2 tablespoons chopped fresh basil
- 1 teaspoon red wine vinegar
- 1 teaspoon minced fresh parsley
- 1 garlic clove, minced
- 1/4 teaspoon salt
- 1/4 teaspoon crushed red pepper flakes
- 1/8 teaspoon pepper
- 1 tablespoon grated Romano cheese

Fresh basil leaves

Using 2 tablespoons oil, lightly brush one side of bread slices. Place the bread oil side up on an ungreased baking sheet. Bake bread at 350° for 15 minutes or until lightly browned.

In a large bowl, combine the tomatoes, pimientos, chopped basil, vinegar, parsley, garlic, salt, pepper flakes and pepper; stir in Romano cheese. Place a whole basil leaf on each slice of toast bread. Top with tomato mixture. Drizzle with remaining olive oil. Serve immediately. **YIELD: 20 appetizers.**

RHONDA COWDEN, QUINCY, ILLINOIS
A warm, creamy bean mixture with colorful toppings is all it takes to create this effortless appetizer that's a tried-and-true favorite at get-togethers. People say the tortilla chips are just a vehicle for the dip!

fiesta dip

PREP/TOTAL TIME: 10 MINUTES

2	cups (16 ounces) sour cream
1	can (16 ounces) refried beans
1	can (4 ounces) chopped green chilies *or* jalapenos
1	envelope fiesta ranch dip mix
2	cups (8 ounces) shredded Mexican cheese blend, *divided*

Sliced ripe olives, chopped tomatoes, sliced green onions and shredded lettuce, optional

Tortilla chips

In a shallow 1-1/2-qt. microwave-safe dish, combine the sour cream, beans, chilies and dip mix. Stir in 1 cup cheese. Cover and microwave on high for 2 minutes; stir.

Cover and microwave 1-1/2 minutes longer or until heated through; stir until blended. Sprinkle with remaining cheese. Top with the olives, tomatoes, onions and lettuce if desired. Serve with tortilla chips. **YIELD: about 5 cups.**

EDITOR'S NOTE: This recipe was tested in a 1,100-watt microwave.

KITCHEN TIP

To keep ground beef from falling out of your burritos or enchiladas—and to up the protein— add a can of refried beans to the meat mixture and heat thoroughly. The filling not only stays in place—the beans stretch the mixture further. Try the ground beef and refried bean mixture in Fiesta Dip, too, for an even heartier snack.

JOANIE ELBOURN, GARDNER, MASSACHUSETTS
I first made this for an open house three years ago and everybody requested the recipe. It is very easy to make and tastes delicious. Cheesecake is popular in these parts—it's fun to have it for an appetizer instead of dessert for a change.

bacon-cheese appetizer pie

PREP: 15 MINUTES / **BAKE:** 50 MINUTES + COOLING

Pastry for a single-crust pie

3	packages (8 ounces *each*) cream cheese, softened
4	eggs, lightly beaten
1/4	cup milk
1	cup (4 ounces) shredded Swiss cheese
1/2	cup sliced green onions
6	bacon strips, cooked and crumbled
1/2	teaspoon salt
1/8	teaspoon pepper
1/8	teaspoon cayenne pepper

Roll the pastry into a 13-1/2-in. circle. Fit into the bottom and up the sides of an ungreased 9-in. springform pan. Lightly prick the bottom. Bake at 450° for 8-10 minutes or until lightly browned. Cool slightly.

In a large bowl, beat cream cheese until fluffy. Add eggs and milk; beat until smooth. Add cheese, onions, bacon, salt, pepper and cayenne; mix well. Pour into the crust.

Bake at 350° for 40-45 minutes or until a knife inserted near the center comes out clean. Cool 20 minutes. Remove sides of pan. Cut the pie into thin slices; serve warm. **YIELD: 16-20 appetizer servings.**

LISA FELD, GRAFTON, WISCONSIN
For an enjoyable and festive presentation of a shrimp appetizer, try these "scoops." People can't seem to stop munching on the savory filled bites.

cheddar shrimp nachos

PREP/TOTAL TIME: 20 MINUTES

3/4	pound deveined peeled cooked shrimp, chopped
1-1/2	cups (6 ounces) shredded cheddar cheese
1	can (4 ounces) chopped green chilies, drained
1/3	cup chopped green onions
1/4	cup sliced ripe olives, drained
1/2	cup mayonnaise
1/4	teaspoon ground cumin
48	tortilla chip scoops

In a large bowl, combine the shrimp, cheese, chilies, onions and olives. Combine the mayonnaise and cumin; add to shrimp mixture and toss to coat.

Drop by tablespoonfuls into tortilla scoops. Place scoops on ungreased baking sheets. Bake at 350° for 5-10 minutes or until cheese is melted. Serve nachos warm. **YIELD: 4 dozen.**

HEATHER COURTNEY, AMES, IOWA
My husband and I love to entertain, and this hearty, seven-ingredient dip is always a hit...as well as a request. It couldn't be much easier to put together, and using our slow cooker leaves us free to share some quality time with our guests.

slow cooker mexican dip

PREP: 15 MINUTES / **COOK:** 1-1/2 HOURS

1-1/2	pounds ground beef
1	pound bulk hot Italian sausage
1	cup chopped onion
1	package (8.8 ounces) ready-to-serve Spanish rice
1	can (16 ounces) refried beans
1	can (10 ounces) enchilada sauce
1	pound process cheese (Velveeta), cubed
1	package tortilla chip scoops

In a Dutch oven, cook the beef, sausage and onion over medium heat until meat is no longer pink; drain. Heat rice according to package directions.

In a 3-qt. slow cooker, combine the meat mixture, rice, beans, enchilada sauce and cheese. Cover and cook on low for 1-1/2 to 2 hours or until cheese is melted. Serve with tortilla scoops. **YIELD: 8 cups.**

MELISSA LANDON, PORT CHARLOTTE, FLORIDA
I was born and raised in Australia, but I moved to the U.S. when I married my husband. When I long for a taste of my childhood home, I bake up a batch of these sausage rolls and share them with neighbors or co-workers.

aussie sausage rolls

PREP: 15 MINUTES / **BAKE:** 20 MINUTES

1-1/4	pounds bulk pork sausage
1	medium onion, finely chopped
2	teaspoons minced chives
2	teaspoons minced fresh basil *or* 1/2 teaspoon dried basil
2	garlic cloves, minced
1	teaspoon paprika, *divided*
1/2	teaspoon salt
1/4	teaspoon pepper
1	package (17.3 ounces) frozen puff pastry, thawed

In a large bowl, combine sausage, onion, chives, basil, garlic, 3/4 teaspoon paprika, salt and pepper. Unfold the pastry onto a lightly floured work surface. Roll each pastry sheet into an 11-in. x 10-1/2-in. rectangle. Cut widthwise into 3-1/2-in. strips.

Spread 1/2 cup of sausage mixture down the center of each strip. Fold pastry over and press edges together to seal. Cut each roll into six pieces. Place seam side down on a rack in a shallow baking pan. Sprinkle with remaining paprika. Bake at 350° for 20-25 minutes or until golden brown. **YIELD: 3 dozen.**

LAURA JIRASEK, HOWELL, MICHIGAN
There's no need to brown ground beef when fixing this gooey, satisfying snack. Instead, I top crunchy chips with warm canned chili and melted cheese, then sprinkle it all with chopped tomato and sliced green onions for fresh flavor and color.

easy cheesy nachos

PREP/TOTAL TIME: 10 MINUTES

1	package (14-1/2 ounces) tortilla chips
2	cans (15 ounces *each*) chili without beans
1	pound process cheese (Velveeta), cubed
4	green onions, sliced
1	medium tomato, chopped

Divide the chips among six plates; set aside. In a saucepan, warm the chili until heated through.

Meanwhile, in another saucepan, heat cheese over medium-low heat until melted, stirring frequently. Spoon the chili over chips; drizzle with the melted cheese. Sprinkle with sliced onions and chopped tomato. **YIELD: 6 servings.**

ANGELA COFFMAN, STEWARTSVILLE, MISSOURI
I first tried these broiled treats at my sister-in-law's house. The juicy mushroom caps and creamy filling are a tempting addition to any appetizer menu.

bacon-stuffed mushrooms

PREP/TOTAL TIME: 20 MINUTES

1	package (8 ounces) cream cheese, softened
1/2	cup real bacon bits
1	tablespoon chopped green onion
1/4	teaspoon garlic powder
1	pound whole fresh mushrooms, stems removed

In a small bowl, beat cream cheese until smooth. Stir in the bacon, onion and garlic powder. Spoon into mushroom caps. Broil 4-6 in. from the heat for 4-6 minutes or until heated through. Serve warm. **YIELD: about 2 dozen.**

CHARLENE CRUMP, MONTGOMERY, ALABAMA
Wrapped in bacon, these irresistible chicken bites can be served with your favorite dipping sauce. I made up this recipe using a few items that were on hand. It was an immediate hit!

chicken poppers

PREP: 15 MINUTES / **COOK:** 20 MINUTES

3	pounds boneless skinless chicken breasts
1	cup ground fully cooked ham
25	to 30 cubed cheddar cheese (1/2-inch cubes)
1	pound sliced bacon
2	to 3 tablespoons olive oil
1	cup chicken broth
1/2	teaspoon salt
1/2	teaspoon pepper

Flatten chicken to 1/4-in. thickness; cut into 1-1/2-in. strips. Spread each strip with 1 teaspoon ham. Place a cheese cube on the end of each strip; roll up. Cut each slice of bacon in half widthwise. Wrap bacon around the chicken roll-up; secure each with a toothpick.

In a large skillet, cook roll-ups in olive oil until bacon is crispy, about 10 minutes. Add the chicken broth, salt and pepper; bring to a boil. Reduce heat; cover and simmer for 10-15 minutes or until the chicken is no longer pink. Serve poppers warm. Refrigerate leftovers. **YIELD: 25-30 appetizers.**

MICHELLE WENTZ, FORT POLK, LOUISIANA
This appealing appetizer takes classic bruschetta to new heights. Instead of olive oil, these savory treats are spread with reduced-fat cream cheese, then topped with tomato, green onion and ripe olives.

basil cream cheese bruschetta

PREP/TOTAL TIME: 20 MINUTES

12	slices French bread (1/2 inch thick)
1/2	cup chopped seeded tomato
2	tablespoons chopped green onion
1	tablespoon chopped ripe olives
4	ounces reduced-fat cream cheese
1	tablespoon minced fresh basil

Place bread on an ungreased baking sheet. Broil 6-8 in. from the heat for 3-4 minutes or until golden brown. Meanwhile, in a small bowl, combine the tomato, onion and olives; set aside.

Combine cream cheese and basil; spread over the untoasted side of bread. Broil 3 minutes longer or until cheese is melted and edges are golden brown. Top with tomato mixture. Serve warm. **YIELD: 1 dozen.**

KITCHEN TIP

To seed a tomato, cut the tomato in half horizontally and remove the stem. Holding the tomato half over a bowl or sink, scrape out the seeds with a small spoon or squeeze the tomato to force out the seeds. Then slice or dice it as directed in the recipe you are using.

LAURA LEMAY, DEERFIELD BEACH, FLORIDA
I created this recipe a few years ago when I was craving something different to do with hard-cooked eggs. I combined three of my favorite foods—bacon, eggs and cheese—in these deliciously different bites.

bacon-cheddar deviled eggs

PREP/TOTAL TIME: 20 MINUTES

12	hard-cooked eggs
1/2	cup mayonnaise
4	bacon strips, cooked and crumbled
2	tablespoons finely shredded cheddar cheese
1	tablespoon honey mustard
1/4	teaspoon pepper

Slice eggs in half lengthwise; remove yolks and set whites aside. In a small bowl, mash yolks. Stir in the mayonnaise, bacon, cheese, mustard and pepper. Stuff or pipe into egg whites. Refrigerate until serving. **YIELD: 2 dozen.**

EDITOR'S NOTE: As a substitute for honey mustard, combine 1-1/2 teaspoons Dijon mustard and 1-1/2 teaspoons honey.

TRISH PERRIN, KEIZER, OREGON
Both crispy and hearty, these filled potato skins are a favorite munchie my family requests often. Feel free to vary the toppings to suit your taste.

baked potato skins

PREP/TOTAL TIME: 20 MINUTES

4	large baking potatoes, baked
3	tablespoons canola oil
1	tablespoon grated Parmesan cheese
1/2	teaspoon salt
1/4	teaspoon garlic powder
1/4	teaspoon paprika
1/8	teaspoon pepper
8	bacon strips, cooked and crumbled
1-1/2	cups (6 ounces) shredded cheddar cheese
1/2	cup sour cream
4	green onions, sliced

Cut potatoes in half lengthwise; scoop out pulp, leaving a 1/4-in. shell (save pulp for another use). Place potatoes skins on a greased baking sheet. Combine oil, Parmesan cheese, salt, garlic powder, paprika and pepper; brush over both sides of skins.

Bake at 475° for 7 minutes; turn. Bake until crisp, about 7 minutes more. Sprinkle bacon and cheddar cheese inside skins. Bake 2 minutes longer or until the cheese is melted. Top with sour cream and onions. Serve immediately. **YIELD: 8 servings.**

LISA BYINGTON, JOHNSON CITY, NEW YORK

These creamy and zippy stuffed jalapenos may be the most popular party fare I make. My husband is always hinting to me that I should prepare a batch.

pepper poppers

PREP: 15 MINUTES / BAKE: 20 MINUTES

- 1 package (8 ounces) cream cheese, softened
- 1 cup (4 ounces) shredded sharp cheddar cheese
- 1 cup (4 ounces) shredded Monterey Jack cheese
- 6 bacon strips, cooked and crumbled
- 1/4 teaspoon salt
- 1/4 teaspoon garlic powder
- 1/4 teaspoon chili powder
- 1 pound fresh jalapenos, halved lengthwise and seeded
- 1/2 cup dry bread crumbs

Sour cream, onion dip *or* ranch salad dressing

In a large bowl, combine the cheeses, bacon and seasonings; mix well. Spoon about 2 tablespoonfuls into each pepper half. Roll in bread crumbs.

Place in a greased 15-in. x 10-in. baking pan. Bake, uncovered, at 300° for 20 minutes for spicy flavor, 30 minutes for medium and 40 minutes for mild. Serve with sour cream, dip or dressing. **YIELD: about 2 dozen.**

EDITOR'S NOTE: When cutting hot peppers, disposable gloves are recommended. Avoid touching your face.

MARINA CASTLE, NORTH HOLLYWOOD, CALIFORNIA

This colorful, freshly made salsa tastes wonderful on fish tacos. The garlic and veggies nicely complement the peach and mango flavors.

fresh peach mango salsa

PREP/TOTAL TIME: 20 MINUTES

- 1-1/2 cups chopped fresh tomatoes
- 3/4 cup chopped peeled fresh peaches
- 1/2 cup chopped red onion
- 1/2 cup chopped sweet yellow pepper
- 1/2 cup chopped peeled mango
- 2 tablespoons chopped seeded jalapeno pepper
- 3 garlic cloves, minced
- 1-1/2 teaspoons lime juice
- 1/2 teaspoon minced fresh cilantro

Tortilla chips

In a large bowl, combine the first nine ingredients. Cover and refrigerate until serving. Serve with tortilla chips. **YIELD: 4 cups.**

EDITOR'S NOTE: When cutting hot peppers, disposable gloves are recommended. Avoid touching your face.

KAREN RIORDAN, FERN CREEK, KENTUCKY

I'm a busy stay-at-home mom, so this recipe is my standby because it's easy to prepare in advance and keep refrigerated. Put it in the oven when guests arrive, and by the time you've poured beverages, the dip is ready.

hot pizza dip

PREP/TOTAL TIME: 30 MINUTES

- 1 package (8 ounces) cream cheese, softened
- 1 teaspoon Italian seasoning
- 1/4 teaspoon garlic powder
- 2 cups (8 ounces) shredded part-skim mozzarella cheese
- 1 cup (4 ounces) shredded cheddar cheese
- 1/2 cup pizza sauce
- 1/2 cup finely chopped green pepper
- 1/2 cup finely chopped sweet red pepper

Tortilla chips *or* breadsticks

In a bowl, combine cream cheese, Italian seasoning and garlic powder; spread on the bottom of a greased 9-in. pie plate. Combine cheeses; sprinkle half over the cream cheese layer. Top with the pizza sauce and peppers. Sprinkle with the remaining cheeses.

Bake at 350° for 20 minutes. Serve dip warm with tortilla chips or breadsticks. **YIELD: about 3-1/2 cups.**

KAREN WYDRINSKI, WOODSTOCK, GEORGIA
I first tasted this quick and easy dip at a friend's Christmas party. The combination of tart apple and sweet brickle chips kept me going back for more.

apple brickle dip

PREP/TOTAL TIME: 10 MINUTES

1	package (8 ounces) cream cheese, softened
1/2	cup packed brown sugar
1/4	cup sugar
1	teaspoon vanilla extract
1	package almond brickle chips (7-1/2 ounces) *or* English toffee bits (10 ounces)
3	medium tart apples, cut into chunks

In a bowl, beat cream cheese, sugars and vanilla. Fold in brickle chips. Serve the dip with apples. Refrigerate any leftovers. **YIELD: 2 cups.**

JANET ANDERSON, CARSON CITY, NEVADA
I need only five ingredients to fix these mouthwatering nibbles. Grape juice and apple jelly are the secrets behind the sweet yet tangy sauce that complements convenient packaged meatballs.

buffet meatballs

PREP: 10 MINUTES / **COOK:** 4 HOURS

1	cup grape juice
1	cup apple jelly
1	cup ketchup
1	can (8 ounces) tomato sauce
4	pounds frozen Italian-style meatballs

In a small saucepan, combine the grape juice, jelly, ketchup and tomato sauce. Cook and stir over medium heat until jelly is melted; remove from the heat. Place meatballs in a 5-qt. slow cooker. Pour sauce over the top and gently stir to coat. Cover and cook on low for 4 hours or until heated through. **YIELD: about 11 dozen.**

VIKKI REBHOLZ, WEST CHESTER, OHIO
These golden-brown rounds have lots of pepperoni flavor. I sometimes serve the simple bites with a side of pizza sauce, but they're just as munchable alone.

pepperoni pinwheels

PREP: 20 MINUTES / **BAKE:** 15 MINUTES

1/2	cup diced pepperoni
1/2	cup shredded part-skim mozzarella cheese
1/4	teaspoon dried oregano
1	egg, *separated*
1	tube (8 ounces) refrigerated crescent rolls

In a small bowl, combine the pepperoni, cheese, oregano and egg yolk. In another small bowl, whisk egg white until foamy; set aside. Separate the crescent dough into four rectangles; seal the perforations.

Spread pepperoni mixture over each rectangle to within 1/4 in. of edges. Roll up jelly-roll style, starting with a short side; pinch seams to seal. Cut each into six slices.

Place cut side down on greased baking sheets; brush tops with egg white. Bake at 375° for 12-15 minutes or until golden brown. Serve warm. Refrigerate leftovers. **YIELD: 2 dozen.**

CELENA CANTRELL, EAU CLAIRE, MICHIGAN
Folks who enjoy the taste of barbecue will gobble up these tender chunks of chicken coated in crushed barbecue potato chips. The crispy, flavorful nuggets are usually the first to go.

barbecue chicken bits

PREP/TOTAL TIME: 25 MINUTES

- 1 egg
- 2 tablespoons milk
- 4 cups barbecue potato chips, crushed
- 1/2 pound boneless skinless chicken breasts, cut into 1-1/2-inch cubes

Barbecue sauce

In a shallow bowl, whisk egg and milk. Place potato chips in another shallow bowl. Dip chicken in egg mixture, then roll in chips. Place in a single layer on a greased baking sheet. Bake at 400° for 10-15 minutes or until juices run clear. Serve with barbecue sauce. **YIELD: 4 servings.**

LESLIE BUENZ, TINLEY PARK, ILLINOIS
These delicious appetizers are always a hit at parties! Zesty strips of chicken and bits of onion sit in jalapeno halves that are wrapped in bacon and grilled. Serve them with blue cheese or ranch salad dressing for dipping.

jalapeno chicken wraps

PREP: 15 MINUTES / **GRILL:** 20 MINUTES

- 1 pound boneless skinless chicken breasts
- 1 tablespoon garlic powder
- 1 tablespoon onion powder
- 1 tablespoon pepper
- 2 teaspoons seasoned salt
- 1 teaspoon paprika
- 1 small onion, cut into strips
- 15 jalapeno peppers, halved and seeded
- 1 pound sliced bacon, halved widthwise

Blue cheese salad dressing

Cut chicken into 2-in. x 1-1/2-in. strips. In a large resealable plastic bag, combine the garlic powder, onion powder, pepper, seasoned salt and paprika; add chicken and shake to coat. Place a chicken and onion strip in each jalapeno half. Wrap each with a piece of bacon and secure with toothpicks.

Grill, uncovered, over indirect medium heat for 9-10 minutes on each side or until chicken is no longer pink and bacon is crisp. Serve with blue cheese dressing. **YIELD: 2-1/2 dozen.**

EDITOR'S NOTE: When cutting hot peppers, disposable gloves are recommended. Avoid touching your face.

CATHLEEN BUSHMAN, GENEVA, ILLINOIS

This is a quick and easy dip to bring to your next potluck. I serve the lip-smacking treat with potato chips, but bagel or pita chips would be equally delicious choices.

blt dip

PREP/TOTAL TIME: 10 MINUTES

1	cup (8 ounces) sour cream
1	cup mayonnaise
1	cup (4 ounces) shredded cheddar cheese
1	cup chopped seeded tomatoes
6	bacon strips, cooked and crumbled
1	tablespoon chopped green onion, optional

Assorted crackers

In a large bowl, combine the sour cream, mayonnaise, cheese, tomatoes and bacon. Refrigerate until serving. Garnish with green onion if desired. Serve with crackers. **YIELD: 3 cups.**

JOAN AIREY, RIVERS, MANITOBA

I received the recipe for these yummy wings from a cousin on Vancouver Island during a visit there a few years ago. They're an appealing appetizer but also a favorite for Sunday lunch with rice and a salad.

glazed chicken wings

PREP: 15 MINUTES / BAKE: 50 MINUTES

12	whole chicken wings (about 2-1/2 pounds)
1/2	cup barbecue sauce
1/2	cup honey
1/2	cup soy sauce

Cut chicken wings into three sections; discard wing tip section. Place in a greased 13-in. x 9-in. baking dish. Combine barbecue sauce, honey and soy sauce; pour over wings. Bake, uncovered, at 350° for 50-60 minutes or until chicken juices run clear. **YIELD: 4 servings.**

EDITOR'S NOTE: Uncooked chicken wing sections (wingettes) may be substituted for whole chicken wings.

KATHY GREEN, LAYTON, NEW JERSEY

So tender and tasty, these chicken appetizers are enhanced by a honey-mustard dipping sauce. I love creating hors d'oeuvres for our holiday open house—these are among the favorites.

sesame chicken bites

PREP/TOTAL TIME: 30 MINUTES

1/2	cup dry bread crumbs
1/4	cup sesame seeds
2	teaspoons minced fresh parsley
1/2	cup mayonnaise
1	teaspoon onion powder
1	teaspoon ground mustard
1/4	teaspoon pepper
1	pound boneless skinless chicken breasts, cut into 1-inch cubes
2	to 4 tablespoons canola oil

HONEY-MUSTARD SAUCE:

3/4	cup mayonnaise
4-1/2	teaspoons honey
1-1/2	teaspoons Dijon mustard

In a large resealable plastic bag, combine the bread crumbs, sesame seeds and parsley; set aside.

In a small bowl, combine the mayonnaise, onion powder, mustard and pepper. Coat chicken in mayonnaise mixture, then add to crumb mixture, a few pieces at a time; shake to coat.

In a large skillet, saute chicken in oil in batches until no longer pink, adding additional oil as needed. In a small bowl, combine sauce ingredients. Serve with chicken. **YIELD: 8-10 servings.**

DOROTHY ANDERSON, OTTAWA, KANSAS

These juicy sausages are cooked in a tangy-sweet sauce that makes them absolutely delectable. The recipe is fast and simple but serves a crowd.

pineapple smokies

PREP/TOTAL TIME: 15 MINUTES

1	cup packed brown sugar
3	tablespoons all-purpose flour
2	teaspoons ground mustard
1	cup pineapple juice
1/2	cup white vinegar
1-1/2	teaspoons soy sauce
2	pounds miniature smoked sausages

In a large saucepan, combine the sugar, flour and mustard. Gradually stir in the pineapple juice, vinegar and soy sauce. Bring to a boil over medium heat; cook and stir for 2 minutes or until thickened. Add sausages; stir to coat. Cook, uncovered, for 5 minutes longer or until heated through. Serve smokies warm. **YIELD: about 8 dozen.**

DEANNE CAUSEY, MIDLAND, TEXAS

These zesty little bites are easy to fix and irresistible to eat. Once you start snacking on them, you'll have a difficult time stopping. They're so popular at parties, I usually double the recipe. Even then, I never have enough!

seasoned fish crackers

PREP: 10 MINUTES / **BAKE:** 15 MINUTES + COOLING

3	packages (6.6 ounces *each*) miniature cheddar cheese fish-shaped crackers
1	envelope ranch salad dressing mix
3	teaspoons dill weed
1/2	teaspoon garlic powder
1/2	teaspoon lemon-pepper seasoning
1/4	teaspoon cayenne pepper
2/3	cup canola oil

Place crackers in a large bowl. Combine the remaining ingredients; drizzle over crackers and toss to coat evenly. Transfer to two ungreased 15-in. x 10-in. baking pans.

Bake the crackers at 250° for 15-20 minutes, stirring occasionally. Cool crackers completely. Store the crackers in an airtight container. **YIELD: about 2-1/2 quarts.**

WENDI WAVRIN LAW, OMAHA, NEBRASKA

My friends and neighbors expect me to bring this wonderful dip to every gathering. When I arrive, they ask, "You brought your bean dip, didn't you?" If there are any leftovers, we use them to make bean and cheese burritos the next day.

championship bean dip

PREP: 10 MINUTES / **COOK:** 2 HOURS

1	can (16 ounces) refried beans
1	cup picante sauce
1	cup (4 ounces) shredded Monterey Jack cheese
1	cup (4 ounces) shredded cheddar cheese
3/4	cup sour cream
1	package (3 ounces) cream cheese, softened
1	tablespoon chili powder
1/4	teaspoon ground cumin

Tortilla chips and salsa

In a large bowl, combine the first eight ingredients; transfer to a 1-1/2-qt. slow cooker. Cover and cook on high for 2 hours or until heated through, stirring once or twice. Serve with tortilla chips and salsa. **YIELD: 4-1/2 cups.**

READERS' RAVES

This is a very addictive dip. My co-workers and family always request this for potlucks. So very good!

—Skoeberg from TasteofHome.com

This is a great standby for me. I find that I can make it just as well in the microwave in less time. Also, leftovers are great wrapped with cooked chicken and salsa in a flour tortilla.

—Herosquad from TasteofHome.com

BRANDI LADNER, GULFPORT, MISSISSIPPI

When a college classmate and I threw a party for our professor, a friend contributed these savory appetizers. Everyone in the class requested the recipe before the party was done. Try the cups with chicken instead of ham if you'd like.

cheddar ham cups

PREP/TOTAL TIME: 30 MINUTES

2	cups (8 ounces) finely shredded cheddar cheese
2	packages (2-1/2 ounces *each*) thinly sliced deli ham, chopped
3/4	cup mayonnaise
1/3	cup real bacon bits
2	to 3 teaspoons Dijon mustard
1	tube (10.2 ounces) large refrigerated flaky biscuits

In a large bowl, combine the cheese, ham, mayonnaise, bacon and mustard. Split biscuits into thirds. Press onto the bottom and up the sides of ungreased miniature muffin cups. Fill each with about 1 tablespoon of cheese mixture.

Bake at 450° for 9-11 minutes or until golden brown and the cheese is melted. Let the appetizers stand for 2 minutes before removing from the pans. Serve warm. **YIELD: 2-1/2 dozen.**

PEGGY FOSTER, FLORENCE, KENTUCKY

This is a great dip my family loves for holidays, birthday gatherings and football parties. People can't seem to get enough of the creamy, spicy mixture.

buffalo chicken dip

PREP/TOTAL TIME: 30 MINUTES

1	package (8 ounces) cream cheese, softened
1	can (10 ounces) chunk white chicken, drained
1/2	cup buffalo wing sauce
1/2	cup ranch salad dressing
2	cups (8 ounces) shredded Colby-Monterey Jack cheese

Tortilla chips

Spread cream cheese into an ungreased shallow 1-qt. baking dish. Layer with chicken, buffalo wing sauce and ranch dressing. Sprinkle with cheese. Bake, uncovered, at 350° for 20-25 minutes or until cheese is melted. Serve warm with tortilla chips. **YIELD: about 2 cups.**

MEARL HARRIS, WEST PLAINS, MISSOURI
Before I retired, these tasty little treats were popular during break time at work. I found they're a good way to use up leftover corn bread, too.

enchilada meatballs

PREP: 20 MINUTES / **BAKE:** 20 MINUTES

> 2 cups crumbled corn bread
> 1 can (10 ounces) enchilada sauce, *divided*
> 1/2 teaspoon salt
> 1-1/2 pounds ground beef
> 1 can (8 ounces) tomato sauce
> 1/2 cup shredded Mexican cheese blend

In a large bowl, combine corn bread, 1/2 cup enchilada sauce and salt. Crumble beef over mixture; mix well. Shape into 1-in. balls. Place meatballs on a greased rack in a shallow baking pan. Bake, uncovered, at 350° for 18-22 minutes or until meat is no longer pink; drain.

Meanwhile, in a small saucepan, heat the tomato sauce and remaining enchilada sauce. Drain meatballs; place the meatballs in a serving dish. Top with sauce and sprinkle with cheese. Serve with toothpicks. **YIELD: about 4-1/2 dozen.**

CARA FLORA, KOKOMO, INDIANA
These cute little sausage and bacon bites are finger-licking good. They have a sweet and salty flavor combo that makes a fantastic as an appetizer...or even a quick breakfast.

smoky bacon wraps

PREP: 20 MINUTES / **BAKE:** 30 MINUTES

> 1 pound sliced bacon
> 1 package (16 ounces) miniature smoked sausage links
> 1 cup packed brown sugar

Cut each bacon strip in half widthwise. Wrap one piece of bacon around each sausage.

Place in a foil-lined 15-in. x 10-in. baking pan. Sprinkle with brown sugar. Bake, uncovered, at 400° for 30-40 minutes or until the bacon is crisp and the sausage is heated through. **YIELD: about 3-1/2 dozen.**

NANCY LESKY, LA CROSSE, WISCONSIN
I'm a beginner cook, so if I can make these delectable chicken wings, anybody can! I prepare the appetizing starter for Christmas, picnics, sports parties...you name it.

crispy chicken wings appetizer

PREP: 15 MINUTES / **BAKE:** 50 MINUTES

> 2 pounds chicken wings
> 1/2 cup butter, melted
> 1/4 teaspoon garlic powder
> 1 cup dry bread crumbs
> 1/2 cup grated Parmesan cheese
> 2 tablespoons minced fresh parsley
> 1/2 teaspoon salt
> 1/4 teaspoon pepper

Cut chicken wings into three sections; discard wing tip sections. In a small shallow bowl, combine butter and garlic powder. In another bowl, combine the remaining ingredients. Dip chicken into butter mixture, then into crumb mixture.

Place the coated wings on greased baking sheet; bake at 350° for 50-60 minutes or until the chicken juices run clear. Serve warm. **YIELD: 20 appetizers.**

EDITOR'S NOTE: Uncooked chicken wing sections (wingettes) may be substituted for whole chicken wings.

breakfast & brunch

Your favorite pancake house just became your very own kitchen thanks to the 5-star morning specialties featured here. From eggs and pancakes to waffles and French toast (and everything in between), you'll never think to skip breakfast again.

HONEY WHEAT PANCAKES / PAGE 58

KAREN SCHROEDER, KANKAKEE, ILLINOIS
This is my husband's favorite breakfast treat and the ultimate comfort food. It's warm, slightly sweet and keeps you going the whole morning through.

fruity baked oatmeal

PREP: 15 MINUTES / **BAKE:** 35 MINUTES

3	cups quick-cooking oats	1	cup fat-free milk
1	cup packed brown sugar	1/2	cup butter, melted
2	teaspoons baking powder	3/4	cup chopped peeled tart apple
1	teaspoon salt	1/3	cup chopped fresh *or* frozen peaches
1/2	teaspoon ground cinnamon	1/3	cup fresh *or* frozen blueberries
2	eggs, lightly beaten		Additional fat-free milk, optional

In a large bowl, combine the oats, brown sugar, baking powder, salt and cinnamon. Combine the eggs, milk and butter; add to the dry ingredients. Stir in the apple, peaches and blueberries.

Pour into an 8-in. square baking dish coated with cooking spray. Bake, uncovered, at 350° for 35-40 minutes or until a knife inserted near the center comes out clean. Cut into squares. Serve with milk if desired. **YIELD: 9 servings.**

EDITOR'S NOTE: If using frozen blueberries, do not thaw before adding to batter.

SUSAN WATT, BASKING RIDGE, NEW JERSEY
I found this recipe a few years ago and made a few changes to suit my family's taste. Every time I serve a brunch, the cheesy, ham-filled frittatas are the first thing to disappear.

mini ham 'n' cheese frittatas

PREP: 15 MINUTES / **BAKE:** 25 MINUTES

- 1/4   **pound cubed fully cooked lean ham**
- 1   **cup (4 ounces) shredded fat-free cheddar cheese**
- 6   **eggs**
- 4   **egg whites**
- 3   **tablespoons minced chives**
- 2   **tablespoons fat-free milk**
- 1/4   **teaspoon salt**
- 1/4   **teaspoon pepper**

Divide ham evenly among eight muffin cups coated with cooking spray; top with cheese. In a large bowl, beat eggs and whites. Beat in the chives, milk, salt and pepper. Pour over cheese, filling each muffin cup three-fourths full.

Bake at 375° for 22-25 minutes or until a knife inserted near the center comes out clean. Carefully run a knife around edges to loosen; remove from pan. Serve warm. **YIELD: 8 frittatas.**

HELEN LIPKO, MARTINSBURG, PENNSYLVANIA
Convenient crescent roll dough hurries along these yummy glazed rolls that are popular with everyone who tries them. It's great with a cup of hot coffee.

morning cinnamon rolls

PREP/TOTAL TIME: 25 MINUTES

- 1   **tube (8 ounces) refrigerated reduced-fat crescent rolls**
- 1/2   **teaspoon ground cinnamon**

Sugar substitute equivalent to 1/2 cup sugar, *divided*

- 1/4   **cup confectioners' sugar**
- 1   **tablespoon fat-free milk**

Unroll crescent dough into a rectangle; seal seams and perforations. Combine the cinnamon and half of the sugar substitute; sprinkle over dough. Roll up jelly-roll style, starting with a long side; seal edge. Cut into eight slices.

Place rolls cut side down in a 9-in. round baking pan coated with cooking spray. Bake at 375° for 12-15 minutes or until golden brown.

For glaze, in a small bowl, combine the confectioners' sugar, milk and remaining sugar substitute; drizzle glaze over warm rolls. **YIELD: 8 servings.**

EDITOR'S NOTE: This recipe was tested with Splenda sugar blend.

TERRY KUEHN, WAUNAKEE, WISCONSIN

For a filling breakfast, I stack cheese, Canadian bacon and a poached egg on an English muffin. The appealing day-break dish is ideal for one, but the delicious open-face sandwich is special enough to make for guests, too.

bacon-egg english muffin

PREP/TOTAL TIME: 15 MINUTES

1	tablespoon white vinegar
2	eggs
1	tablespoon cream cheese, softened
1	English muffin, split and toasted
2	slices process American cheese
2	slices Canadian bacon

Place 2-3 in. of water in a large skillet with high sides; add vinegar. Bring to a boil; reduce heat and simmer gently. Break cold eggs, one at a time, into a custard cup or saucer; holding the cup close to the surface of the water, slip egg into water. Cook, uncovered, until whites are completely set, about 4 minutes.

Meanwhile, spread cream cheese over muffin halves. Top with cheese slices and Canadian bacon. Using a slotted spoon, lift eggs out of water and place over bacon. **YIELD: 2 servings.**

KITCHEN TIP

You can also poach eggs using your microwave. Place 2 tablespoons of water in a 6-ounce custard cup. Microwave, uncovered, on high until boiling. Carefully break 1 egg into the cup. Pierce the egg yolk several times with a toothpick. Cover and cook at 50% power for 1 to 1-1/2 minutes or until egg is almost set. Let stand, covered, for 1 minute. Whether prepared in the microwave or on the stovetop, be sure you are using the freshest eggs possible.

PRISCILLA DETRICK, CATOOSA, OKLAHOMA

BLT's are a favorite at my house, so I created this recipe to combine those flavors in a "dressier" morning dish. It was such a hit when I served it at a brunch I hosted. I received many compliments and wrote out the recipe several times that day.

blt egg bake

PREP/TOTAL TIME: 30 MINUTES

1/4	cup mayonnaise
5	slices bread, toasted
4	slices process American cheese
12	bacon strips, cooked and crumbled
4	eggs
1	medium tomato, halved and sliced
2	tablespoons butter
2	tablespoons all-purpose flour
1/4	teaspoon salt
1/8	teaspoon pepper
1	cup milk
1/2	cup shredded cheddar cheese
2	green onions, thinly sliced

Shredded lettuce

Spread mayonnaise on one side of each slice of toast and cut into small pieces. Arrange toast, mayonnaise side up, in a greased 8-in. square baking dish. Top with cheese slices and bacon.

In a large skillet, fry eggs over medium heat until completely set; place over bacon. Top with tomato slices; set aside.

In a small saucepan, melt butter. Stir in flour, salt and pepper until smooth. Gradually add milk. Bring to a boil; cook and stir for 2 minutes or until thickened.

Pour over tomato. Sprinkle with cheddar cheese and onions. Bake, uncovered, at 325° for 10 minutes. Cut in squares; serve with lettuce. **YIELD: 4 servings.**

KAY CLARK, LAWRENCEBURG, KENTUCKY
This is an elegant breakfast dish to make ahead for holidays or Sunday brunch. I run a bed and breakfast and tea room cafe, and this recipe is a frequent request from my customers.

apple-stuffed french toast

PREP: 20 MINUTES + CHILLING / **BAKE:** 35 MINUTES

1	cup packed brown sugar
1/2	cup butter, cubed
2	tablespoons light corn syrup
1	cup chopped pecans
12	slices Italian bread (1/2 inch thick)
2	large tart apples, peeled and thinly sliced
6	eggs
1-1/2	cups milk
1-1/2	teaspoons ground cinnamon
1	teaspoon vanilla extract
1/4	teaspoon salt
1/4	teaspoon ground nutmeg

CARAMEL SAUCE:

1/2	cup packed brown sugar
1/4	cup butter, cubed
1	tablespoon light corn syrup

In a small saucepan, combine the brown sugar, butter and corn syrup; cook and stir over medium heat until thickened. Pour into a greased 13-in. x 9-in. baking dish; top with half of the pecans, a single layer of bread and remaining pecans. Arrange apples and remaining bread over the top.

In a large bowl, whisk the eggs, milk, cinnamon, vanilla, salt and nutmeg. Pour over bread. Cover and refrigerate overnight.

Remove from the refrigerator 30 minutes before baking. Bake, uncovered, at 350° for 35-40 minutes or until lightly browned.

In a small saucepan, combine the sauce ingredients. Cook and stir over medium heat until thickened. Serve with French toast. **YIELD: 6 servings.**

ARLENE BUTLER, OGDEN, UTAH
Ham, zucchini, mushrooms, green pepper and cheese flavor this rich, hearty egg bake. It adds appeal to a breakfast or lunch buffet and cuts easily, too. Make sure you bring the recipe—everyone will want it!

brunch strata

PREP: 45 MINUTES / **BAKE:** 35 MINUTES + STANDING

3	cups sliced fresh mushrooms
3	cups chopped zucchini
2	cups cubed fully cooked ham
1-1/2	cups chopped onions
1-1/2	cups chopped green peppers
2	garlic cloves, minced
1/3	cup canola oil
2	packages (8 ounces *each*) cream cheese, softened
1/2	cup half-and-half cream
12	eggs
4	cups cubed day-old bread
3	cups (12 ounces) shredded cheddar cheese
1	teaspoon salt
1/2	teaspoon pepper

In a large skillet, saute the mushrooms, zucchini, ham, onions, green peppers and garlic in oil until vegetables are tender. Drain and pat dry; set aside.

In a large bowl, beat the cream cheese and cream until smooth. Beat in eggs. Stir in the bread, cheddar cheese, salt, pepper and vegetable mixture.

Pour into two greased 11-in. x 7-in. baking dishes. Bake, uncovered, at 350° for 35-40 minutes or until a knife inserted near the center comes out clean. Let stand for 10 minutes before serving. **YIELD: 2 casseroles (8 servings each).**

PATRICIA WALLS, AURORA, MINNESOTA
This is the best breakfast dish I've ever tasted. With luscious blueberries tucked inside every bite, it's almost more like a dessert. A local blueberry grower shared the recipe with me.

blueberry french toast

PREP: 30 MINUTES + CHILLING / **BAKE:** 55 MINUTES

12	slices day-old white bread, crusts removed
2	packages (8 ounces *each*) cream cheese
1	cup fresh *or* frozen blueberries
12	eggs
2	cups milk
1/3	cup maple syrup *or* honey

SAUCE:

1	cup sugar
2	tablespoons cornstarch
1	cup water
1	cup fresh *or* frozen blueberries
1	tablespoon butter

Cut bread into 1-in. cubes; place half in a greased 13-in. x 9-in. baking dish. Cut cream cheese into 1-in. cubes; place over bread. Top with blueberries and remaining bread cubes.

In a large bowl, beat the eggs. Add the milk and syrup; mix well. Pour over the bread mixture. Cover and refrigerate for 8 hours or overnight.

Remove from the refrigerator 30 minutes before baking. Cover and bake at 350° for 30 minutes. Uncover; bake 25-30 minutes longer or until golden brown and center is set.

In a small saucepan, combine sugar, cornstarch and water until smooth. Bring to a boil over medium heat; cook and stir for 3 minutes. Stir in blueberries; reduce heat. Simmer for 8-10 minutes or until berries have burst. Stir in butter until melted. Serve with French toast. **YIELD: 6-8 servings (1-3/4 cups sauce).**

LINDA BERNHAGEN, PLAINFIELD, ILLINOIS
These French toast slices have creamy vanilla flavor from a convenient pudding mix, plus a hint of cinnamon. We like to top the scrumptious slices with syrup or powdered sugar and fresh berries. You can also use butterscotch pudding instead of vanilla.

very vanilla french toast

PREP/TOTAL TIME: 10 MINUTES

1	cup milk
1	package (3 ounces) cook-and-serve vanilla pudding mix
1	egg
1/2	teaspoon ground cinnamon
8	slices Texas toast
2	teaspoons butter

In a large bowl, whisk the milk, pudding mix, egg and cinnamon for 2 minutes or until well blended. Dip Texas toast slices in pudding mixture, coating both sides.

In a large skillet, melt butter over medium heat. Cook Texas toast on both sides until golden brown. **YIELD: 4 servings.**

READERS' RAVES

"This has been one of my all-time favorite recipes since I found it in *Taste of Home* years ago! The number of reviews, and the fact that people took the time to write about this recipe, should tell anyone of its wonders! This is in my top five foods of all time!

—Whisk-Karrs from TasteofHome.com"

ROCHELLE FELSBURG, FREDERICKSBURG, VIRGINIA
I'm a music teacher, and I made this for a teachers' breakfast. It was heartily received! The nutmeg adds a rich, homey flavor.

nutmeg syrup

PREP/TOTAL TIME: 15 MINUTES

- 1 cup sugar
- 2 tablespoons all-purpose flour
- 1 teaspoon ground cinnamon
- 1/2 teaspoon ground nutmeg
- 2 cups cold water
- 2 tablespoons butter
- 1 teaspoon vanilla extract
- 1/4 teaspoon rum extract, optional

In a large saucepan, combine sugar, flour, cinnamon, nutmeg and water until smooth. Bring to a boil; cook and stir for 2 minutes or until thickened. Remove from the heat; stir in the butter, vanilla and extract if desired. **YIELD: 2-1/3 cups.**

BARBARA MCCALLEY, ALLISON PARK, PENNSYLVANIA
This eye-opening quiche features chicken, spinach and cheddar cheese, but you can use Swiss cheese if you'd like. This easy-to-prepare quiche cuts beautifully and always impresses.

chicken spinach quiche

PREP: 10 MINUTES / **BAKE:** 40 MINUTES + STANDING

- 1 cup (4 ounces) shredded cheddar cheese, *divided*
- 1 unbaked pastry shell (9 inches)
- 1 cup diced cooked chicken
- 1 package (10 ounces) frozen chopped spinach, thawed and squeezed dry
- 1/4 cup finely chopped onion
- 2 eggs
- 3/4 cup milk
- 3/4 cup mayonnaise
- 1/4 teaspoon salt
- 1/8 teaspoon pepper

Sprinkle 1/4 cup cheese into the pastry shell. In a bowl, combine the chicken, 1/2 cup spinach, onion and remaining cheese (save remaining spinach for another use). Spoon into pastry shell. In a bowl, whisk the eggs, milk, mayonnaise, salt and pepper; pour over the chicken mixture.

Bake at 350° for 40-45 minutes or until a knife inserted near the center comes out clean. Let quiche stand for 15 minutes before cutting. **YIELD: 6-8 servings.**

EDITOR'S NOTE: Reduced-fat or fat-free mayonnaise is not recommended for this recipe.

BRANDI DAVIS, PULLMAN, WASHINGTON
For the perfect autumn wake-up call, turn to these deliciously different waffles. The orange walnut butter adds plenty of fall flavor in every bite.

pumpkin waffles with orange walnut butter

PREP/TOTAL TIME: 30 MINUTES

- 1 cup plus 2 tablespoons all-purpose flour
- 2 tablespoons brown sugar
- 1 teaspoon ground cinnamon
- 1/2 teaspoon salt
- 1/2 teaspoon baking powder
- 1/4 teaspoon baking soda
- 2 eggs
- 1 cup milk
- 1/2 cup canned pumpkin
- 2 tablespoons butter, melted

ORANGE WALNUT BUTTER:
- 1/2 cup butter, softened
- 1/4 cup chopped walnuts
- 1 tablespoon grated orange peel

Maple syrup

In a large bowl, combine the first six ingredients. In another bowl, combine the eggs, milk, pumpkin and butter; stir into dry ingredients just until combined.

Bake in a preheated waffle iron according to the manufacturer's directions until golden brown.

Meanwhile, for orange walnut butter, in a small bowl, combine the butter, walnuts and orange peel until blended. Serve waffles with butter mixture and maple syrup. **YIELD: 4 servings.**

PAULA HADLEY, SOMERVILLE, LOUISIANA

When our family goes blueberry picking, we have a bounty of berries in no time. Our favorite way to enjoy them is in these melt-in-your-mouth pancakes topped with a satisfying blueberry sauce.

blueberry sour cream pancakes

PREP: 20 MINUTES / **COOK:** 30 MINUTES

1/2	cup sugar
2	tablespoons cornstarch
1	cup cold water
4	cups fresh *or* frozen blueberries

PANCAKES:

2	cups all-purpose flour
1/4	cup sugar
4	teaspoons baking powder
1/2	teaspoon salt
2	eggs
1-1/2	cups milk
1	cup (8 ounces) sour cream
1/3	cup butter, melted
1	cup fresh *or* frozen blueberries

In a large saucepan, combine sugar and cornstarch. Stir in water until smooth. Add blueberries. Bring to a boil over medium heat; cook and stir for 2 minutes or until thickened. Remove from the heat; cover and keep warm.

For pancakes, in a large bowl, combine the flour, sugar, baking powder and salt. Combine the eggs, milk, sour cream and butter. Stir into dry ingredients just until moistened. Fold in blueberries.

Pour batter by 1/4 cupful onto a greased hot griddle. Turn when bubbles form on top; cook until the second side is golden brown. Serve with blueberry topping. **YIELD: about 20 pancakes (3-1/2 cups topping).**

EDITOR'S NOTE: If using frozen blueberries, do not thaw before adding to batter.

SUE ELLEN BUMPUS, LAMPASAS, TEXAS

This sunny morning slush always comes together in a wink thanks to a handful of convenient ingredients. It's sure to put a little extra zip in your day!

frothy orange drink

PREP/TOTAL TIME: 10 MINUTES

1	cup water
1	cup milk
1	can (6 ounces) frozen orange juice concentrate, thawed
1/2	cup sugar
1	teaspoon vanilla extract
8	to 10 ice cubes

In a blender, combine all ingredients; cover and process until thickened and slushy. Pour into chilled glasses; serve immediately. **YIELD: 4 cups.**

MARTINA BIAS, BELLEVILLE, ILLINOIS
Even my kids can't wait to dig into these wholesome pancakes! The thick yet tender flapjacks have a delightful hint of honey and cinnamon flavor that wakes up the taste buds.

honey wheat pancakes

PREP: 10 MINUTES / **COOK:** 5 MINUTES/BATCH

1-1/2	cups reduced-fat biscuit/baking mix
1/2	cup whole wheat flour
1/4	cup wheat germ
1	teaspoon baking powder
1	teaspoon ground cinnamon
2	eggs, lightly beaten
1-1/2	cups buttermilk
1	medium ripe banana, mashed
2	tablespoons honey

Assorted fresh fruit *and/or* maple syrup, optional

In a small bowl, combine the first five ingredients. Combine the eggs, buttermilk, banana and honey; add to dry ingredients just until moistened.

Pour batter by 1/4 cupfuls onto a hot griddle coated with cooking spray; turn when bubbles form on top. Cook pancakes until the second side is golden brown. Serve with fruit and/or syrup if desired. **YIELD: 12 pancakes.**

JUANITA CARLSEN, NORTH BEND, OREGON
Maple syrup sweetens these lovely cinnamon buns. I make the dough in my bread machine before popping the rolls in the oven. They're wonderful served warm.

mini maple cinnamon rolls

PREP: 20 MINUTES + RISING / **BAKE:** 20 MINUTES

2/3	cup milk
1/3	cup maple syrup
1/3	cup butter, softened
1	egg
3/4	teaspoon salt
3	cups bread flour
1	package (1/4 ounce) active dry yeast

TOPPING:

1/2	cup packed brown sugar
2	tablespoons bread flour
4	teaspoons ground cinnamon
6	tablespoons cold butter

MAPLE ICING:

1	cup confectioners' sugar
3	tablespoons butter, melted
3	tablespoons maple syrup
1	to 2 teaspoons milk

In bread machine pan, place the first seven ingredients in order suggested by manufacturer. Select dough setting (check dough after 5 minutes of mixing; add 1 to 2 tablespoons of water or bread flour if needed).

When the cycle is completed, turn dough onto a lightly floured surface. Roll into two 12-in. x 7-in. rectangles. In a small bowl, combine the brown sugar, flour and cinnamon; cut in butter until mixture resembles coarse crumbs. Sprinkle half over each rectangle. Roll up jelly-roll style, starting from a long side; pinch seam to seal.

Cut each roll into 12 slices. Place cut side down in one greased 13-in. x 9-in. baking pan. Cover and let rise in a warm place until doubled, about 20 minutes.

Bake at 375° for 20-25 minutes or until golden brown. Cool on a wire rack for 5 minutes. Meanwhile, in a small bowl, combine the confectioners' sugar, butter, syrup and enough milk to achieve desired consistency. Spread maple icing over warm rolls. **YIELD: 2 dozen.**

EDITOR'S NOTE: We recommend you do not use a bread machine's time-delay feature for this recipe.

JENNIFER HOWELL, FORT COLLINS, COLORADO
I love how easy it is to assemble this savory egg casserole that features hash browns, ham and cheese. Putting it together the night before really frees up your time the next morning.

overnight
egg casserole

PREP: 10 MINUTES + CHILLING
BAKE: 1 HOUR + STANDING

4	cups frozen shredded hash brown potatoes, thawed
1	cup cubed fully cooked ham
1	can (4 ounces) chopped green chilies
1/2	cup shredded Monterey Jack cheese
1/2	cup shredded cheddar cheese
6	eggs
1	can (12 ounces) evaporated milk
1/4	teaspoon pepper

Salsa, optional

In a greased 8-in. square baking dish, layer the hash browns, ham, chilies, Monterey Jack cheese and cheddar cheese. In a large bowl, whisk the eggs, milk and pepper; pour over the casserole. Cover and refrigerate overnight.

Remove from the refrigerator 30 minutes before baking. Bake, uncovered, at 350° for 1 hour or until a knife inserted near the center comes out clean. Let stand for 5-10 minutes. Serve with salsa if desired. **YIELD: 9 servings.**

NANCY DAUGHERTY, CORTLAND, OHIO
I love hosting brunch...and this special omelet roll is one reason why. It's stuffed with mouthwatering ingredients and offers an impressive look—all rolled into one! A platter of these pretty swirled slices never lasts long.

ham 'n' cheese
omelet roll

PREP: 15 MINUTES / **BAKE:** 35 MINUTES

4	ounces cream cheese, softened
3/4	cup milk
2	tablespoons all-purpose flour
1/4	teaspoon salt
12	eggs
2	tablespoons Dijon mustard
2-1/4	cups shredded cheddar cheese, *divided*
2	cups finely chopped fully cooked ham
1/2	cup thinly sliced green onions

Line the bottom and sides of a greased 15-in. x 10-in. baking pan with parchment paper; grease the paper and set aside.

In a small bowl, beat cream cheese and milk until smooth. Add flour and salt; mix until combined. In a large bowl, beat the eggs until blended. Add cream cheese mixture; mix well. Pour into prepared pan.

Bake at 375° for 30-35 minutes or until eggs are puffed and set. Remove from the oven. Immediately spread with mustard and sprinkle with 1 cup cheese. Sprinkle with ham, onions and 1 cup cheese.

Roll up from a short side, peeling parchment paper away while rolling. Sprinkle top of roll with the remaining cheese; bake 3-4 minutes longer or until cheese is melted. **YIELD: 12 servings.**

BETH NOTARO, KOKOMO, INDIANA
We enjoyed a hearty breakfast bake during a visit to an Amish inn. When I asked for the recipe, one of the ladies recited it right off the top of her head. I modified a few things to create this version my family raves about. You can even try breakfast sausage in place of the bacon.

amish breakfast
casserole

PREP: 15 MINUTES / **BAKE:** 35 MINUTES + STANDING

1	pound sliced bacon, diced
1	medium sweet onion, chopped
6	eggs, lightly beaten
4	cups frozen shredded hash brown potatoes, thawed
2	cups (8 ounces) shredded cheddar cheese
1-1/2	cups (12 ounces) 4% cottage cheese
1-1/4	cups shredded Swiss cheese

In a large skillet, cook bacon and onion until bacon is crisp; drain. In a large bowl, combine the remaining ingredients; stir in the bacon mixture. Transfer all to a greased 13-in. x 9-in. baking dish.

Bake, uncovered, at 350° for 35-40 minutes or until a knife inserted near the center comes out clean. Let casserole stand for 10 minutes before cutting. **YIELD: 12 servings.**

VICKY DEMPSEY, LOUISVILLE, MISSISSIPPI
This is one of my son's favorites. Buttered hash browns form a mouthwatering crust for a yummy filling of sausage and cheese. It's sure to please at breakfast, brunch or even dinner.

hash brown sausage bake

PREP: 30 MINUTES / **BAKE:** 40 MINUTES

1	package (20 ounces) refrigerated shredded hash brown potatoes
1/3	cup butter, melted
1	teaspoon beef bouillon granules
1	pound bulk pork sausage
1/3	cup chopped onion
1	cup (8 ounces) 4% cottage cheese
3	eggs, lightly beaten
4	slices process American cheese, chopped

In a large bowl, combine the hash browns, butter and bouillon. Press hash brown mixture onto the bottom and up the sides of a greased 10-in. pie plate. Bake at 350° for 25-30 minutes or until edges are lightly browned.

Meanwhile, in a large skillet, cook sausage and onion over medium heat until meat is no longer pink; drain. In a large bowl, combine the sausage mixture, cottage cheese, eggs and American cheese.

Pour into crust. Bake at 350° for 40-45 minutes or until a knife inserted near the center comes out clean. Let stand for 5 minutes before cutting. **YIELD: 6-8 servings.**

NANCY HAWTHORNE, GETTYSBURG, PENNSYLVANIA
My son begged me to try making the stuffed French toast we enjoyed when our family visited Walt Disney World. His encouragement resulted in this effortless and delicious creation that's a favorite on Saturday mornings.

fruity french toast

PREP/TOTAL TIME: 15 MINUTES

1	medium firm banana, sliced
4	slices Texas toast
2	teaspoons confectioners' sugar, *divided*
2	large strawberries, sliced
1	egg
1/2	cup milk
1/2	teaspoon vanilla extract
1/4	teaspoon ground cinnamon
2	teaspoons butter

Maple syrup

Place banana slices on two slices of toast. Sprinkle each with 1/2 teaspoon confectioners' sugar. Top with strawberries and remaining toast. In a shallow bowl, whisk the egg, milk, vanilla extract and cinnamon. Dip the toast in the egg mixture, coating both sides.

In a large skillet, melt butter over medium heat; cook toast for 2-4 minutes on each side or until golden brown. Sprinkle with remaining confectioners' sugar. Serve with maple syrup. **YIELD: 2 servings.**

SORREL PICKLE, ARCADIA, FLORIDA

This is an excellent morning meal when you're short on time. The yummy egg bake is simple to prepare, plus it can be made ahead of time and frozen until needed.

breakfast casserole

PREP: 20 MINUTES / **BAKE:** 30 MINUTES

2	slices bread
1/2	pound bulk pork sausage
1/2	cup shredded cheddar cheese
3	eggs
1	cup milk
1/2	teaspoon ground mustard
1/4	teaspoon salt
1/8	teaspoon pepper

Remove the crust from the bread and cut into 1-in. cubes. (Discard crust or save for another use.) Place in a greased 8-in. square baking dish.

In a skillet, brown the sausage over medium heat until no longer pink; drain. Sprinkle the sausage and cheese over bread cubes.

In a bowl, whisk the eggs, milk, mustard, salt and pepper. Pour over the sausage and cheese. Bake at 350° for 30 minutes or until puffed and golden. **YIELD: 2-4 servings.**

KITCHEN TIP

Save time and money by purchasing shredded cheddar cheese in bulk. Buy a 5-pound bag and put small amounts in resealable freezer bags and freeze individually. When a recipe calls for it, just thaw a bag. It tastes the same without being wasteful of time, money...or cheese.

—Rose M., Plaxo, Texas

REBECCA CLARK, WARRIOR, ALABAMA

A few tubes of convenient crescent roll dough make this impressive recipe a snap. I fill the flaky crescent roll ring with chicken salad, and then serve the warm slices with a mustard-flavored mayonnaise.

chicken club brunch ring

PREP: 20 MINUTES / **BAKE:** 20 MINUTES

1/2	cup mayonnaise
1	tablespoon minced fresh parsley
2	teaspoons Dijon mustard
1-1/2	teaspoons finely chopped onion
1-3/4	cups cubed cooked chicken breast (1/2-inch cubes)
2	bacon strips, cooked and crumbled
1	cup (4 ounces) shredded Swiss cheese, *divided*
2	tubes (8 ounces *each*) refrigerated crescent rolls
2	plum tomatoes
2	cups shredded lettuce

In a large bowl, combine the mayonnaise, parsley, mustard and onion. Stir in the chicken, bacon and 3/4 cup Swiss cheese.

Unroll crescent dough; separate into 16 triangles. Arrange on an ungreased 12-in. round pizza pan, forming a ring with pointed ends facing outer edge of pan and wide ends overlapping.

Spoon chicken mixture over wide ends; fold points over filling and tuck under wide ends (filling will be visible). Chop half of a tomato; set aside. Slice remaining tomatoes; place over filling and tuck into dough.

Bake at 375° for 20-25 minutes or until golden brown. Sprinkle with remaining Swiss cheese. Let stand for 5 minutes. Place lettuce in center of ring; sprinkle lettuce with chopped tomato. **YIELD: 16 servings.**

NANCY ROPER, ETOBICOKE, ONTARIO

Chopped cranberries and orange peel give this coffee cake a burst of tart flavor that complements the sweet cream cheese layer so well. The pretty appearance makes it a treat you'll look forward to serving your guests.

creamy cranberry coffee cake

PREP: 15 MINUTES / **BAKE:** 70 MINUTES + COOLING

2	cups all-purpose flour
1	cup sugar
1-1/2	teaspoons baking powder
1/2	teaspoon baking soda
1	egg
3/4	cup orange juice
1/4	cup butter, melted
1	teaspoon vanilla extract
2	cups coarsely chopped fresh *or* frozen cranberries
1	tablespoon grated orange peel

CREAM CHEESE LAYER:

1	package (8 ounces) cream cheese, softened
1/3	cup sugar
1	egg
1	teaspoon vanilla extract

TOPPING:

3/4	cup all-purpose flour
1/2	cup sugar, cubed
1/2	cup cold butter

In a large bowl, combine the first four ingredients. Combine the egg, orange juice, butter and vanilla; stir into dry ingredients until well combined. Fold in the cranberries and orange peel. Pour into a greased 9-in. springform pan.

In a small bowl, beat cream cheese and sugar until smooth. Beat in egg and vanilla. Spread over batter. Combine flour and sugar; cut in the cold butter until the mixture resembles coarse crumbs. Sprinkle over top.

Place pan on a baking sheet. Bake at 350° for 70-75 minutes or until golden brown. Cool coffee cake on a wire rack for 15 minutes before removing sides of pan. **YIELD: 12 servings.**

MARY ANN TAYLOR, ROCKWELL, IOWA

Fresh asparagus stars along with crispy bacon, flavorful onion and mellow Swiss cheese in this hearty quiche. It's the perfect breakfast main dish for a spring brunch.

asparagus swiss quiche

PREP: 25 MINUTES / **BAKE:** 30 MINUTES + STANDING

10	bacon strips, diced
1/2	cup chopped onion
1	pound fresh asparagus, trimmed
1	cup (4 ounces) shredded Swiss cheese
1	tablespoon all-purpose flour
1/4	teaspoon salt
1/8	teaspoon pepper
1	unbaked pastry shell (9 inches)
3	eggs
1/2	cup half-and-half cream

In a skillet, cook bacon over medium heat until crisp. Remove the bacon with a slotted spoon to paper towels; drain, reserving 1 tablespoon drippings. In the drippings, saute the onion until browned; drain.

Cut eight asparagus spears into 4-in.-long spears for garnish. Cut remaining asparagus into 1-in. pieces. In a saucepan, cook all of the asparagus in a small amount of boiling water until crisp-tender; drain.

In a bowl, toss the bacon, onion, asparagus pieces, cheese, flour, salt and pepper. Pour into pastry shell. In a bowl, beat eggs and cream; pour over bacon mixture. Top with asparagus spears. Bake at 400° for 30-35 minutes or until a knife inserted near the center comes out clean and crust is golden brown. Let stand for 10 minutes before cutting. **YIELD: 6-8 servings.**

GAIL SYKORA, MENOMONEE FALLS, WISCONSIN
When I'm expecting company for brunch, the menu often features this tried-and-true casserole. With ham, eggs and plenty of cheese, the enchiladas are flavorful, hearty and fun. Plus, they can be assembled the day before.

brunch enchiladas

PREP: 15 MINUTES + CHILLING
BAKE: 40 MINUTES + STANDING

2	cups cubed fully cooked ham
1/2	cup chopped green onions
10	flour tortillas (8 inches)
2	cups (8 ounces) shredded cheddar cheese, *divided*
1	tablespoon all-purpose flour
2	cups half-and-half cream
6	eggs, beaten
1/4	teaspoon salt, optional

Combine ham and onions; place about 1/3 cup down the center of each tortilla. Top with 2 tablespoons cheese. Roll up and place seam side down in a greased 13-in. x 9-in. baking dish.

In a bowl, combine flour, cream, eggs and salt if desired until smooth. Pour over tortillas. Cover and refrigerate for 8 hours or overnight.

Remove from the refrigerator 30 minutes before baking. Cover and bake at 350° for 25 minutes. Uncover; bake for 10 minutes. Sprinkle with remaining cheese; bake 3 minutes longer or until the cheese is melted. Let stand for 10 minutes before serving.
YIELD: 10 enchiladas.

JAIME KEELING, KEIZER, OREGON
The first time I made this delightful breakfast treat, it was a huge hit. Now I get requests every time family or friends do anything around the breakfast hour. I'm always certain to keep the four simple ingredients on hand.

pull-apart caramel coffee cake

PREP: 10 MINUTES / **BAKE:** 25 MINUTES

2	tubes (12 ounces *each*) refrigerated flaky buttermilk biscuits
1	cup packed brown sugar
1/2	cup heavy whipping cream
1	teaspoon ground cinnamon

Cut each biscuit into four pieces; arrange evenly in a 10-in. fluted tube pan coated with cooking spray. Combine the brown sugar, cream and cinnamon; pour over biscuits.

Bake at 350° for 25-30 minutes or until golden brown. Cool for 5 minutes before inverting coffee cake onto a serving platter.
YIELD: 12 servings.

SHELLY SOULE, LAS VEGAS, NEVADA
My family often has company over for breakfast or brunch, and these light, fruit-topped crepes are one of our favorites. The sweet sensations are as fast to make as they are fabulous. You can cook the crepes the night before, refrigerate them with waxed paper in between, then fill and top them in the morning.

strawberry banana crepes

PREP: 20 MINUTES + CHILLING / **COOK:** 10 MINUTES

1	cup all-purpose flour
1	tablespoon sugar
1/2	teaspoon ground cinnamon
1-1/2	cups milk
2	eggs
1	to 2 tablespoons butter

FILLING:

1	package (8 ounces) cream cheese, softened
1	carton (8 ounces) frozen whipped topping, thawed
1/2	cup confectioners' sugar

TOPPING:

2	cups sliced fresh strawberries
2	medium firm bananas, sliced
1/4	cup sugar, optional

In a large bowl, combine the flour, sugar, cinnamon, milk and eggs. Cover and refrigerate for 1 hour.

In an 8-in. nonstick skillet, melt 1 teaspoon butter. Stir batter; pour about 2 tablespoons into the center of skillet. Lift and tilt pan to evenly coat bottom. Cook until top appears dry; turn and cook 15-20 seconds longer. Remove to a wire rack.

Repeat with remaining batter, add butter to a skillet as needed. When cool, stack crepes with waxed paper on paper towels in between.

In a large bowl, beat the filling ingredients until smooth. Spread 2 rounded tablespoonfuls on each crepe; roll up. In a large bowl, combine topping ingredients; spoon topping over crepes.
YIELD: 18 crepes.

DOROTHY MOREHOUSE, MASSENA, NEW YORK
Although this strawberry and rhubarb-laden coffee cake serves a crowd, it never lasts very long! It's just as nice for a Sunday brunch as it is to bring to family reunions.

strawberry rhubarb coffee cake

PREP: 45 MINUTES / **BAKE:** 40 MINUTES

FILLING:

3	cups sliced fresh *or* frozen rhubarb (1-inch pieces)
1	quart fresh strawberries, mashed
2	tablespoons lemon juice
1	cup sugar
1/3	cup cornstarch

CAKE:

3	cups all-purpose flour
1	cup sugar
1	teaspoon baking powder
1	teaspoon baking soda
1/2	teaspoon salt
1	cup butter, cut into pieces
1-1/2	cups buttermilk
2	eggs
1	teaspoon vanilla extract

TOPPING:

1/4	cup butter
3/4	cup all-purpose flour
3/4	cup sugar

In a large saucepan, combine rhubarb, strawberries and lemon juice. Cover and cook over medium heat about 5 minutes. Combine sugar and cornstarch; stir into saucepan. Bring to a boil, cook and stir for 2 minutes or until thickened. Remove from heat and set aside.

In a large bowl, combine flour, sugar, baking powder, baking soda and salt. Cut in butter until mixture resembles coarse crumbs. Beat the buttermilk, eggs and vanilla extract; stir into crumb mixture.

Spread half of the batter evenly into a greased 13-in. x 9-in. baking dish. Carefully spread filling on top. Drop remaining batter by tablespoonfuls over filling.

For topping, melt butter in a saucepan over low heat. Remove from heat; stir in flour and sugar until mixture resembles coarse crumbs. Sprinkle over batter. Lay foil on lower rack to catch any juice fruit spillovers.

Place coffee cake on middle rack; bake at 350° for 40-45 minutes. Cool in pan. Cut in squares. **YIELD: 16-20 servings.**

KAREN HOWARD, LAKEVILLE, MASSACHUSETTS
A few years ago, I found this zucchini recipe that's quick to prepare and freezes well. Just put it in the refrigerator to thaw in the morning and pop it into the oven after work!

zucchini quiche

PREP: 25 MINUTES / **BAKE:** 35 MINUTES

4	cups thinly sliced zucchini
1	large onion, thinly sliced
3	tablespoons butter
2	eggs
2	teaspoons dried parsley flakes
1/2	teaspoon salt
1/2	teaspoon *each* garlic powder, dried basil and oregano
1/4	teaspoon pepper
2	cups (8 ounces) part-skim shredded mozzarella cheese
2	teaspoons prepared mustard
1	pastry shell (9 inches)

In a large skillet, saute the zucchini and onion in butter until tender; drain. In a large bowl, whisk the eggs, parsley, salt, garlic powder, basil, oregano and pepper. Stir in cheese and zucchini mixture. Spread mustard over pastry shell; add egg mixture.

Cover and freeze for up to 2 months. Or bake, uncovered, at 400° for 35-40 minutes or until a knife inserted near the center comes out clean and crust is golden brown (cover loosely with foil after 25 minutes if needed to prevent overbrowning). Let stand for 5 minutes before cutting. **YIELD: 6-8 servings.**

TO USE FROZEN QUICHE: Thaw in the refrigerator. Bake, uncovered, at 400° for 50-55 minutes or until a knife inserted near the center comes out clean and crust is golden brown (cover loosely with foil after 35 minutes if needed to prevent overbrowning). Let stand for 5 minutes before cutting.

LINDA KRIVANEK, OAK CREEK, WISCONSIN
When we go camping, I'm always asked to make this campfire favorite. We enjoy it just as much at home.

camper's breakfast hash

PREP/TOTAL TIME: 25 MINUTES

1/4	cup butter, cubed
2	packages (20 ounces *each*) refrigerated shredded hash brown potatoes
1	package (7 ounces) brown-and-serve sausage links, cut into 1/2-inch pieces
1/4	cup chopped onion
1/4	cup chopped green pepper
12	eggs, lightly beaten

Salt and pepper to taste
1	cup (4 ounces) shredded cheddar cheese

In a large skillet, melt butter. Add the potatoes, sausage, onion and green pepper. Cook, uncovered, over medium heat for 10-15 minutes or until potatoes are lightly browned, turning once.

Push potato mixture to the sides of pan. Pour eggs into center of pan. Cook and stir over medium heat until eggs are completely set. Season with salt and pepper. Reduce heat; stir eggs into potato mixture. Top with cheese; cover and cook for 1-2 minutes or until cheese is melted. **YIELD: 8 servings.**

IRIS FRANK, EUREKA, ILLINOIS
You'll find everything you want for breakfast—potatoes, eggs, cheese and ham—in this satisfying bake. I frequently make it for church potlucks and special occasions.

wake-up casserole

PREP: 15 MINUTES / **BAKE:** 1-1/4 HOURS

8	frozen hash brown patties
4	cups (16 ounces) shredded cheddar cheese
1	pound cubed fully cooked ham (2 cups)
7	eggs
1	cup milk
1/2	teaspoon salt
1/2	teaspoon ground mustard

Place the hash brown patties in a single layer in a greased 13-in. x 9-in. baking dish. Sprinkle with cheese and ham. In a large bowl, beat eggs, milk, salt and mustard. Pour over ham.

Cover and bake at 350° for 1 hour. Uncover; bake 15 minutes longer or until edges are golden brown and a knife inserted near the center comes out clean. **YIELD: 8 servings.**

AMELIA MEAUX, CROWLEY, LOUISIANA
I created this sausage-stuffed bread when I needed something special to bring to a party. Not only can the versatile braid be served as a morning mainstay, it makes a great appetizer, too.

sausage brunch braid

PREP: 30 MINUTES / **BAKE:** 20 MINUTES

12	ounces bulk pork sausage
1/2	cup chopped onion
1/4	cup chopped celery
1/4	cup chopped green pepper
1	garlic clove, minced
1	package (3 ounces) cream cheese, cubed
2	tablespoons chopped green onion tops
2	tablespoons minced fresh parsley
1	tube (8 ounces) refrigerated crescent rolls
1	egg, lightly beaten

In a large skillet, cook the sausage, onion, celery, green pepper and garlic until meat is no longer pink and the vegetables are tender; drain. Add cream cheese, green onion and parsley. Cook and stir over low heat until cheese is melted; set aside.

Unroll crescent dough on a greased baking sheet; seal perforations. Roll into a 12-in. x 10-in. rectangle. Spoon sausage mixture to within 3 in. of long sides and 1 in of ends. On each long side, cut 3/4-in.-wide strips 3 in. into center. Starting at one end, fold alternately strips at an angle, forming a braid.

Brush dough with egg. Bake at 350° for 20-25 minutes or until golden brown. Refrigerate leftovers. **YIELD: 8-10 servings.**

BARBARA WADDEL, LINCOLN, NEBRASKA

This layered tortilla dish is not only delicious, but its simple-to-follow instructions make it a real timer-saver, too. The tomato slices provide a nice touch of color. I like to serve this crowd-pleasing casserole with muffins and fresh fruit.

southwest sausage bake

PREP: 15 MINUTES + CHILLING
BAKE: 1 HOUR + STANDING

6	flour tortillas (10 inches), cut into 1/2-inch strips
4	cans (4 ounces *each*) chopped green chilies, drained
1	pound bulk pork sausage, cooked and drained
2	cups (8 ounces) shredded Monterey Jack cheese
10	eggs
1/2	cup milk
1/2	teaspoon *each* salt, garlic salt, onion salt, pepper and ground cumin

Paprika

2	medium tomatoes, sliced

Sour cream and salsa

In a greased 13-in. x 9-in. baking dish, layer half of the tortilla strips, chilies, sausage and cheese. Repeat layers.

In a bowl, beat the eggs, milk and seasonings; pour over cheese. Sprinkle with paprika. Cover and refrigerate overnight.

Remove from the refrigerator 30 minutes before baking. Bake, uncovered, at 350° for 50 minutes. Arrange tomato slices over the top. Bake 10-15 minutes longer or until a knife inserted near the center comes out clean. Let stand for 10 minutes before cutting. Serve with sour cream and salsa. **YIELD: 12 servings.**

COLLEEN BUTLER, INWOOD, WEST VIRGINIA

The first time I enjoyed this morning specialty was at a bed-and-breakfast in Lancaster, Pennsylvania. To me, it tasted just like a big warm-from-the-oven oatmeal cookie!

amish baked oatmeal

PREP: 10 MINUTES / **BAKE:** 25 MINUTES

1-1/2	cups quick-cooking oats
1/2	cup sugar
1/2	cup milk
1/4	cup butter, melted
1	egg
1	teaspoon baking powder
3/4	teaspoon salt
1	teaspoon vanilla extract

Warm milk

Fresh fruit *and/or* brown sugar, optional

Combine the first eight ingredients; mix well. Spread evenly in a greased 13-in. x 9-in. baking pan.

Bake at 350° for 25-30 minutes or until edges are golden brown. Immediately spoon into bowls; add milk. Top with fruit and/or brown sugar if desired. **YIELD: 6 servings.**

CHRISTENA PALMER, GREEN RIVER, WYOMING

These cheesy quiches freeze wonderfully. It's so nice to have breakfast in the freezer and ready to go on busy mornings or when unexpected guests drop by.

ham 'n' cheese quiche

PREP: 15 MINUTES / **BAKE:** 35 MINUTES

2	pastry shells (9 inches)
2	cups diced fully cooked ham
2	cups (8 ounces) shredded sharp cheddar cheese
2	teaspoons dried minced onion
4	eggs
2	cups half-and-half cream
1/2	teaspoon salt
1/4	teaspoon pepper

Line unpricked pastry shells with a double thickness of heavy-duty foil. Bake at 400° for 5 minutes. Remove foil; bake for 5 minutes longer.

Divide ham, cheese and onion between the shells. In a bowl, whisk eggs, cream, salt and pepper. Pour into shells. Cover and freeze for up to 3 months. Or cover edges with foil and bake at 400° for 35-40 minutes or until a knife inserted near the center comes out clean. Let stand for 5-10 minutes before cutting. **YIELD: 2 quiches (6 servings each).**

TO USE FROZEN QUICHE: Completely thaw in the refrigerator. Remove 30 minutes before baking as directed.

SHARYN ADAMS, CRAWFORDSVILLE, INDIANA

Cinnamon and sugar top this fuss-free casserole that tastes like French toast. Since you assemble it the previous night, you save a lot of time in the morning.

french toast casserole

PREP: 15 MINUTES + CHILLING / **BAKE:** 45 MINUTES + STANDING

1	loaf (10 ounces) French bread, cut into 1-inch cubes (10 cups)
8	eggs
3	cups milk
4	teaspoons sugar
1	teaspoon vanilla extract
3/4	teaspoon salt, optional

TOPPING:

2	tablespoons butter
3	tablespoons sugar
2	teaspoons ground cinnamon

Maple syrup, optional

Place bread cubes in a greased 13-in. x 9-in. baking dish. In a large bowl, whisk the eggs, milk, sugar, vanilla and salt if desired. Pour over bread. Cover and refrigerate for 8 hours or overnight.

Remove from refrigerator 30 minutes before baking. Dot with butter. Combine sugar and cinnamon; sprinkle over the top.

Cover and bake at 350° for 45-50 minutes or until a knife inserted near the center comes out clean. Let stand for 5 minutes. Serve with maple syrup if desired. **YIELD: 12 servings.**

SUSAN MCCARTNEY, ONALASKA, WISCONSIN

My kids love smoothies—especially this fruity strawberry and pineapple sensation. I make it so often, I almost know this recipe by heart. It's great as a quick breakfast, after-school snack or guilt-free dessert.

fruit smoothies

PREP/TOTAL TIME: 10 MINUTES

1	cup fat-free milk
1/2	cup plain yogurt
1/4	teaspoon vanilla extract
1-1/2	cups fresh *or* frozen strawberries, thawed
1/2	cup canned unsweetened pineapple chunks
1/4	cup nonfat dry milk powder
4	ice cubes
2	tablespoons sugar

In a blender, combine all ingredients; cover and process for 30-45 seconds or until smooth. Stir if necessary. Pour into chilled glasses; serve immediately. **YIELD: 4 servings.**

soups & sandwiches

Nothing says comfort like a pot of homemade soup simmering on the stovetop. And when it's paired with a hearty sandwich piled high with the freshest ingredients, you've got yourself a winning combination that will warm you up from head to toe.

BAKED DELI FOCACCIA SANDWICH / PAGE 78

JAN PERI-WYRICK, FORT WORTH, TEXAS

This recipe is really a snap to prepare. Don't be scared by the long list of ingredients—most of them are probably already in your pantry.

tortilla-vegetable chicken soup

PREP: 20 MINUTES / **COOK:** 15 MINUTES

3	flour tortillas (6 inches), cut into 1-inch strips
1/4	cup chicken drippings, optional
1	cup chopped celery
3/4	cup finely chopped carrot
1/2	cup chopped red onion
2	tablespoons olive oil
3	cans (14-1/2 ounces *each*) reduced-sodium chicken broth
1	can (15 ounces) black beans, rinsed and drained
1	can (14-1/2 ounces) beef broth
1	can (10 ounces) diced tomatoes with mild green chilies
2	cups cubed cooked chicken breast
2	cups frozen corn
2	teaspoons dried parsley flakes
1	teaspoon garlic powder
1	teaspoon dried basil
1	teaspoon ground cumin
1	teaspoon ground coriander
	Shredded Monterey Jack cheese, optional

Place tortilla strips on a baking sheet coated with cooking spray; bake at 350° for 8-10 minutes or until lightly browned. Set aside.

Meanwhile, skim fat from chicken drippings if desired. In a Dutch oven, saute the celery, carrot and onion in oil until tender. Stir in the chicken broth, black beans, beef broth, tomatoes, chicken, corn, seasonings and drippings if desired. Bring to a boil. Reduce heat; simmer, uncovered, for 15 minutes.

Serve soup with cheese if desired and tortilla strips. **YIELD: 6 servings**.

MARGERY BRYAN, MOSES LAKE, WASHINGTON

Basic ingredients make this hearty stew a favorite at our home. I usually have everything on hand for this soul-soothing recipe, so it's simple to load up the slow cooker at noon. Come evening, dinner's ready and waiting.

hobo meatball stew

PREP: 20 MINUTES / **COOK:** 4 HOURS

1	pound ground beef
1-1/2	teaspoons salt *or* salt-free seasoning blend, *divided*
1/2	teaspoon pepper, *divided*
4	medium potatoes, peeled and cut into chunks
4	medium carrots, cut into chunks
1	large onion, cut into chunks
1/2	cup water
1/2	cup ketchup
1-1/2	teaspoons cider vinegar
1/2	teaspoon dried basil

In a bowl, combine the beef, 1 teaspoon salt and 1/4 teaspoon pepper. Shape into 1-in. balls. In a skillet over medium heat, brown meatballs on all sides; drain.

Place the potatoes, carrots and onion in a 3-qt. slow cooker; top with meatballs. Combine the water, ketchup, vinegar, basil, and remaining salt and pepper; pour over meatballs. Cover and cook on high for 4-5 hours or until the vegetables are tender. **YIELD: 4 servings.**

NANCY TUCK, ELK FALLS, KANSAS

Perfect for cool autumn nights, this comforting main course is speedy, low in fat and a delicious one-dish meal.

easy chicken and dumplings

PREP/TOTAL TIME: 30 MINUTES

3	celery ribs, chopped
1	cup sliced fresh carrots
3	cans (14-1/2 ounces *each*) reduced-sodium chicken broth
1/2	teaspoon poultry seasoning
1/8	teaspoon pepper
3	cups cubed cooked chicken breast
1-2/3	cups reduced-fat biscuit/baking mix
2/3	cup fat-free milk

In a Dutch oven coated with cooking spray, saute celery and carrots for 5 minutes. Stir in the chicken broth, poultry seasoning and pepper. Bring to a boil. Reduce heat; simmer, uncovered. Add the chicken.

For dumplings, combine biscuit mix and milk. Drop the batter by tablespoonfuls onto simmering broth. Cover and simmer for 10-15 minutes or until a toothpick inserted into a dumpling comes out clean (do not lift cover while simmering). **YIELD: 6 servings.**

RHODA TROYER, GLENFORD, OHIO
I can't take all the credit for these winning burgers. My husband's uncle passed down the special barbecue sauce recipe. We love it on everything...it was only natural to try it on, and in, these big-bite burgers.

barbecued burgers

PREP: 25 MINUTES / **GRILL:** 15 MINUTES

SAUCE:

1	cup ketchup
1/2	cup packed brown sugar
1/3	cup sugar
1/4	cup honey
1/4	cup molasses
2	teaspoons prepared mustard
1-1/2	teaspoons Worcestershire sauce
1/4	teaspoon salt
1/4	teaspoon Liquid Smoke
1/8	teaspoon pepper

BURGERS:

1	egg, lightly beaten
1/3	cup quick-cooking oats
1/4	teaspoon onion salt
1/4	teaspoon garlic salt
1/4	teaspoon pepper
1/8	teaspoon salt
1-1/2	pounds ground beef
6	hamburger buns, split

Toppings of your choice

In a small saucepan, combine the first 10 ingredients. Bring to a boil. Remove from the heat. Set aside 1 cup barbecue sauce to serve with burgers.

In a large bowl, combine the egg, oats, 1/4 cup of the remaining barbecue sauce, onion salt, garlic salt, pepper and salt. Crumble beef over mixture and mix well. Shape into six patties.

Grill, covered, over medium heat for 6-8 minutes on each side or until a meat thermometer reads 160°, basting with 1/2 cup barbecue sauce during the last 5 minutes. Serve on buns with toppings of your choice and reserved barbecue sauce. **YIELD: 6 servings.**

LAURA BREWER, LAFAYETTE, INDIANA
I got this wonderful recipe from my sister-in-law, who made a huge batch and served a crowd one night. I've never had another dish receive so many compliments.

creamy white chili

PREP: 10 MINUTES / **COOK:** 40 MINUTES

1	pound boneless skinless chicken breasts, cut into 1/2-inch cubes
1	medium onion, chopped
1-1/2	teaspoons garlic powder
1	tablespoon canola oil
2	cans (15-1/2 ounces *each*) great northern beans, rinsed and drained
1	can (14-1/2 ounces) chicken broth
2	cans (4 ounces *each*) chopped green chilies
1	teaspoon salt
1	teaspoon ground cumin
1	teaspoon dried oregano
1/2	teaspoon pepper
1/4	teaspoon cayenne pepper
1	cup (8 ounces) sour cream
1/2	cup heavy whipping cream

In a large saucepan, saute the chicken, onion and garlic powder in oil until chicken is no longer pink. Add the beans, broth, chilies and seasonings. Bring to a boil. Reduce heat; simmer, uncovered, for 30 minutes.

Remove from the heat; stir in the sour cream and whipping cream. **YIELD: 7 servings.**

CHRISTIE GARDINER, EAGLE MOUNTAIN, UTAH

Sometimes we don't even bother with a bun for these moist, flavorful burgers. Smoked cheese, grilled onions and a special sauce make them out of the ordinary!

sweet onion bbq burgers

PREP: 30 MINUTES + MARINATING / **GRILL:** 15 MINUTES

1/2	cup dry bread crumbs
2	teaspoons onion salt
2	teaspoons brown sugar
1	egg, lightly beaten
1	pound ground beef
1-1/4	cups barbecue sauce

SAUCE:

1/2	cup mayonnaise
1/2	cup barbecue sauce
1	teaspoon brown sugar

ONION TOPPING:

2	tablespoons butter
1/4	cup honey
2	large sweet onions, thinly sliced
4	slices smoked cheddar cheese
4	hamburger buns, split

In a large bowl, combine the bread crumbs, onion salt and brown sugar. Add egg. Crumble beef over mixture and mix well. Shape into four patties. Place in a shallow dish; pour barbecue sauce over patties. Cover and refrigerate for 2-4 hours.

In a small bowl, combine the sauce ingredients; cover and refrigerate until serving. For topping, melt butter in a small skillet. Stir in honey until blended. Add onions; saute for 15-20 minutes or until tender and lightly browned. Remove from the heat and keep warm.

Drain and discard barbecue sauce. Grill patties, uncovered, over medium-hot heat for 5-7 minutes on each side or until juices run clear. Top each with a cheese slice; grill 1 minute longer or until cheese is melted. Serve patties on buns with sauce and onion topping. **YIELD: 4 servings.**

JUDY METZENTINE, THE DALLES, OREGON

It's so easy to fill my slow cooker and forget about supper...until the kitchen is filled with the wonderful aroma of this hearty soup. I've served this soup often to family and friends on cold winter evenings, along with homemade rolls and a green salad.

beef barley lentil soup

PREP: 5 MINUTES / **COOK:** 8 HOURS

1	pound lean ground beef
1	medium onion, chopped
2	cups cubed red potatoes (1/4-inch pieces)
1	cup chopped celery
1	cup chopped carrots
1	cup dried lentils, rinsed
1/2	cup medium pearl barley
8	cups water
2	teaspoons beef bouillon granules
1	teaspoon salt
1/2	teaspoon lemon-pepper seasoning
2	cans (14-1/2 ounces *each*) stewed tomatoes

In a nonstick skillet, cook beef and onion over medium heat until meat is no longer pink; drain. Transfer to a 5-qt. slow cooker. Layer with the potatoes, celery, carrots, lentils and barley. Combine the water, bouillon, salt and lemon-pepper; pour over vegetables. Cover and cook on low for 6 hours or until vegetables and barley are tender. Add the tomatoes; cook 2 hours longer. **YIELD: 10 servings.**

NOELLE MYERS, GRAND FORKS, NORTH DAKOTA
I enjoyed a similar soup for lunch at work one day and decided to re-create it at home. I love the combination of robust meatballs, vegetables and pasta.

italian wedding soup

PREP: 30 MINUTES / **COOK:** 45 MINUTES

2	eggs, lightly beaten
1/2	cup seasoned bread crumbs
1	pound ground beef
1	pound bulk Italian sausage
3	medium carrots, sliced
3	celery ribs, diced
1	large onion, chopped
3	garlic cloves, minced
4-1/2	teaspoons olive oil
4	cans (14-1/2 ounces *each*) reduced-sodium chicken broth
2	cans (14-1/2 ounces *each*) beef broth
1	package (10 ounces) frozen chopped spinach, thawed and squeezed dry
1/4	cup minced fresh basil
1	envelope onion soup mix
4-1/2	teaspoons ketchup
1/2	teaspoon dried thyme
3	bay leaves
1-1/2	cups uncooked penne pasta

In a large bowl, combine eggs and bread crumbs. Crumble beef and sausage over mixture; mix well. Shape into 3/4-in. balls.

Place meatballs on a greased rack in a foil-lined 15-in. x 10-in. baking pan. Bake at 350° for 15-18 minutes or until no longer pink. Meanwhile, in a soup kettle or Dutch oven, saute carrots, celery, onion and garlic in oil until tender. Stir in the broths, spinach, basil, soup mix, ketchup, thyme and bay leaves.

Drain meatballs on paper towels. Bring soup to a boil; add meatballs. Reduce heat; simmer, uncovered, for 30 minutes. Add the pasta; cook 13-15 minutes longer or until tender, stirring occasionally. Discard bay leaves before serving. **YIELD: 10 servings (2-1/2 quarts).**

SUE SHEA, DEFIANCE, OHIO
This tasty Italian-style sandwich can be served warm or at room temperature. Leftovers, if there are any, heat up nicely in the microwave. Because it serves a crowd, it's perfect for parties and potlucks.

meat 'n' cheese stromboli

PREP: 25 MINUTES / **BAKE:** 15 MINUTES

1	medium onion, sliced and separated into rings
1	medium green pepper, sliced into rings
1	tablespoon butter
2	loaves (16 ounces *each*) frozen bread dough, thawed
1/2	pound thinly sliced hard salami
1/2	pound thinly sliced deli ham
8	ounces sliced part-skim mozzarella cheese
1/2	pound sliced mild cheddar cheese
1/2	teaspoon Italian seasoning
1/4	teaspoon garlic powder
1/8	teaspoon pepper
1	egg, beaten
1	teaspoon poppy seeds

In a large skillet, saute onion and green pepper in butter until crisp-tender; set aside.

On two greased baking sheets, roll each loaf of bread dough into a 15-in. x 12-in. rectangle. Arrange the salami, ham and cheeses lengthwise over half of each rectangle to within 1/2 in. of edges. Top with onion mixture; sprinkle onion mixture with the Italian seasoning, garlic powder and pepper. Fold dough over filling; pinch the edges to seal.

Brush with egg and sprinkle with poppy seeds. Bake at 400° for 15-20 minutes or until golden brown. Cool loaf for 5 minutes before slicing. **YIELD: 2 loaves (8 servings each).**

KEVIN WEEKS, NORTH PALM BEACH, FLORIDA
This spicy soup, featuring shrimp, crabmeat and tomatoes, gets its zip from hot pepper sauce and cayenne pepper. It's easy to prepare and dresses up any meal quite readily. Of all the recipes I have borrowed from my mom, this soup is the one that I've made most often.

spicy seafood bisque

PREP/TOTAL TIME: 30 MINUTES

1/2	cup chopped onion
1/2	cup chopped celery
2	tablespoons butter
4	cups chicken broth
3	cups tomato juice
1	can (14-1/2 ounces) diced tomatoes, undrained
1	tablespoon Worcestershire sauce
1	teaspoon seafood seasoning
1	teaspoon dried oregano
1/2	teaspoon garlic powder
1/2	teaspoon hot pepper sauce
1/4	teaspoon cayenne pepper
1	bay leaf
1/2	cup uncooked small shell pasta *or* elbow macaroni
1	pound uncooked medium shrimp, peeled and deveined
1	can (6 ounces) crabmeat, drained, flaked and cartilage removed

In a large saucepan, saute the onion and celery in butter until tender. Add the broth, tomato juice, tomatoes, Worcestershire sauce and seasonings; bring to a boil. Reduce heat; cover and simmer for 20 minutes.

Discard bay leaf. Add pasta to the soup; cook, uncovered, until tender. Add shrimp and crab; simmer 5 minutes longer or until the shrimp turn pink. **YIELD: 10-12 servings (about 3 quarts).**

RUTH STAHL, SHEPHERD, MONTANA
If your family likes gyros as much as mine, they'll love this quick version that's made with ground beef instead of lamb. I found the recipe in a newspaper and adapted it to fit our tastes. They're very much like the ones served at a local restaurant. A cucumber-yogurt sauce adds an authentic finishing touch.

ground beef gyros

PREP/TOTAL TIME: 30 MINUTES

1	carton (8 ounces) plain yogurt
1/3	cup chopped seeded cucumber
2	tablespoons finely chopped onion
1	garlic clove, minced
1	teaspoon sugar

FILLING:

1-1/2	teaspoons dried oregano
1	teaspoon garlic powder
1	teaspoon onion powder
1	teaspoon salt, optional
3/4	teaspoon pepper
1	pound ground beef
4	pita breads (6 inches), halved, warmed
3	cups shredded lettuce
1	large tomato, chopped
1	small onion, sliced

In a small bowl, combine the first five ingredients. Chill.

In a large bowl, combine seasonings; crumble beef over mixture and mix well. Shape into four patties. Grill, covered, over medium-hot heat for 6-7 minutes on each side or until a meat thermometer reads 160°. Cut patties into thin slices; stuff into pita halves. Add lettuce, tomato and onion. Serve with the yogurt sauce. **YIELD: 4 servings.**

BEKI KOSYDAR-KRANTZ, CLARKS SUMMIT, PENNSYLVANIA
The slow cooker not only makes this a simple meal, but it keeps the pork tender, moist and loaded with flavor. The sandwiches' flavor is so satisfying, they seem anything but light.

tangy pulled pork sandwiches

PREP: 10 MINUTES / **COOK:** 4 HOURS

1	pork tenderloin (1 pound)
1	cup ketchup
2	tablespoons plus 1-1/2 teaspoons brown sugar
2	tablespoons plus 1-1/2 teaspoons cider vinegar
1	tablespoon plus 1-1/2 teaspoons Worcestershire sauce
1	tablespoon spicy brown mustard
1/4	teaspoon pepper
4	kaiser rolls, split

Cut the tenderloin in half; place in a 3-qt. slow cooker. Combine the ketchup, brown sugar, vinegar, Worcestershire sauce, mustard and pepper; pour over pork.

Cover and cook on low for 4-5 hours or until meat is tender. Remove meat; shred with two forks. Return meat to the slow cooker; heat through. Serve on kaiser rolls. **YIELD: 4 servings.**

JULIE SMITHOUSER, COLORADO SPRINGS, COLORADO
I came up with this comforting soup when I was crunched for time and wanted to use up leftover baked potatoes. Since then, it has become a trusted mealtime staple. Its wonderful aroma always gets cheers from my husband when he arrives home.

easy baked potato soup

PREP/TOTAL TIME: 30 MINUTES

3	to 4 medium baking potatoes, baked
5	bacon strips, diced
2	cans (10-3/4 ounces *each*) condensed cream of potato soup, undiluted
1	can (10-3/4 ounces) condensed cheddar cheese soup, undiluted
3-1/2	cups milk
2	teaspoons garlic powder
2	teaspoons Worcestershire sauce
1/2	teaspoon onion powder
1/4	teaspoon pepper

Dash Liquid Smoke, optional

| 1 | cup (8 ounces) sour cream |

Shredded cheddar cheese

Peel and dice the baked potatoes; set aside. In a Dutch oven or soup kettle, cook the bacon over medium heat until crisp. Using a slotted spoon, remove to paper towels. Drain, reserving 1-1/2 teaspoons drippings.

Add the soups, milk, garlic powder, Worcestershire sauce, onion powder, pepper, Liquid Smoke if desired and reserved potatoes to the drippings.

Cook, uncovered, for 10 minutes or until heated through, stirring occasionally. Stir in sour cream; cook for 1-2 minutes or until heated through (do not boil). Garnish with cheddar cheese and bacon. **YIELD: 10 servings (2-1/2 quarts).**

NADINA LADIMARCO, BURTON, OHIO

I've never met a person who didn't enjoy this creamy, cheesy soup. Brimming with carrots, potatoes, green pepper and ground beef, it's hearty enough to serve as a main course with your favorite bread or rolls.

cheeseburger paradise soup

PREP: 30 MINUTES / **COOK:** 25 MINUTES

6	medium potatoes, peeled and cubed
1	small carrot, grated
1	small onion, chopped
1/2	cup chopped green pepper
2	tablespoons chopped seeded jalapeno pepper
3	cups water
2	tablespoons plus 2 teaspoons beef bouillon granules
2	garlic cloves, minced
1/8	teaspoon pepper
2	pounds ground beef
1/2	pound sliced fresh mushrooms
2	tablespoons butter
5	cups milk, *divided*
6	tablespoons all-purpose flour
1	package (16 ounces) process cheese (Velveeta), cubed

Crumbled cooked bacon

In a soup kettle, combine the first nine ingredients; bring to a boil. Reduce heat; cover and simmer for 15-20 minutes or until potatoes are tender.

Meanwhile, in a large skillet, cook ground beef and mushrooms in butter over medium heat until meat is no longer pink; drain. Add to soup. Stir in 4 cups milk; heat through.

In a small bowl, combine flour and remaining milk until smooth; gradually stir into soup. Bring to a boil; cook and stir for 2 minutes or until thickened. Reduce heat; stir in cheese until melted. Garnish with bacon. **YIELD: 14 servings (about 3-1/2 quarts).**

EDITOR'S NOTE: When cutting hot peppers, disposable gloves are recommended. Avoid touching your face.

ELLEN STRINGER, BOURBONNAIS, ILLINOIS

Mother made these fresh-tasting sloppy joes many times when I was growing up. She passed the recipe on to me when I got married. My brother-in-law says they're the best sandwiches he's ever tasted, and I couldn't agree more.

super sloppy joes

PREP: 15 MINUTES / **COOK:** 35 MINUTES

2	pounds ground beef
1/2	cup chopped onion
2	celery ribs with leaves, chopped
1/4	cup chopped green pepper
1-2/3	cups canned crushed tomatoes
1/4	cup ketchup
2	tablespoons brown sugar
1	tablespoon white vinegar
1	tablespoon Worcestershire sauce
1	tablespoon steak sauce
1/2	teaspoon garlic salt
1/4	teaspoon ground mustard
1/4	teaspoon paprika
8	to 10 hamburger buns, split

In a Dutch oven over medium heat, cook beef, onion, celery and green pepper until the meat is no longer pink and vegetables are tender; drain.

Add the next nine ingredients; mix well. Simmer, uncovered, for 35-40 minutes, stirring occasionally. Spoon 1/2 cup meat mixture onto each bun. **YIELD: 8-10 servings.**

READERS' RAVES

> I love this recipe. It is a fantastic blend of flavors—even my very picky family loves them. It isn't often that they ask for repeats in my adventures in recipes, but this one is a keeper.
>
> —Christinegibbons
>   from TasteofHome.com

ATHENA RUSSELL, FLORENCE, SOUTH CAROLINA
Blue cheese dressing and hot pepper sauce enhance these yummy tortilla wraps. Filled with spicy chicken, cheese, lettuce and tomatoes, they're colorful and flavorful.

buffalo chicken wraps

PREP/TOTAL TIME: 25 MINUTES

1	cup all-purpose flour
1	teaspoon salt
1/4	teaspoon pepper
1/2	cup buttermilk
4	boneless skinless chicken breast halves (4 ounces *each*)
1	cup canola oil
1/2	cup hot pepper sauce
1/4	cup butter, melted
4	spinach tortillas (10 inches)
1	cup shredded lettuce
1	cup (4 ounces) shredded cheddar cheese
2/3	cup chopped tomatoes
1/2	cup blue cheese salad dressing

In a shallow bowl, combine the flour, salt and pepper. Place the buttermilk in another shallow bowl. Dip chicken in buttermilk, then roll in flour mixture.

In a large skillet, cook chicken in oil for 4-5 minutes on each side or until a meat thermometer reads 170°. Drain on paper towels; cut into strips.

In a small bowl, combine hot pepper sauce and butter. Dip chicken strips into mixture, coating both sides. Place chicken in the center of each tortilla. Layer with the lettuce, cheese and tomatoes; drizzle with salad dressing. Bring up sides of tortillas; secure with toothpicks if desired. **YIELD: 4 servings.**

CHERYL TROWBRIDGE, WINDSOR, ONTARIO
I make multiple servings of everything I cook—as reflected in the name of my soup! Chock-full of great northern beans, onion, carrots and celery simmered in a well-seasoned broth, this soup is sure to warm you up in no time.

neighborhood bean soup

PREP: 30 MINUTES + STANDING / **COOK:** 3 HOURS

2	cups dried great northern beans
5	cups chicken broth
3	cups water
1	meaty ham bone *or* 2 smoked ham hocks
2	to 3 tablespoons chicken bouillon granules
1	teaspoon dried thyme
1/2	teaspoon dried marjoram
1/2	teaspoon pepper
1/4	teaspoon rubbed sage
1/4	teaspoon dried savory
2	medium onions, chopped
3	medium carrots, chopped
3	celery ribs, chopped
1	tablespoon canola oil

Place beans in a Dutch oven or soup kettle; add water to cover by 2 in. Bring to a boil; boil for 2 minutes. Remove from the heat; cover and let stand for 1 hour. Drain.

Add broth, water, ham bone, bouillon and seasonings; bring to a boil. Reduce heat; cover and simmer for 2 hours. Meanwhile, saute the onions, carrots and celery in oil; add vegetables to soup. Cover and simmer 1 hour longer.

Remove ham bone from soup. Debone ham and cut meat into chunks; return to soup. Skim fat. **YIELD: 10 servings (2-3/4 quarts).**

MARY HUMENIUK-SMITH, PERRY HALL, MARYLAND
Pesto and focaccia bread make this pretty sandwich deliciously different from most deli specialties. This hearty, handheld bite is perfect for football parties and other group gatherings as it seems to please hungry crowds.

baked deli focaccia sandwich

PREP: 10 MINUTES / **BAKE:** 20 MINUTES + STANDING

1	loaf (12 ounces) focaccia bread
1/4	cup prepared pesto
1/4	pound sliced deli ham
1/4	pound sliced deli smoked turkey
1/4	pound sliced deli pastrami
5	slices process American cheese
1/3	cup thinly sliced onion
1	small tomato, sliced
1/4	teaspoon Italian seasoning

Cut focaccia horizontally in half; spread pesto over cut sides. On bread bottom, layer the ham, turkey, pastrami, cheese, onion and tomato. Sprinkle with Italian seasoning. Replace bread top; wrap in foil.

Place on a baking sheet. Bake at 350° for 20-25 minutes or until heated through. Let stand for 10 minutes. Cut into wedges. **YIELD: 8 servings.**

AMI PATON, WACONIA, MINNESOTA
Flavored with crab, shrimp and cheddar cheese, this chowder is so good that I make it weekly. Sometimes I substitute chicken or ham for the seafood and leave out the juice. Either way, this pretty soup is a winner.

golden seafood chowder

PREP: 25 MINUTES / **COOK:** 25 MINUTES

1/2	cup finely chopped onion
1/4	cup butter, cubed
1	can (14-1/2 ounces) chicken broth
1	cup cubed peeled potato
2	celery ribs, chopped
2	medium carrots, chopped
1/4	cup Clamato juice
1/4	teaspoon lemon-pepper seasoning
1/4	cup all-purpose flour
2	cups milk
2	cups (8 ounces) shredded sharp cheddar cheese
1	can (6 ounces) crabmeat, drained, flaked and cartilage removed
1	cup cooked medium shrimp, peeled and deveined

In a large saucepan, saute onion in butter until tender. Stir in the chicken broth, potato, celery, carrots, Clamato juice and lemon-pepper. Bring to a boil. Reduce heat; cover and simmer for 15-20 minutes or until vegetables are tender.

In a small bowl, whisk flour and milk until smooth; add to soup. Bring to a boil; cook and stir for 2 minutes or until thickened. Reduce heat. Add the cheese, crab and shrimp; cook and stir until cheese is melted. **YIELD: 4 servings.**

BARBARA LINK, RANCHO CUCAMONGA, CALIFORNIA
For a different spin on traditional split pea soup, try this recipe. The flavor is peppery rather than smoky, and the corned beef is an unexpected and tasty change of pace.

hearty split pea soup

PREP: 15 MINUTES / **COOK:** 1-1/2 HOURS

1	package (16 ounces) dried split peas
8	cups water
2	medium potatoes, peeled and cubed
2	large onions, chopped
2	medium carrots, chopped
2	cups cubed cooked corned beef *or* ham
1/2	cup chopped celery
5	teaspoons chicken bouillon granules
1	teaspoon dried marjoram
1	teaspoon poultry seasoning
1	teaspoon rubbed sage
1/2	to 1 teaspoon pepper
1/2	teaspoon dried basil
1/2	teaspoon salt, optional

In a Dutch oven or soup kettle, combine all ingredients; bring to a boil. Reduce heat; cover and simmer soup for 1-1/4 to 1-1/2 hours or until the peas and vegetables are tender. **YIELD: 12 servings (3 quarts).**

CARLA KIMBALL, CALLAWAY, NEBRASKA
A chuck roast slow-simmered in a beefy broth is delicious when shredded and spooned onto freshly baked rolls. I usually serve the cooking juices in individual cups for dipping.

shredded french dip

PREP: 5 MINUTES / **COOK:** 6 HOURS

1	boneless beef chuck roast (3 pounds), trimmed
1	can (10-1/2 ounces) condensed French onion soup, undiluted
1	can (10-1/2 ounces) condensed beef consomme, undiluted
1	can (10-1/2 ounces) condensed beef broth, undiluted
1	teaspoon beef bouillon granules
8	to 10 French *or* Italian rolls, split

Halve roast and place in a 3-qt. slow cooker. Combine the soup, consomme, broth and bouillon; pour over roast. Cover and cook on low for 6-8 hours or until meat is tender.

Remove meat and shred with two forks. Serve shredded beef on French or Italian rolls. Skim fat from cooking juices and serve as a dipping sauce. **YIELD: 10 servings.**

AMBER PETERSON, OAKES, NORTH DAKOTA
This is my favorite sandwich thanks to the zesty seasoning mixture. Use it on several chicken breasts for a more mild flavor or just a few to turn the heat up a notch.

cajun chicken sandwiches

PREP: 10 MINUTES + MARINATING / **GRILL:** 10 MINUTES

6	boneless skinless chicken breast halves (4 ounces each)
1	tablespoon olive oil
1/2	teaspoon celery salt
1/2	teaspoon garlic salt
1/2	teaspoon lemon-pepper seasoning
1/4	teaspoon cayenne pepper
1/4	teaspoon paprika
1/4	teaspoon pepper
6	kaiser rolls, split and toasted
12	slices tomato
6	lettuce leaves

Flatten chicken to 1/2-in. thickness. Brush both sides with oil. Combine the seasonings; rub over both sides of chicken. Arrange in a 13-in. x 9-in. baking dish. Cover and refrigerate for at least 2 hours or overnight.

Coat grill rack with cooking spray before starting the grill. Grill, covered, over medium heat for 3-5 minutes on each side or until chicken is no longer pink. Serve chicken on rolls with tomato and lettuce. **YIELD: 6 servings.**

JANICE BRIGHTWELL, JEFFERSONVILLE, INDIANA

The original recipe for this savory bread called for salami, but I use ham instead. People are always amazed that the stuffed loaf only takes about 15 minutes to assemble. I usually serve it with tomato soup.

mozzarella ham stromboli

PREP: 20 MINUTES / **BAKE:** 20 MINUTES

1	tube (11 ounces) refrigerated crusty French loaf
2	cups (8 ounces) shredded part-skim mozzarella cheese
1/4	pound thinly sliced deli ham
1	tablespoon butter, melted
1	tablespoon grated Parmesan cheese

On a lightly floured surface, unroll dough at seam. Pat dough into a 14-in. x 12-in. rectangle. Sprinkle mozzarella cheese over dough to within 1/2 in. of edges. Top with a single layer of ham.

Roll up tightly from a short side; pinch seam to seal. Place seam side down on an ungreased baking sheet. Brush the top of the loaf with butter; sprinkle top with Parmesan cheese.

Bake at 375° for 20-25 minutes or until golden brown. Cool loaf on a wire rack for 5 minutes. Cut with a serrated knife. **YIELD: 6 servings.**

KATHY NORRIS, STREATOR, ILLINOIS

These gooey grilled cheese sandwiches, subtly seasoned with garlic, taste great for lunch with sliced apples. And they're really fast to whip up, too. To save time, I soften the cream cheese in the microwave, then blend it with the rest of the ingredients in the same bowl, which makes cleanup a breeze.

the ultimate grilled cheese

PREP/TOTAL TIME: 15 MINUTES

1	package (3 ounces) cream cheese, softened
3/4	cup mayonnaise
1	cup (4 ounces) shredded part-skim mozzarella cheese
1	cup (4 ounces) shredded cheddar cheese
1/2	teaspoon garlic powder
1/8	teaspoon seasoned salt
10	slices Italian bread (1/2 inch thick)
2	tablespoons butter, softened

In a large bowl, beat cream cheese and mayonnaise until smooth. Stir in the cheeses, garlic powder and seasoned salt. Spread five slices of bread with the cheese mixture, about 1/3 cup on each. Top with remaining bread.

Butter the outsides of sandwiches. In a skillet over medium heat, toast sandwiches for 4-5 minutes on each side or until bread is lightly browned and cheese is melted. **YIELD: 5 servings.**

DORIS SLEETH, NAPLES, FLORIDA

This is such an easy way to make a wonderful beef stew. You don't need to brown the meat first—just combine it with hearty chunks of carrots, potatoes and celery and let it cook together in a flavorful gravy. My daughter Karen came up with this recipe for her busy family and shared it with me.

baked beef stew

PREP: 15 MINUTES / **BAKE:** 1-3/4 HOURS

1	can (14-1/2 ounces) diced tomatoes, undrained
1	cup water
3	tablespoons quick-cooking tapioca
2	teaspoons sugar
1-1/2	teaspoons salt
1/2	teaspoon pepper
2	pounds beef stew meat, cut into 1-inch cubes
4	medium carrots, cut into 1-inch chunks
3	medium potatoes, peeled and quartered
2	celery ribs, cut into 3/4-inch chunks
1	medium onion, cut into chunks
1	slice bread, cubed

In a large bowl, combine the tomatoes, water, tapioca, sugar, salt and pepper. Stir in the remaining ingredients.

Pour into a greased 13-in. x 9-in. or 3-qt. baking dish. Cover and bake at 375° for 1-3/4 to 2 hours or until meat and vegetables are tender. Serve in bowls. **YIELD: 6-8 servings.**

JESSICA MERGEN, CUBA CITY, WISCONSIN

I've always liked sloppy joes but was feeling that my own recipe lacked character. Then a co-worker shared hers with me, and I guarantee I'll never go back to my own! Grape jelly adds a hint of sweetness to this fun, flavorful mixture, but I often use more than called for because my husband likes it extra sweet.

sensational sloppy joes

PREP/TOTAL TIME: 30 MINUTES

1	pound ground beef
1/2	cup chopped onion
1/2	cup condensed tomato soup, undiluted
1/2	cup ketchup
3	tablespoons grape jelly
1	tablespoon brown sugar
1	tablespoon cider vinegar
1	tablespoon prepared mustard
1/2	teaspoon salt
1/2	teaspoon celery seed
5	hamburger buns, split

In a large skillet, cook beef and onion over medium heat until meat is no longer pink; drain. Stir in the soup, ketchup, jelly, brown sugar, vinegar, mustard, salt and celery seed. Bring to a boil. Reduce heat; simmer, uncovered, for 10 minutes or until heated through. Serve on buns. **YIELD: 5 servings.**

AUDREY WALL, INDUSTRY, PENNSYLVANIA

This recipe originally came courtesy of my sister-in-law, who is from Mexico. Since she prefers her foods much spicier than we do, I've cut back on the "heat" by reducing the amount of hot pepper sauce.

spicy potato soup

PREP: 5 MINUTES / **COOK:** 1 HOUR 5 MINUTES

1	pound ground beef
4	cups cubed peeled potatoes (1/2-inch cubes)
1	small onion, chopped
3	cans (8 ounces *each*) tomato sauce
4	cups water
2	teaspoons salt
1-1/2	teaspoons pepper
1/2	to 1 teaspoon hot pepper sauce

In a Dutch oven or large kettle, brown ground beef over medium heat until no longer pink; drain. Add the potatoes, onion and tomato sauce. Stir in the water, salt, pepper and hot pepper sauce; bring to a boil. Reduce heat and let soup simmer for 1 hour or until the potatoes are tender and the soup has thickened. **YIELD: 6-8 servings (2 quarts).**

DEBBI SMITH, CROSSETT, ARKANSAS
Since I prepare the beef for these robust sandwiches in the slow cooker, it's easy to fix a meal for a hungry bunch. The savory homemade sauce assures I come home with no leftovers.

tangy barbecue sandwiches

PREP: 10 MINUTES / **COOK:** 8 HOURS

3	cups chopped celery
1	cup chopped onion
1	cup ketchup
1	cup barbecue sauce
1	cup water
2	tablespoons white vinegar
2	tablespoons Worcestershire sauce
2	tablespoons brown sugar
1	teaspoon chili powder
1	teaspoon salt
1/2	teaspoon pepper
1/2	teaspoon garlic powder
1	boneless beef chuck roast (3 to 4 pounds), trimmed and cut in half
14	to 18 hamburger buns, split

In a 5-qt. slow cooker, combine the first 12 ingredients. Add roast. Cover and cook on high for 1 hour. Reduce heat to low and cook roast 7-8 hours longer or until the meat is tender.

Remove roast; cool. Shred meat and return to sauce; heat through. Using a slotted spoon, fill each bun with about 1/2 cup of meat mixture. **YIELD: 14-18 servings.**

IVY ERESMAS, DADE CITY, FLORIDA
My husband and his buddies love to pack these sandwiches when they go on fishing trips. The tangy tuna salad gets fun flavor from sweet pickle relish and lots of crunch from apples, celery and walnuts. The satisfying sandwiches are a complete meal in themselves.

apple tuna sandwiches

PREP/TOTAL TIME: 15 MINUTES

1/3	cup fat-free mayonnaise
1/4	cup finely chopped celery
1/4	cup finely chopped walnuts
2	tablespoons finely chopped onion
1	tablespoon sweet pickle relish
1	teaspoon sugar
1/4	teaspoon salt
1	can (6 ounces) light water-packed tuna, drained
1/2	cup chopped red apple
6	slices reduced-calorie bread, toasted
6	lettuce leaves

In a large bowl, combine the first seven ingredients; stir in tuna and apple. Spread 1/2 cup tuna mixture on three slices of bread. Top with lettuce and remaining bread. **YIELD: 3 servings.**

JOANIE SHAWHAN, MADISON, WISCONSIN

A local restaurant serves a similar soup but wouldn't share their recipe with me. So I developed my own, modifying a recipe for potato soup. I was really pleased at how good this rich and cheesy "all-American" soup turned out.

cheeseburger soup

PREP: 45 MINUTES / **COOK:** 10 MINUTES

1/2	pound ground beef
3/4	cup chopped onion
3/4	cup shredded carrots
3/4	cup diced celery
1	teaspoon dried basil
1	teaspoon dried parsley flakes
4	tablespoons butter, *divided*
3	cups chicken broth
4	cups diced peeled potatoes (1-3/4 pounds)
1/4	cup all-purpose flour
2	cups (8 ounces) process cheese (Velveeta)
1-1/2	cups milk
3/4	teaspoon salt
1/4	to 1/2 teaspoon pepper
1/4	cup sour cream

In a 3-qt. saucepan, brown beef; drain and set aside. In the same saucepan, saute onion, carrots, celery, basil and parsley flakes in 1 tablespoon butter until vegetables are tender, about 10 minutes. Add broth, potatoes and beef; bring to a boil. Reduce heat; cover and simmer for 10-12 minutes or until potatoes are tender.

Meanwhile, in a small skillet, melt remaining butter. Add flour; cook and stir for 3-5 minutes or until bubbly. Add to soup; bring to a boil. Cook and stir for 2 minutes. Reduce heat to low. Add cheese, milk, salt and pepper; cook and stir until cheese melts. Remove from the heat; blend in sour cream. **YIELD: 8 servings (2-1/4 quarts).**

LINDA REIS, SALEM, OREGON

I make this zippy, comforting soup very often. The recipe makes a lot, but thankfully I've found that it freezes well.

minestrone with italian sausage

PREP: 25 MINUTES / **COOK:** 1 HOUR

1	pound bulk Italian sausage
1	large onion, chopped
2	large carrots, chopped
2	celery ribs, chopped
1	medium leek (white portion only), chopped
3	garlic cloves, minced
1	medium zucchini, cut into 1/2-inch pieces
1/4	pound fresh green beans, trimmed and cut into 1/2-inch pieces
6	cups beef broth
2	cans (14-1/2 ounces *each*) diced tomatoes with basil, oregano and garlic
3	cups shredded cabbage
1	teaspoon dried basil
1	teaspoon dried oregano
1/4	teaspoon pepper
1	can (15 ounces) garbanzo beans *or* chickpeas, rinsed and drained
1/2	cup uncooked small pasta shells
3	tablespoons minced fresh parsley
1/3	cup grated Parmesan cheese

In a soup kettle, cook sausage and onion over medium heat until meat is no longer pink; drain. Stir in the carrots, celery, leek and garlic; cook for 3 minutes. Add zucchini and green beans; cook 2 minutes longer.

Stir in the beef broth, tomatoes, cabbage, basil, oregano and pepper. Bring all to a boil. Reduce heat; cover and let simmer for 45 minutes. Return to a boil. Stir in the garbanzo beans, pasta and parsley. Cook for 6-9 minutes or until pasta is tender. Serve with cheese. **YIELD: 11 servings (about 3 quarts).**

READERS' RAVES

> Incredible soup! I used garden Roma tomatoes; I ran them under hot water to peel them, then coarsely chopped them. I added salt, pepper and Italian seasoning to bring their flavor up.
>
> —Elfman42 from TasteofHome.com

> I suggest preparing the recipe up to adding the pasta, then giving it a night in the fridge to let the flavors blend.
>
> —150113 from TasteofHome.com

SUSAN GAROUTTE, GEORGETOWN, TEXAS

I like to make this smooth, creamy soup when company comes to visit. Its zippy flavor is full of Southwestern flair people seem to rave about. Dip slices of homemade bread in this chowder to soak up every comforting bite!

mexican chicken corn chowder

PREP/TOTAL TIME: 30 MINUTES

1-1/2	pounds boneless skinless chicken breasts, cut into 1-inch pieces
1/2	cup chopped onion
1	to 2 garlic cloves, minced
3	tablespoons butter
1	cup hot water
2	teaspoons chicken bouillon granules
1/2	to 1 teaspoon ground cumin
2	cups half-and-half cream
2	cups (8 ounces) shredded Monterey Jack cheese
1	can (14-3/4 ounces) cream-style corn
1	can (4 ounces) chopped green chilies, undrained
1/4	to 1 teaspoon hot pepper sauce
1	medium tomato, chopped

Minced fresh cilantro, optional

In a Dutch oven, brown chicken, onion and garlic in butter until chicken is no longer pink. Add the water, bouillon and cumin; bring to a boil. Reduce heat; cover and simmer for 5 minutes.

Stir in the cream, cheese, corn, chilies and hot pepper sauce. Cook and stir over low heat until the cheese is melted; add tomato. Sprinkle soup with cilantro if desired. **YIELD: 6-8 servings (2 quarts).**

JENNY BROWN, WEST LAFAYETTE, INDIANA

This savory stromboli relies on frozen bread dough, so it comes together in no time. The golden loaf is stuffed with cheese, pepperoni, mushrooms, peppers and olives. I often add a few slices of ham, too. I think it's especially tasty served with warm pizza sauce for dipping.

pizza loaf

PREP: 20 MINUTES / **BAKE:** 35 MINUTES

1	loaf (1 pound) frozen bread dough, thawed
2	eggs, *separated*
1	tablespoon grated Parmesan cheese
1	tablespoon olive oil
1	teaspoon minced fresh parsley
1	teaspoon dried oregano
1/2	teaspoon garlic powder
1/4	teaspoon pepper
8	ounces sliced pepperoni
2	cups (8 ounces) shredded part-skim mozzarella cheese
1	can (4 ounces) mushroom stems and pieces, drained
1/4	to 1/2 cup pickled pepper rings
1	medium green pepper, diced
1	can (2-1/4 ounces) sliced ripe olives
1	can (15 ounces) pizza sauce

On a greased baking sheet, roll out dough into a 15-in. x 10-in. rectangle. In a small bowl, combine the egg yolks, Parmesan cheese, oil, parsley, oregano, garlic powder and pepper. Brush over the dough.

Sprinkle with the pepperoni, mozzarella cheese, mushrooms, pepper rings, green pepper and olives. Roll up jelly-roll style, starting with a long side; pinch seam to seal and tuck the ends under.

Place seam side down; brush with egg whites. Do not let rise. Bake at 350° for 35-40 minutes or until golden brown. Warm the pizza sauce; serve with sliced loaf. **YIELD: 10-12 slices.**

VADA McROBERTS, SILVER LAKE, KANSAS
I've had a hundred requests for this recipe over the years. It's perfect for a light lunch or as an evening snack, plus it isn't tricky to make at all. I never have to worry about storing leftovers!

cheesy sausage stromboli

PREP: 30 MINUTES + RISING / **BAKE:** 20 MINUTES

5	cups all-purpose flour
2	tablespoons sugar
2	teaspoons salt
2	packages (1/4 ounce *each*) active dry yeast
1-1/2	cups warm water (120° to 130°)
1/2	cup warm milk (120° to 130°)
2	tablespoons butter, melted
2	pounds bulk pork sausage
4	cups (16 ounces) shredded part-skim mozzarella cheese
3	eggs
1	teaspoon minced fresh basil *or* 1/4 teaspoon dried basil
2	tablespoons grated Parmesan cheese

In a large bowl, combine flour, sugar, salt and yeast. Add water, milk and butter; beat on low until well combined. Turn onto a well-floured surface; knead until smooth and elastic, about 6-8 minutes. Place in a greased bowl, turning once to grease top. Cover and let rise in a warm place until doubled, about 1 hour.

Meanwhile, in a skillet, cook sausage until no longer pink; drain and cool. Stir in mozzarella, 2 eggs and basil; set aside. Punch dough down; divide in half. Roll one portion into a 15-in. x 10-in. rectangle on a greased baking sheet. Spoon half of the sausage mixture lengthwise down one side of rectangle to within 1 in. of edges.

Fold dough over filling; pinch edges to seal. Cut four diagonal slits on top of stromboli. Repeat with remaining dough and filling. Beat remaining egg; brush over loaves. Sprinkle with Parmesan cheese. Cover and let rise until doubled, about 45 minutes. Bake at 375° for 20-25 minutes or until golden brown. Slice; serve warm. **YIELD: 2 loaves (16 slices each).**

CINDIE HENF, SEBASTIAN, FLORIDA
My husband loves Alfredo sauce, so I'm always looking for new variations. This easy-to-make soup is wonderful with crusty Italian bread and a tomato-mozzarella-basil salad. Best of all, it's the perfect amount for two of us.

florentine chicken soup

PREP/TOTAL TIME: 30 MINUTES

1	cup uncooked penne pasta
1	package (6 ounces) ready-to-use chicken breast cuts
4	cups chopped fresh spinach
1	jar (7 ounces) roasted sweet red peppers, drained and sliced
3	fresh rosemary sprigs, chopped
1/2	teaspoon garlic powder
1/4	teaspoon pepper
1	tablespoon butter
1-1/2	cups reduced-sodium chicken broth
3/4	cup Alfredo sauce
3	tablespoons prepared pesto
2	tablespoons pine nuts, toasted
1	tablespoon shredded Parmesan cheese

Cook pasta according to package directions. Meanwhile, in a large saucepan, saute the chicken, spinach, red peppers, rosemary, garlic powder and pepper in butter until spinach is wilted. Stir in the broth, Alfredo sauce and pesto; cook for 4-5 minutes or until heated through.

Drain pasta and add to the soup. Sprinkle with pine nuts and Parmesan cheese. **YIELD: 5 cups.**

JENNIFER TRENHAILE, EMERSON, NEBRASKA
This comforting soup is a favorite of my five children. It's chock-full of potatoes, carrots and ham. The best part is that I can get it on the table in a half hour.

cheesy ham chowder

PREP: 30 MINUTES / **COOK:** 20 MINUTES

10	bacon strips, diced
1	large onion, chopped
1	cup diced carrots
3	tablespoons all-purpose flour
3	cups milk
1-1/2	cups water
2-1/2	cups cubed potatoes
1	can (15-1/4 ounces) whole kernel corn, drained
2	teaspoons chicken bouillon granules

Pepper to taste

3	cups (12 ounces) shredded cheddar cheese
2	cups cubed fully cooked ham

In a Dutch oven or large soup kettle, cook the bacon over medium heat until crisp. Using a slotted spoon, remove to paper towels to drain. In the drippings, saute onion and carrots until tender. Stir in flour until blended. Gradually add milk and water.

Bring to a boil; cook and stir for 2 minutes or until thickened. Add the potatoes, corn, bouillon and pepper. Reduce heat; simmer, uncovered, for 20 minutes or until potatoes are tender. Add cheese and ham; heat until cheese is melted. Stir in bacon. **YIELD: 10 servings.**

COLLEEN NELSON, MANDAN, NORTH DAKOTA
This juicy shredded beef is so popular at summer gatherings. The tender meat is slow-cooked in a savory sauce that includes tomato paste, brown sugar, molasses and chili powder. It makes a big batch...enough for seconds.

slow cooker barbecue beef

PREP: 15 MINUTES / **COOK:** 8 HOURS

1	beef sirloin tip roast (3 pounds), cut into large chunks
3	celery ribs, chopped
1	large onion, chopped
1	medium green pepper, chopped
1	cup ketchup
1	can (6 ounces) tomato paste
1/2	cup packed brown sugar
1/4	cup cider vinegar
3	tablespoons chili powder
2	tablespoons lemon juice
2	tablespoons molasses
2	teaspoons salt
2	teaspoons Worcestershire sauce
1	teaspoon ground mustard
8	to 10 sandwich rolls, split

Place beef in a 5-qt. slow cooker. Add the celery, onion and green pepper. In a bowl, combine the ketchup, tomato paste, brown sugar, vinegar, chili powder, lemon juice, molasses, salt, Worcestershire sauce and mustard. Pour over beef mixture. Cover and cook on low for 8-9 hours or until meat is tender.

Skim fat from cooking juices if necessary. Shred beef. Toast rolls if desired. Use a slotted spoon to serve the beef on rolls. **YIELD: 8-10 servings.**

GLADYS DEBOER, CASTLEFORD, IDAHO
Having grown up on a dairy farm in Holland, I love our rural life in here Idaho's "potato country." My favorite potato soup originally called for heavy cream and bacon fat, but I've trimmed down the recipe to create this tempting version.

hearty potato soup

PREP: 10 MINUTES / **COOK:** 30 MINUTES

6	medium potatoes, peeled and sliced
2	carrots, chopped
6	celery ribs, chopped
8	cups water
1	onion, chopped
6	tablespoons butter, cubed
6	tablespoons all-purpose flour
1	teaspoon salt
1/2	teaspoon pepper
1-1/2	cups milk

In a large kettle, cook potatoes, carrots and celery in water until tender, about 20 minutes. Drain, reserving liquid and setting vegetables aside.

In the same kettle, saute onion in butter until soft. Stir in flour, salt and pepper; gradually add milk, stirring constantly until thickened. Gently stir in the cooked vegetables. Add 1 cup or more of reserved cooking liquid until the soup is desired consistency. **YIELD: 8-10 servings (about 2-1/2 quarts).**

TRINA BIGHAM, FAIRHAVEN, MASSACHUSETTS
When I turned 40, I decided to live an improved lifestyle, which included cooking healthier for my family. I make this soup every week. Everyone loves the full flavor and mix of ingredients so much, they forget it's nutritious.

colorful chicken 'n' squash soup

PREP: 25 MINUTES / **COOK:** 1-1/2 HOURS

1	broiler/fryer chicken (4 pounds), cut up
13	cups water
5	pounds butternut squash, peeled and cubed (about 10 cups)
1	bunch kale, trimmed and chopped
6	medium carrots, chopped
2	large onions, chopped
3	teaspoons salt

Place chicken and water in a stockpot. Bring to a boil. Reduce heat; cover and simmer for 1 hour or until chicken is tender.

Remove chicken from broth. Strain broth and skim fat. Return broth to the pan; add the squash, kale, carrots and onions. Bring to a boil. Reduce heat; cover and simmer for 25-30 minutes or until vegetables are tender.

When chicken is cool enough to handle, remove meat from bones and cut into bite-size pieces. Discard bones and skin. Add chicken and salt to soup; heat through. **YIELD: 14 servings (5-1/2 quarts).**

sides, salads & breads

Complete your main course with a home-style side, crisp, green salad or just-baked loaf of bread. From trusted standbys such as mac 'n' cheese and potato salad to new muffin flavors and creative salad combinations, you are sure to discover the most delicious dinner sidekicks in this chapter.

ROASTED VEGETABLE MEDLEY / PAGE 93

MARCIA VERMAIRE, NEW ERA, MICHIGAN

During the holidays, I sometimes make a couple of these golden loaves a day to give as gifts, but every one in my family loves the chewy egg bread any time of year. The recipe originated with one for Jewish challah, which I began making over a decade ago. Leftover slices make wonderful French toast.

celebration braid

PREP: 35 MINUTES + RISING / **BAKE:** 20 MINUTES + COOLING

2	packages (1/4 ounce *each*) active dry yeast	2	eggs
1	cup warm water (110° to 115°)	4-1/2	to 5 cups all-purpose flour
1/3	cup butter, softened	1	egg yolk
1/4	cup sugar	1	tablespoon cold water
1	teaspoon salt		

In a large bowl, dissolve yeast in warm water. Add the butter, sugar, salt, eggs and 3 cups flour. Beat on medium speed for 3 minutes. Stir in enough remaining flour to form a soft dough.

Turn onto a floured surface; knead until smooth and elastic, about 6-8 minutes. Place in a greased bowl, turning once to grease top. Cover and let rise in a warm place until doubled, about 1 hour.

Punch dough down. Turn onto a lightly floured surface; divide into four pieces. Shape each piece into an 18-in. rope. Place ropes parallel to each other on a greased baking sheet.

Beginning from the right side, braid dough by placing the first rope over the second rope, under the third and over the fourth. Repeat three or four times, beginning each time from the right side. Pinch ends to seal and tuck under.

Cover and let rise until doubled, about 45 minutes. Beat egg yolk and water; brush over braid. Bake at 350° for 20-25 minutes or until golden brown. Remove from pan to a wire rack to cool. **YIELD: 1 loaf.**

DARLIS WILFER, WEST BEND, WISCONSIN

I can remember my Grandma Wheeler making these delectable muffins—we'd eat them nice and warm, fresh from the oven! She was a "pinch of this" and "handful of that" kind of cook, so getting the ingredient amounts correct for the recipe was a challenge. Now it's a family treasure!

grandma's honey muffins

PREP/TOTAL TIME: 30 MINUTES

2	cups all-purpose flour
1/2	cup sugar
3	teaspoons baking powder
1/2	teaspoon salt
1	egg
1	cup 2% milk
1/4	cup butter, melted
1/4	cup honey

In a large bowl, combine the flour, sugar, baking powder and salt. In another bowl, combine the egg, milk, butter and honey; stir into dry ingredients just until moistened.

Fill greased or paper-lined muffin cups three-fourths full. Bake at 400° for 15-18 minutes or until a toothpick inserted near the center comes out clean. Remove from pan to a wire rack. Serve warm. **YIELD: 1 dozen.**

SUZETTE JURY, KEENE, CALIFORNIA

Everyone in our extended family loves to cook, so I put together all of our favorite recipes in a cookbook to be handed down from generation to generation. This mouthwatering twist on traditional potato salad comes from that collection.

grilled three-potato salad

PREP: 25 MINUTES / **GRILL:** 10 MINUTES

3/4	pound Yukon Gold potatoes (about 3 medium)
3/4	pound red potatoes (about 3 medium)
1	medium sweet potato, peeled
1/2	cup thinly sliced green onions
1/4	cup canola oil
2	to 3 tablespoons white wine vinegar
1	tablespoon Dijon mustard
1	teaspoon salt
1/2	teaspoon celery seed
1/4	teaspoon pepper

Place all of the potatoes in a Dutch oven; cover with water. Bring to a boil. Reduce heat; cover and simmer for 15-20 minutes or until tender. Drain and rinse in cold water. Cut into 1-in. chunks.

Place the potatoes in a grill wok or basket. Grill, uncovered, over medium heat for 8-12 minutes or browned, stirring frequently. Transfer to a large salad bowl; add onions.

In a small bowl, whisk oil, vinegar, mustard, salt, celery seed and pepper. Drizzle over potato mixture and toss to coat. Serve warm or at room temperature. **YIELD: 6 servings.**

EDITOR'S NOTE: If you do not have a grill wok or basket, use a disposable foil pan. Poke holes in the bottom of the pan with a meat fork to allow liquid to drain.

CHRYSA DURAN, CAMBRIDGE, MINNESOTA

Classic pear salad gets an innovative makeover with juicy chunks of cooked chicken breast and a deliciously different maple vinaigrette. This special salad is served over crisp romaine for a delightful taste experience.

pear chicken salad with maple vinaigrette

PREP/TOTAL TIME: 15 MINUTES

3	cups torn romaine
1	cup cubed cooked chicken breast
1	medium pear, sliced
1/4	cup crumbled blue cheese
1/4	cup dried cranberries
2	tablespoons balsamic vinegar
2	teaspoons maple syrup

Dash salt

2	tablespoons olive oil

In a large bowl, combine the romaine, chicken, pear, cheese and cranberries. In a small bowl, combine the vinegar, maple syrup and salt; whisk in oil. Drizzle over salad; toss to coat. Serve immediately. **YIELD: 2 servings.**

MARGARET O'BRYON, BEL AIR, MARYLAND

Baby spinach, mandarin oranges and avocado are teamed in this refreshing springtime salad. You can also substitute fresh orange slices for the mandarin oranges—regardless, it's one way to guarantee your family will enjoy eating right.

avocado-orange spinach toss

PREP/TOTAL TIME: 20 MINUTES

1/4	cup orange juice
4-1/2	teaspoons lemon juice
1	tablespoon sugar
1	tablespoon white wine vinegar
1	tablespoon canola oil
1/4	teaspoon grated orange peel

Dash salt

6	cups fresh baby spinach
1	can (11 ounces) mandarin oranges, drained
1	small cucumber, thinly sliced
1/2	medium ripe avocado, peeled and sliced

For dressing, in a small bowl, combine first seven ingredients. Place the spinach in a large salad bowl; top with the oranges, cucumber and avocado. Drizzle with dressing and gently toss to coat. **YIELD: 8 servings.**

MICHELE LARSON, BADEN, PENNSYLVANIA

Everybody just loves this tempting blend of meats, veggies and pasta. It goes together in no time, serves a crowd and tastes as delicious at room temperature as it does cold. Also, it's chunky enough for the kids to pick out any individual ingredient they might not like!

antipasto picnic salad

PREP: 30 MINUTES / **COOK:** 15 MINUTES

1	package (16 ounces) medium pasta shells
2	jars (16 ounces *each*) giardiniera
1	pound fresh broccoli florets
1/2	pound cubed part-skim mozzarella cheese
1/2	pound hard salami, cubed
1/2	pound deli ham, cubed
2	packages (3-1/2 ounces *each*) sliced pepperoni, halved
1	large green pepper, cut into chunks
1	can (6 ounces) pitted ripe olives, drained

DRESSING:

1/2	cup olive oil
1/4	cup red wine vinegar
2	tablespoons lemon juice
1	teaspoon Italian seasoning
1	teaspoon coarsely ground pepper
1/2	teaspoon salt

Cook pasta according to package directions. Meanwhile, drain giardiniera, reserving 3/4 cup liquid. In a large bowl, combine the giardiniera, broccoli, mozzarella, salami, ham, pepperoni, green pepper and olives. Drain pasta and rinse in cold water; stir into meat mixture.

For dressing, in a small bowl, whisk the oil, vinegar, lemon juice, Italian seasoning, pepper, salt and reserved giardiniera liquid. Pour over salad and toss to coat. Refrigerate until serving. **YIELD: 25 servings.**

EDITOR'S NOTE: Giardiniera, a pickled vegetable mixture, is available in mild and hot varieties and can be found in the Italian or pickle section of your grocery store.

ARLENE BUTLER, OGDEN, UTAH

Because these soft, hearty rolls require only one rising, they are relatively quick to make. Whole wheat flour and good-for-you oats make them nutritious, too.

honey-oat pan rolls

PREP: 45 MINUTES + RISING / **BAKE:** 20 MINUTES

2-1/2	to 2-3/4 cups all-purpose flour
3/4	cup whole wheat flour
1/2	cup old-fashioned oats
2	packages (1/4 ounce *each*) active dry yeast
1	teaspoon salt
1	cup water
1/4	cup honey
5	tablespoons butter, *divided*
1	egg

In a large bowl, combine 1 cup all-purpose flour, whole wheat flour, oats, yeast and salt. In a small saucepan, heat the water, honey and 4 tablespoons butter to 120°-130°. Add to dry ingredients; beat just until moistened. Add egg; beat until well combined. Stir in enough remaining all-purpose flour to form a soft dough.

Turn onto a floured surface; knead until smooth and elastic, about 6-8 minutes. Place in a greased bowl, turning once to grease top. Cover and let rise in a warm place until doubled, about 1 hour.

Punch dough down. Turn onto a lightly floured surface; divide into 24 pieces. Shape each into a ball. Place in a greased 13-in. x 9-in. baking pan. Cover and let rise until doubled, about 30 minutes.

Bake at 375° for 20-22 minutes or until golden brown. Melt the remaining butter; brush over rolls. Remove from pan to a wire rack. **YIELD: 2 dozen.**

JULIE HEWITT, UNION MILLS, INDIANA
Fresh green beans are wrapped in bacon and covered in a sweet sauce in this fast and simple side dish. Every time I take these green bean bundles to a luncheon or family dinner, people beg me for the recipe.

bacon-wrapped green beans

PREP/TOTAL TIME: 30 MINUTES

3/4	pound fresh green beans
4	bacon strips
3	tablespoons butter, melted
1/4	cup packed brown sugar
1/4	teaspoon garlic salt
1/8	teaspoon soy sauce

Place the beans in a large saucepan and cover with water. Bring to a boil. Cook, uncovered, for 8 minutes or until crisp-tender. Meanwhile, in a skillet, cook the bacon over medium heat until cooked but not crisp, about 3 minutes. Remove to paper towels.

Drain beans; place about 12 beans on each bacon strip. Wrap bacon around beans and secure with a toothpick. Place on an ungreased baking sheet.

In a small bowl, combine butter, brown sugar, garlic salt and soy sauce; brush over bundles. Bake at 400° for 10-15 minutes or until bacon is crisp. **YIELD: 4 servings.**

SHIRLEY BEAUREGARD, GRAND JUNCTION, COLORADO
This eye-fetching veggie side dish is good with any meat entree, but I especially enjoy it alongside roast pork. Because the tender vegetables can be prepared in advance, I have more time to enjoy with my dinner guests.

roasted vegetable medley

PREP: 25 MINUTES / **BAKE:** 30 MINUTES

3	Yukon Gold potatoes, cut into small wedges
2	medium sweet red peppers, cut into 1-inch pieces
1	small butternut squash, peeled and cubed
1	medium sweet potato, peeled and cubed
1	medium red onion, quartered
3	tablespoons olive oil
2	tablespoons balsamic vinegar
2	tablespoons minced fresh rosemary *or* 2 teaspoons dried rosemary, crushed
1	tablespoon minced fresh thyme *or* 1 teaspoon dried thyme
1	teaspoon salt
1/2	teaspoon pepper

In a large bowl, combine the Yukon Gold potatoes, red peppers, squash, sweet potato and onion. In a small bowl, whisk the oil, vinegar and seasonings. Pour dressing over vegetables and toss to coat.

Transfer to two greased 15-in. x 10-in. baking pans. Bake, uncovered, at 425° for 30-40 minutes or until tender, stirring occasionally. **YIELD: 7 servings.**

KATHERINE MCCLELLAND, DEEP BROOK, NOVA SCOTIA
Love banana bread? Then these yummy handheld muffins, drizzled with sweet caramel icing, will fill the bill in a big way.

jumbo caramel banana muffins

PREP: 20 MINUTES / **COOK:** 25 MINUTES

1/4	cup shortening
1	cup sugar
1	egg
1-1/2	cups mashed ripe bananas (about 3 large)
1	teaspoon vanilla extract
1-1/2	cups all-purpose flour
1	teaspoon baking soda
1/4	teaspoon salt

CARAMEL ICING:

2	tablespoons butter
1/4	cup packed brown sugar
1	tablespoon milk
1/2	cup confectioners' sugar

In a small bowl, cream shortening and sugar. Add egg; mix well. Beat in bananas and vanilla. Combine the flour, baking soda and salt; add to creamed mixture just until moistened.

Fill paper-lined jumbo muffin cups three-fourths full. Bake at 350° for 23-28 minutes or until a toothpick inserted near the center comes out clean. Cool for 5 minutes before removing from pan to a wire rack to cool completely.

For icing, in a small saucepan, melt butter over medium heat. Stir in brown sugar and milk; bring to a boil. Cool slightly. Whisk in confectioners' sugar. Transfer to a small resealable plastic bag; cut a small hole in a corner of bag and drizzle over muffins. **YIELD: 6 muffins.**

SHEILA SAUNDERS, PLEASANT GROVE, UTAH
Whenever I take this salad to an event, people want the recipe to bring home. It's a delicious way to introduce people to pomegranate.

pomegranate spinach salad

PREP/TOTAL TIME: 25 MINUTES

1	package (6 ounces) fresh baby spinach
1/2	cup shredded reduced-fat Swiss cheese
1/3	cup slivered almonds, toasted
1/2	cup pomegranate seeds

DRESSING:

3	tablespoons canola oil
2	tablespoons sugar
2	tablespoons white vinegar
3/4	teaspoon poppy seeds
1/4	teaspoon salt
1/8	teaspoon ground mustard

In a large salad bowl, combine the spinach, cheese, almonds and pomegranate seeds. In a blender, combine the dressing ingredients; cover and process until blended. Drizzle over salad and toss to coat. Serve immediately. **YIELD: 6 servings.**

KITCHEN TIP

Pomegranates are available from late September to November. Select pomegranates with fresh leather-like skin free from cracks and splits. Skin color varies from bright to deep red.

The seeds and surrounding juice sacs are the only parts of the pomegranate that are edible. You can refrigerate pomegranate seeds for up to 3 days. Or, to freeze them, place in a single layer in a baking pan. When frozen, transfer to an airtight container and freeze for up to 6 months.

RUTH BIANCHI, APPLE VALLEY, MINNESOTA

The recipe for this flavorful, colorful salad has been in my family for years. My mother used to bring it to many different functions, and I'm carrying on her tradition.

southwestern rice salad

PREP/TOTAL TIME: 30 MINUTES

1-1/3	cups water
2/3	cup uncooked long grain rice
3/4	cup chopped green pepper
1/2	cup chopped red onion
1	medium carrot, chopped
1	tablespoon canola oil
3	garlic cloves, minced
1	package (16 ounces) frozen corn, thawed
1	can (15 ounces) black beans, rinsed and drained
2	medium plum tomatoes, chopped
1	cup salted peanuts
1/3	cup minced fresh cilantro
2/3	cup olive oil
1/3	cup lemon juice
1/2	to 1-1/2 teaspoons cayenne pepper
1/2	teaspoon ground cumin

In a large saucepan, bring water and rice to a boil. Reduce heat; cover and simmer for 15 minutes. Remove from the heat. Let stand for 5 minutes or until rice is tender. Rinse rice with cold water and drain. Place in a large bowl.

In a small skillet, saute the green pepper, onion and carrot in oil until crisp-tender. Add garlic; cook 1 minute longer. Add to rice. Stir in the corn, beans, tomatoes, peanuts and cilantro.

In a small bowl, combine the oil, lemon juice, cayenne and cumin. Pour over rice mixture; stir to coat. Cover and refrigerate until serving. **YIELD: 12 servings.**

HOPE TOOLE, MUSCLE SHOALS, ALABAMA

This recipe has evolved over the past several years since I began making it. After I added the thyme, ham and sour cream, my husband declared, "This is it!" I like to serve this rich, saucy entree with homemade French bread.

white cheddar scalloped potatoes

PREP: 40 MINUTES / **BAKE:** 70 MINUTES

1	medium onion, finely chopped
1/4	cup butter, cubed
1/4	cup all-purpose flour
1	teaspoon dried parsley flakes
1	teaspoon salt
1/2	teaspoon pepper
1/2	teaspoon dried thyme
3	cups milk
1	can (10-3/4 ounces) condensed cream of mushroom soup, undiluted
1	cup (8 ounces) sour cream
8	cups thinly sliced peeled potatoes
3-1/2	cups cubed fully cooked ham
2	cups (8 ounces) shredded white cheddar cheese

In a large saucepan, saute onion in butter until tender. Stir in the flour, parsley, salt, pepper and thyme until blended. Gradually add milk. Bring to a boil; cook and stir for 2 minutes or until thickened. Stir in the soup. Remove from the heat; stir in sour cream until blended.

In a large bowl, combine the potatoes and ham. In a greased 13-in. x 9-in. baking dish, layer half of the potato mixture, cheese and white sauce. Repeat layers. Cover and bake at 375° for 30 minutes. Uncover; bake 40-50 minutes longer or until potatoes are tender. **YIELD: 6-8 servings.**

KARA COOK, ELK RIDGE, UTAH
I've tried many chicken salad recipes over the years, but this is my very favorite. It's fresh, fruity and refreshing, and the cashews add a delightful crunch. Every time I serve it at a potluck or picnic, I get rave reviews...and always come home with an empty bowl!

cashew-chicken rotini salad

PREP: 30 MINUTES + CHILLING

1	package (16 ounces) spiral *or* rotini pasta
4	cups cubed cooked chicken
1	can (20 ounces) pineapple tidbits, drained
1-1/2	cups sliced celery
3/4	cup thinly sliced green onions
1	cup seedless red grapes
1	cup seedless green grapes
1	package (6 ounces) dried cranberries
1	cup ranch salad dressing
3/4	cup mayonnaise
2	cups salted cashews

Cook pasta according to package directions. Meanwhile, in a large bowl, combine the chicken, pineapple, celery, onions, grapes and cranberries. Drain pasta and rinse in cold water; stir into chicken mixture.

In a small bowl, whisk the ranch dressing and mayonnaise. Pour over salad and toss to coat. Cover and refrigerate for at least 1 hour. Just before serving, stir in cashews. **YIELD: 12 servings.**

TASTE OF HOME TEST KITCHEN
With just a few minutes of prep, our team of home economists tossed together this pleasing potato side dish. Seasoned with fresh rosemary and herbs, the golden potatoes bring a pleasantly bold flavor to any meal.

herb-crusted potatoes

PREP: 10 MINUTES / **BAKE:** 40 MINUTES

1-1/2	pounds Yukon Gold potatoes, cut into wedges
1	tablespoon olive oil
1	tablespoon minced fresh rosemary
1	teaspoon dried thyme
1	teaspoon dried oregano
1/2	teaspoon salt
1/4	to 1/2 teaspoon pepper

In a large bowl, toss potato wedges with oil. Combine the rosemary, thyme, oregano, salt and pepper. Sprinkle seasoning mixture over the potatoes and toss to coat.

Arrange the potatoes in a single layer in a 15-in. x 10-in. baking pan coated with cooking spray. Bake at 425° for 40-45 minutes or until the potatoes are tender, stirring once. **YIELD: 4 servings.**

GWEN MILLER, ROLLING HILLS, ALBERTA

This home-style dish puts a new twist on a traditional comfort food standby. At first the three different cheese flavors sounded interesting, but they blend together wonderfully.

rich 'n' cheesy macaroni

PREP: 30 MINUTES / **BAKE:** 30 MINUTES

2-1/2	cups uncooked elbow macaroni
6	tablespoons butter, *divided*
1/4	cup all-purpose flour
1	teaspoon salt
1	teaspoon sugar
2	cups milk
8	ounces process American cheese (Velveeta), cubed
1-1/3	cups 4% cottage cheese
2/3	cup sour cream
2	cups (8 ounces) shredded sharp cheddar cheese
1-1/2	cups soft bread crumbs

Cook the macaroni according to the package directions; drain. Place in a greased 2-1/2-qt. baking dish. In a saucepan, melt 4 tablespoons butter. Stir in the flour, salt and sugar until smooth. Gradually stir in milk. Bring to a boil; cook and stir for 2 minutes or until thickened.

Reduce heat; stir in American cheese until melted. Stir in the cottage cheese and sour cream. Pour over macaroni. Sprinkle with cheddar cheese. Melt remaining butter and toss with bread crumbs; sprinkle over top.

Bake, uncovered, at 350° for 30 minutes or until golden brown. **YIELD: 6-8 servings.**

WENDY MASTERS, GRAND VALLEY, ONTARIO

This is one of my very best recipes. It has all the goodness of homemade banana bread in the form of a cute muffin.

banana crumb muffins

PREP: 15 MINUTES / **BAKE:** 20 MINUTES + COOLING

1-1/2	cups all-purpose flour
1	teaspoon baking soda
1	teaspoon baking powder
1/2	teaspoon salt
3	large ripe bananas, mashed
3/4	cup sugar
1	egg, lightly beaten
1/2	cup butter, melted

TOPPING:

1/3	cup packed brown sugar
1	tablespoon all-purpose flour
1/8	teaspoon ground cinnamon
1	tablespoon cold butter

In a large bowl, combine dry ingredients. Combine bananas, sugar, egg and butter; mix well. Stir into dry ingredients just until moistened. Fill greased or paper-lined muffin cups three-fourths full. Combine the first three topping ingredients; cut in butter until crumbly. Sprinkle over muffins.

Bake at 375° for 18-20 minutes or until a toothpick inserted near the center comes out clean. Cool muffins in pan 10 minutes before removing to a wire rack. **YIELD: about 1 dozen.**

MARCIA BRAUN, SCOTT CITY, KANSAS

I stir together corn bread mix, French onion dip and canned corn to make this super-moist side dish. It went over so well at Thanksgiving that it's now served at all our holiday gatherings.

golden corn casserole

PREP: 10 MINUTES / **BAKE:** 35 MINUTES

3	eggs
1	carton (8 ounces) French onion dip
1/4	cup butter, softened
1	package (8-1/2 ounces) corn bread/muffin mix
1/2	teaspoon salt
1/2	teaspoon pepper
1	can (15-1/4 ounces) whole kernel corn, drained
1	can (14-3/4 ounces) cream-style corn

In a large bowl, beat the eggs, French onion dip, butter, corn bread mix, salt and pepper until combined. Stir in the corn.

Pour into a greased 11-in. x 7-in. baking dish. Bake, uncovered, at 350° for 35-40 minutes or until edges are lightly browned and pull away from sides of dish. **YIELD: 8-10 servings.**

KELLI RITZ, INNISFAIL, ALBERTA

My family loves this recipe because it brings out the lovely flavors of the root vegetables. Even my children enjoy it thanks to the drizzle of maple syrup! It's a tasty—and successful—way to introduce kids to turnips, rutabaga and parsnips.

maple-ginger root vegetables

PREP: 35 MINUTES / **BAKE:** 45 MINUTES

5	medium parsnips, peeled and sliced
5	small carrots, sliced
3	medium turnips, peeled and cubed
1	large sweet potato, peeled and cubed
1	small rutabaga, peeled and cubed
1	large sweet onion, cut into wedges
1	small red onion, cut into wedges
2	tablespoons olive oil
1	tablespoon minced fresh gingerroot
1	teaspoon salt
1/2	teaspoon pepper
1	cup maple syrup

Place the first seven ingredients in a large resealable plastic bag; add the oil, ginger, salt and pepper. Seal bag and shake to coat. Arrange vegetables in a single layer in two 15-in. x 10-in. baking pans coated with cooking spray.

Bake, uncovered, at 425° for 25 minutes, stirring once. Drizzle with syrup. Bake 20-25 minutes longer or until vegetables are tender, stirring once. **YIELD: 24 servings.**

JEANNETTE TRAVIS, FORTH WORTH, TEXAS

This tasty corn casserole gets plenty of flavor from sweet onions, cream-style corn and cheddar cheese, plus a little zip from hot pepper sauce. The comfy-cozy dish is a popular addition to our church potlucks.

sweet onion corn bake

PREP: 15 MINUTES / **BAKE:** 45 MINUTES + STANDING

2	large sweet onions, thinly sliced
1/2	cup butter, cubed
1	cup (8 ounces) sour cream
1/2	cup milk
1/2	teaspoon dill weed
1/4	teaspoon salt
2	cups (8 ounces) shredded cheddar cheese, *divided*
1	egg, lightly beaten
1	can (14-3/4 ounces) cream-style corn
1	package (8-1/2 ounces) corn bread/muffin mix
4	drops hot pepper sauce

In a large skillet, saute onions in butter until tender. In a small bowl, combine the sour cream, milk, dill and salt until blended; stir in 1 cup of cheese. Stir into the onion mixture; remove from the heat and set aside.

In a large bowl, combine the egg, corn, corn bread mix and hot pepper sauce. Pour into a greased 13-in. x 9-in. baking dish. Spoon onion mixture over top. Sprinkle with remaining cheese.

Bake, uncovered, at 350° for 45-50 minutes or until a thermometer reaches 160°. Let stand for 10 minutes before cutting. **YIELD: 12-15 servings.**

NANCY MONTGOMERY, HARTVILLE, OHIO

When I started making this bread, my husband and our six children liked it so much I was baking every day. I was thrilled when the judges at our county fair gave these pretty braids both a blue ribbon and best of show award!

sesame wheat braids

PREP: 30 MINUTES + RISING / **BAKE:** 20 MINUTES + COOLING

2	packages (1/4 ounce *each*) active dry yeast
2-1/4	cups warm water (110° to 115°)
1/3	cup sugar
1	tablespoon canola oil
1	cup whole wheat flour
2	eggs
1	tablespoon water
1	tablespoon salt
5	to 6 cups all-purpose flour
2	teaspoons sesame seeds

In a large bowl, dissolve yeast in water. Add the sugar and oil; mix well. Stir in whole wheat flour; let stand until the mixture bubbles, about 5 minutes.

In a small bowl, beat eggs and water. Remove 2 tablespoons to a small bowl; cover and refrigerate. Add remaining egg mixture and salt to batter; mix until smooth. Add 4 cups all-purpose flour and beat until smooth. Add enough remaining flour to form a soft dough.

Turn onto a floured surface; knead until smooth and elastic, about 6-8 minutes. Place in a greased bowl, turning once to grease top. Cover and let rise in a warm place until doubled, about 1 hour. Punch dough down and divide in half. Divide each half into thirds.

Shape each portion into a rope about 15 in. long. Place three ropes on a greased baking sheet; braid ropes. Pinch each end firmly and tuck under.

Brush braids with the reserved egg mixture; sprinkle with sesame seeds. Repeat, placing second braid on the same baking sheet. Let rise until doubled, about 45 minutes. Bake at 350° for 20-25 minutes. Remove from baking sheet to cool on a wire rack. **YIELD: 2 loaves.**

BETTY LAMB, OREM, UTAH

When a friend shared this recipe, it had a fancy French name. My children can never remember the salad's real name, so they just say, "Mom, please make that good salad." Now our friends and neighbors request it—by that same name—for potluck dinners.

that good salad

PREP/TOTAL TIME: 20 MINUTES

3/4	cup canola oil
1/4	cup lemon juice
2	garlic cloves, minced
1/2	teaspoon salt
1/2	teaspoon pepper
2	bunches (1 pound *each*) romaine, torn
2	cups chopped tomatoes
1	cup (4 ounces) shredded Swiss cheese
2/3	cup slivered almonds, toasted, optional
1/2	cup grated Parmesan cheese
8	bacon strips, cooked and crumbled
1	cup Caesar salad croutons

In a jar with tight-fitting lid, combine the oil, lemon juice, garlic, salt and pepper; cover and shake well. Chill.

In a large serving bowl, toss the romaine, tomatoes, Swiss cheese, almonds if desired, Parmesan cheese and bacon. Shake dressing; pour over salad and toss. Add croutons and serve immediately. **YIELD: 14 servings.**

RHODA MCFALL, LINCOLN, KANSAS

This delicious veggie salad is flavorful and so pretty when set on the table. I fixed it for a family reunion and everyone couldn't get enough, especially my Italian son-in-law.

tomato corn salad

PREP/TOTAL TIME: 10 MINUTES

1	package (16 ounces) frozen corn
3	medium tomatoes, diced
1/3	cup Italian salad dressing
1/4	cup minced fresh basil
1/2	to 1 teaspoon salt

In a microwave-safe bowl, combine corn and a small amount of water. Cover and microwave on high for 3 to 3-1/2 minutes or until corn is crisp-tender; drain.

In a large bowl, combine the tomatoes, salad dressing, basil and salt. Stir in corn. Serve immediately or refrigerate. Serve with a slotted spoon. **YIELD: 8 servings.**

EDITOR'S NOTE: This recipe was tested in a 1,100-watt microwave.

KITCHEN TIP

Homegrown basil is a wonderful addition to recipes and can be used as a pretty garnish, too. However, chopping one leaf at a time can be tedious. To quickly chop a large amount of basil, stack several basil leaves and roll them into a tight tube. Slice the leaves widthwise into narrow pieces to create long thin strips. If you'd like smaller pieces, simply chop the strips.

BEVERLY SPRAGUE, CATONSVILLE, MARYLAND

My extra-special banana bread makes a wonderful homemade gift for friends and neighbors. The recipe makes two loaves, so I can serve one and keep the other one in the freezer so I have a last-minute gift on hand.

special banana nut bread

PREP: 25 MINUTES / **BAKE:** 1 HOUR + COOLING

3/4	cup butter, softened
1	package (8 ounces) cream cheese, softened
2	cups sugar
2	eggs
1-1/2	cups mashed ripe bananas (about 4 medium)
1/2	teaspoon vanilla extract
3	cups all-purpose flour
1/2	teaspoon baking powder
1/2	teaspoon baking soda
1/2	teaspoon salt
2	cups chopped pecans, *divided*

ORANGE GLAZE:

1	cup confectioners' sugar
3	tablespoons orange juice
1	teaspoon grated orange peel

In a large bowl, cream the butter, cream cheese and sugar until light and fluffy. Add eggs, one at a time, beating well after each addition. Beat in bananas and vanilla. Combine the flour, baking powder, baking soda and salt; gradually add to the creamed mixture. Fold in 1 cup pecans.

Transfer to two greased 8-in. x 4-in. loaf pans. Sprinkle with the remaining pecans. Bake at 350° for 1 to 1-1/4 hours or until a toothpick inserted near the center comes out clean.

In a small bowl, whisk the glaze ingredients; drizzle over loaves. Cool for 10 minutes before removing from pans to wire racks. **YIELD: 2 loaves (12 slices each).**

PAT STEVENS, GRANBURY, TEXAS

Homemade bread can be time-consuming, difficult and tricky to make. But this fun-to-eat "monkey bread," baked in a fluted tube pan, is almost foolproof. If I'm serving it for breakfast, I add some cinnamon and drizzle it with icing.

buttery bubble bread

PREP: 25 MINUTES + RISING / **BAKE:** 30 MINUTES

1	package (1/4 ounce) active dry yeast
1	cup warm water (110° to 115°)
1/2	cup sugar
1/2	cup shortening
1	egg
1/2	teaspoon salt
4	to 4-1/2 cups all-purpose flour, *divided*
6	tablespoons butter, melted

In a large bowl, dissolve the yeast in warm water. Add the sugar, shortening, egg, salt and 1 cup of flour. Beat until smooth. Stir in enough remaining flour to form a soft dough.

Turn dough onto a floured surface; knead until smooth and elastic, about 6-8 minutes. Place in a greased bowl, turning once to grease top. Cover and let rise in a warm place until doubled, about 1 hour.

Punch dough down. Turn onto a lightly floured surface; shape into 1-1/2-in. balls. Dip the balls in butter and arrange evenly in a greased 9-in. fluted tube pan. Drizzle with the remaining butter. Cover and let rise in a warm place until doubled, about 45 minutes.

Bake at 350° for 30-35 minutes or until golden brown. Cool for 5 minutes before inverting onto a serving platter. Serve warm. **YIELD: 1 loaf.**

NORENE WRIGHT, MANILLA, INDIANA

This pleasing pasta salad is like eating a BLT in a bowl. Full of crispy crumbled bacon, chopped tomato, celery and green onion, the sensational salad is draped in a tangy mayonnaise and vinegar dressing to create a real crowd-pleaser!

blt macaroni salad

PREP: 20 MINUTES + CHILLING

2	cups uncooked elbow macaroni
5	green onions, finely chopped
1	large tomato, diced
1-1/4	cups diced celery
1-1/4	cups mayonnaise
5	teaspoons white vinegar
1/4	teaspoon salt
1/8	to 1/4 teaspoon pepper
1	pound sliced bacon, cooked and crumbled

Cook macaroni according to package directions; drain and rinse in cold water. In a large bowl, combine the macaroni, green onions, tomato and celery. In a small bowl, combine the mayonnaise, vinegar, salt and pepper. Pour over macaroni mixture and toss to coat. Cover and refrigerate for at least 2 hours. Just before serving, add bacon. **YIELD: 12 servings.**

JAUNEEN HOSKING, GREENFIELD, WISCONSIN

With its unique medley of fruits and showstopping festive look, this salad is a holiday tradition at our house. Our three grown daughters have come to expect it. One forkful reminds us of all the things we can be thankful for.

festive tossed salad

PREP/TOTAL TIME: 15 MINUTES

1/2	cup sugar
1/3	cup red wine vinegar
2	tablespoons lemon juice
2	tablespoons finely chopped onion
1/2	teaspoon salt
2/3	cup canola oil
2	to 3 teaspoons poppy seeds
10	cups torn romaine
1	cup (4 ounces) shredded Swiss cheese
1	medium apple, chopped
1	medium pear, chopped
1/4	cup dried cranberries
1/2	to 1 cup chopped cashews

In a blender or food processor, combine the sugar, vinegar, lemon juice, onion and salt. Cover and process until blended. With the blender running, gradually add oil. Add the poppy seeds and blend.

In a salad bowl, combine the romaine, Swiss cheese, apple, pear and cranberries. Drizzle with desired amount of dressing. Add cashews; toss to coat. Serve immediately. **YIELD: 8-10 servings.**

DANA LOWRY, HICKORY, NORTH CAROLINA

After I had my sixth child, a friend dropped off dinner, including these tender rolls, which start in a bread machine. They were so delicious that I quickly bought my own machine so I could make them myself whenever I wanted.

herbed dinner rolls

PREP: 20 MINUTES + RISING / **BAKE:** 15 MINUTES

1	cup water (70° - 80°)
2	tablespoons butter, softened
1	egg
1/4	cup sugar
1	teaspoon salt
1/2	teaspoon *each* dried basil, oregano, thyme and rosemary, crushed
3-1/4	cups bread flour
2-1/4	teaspoons active dry yeast

Additional butter, melted

Coarse salt, optional

In a bread machine pan, place the water, butter, egg, sugar, salt, seasonings, flour and yeast in order suggested by manufacturer. Select dough setting (check dough after 5 minutes of mixing; add 1 to 2 tablespoons of water or flour if needed).

When cycle is completed, turn dough onto a lightly floured surface. Divide dough into 16 portions; shape each into a ball. Place 2 in. apart on greased baking sheets. Cover and let rise in a warm place until doubled, about 30 minutes.

Bake at 375° for 12-15 minutes or until golden brown. If desired, brush with butter and sprinkle with coarse salt. Remove from pans to wire racks. **YIELD: 16 rolls.**

EDITOR'S NOTE: We recommend you do not use a bread machine's time-delay feature for this recipe.

IDALEE SCHOLZ, COCOA BEACH, FLORIDA
A sweet, out-of-the-ordinary dressing makes this macaroni salad special. My aunt gave me the recipe, and it has become a treasure. I occasionally leave out the green pepper if I know that people don't like it, and it still tastes great.

sweet macaroni salad

PREP: 20 MINUTES + CHILLING

1	package (16 ounces) elbow macaroni
4	medium carrots, shredded
1	large green pepper, chopped
1	medium red onion, chopped
2	cups mayonnaise
1	can (14 ounces) sweetened condensed milk
1	cup sugar
1	cup cider vinegar
1	teaspoon salt
1/2	teaspoon pepper

Cook macaroni according to package directions; drain and rinse in cold water. In a large serving bowl, combine the macaroni, carrots, green pepper and onion.

In a small bowl, whisk the mayonnaise, milk, sugar, vinegar, salt and pepper until smooth. Pour over macaroni mixture and toss to coat. Cover and refrigerate overnight. **YIELD: 14 servings.**

READERS' RAVES

> I've found that it's very important to make Sweet Macaroni Salad ahead of time so that the pasta has time to absorb the "dressing." I usually make it a day ahead and refrigerate it until serving. I always get lots of requests for the recipe, too. Definitely a keeper.
>
> —Boadecia from TasteofHome.com

NICOLE CALLEN, AUBURN, CALIFORNIA
I got this recipe from a long-time friend several years ago, and it's one of my most-used. I love to serve this melt-in-your-mouth corn bread hot from the oven with butter and syrup. It gets rave reviews at holiday and potluck dinners alike.

buttery corn bread

PREP: 15 MINUTES / **BAKE:** 25 MINUTES

2/3	cup butter, softened
1	cup sugar
3	eggs
1-2/3	cups milk
2-1/3	cups all-purpose flour
1	cup cornmeal
4-1/2	teaspoons baking powder
1	teaspoon salt

In a bowl, cream butter and sugar. Combine the eggs and milk. Combine flour, cornmeal, baking powder and salt; add to creamed mixture alternately with egg mixture.

Pour batter into a greased 13-in. x 9-in. baking pan. Bake at 400° for 22-27 minutes or until a toothpick inserted near the center comes out clean. Cut the bread into squares; serve warm. **YIELD: 12-15 servings.**

JULIANNE JOHNSON, GROVE CITY, MINNESOTA
Of all the quick breads I enjoyed while growing up, this beautifully glazed, berry-studded loaf is the best! The flavor duo of tangy lemon and sweet blueberries shines through in every bite.

lemon blueberry bread

PREP: 15 MINUTES / **BAKE:** 1 HOUR + COOLING

1/3	cup butter, melted
1	cup sugar
2	eggs
3	tablespoons lemon juice
1-1/2	cups all-purpose flour
1	teaspoon baking powder
1/2	teaspoon salt
1/2	cup milk
2	tablespoons grated lemon peel
1/2	cup chopped nuts
1	cup fresh *or* frozen blueberries

GLAZE:

2	tablespoons lemon juice
1/4	cup sugar

In a large bowl, cream butter and sugar until light and fluffy. Beat in eggs and lemon juice.

Combine flour, baking powder and salt; stir into egg mixture alternately with milk; beating well after each addition. Fold in lemon peel, nuts and blueberries.

Pour into a greased 8-in. x 4-in. loaf pan. Bake at 350° for 60-70 minutes or until a toothpick inserted near the center comes out clean. Cool for 10 minutes before removing from pan to a wire rack. Combine the glaze ingredients; drizzle the glaze over the warm bread. Let bread cool completely before serving. **YIELD: 1 loaf.**

EDITOR'S NOTE: If using frozen blueberries, do not thaw before adding to batter.

NANCY HOLLAND, MORGAN HILL, CALIFORNIA
Dill pickles add pizzazz to this old-fashioned chilled salad. The creamy, well-dressed side makes an attractive addition to any picnic or bring-a-dish event. You can expect to leave with an empty bowl.

dill pickle potato salad

PREP: 20 MINUTES + CHILLING
BAKE: 20 MINUTES + COOLING

3	pounds potatoes (about 8 medium)
6	hard-cooked eggs, chopped
3	celery ribs, chopped
6	green onions, chopped
2	medium dill pickles, finely chopped
1-1/2	cups mayonnaise
1/4	cup dill pickle juice
4-1/2	teaspoons prepared mustard
1	teaspoon celery seed
1	teaspoon salt
1/2	teaspoon pepper

Leaf lettuce, optional

Place the potatoes in a Dutch oven or large kettle and cover with water; bring to a boil. Reduce heat; cover and simmer for 20-30 minutes or until tender. Drain and cool. Peel and cube potatoes; place in a large bowl. Add the eggs, celery, onions and pickles.

In a small bowl, combine the mayonnaise, pickle juice, mustard, celery seed, salt and pepper. Pour over the potato mixture; mix well. Cover and refrigerate for at least 4 hours. Serve in a lettuce-lined bowl if desired. **YIELD: 8-10 servings.**

TASTE OF HOME TEST KITCHEN
Tender tortellini pairs wonderfully with crunchy fresh spinach in this popular salad whipped up by our home economists. Caramelized onions add a flavorful element.

caramelized onion-tortellini spinach salad

PREP: 15 MINUTES / **COOK:** 25 MINUTES

4	cups thinly sliced sweet onions
3	tablespoons butter
3	tablespoons olive oil
2	teaspoons brown sugar
1	package (19 ounces) frozen cheese tortellini
3	tablespoons balsamic vinegar
1/4	teaspoon salt
1/4	teaspoon pepper
1	package (10 ounces) fresh spinach, stems removed and torn
1/3	cup shredded Parmesan cheese

In a large skillet over medium-low heat, cook onions in butter and oil for 5 minutes or until tender. Add brown sugar; cook over low heat for 20 minutes or until onions are golden brown, stirring frequently. Meanwhile, cook the tortellini according to the package directions.

Add the vinegar, salt and pepper to onion mixture. Bring to a boil. Reduce heat; cook 1-2 minutes longer or until syrupy.

Drain tortellini and rinse in cold water. In a large serving bowl, combine the tortellini, spinach and Parmesan cheese. Add onion mixture and toss to coat. **YIELD: 12 servings.**

JANICE BASSING, RACINE, WISCONSIN
These are my favorite muffins to serve with a cup of coffee or a tall glass of cold milk. Not only are they great for breakfast, they make a tasty dessert or midnight snack, too. The espresso spread is also super on bagels. I get lots of recipe requests whenever I serve them.

cappuccino muffins

PREP: 15 MINUTES / **BAKE:** 20 MINUTES

ESPRESSO SPREAD:

4	ounces cream cheese, cubed
1	tablespoon sugar
1/2	teaspoon instant coffee granules
1/2	teaspoon vanilla extract
1/4	cup miniature semisweet chocolate chips

MUFFINS:

2	cups all-purpose flour
3/4	cup sugar
2-1/2	teaspoons baking powder
1	teaspoon ground cinnamon
1/2	teaspoon salt
1	cup milk
2	tablespoons instant coffee granules
1/2	cup butter, melted
1	egg
1	teaspoon vanilla extract
3/4	cup miniature semisweet chocolate chips

In a food processor or blender, combine the spread ingredients; cover and process until well blended. Transfer to a small bowl; cover and refrigerate until serving.

In a large bowl, combine flour, sugar, baking powder, cinnamon and salt. In another bowl, stir milk and coffee granules until coffee is dissolved. Add butter, egg and vanilla; mix well. Stir into dry ingredients just until moistened. Fold in chocolate chips.

Fill greased or paper-lined muffin cups two-thirds full. Bake at 375° for 17-20 minutes or until a toothpick comes out clean. Let muffins cool for 5 minutes before removing from pans to wire racks. Serve with espresso spread. **YIELD: about 14 muffins (1 cup spread).**

ANNA MINEGAR, ZOLFO SPRINGS, FLORIDA
I've loved corn served with this simple seasoning since I was a child. It makes corn on the cob extra special.

garlic pepper corn

PREP/TOTAL TIME: 25 MINUTES

1	tablespoon dried parsley flakes
1	tablespoon garlic pepper blend
1/2	teaspoon paprika
1/4	teaspoon salt
8	medium ears sweet corn, husked
1/4	cup butter, melted

In a small bowl, combine the parsley, garlic pepper, paprika and salt; set aside. Place corn in a Dutch oven or kettle; cover with water. Bring to a boil; cover and cook for 3 minutes or until tender. Drain.

Brush corn with butter; sprinkle with seasoning mixture. Serve immediately. **YIELD: 8 servings.**

LYNN BREUNIG, WIND LAKE, WISCONSIN

Here's a simple way to jazz up your usual potato salad—add cheese, bacon and ranch salad dressing. Who knew so few ingredients could create such a special, palate-pleasing dish!

ranch potato salad

PREP/TOTAL TIME: 30 MINUTES

2	pounds red potatoes
1	bottle (8 ounces) ranch salad dressing
1	cup (4 ounces) shredded cheddar cheese
1	package (2.8 ounces) real bacon bits
1/4	teaspoon pepper

Dash garlic powder

Place potatoes in a large saucepan and cover with water. Bring to a boil. Reduce heat; cover and simmer for 20-25 minutes or until tender.

In a large bowl, combine the remaining ingredients (dressing will be thick). Drain potatoes and cut into cubes; add to the dressing and gently toss to coat. Cover and refrigerate for 2 hours or until chilled. Refrigerate leftovers. **YIELD: 6-8 servings.**

TRACI COLLINS, CHEYENNE, WYOMING

I stumbled across this recipe while looking for something different to take to a potluck. Boy, am I glad I did! The fun-to-eat loaf tastes fabulous, and no one could believe it only called for five ingredients. It's the perfect item to bake if you're attending an informal get-together.

pull-apart bacon bread

PREP: 20 MINUTES + RISING / BAKE: 20 MINUTES

12	bacon strips, diced
1	loaf (1 pound) frozen bread dough, thawed
2	tablespoons olive oil, *divided*
1	cup (4 ounces) shredded part-skim mozzarella cheese
1	envelope (1 ounce) ranch salad dressing mix

In a skillet, cook bacon over medium heat for 5 minutes or until partially cooked; drain on paper towels. Roll out dough to 1/2-in. thickness; brush with 1 tablespoon of oil. Cut into 1-in. pieces; place in a large bowl. Add the bacon, cheese, dressing mix and remaining oil; toss to coat.

Arrange pieces in a 9-in. x 5-in. oval on a greased baking sheet, layering as needed. Cover and let rise in a warm place for 30 minutes or until doubled. Bake at 350° for 15 minutes. Cover with foil; bake 5-10 minutes longer or until golden brown. **YIELD: 1 loaf.**

KATIE SLOAN, CHARLOTTE, NORTH CAROLINA
No truly Southern meal is complete without macaroni and cheese. Three types of cheese and a squirt of mustard make this comforting dish sing!

triple-cheese macaroni

PREP: 20 MINUTES / **BAKE:** 25 MINUTES

1	package (16 ounces) elbow macaroni
2	eggs
1	can (12 ounces) evaporated milk
1/4	cup butter, melted
2	tablespoons prepared mustard
1	teaspoon seasoned salt
1	teaspoon pepper
8	ounces process cheese (Velveeta), melted
2	cups (8 ounces) shredded mild cheddar cheese, *divided*
2	cups (8 ounces) shredded sharp cheddar cheese, *divided*

Cook macaroni according to package directions. Meanwhile, in a large bowl, whisk the eggs, milk, butter, mustard, seasoned salt and pepper until combined. Stir in the process cheese and 1-1/2 cups of each cheddar cheese.

Drain the macaroni; stir into the cheese mixture. Pour into a greased 3-qt. baking dish. Top with remaining cheeses. Bake, uncovered, at 350° for 25-30 minutes or until cheese is melted and edges are bubbly. **YIELD: 6 servings.**

STEPHANIE KIENZLE, NORTH MIAMI BEACH, FLORIDA
I bake something almost everyday—either early in the morning before everyone's awake or in the evening. I whip up these tender muffins in no time and serve them with jam for breakfast or ice cream and chocolate syrup for dessert.

chocolate banana muffins

PREP: 25 MINUTES / **BAKE:** 15 MINUTES + COOLING

1/2	cup butter, softened
1/2	cup sugar
1/2	cup packed brown sugar
2	eggs
1-1/2	cups mashed ripe bananas (about 3 large)
3	teaspoons vanilla extract
2	cups all-purpose flour
3	teaspoons baking soda
1	cup chopped walnuts
1	cup (6 ounces) semisweet chocolate chips

In a bowl, cream the butter and sugars. Beat in eggs, bananas and vanilla. Combine flour and baking soda; add to creamed mixture just until combined. Stir in the walnuts and chocolate chips. Fill greased or paper-lined muffin cups half full.

Bake at 350° for 15-20 minutes or until a toothpick comes out clean. Cool for 5 minutes before removing from pans to wire racks. **YIELD: 2 dozen.**

P. LAUREN FAY-NERI, SYRACUSE, NEW YORK
The pleasing corn flavor of this golden side dish makes it a real comfort food favorite. It's easy to prepare because the recipe calls for a packaged corn mix.

corn pudding

PREP: 20 MINUTES / **BAKE:** 45 MINUTES

- 1/2 cup butter, softened
- 1/2 cup sugar
- 2 eggs
- 1 cup (8 ounces) sour cream
- 1 package (8-1/2 ounces) corn bread/muffin mix
- 1/2 cup milk
- 1 can (15-1/4 ounces) whole kernel corn, drained
- 1 can (14-3/4 ounces) cream-style corn

In a large bowl, cream butter and sugar until light and fluffy. Add eggs, one at a time, beating well after each addition. Beat in sour cream. Gradually add muffin mix alternately with milk. Fold in corn.

Pour into a greased 3-qt. baking dish. Bake, uncovered, at 325° for 45-50 minutes or until set and lightly browned. **YIELD: 8 servings.**

SALLY DURRETT, PALO CEDRO, CALIFORNIA
The day after Thanksgiving, I prepare three of these golden brown bakes for our large family gathering. I complete the feast with an egg bake, banana nut bread and fruit.

golden potato casserole

PREP: 20 MINUTES / **BAKE:** 40 MINUTES + STANDING

- 6 large potatoes, peeled and cut into 1/2-inch cubes
- 4 cups (16 ounces) shredded cheddar cheese
- 1 can (10-3/4 ounces) condensed cream of chicken soup, undiluted

- 1 cup (8 ounces) sour cream
- 1/4 cup butter, melted
- 8 green onions, chopped

Dash salt and pepper

Place the potatoes in a large saucepan and cover with water. Bring to a boil. Reduce heat; cover and cook for 12-15 minutes or until tender. Drain.

In a large bowl, combine the cheese, soup, sour cream, butter, onions, salt and pepper. Gently stir in potatoes. Transfer to a greased 13-in. x 9-in. baking dish (dish will be full). Bake, uncovered, at 350° for 40-45 minutes or until bubbly. Let stand for 10 minutes before serving. **YIELD: 12-14 servings.**

PAT SCHRAND, ENTERPRISE, ALABAMA
While these little gems are delicious year-round, you could easily turn the decadent muffins into an edible Christmas gift. They look festive on a decorative tray wrapped in red or green cellophane or tucked into a giveaway cookie tin. And don't forget to include the recipe so your recipient can enjoy this treat again and again.

pecan pie mini muffins

PREP: 10 MINUTES / **BAKE:** 25 MINUTES

- 1 cup packed brown sugar
- 1/2 cup all-purpose flour
- 1 cup chopped pecans
- 2/3 cup butter, melted
- 2 eggs, lightly beaten

In a large bowl, combine the brown sugar, flour and pecans; set aside. Combine butter and eggs. Stir into brown sugar mixture.

Fill greased and floured miniature muffin cups two-thirds full. Bake at 350° for 22-25 minutes or until a toothpick inserted near the center comes out clean. Immediately remove from pans to wire racks to cool. **YIELD: about 2-1/2 dozen.**

EDITOR'S NOTE: This recipe uses only 1/2 cup flour.

KAREN BOURNE, MAGRATH, ALBERTA

The orange dressing that adorns this salad complements the fresh fruit flavors beautifully. It's perfect for a summer event.

glazed fruit medley

PREP: 20 MINUTES + CHILLING

1	cup sugar
2	tablespoons cornstarch
2	cups orange juice
3	cups cubed honeydew
3	medium firm bananas, sliced
2	cups green grapes
2	cups halved fresh strawberries

In a small saucepan, combine the sugar, cornstarch and orange juice until smooth. Bring to a boil; cook and stir for 2 minutes or until thickened. Transfer to a bowl. Cover and chill for 2 hours.

In a large serving bowl, combine the honeydew, bananas, grapes and strawberries. Drizzle with glaze; gently toss to coat. **YIELD: 10 servings.**

READERS' RAVES

> Best Ever Banana Bread is wonderfully moist and tasty. I also substituted the oil with applesauce and added chocolate chips. Loved it, and will definitely make it again.
>
> —Misspriss1 from TasteofHome.com

> I always double the recipe since it goes so fast. I get 3 loaves from a double batch by baking them in 8 x 4 x 2.5 inch glass loaf pans. Oven temperatures may vary, so check them after an hour; generally mine take 1-1/4 hours. It's hard to resist having a slice fresh from the oven. Yum!!
>
> —Joscy from TasteofHome.com

GERT KAISER, KENOSHA, WISCONSIN

Whenever I pass bananas in the grocery store, I can almost smell the aroma of this bread baking in the oven. The chopped walnuts add a wonderful nutty texture.

best ever banana bread

PREP: 15 MINUTES / **BAKE:** 70 MINUTES

1-3/4	cups all-purpose flour
1-1/2	cups sugar
1	teaspoon baking soda
1/2	teaspoon salt
2	eggs
2	medium ripe bananas, mashed (1 cup)
1/2	cup canola oil
1/4	cup plus 1 tablespoon buttermilk
1	teaspoon vanilla extract
1	cup chopped walnuts

In a large bowl, stir together the flour, sugar, baking soda and salt. In another bowl, combine the eggs, bananas, oil, buttermilk and vanilla; add to flour mixture, stirring just until combined. Fold in nuts.

Pour into a greased 9-in. x 5-in. loaf pan. Bake at 325° for 1 hour 20 minutes or until a toothpick comes out clean. Cool on wire rack. **YIELD: 1 loaf.**

KRISTA FRANK, RHODODENDRON, OREGON

This bread is so full of flavor that spreading butter on it is not necessary. I always hear yums, oohs and aahs when guests take their first bite. It's best served warm, and the next day, it makes the best toast you've ever had!

herbed onion focaccia

PREP: 30 MINUTES + RISING / **BAKE:** 20 MINUTES

1	cup water (70° to 80°)
1/3	cup finely chopped onion
1	tablespoon sugar
1-1/2	teaspoons salt
1	teaspoon grated Parmesan cheese
1/2	teaspoon garlic powder
1/2	teaspoon dried basil
1/2	teaspoon dill weed
1/2	teaspoon pepper
3	cups all-purpose flour
2	teaspoons active dry yeast

TOPPING:

1	tablespoon olive oil
1/2	teaspoon grated Parmesan cheese
1/2	teaspoon dried parsley flakes
1/4	teaspoon salt
1/8	teaspoon pepper

In bread machine pan, place the first 11 ingredients in order suggested by manufacturer. Select dough setting (check dough after 5 minutes of mixing; add 1 to 2 tablespoons of water or flour if needed).

When cycle is completed, turn dough onto a greased baking sheet and punch down (dough will be sticky). With lightly oiled hands, pat dough into a 9-in. circle. Brush with oil; sprinkle with the cheese, parsley, salt and pepper. Cover and let rise in a warm place until doubled, about 45 minutes.

Bake at 400° for 18-20 minutes or until golden brown. Cut into wedges; serve warm. **YIELD: 1 loaf (1-1/2 pounds, 16 slices).**

JACKIE DECKARD, SOLSBERRY, INDIANA

I revamped my mother's potato salad recipe to taste more like baked potatoes with all the toppings. It is now the most requested dish at our family gatherings...even my mother asked for the recipe!

loaded baked potato salad

PREP: 20 MINUTES / **BAKE:** 40 MINUTES + COOLING

5	pounds small unpeeled red potatoes, cubed
1	teaspoon salt
1/2	teaspoon pepper
8	hard-cooked eggs, chopped
1	pound sliced bacon, cooked and crumbled
2	cups (8 ounces) shredded cheddar cheese
1	sweet onion, chopped
3	dill pickles, chopped
1-1/2	cups (12 ounces) sour cream
1	cup mayonnaise
2	to 3 teaspoons prepared mustard

Place the potatoes in a greased 15-in. x 10-in. baking pan; sprinkle with salt and pepper. Bake, uncovered, at 425° for 40-45 minutes or until tender. Cool in pan on a wire rack.

In a large bowl, combine the potatoes, eggs, bacon, cheese, onion and pickles. In a small bowl, combine the sour cream, mayonnaise and mustard; pour over the potato mixture and toss to coat. **YIELD: 20 servings.**

CARRINA COOPER, MCALPIN, FLORIDA

Because my husband likes spicy foods, I frequently sprinkle chopped jalapeno peppers over half of this casserole for him. The sweetness from the corn and kick of the peppers are a lively combination we can't resist.

corn bread casserole

PREP: 5 MINUTES / **BAKE:** 30 MINUTES

- 1 can (15-1/4 ounces) whole kernel corn, drained
- 1 can (14-3/4 ounces) cream-style corn
- 1 package (8-1/2 ounces) corn bread/muffin mix
- 1 egg
- 2 tablespoons butter, melted
- 1/4 teaspoon garlic powder
- 1/4 teaspoon paprika

In a large bowl, combine all ingredients. Pour into a greased 11-in. x 7-in. baking dish. Bake, uncovered, at 400° for 25-30 minutes or until the top and edges are golden brown. **YIELD: 4-6 servings.**

BRENDA NICKERSON, CLYMER, NEW YORK

I rely on this refreshing chicken salad often for lunch or a healthy supper. It can be made ahead of time and popped in the refrigerator, which is perfect for my busy schedule.

almond chicken salad

PREP: 10 MINUTES + CHILLING

- 4 cups cubed cooked chicken
- 1 cup chopped celery
- 1 cup green grapes, halved
- 1/2 cup fat-free mayonnaise
- 1/2 cup fat-free plain yogurt
- 1/4 teaspoon pepper
- 1/4 cup chopped almonds, toasted

In a large bowl, combine chicken, celery, grapes, mayonnaise, yogurt and pepper; mix well. Cover and refrigerate for several hours. Stir in almonds just before serving. **YIELD: 8 servings.**

READERS' RAVES

> "This is by far one of the very best chicken salads I have ever tasted! I love it! Thanks.
> —5hungrykids
> from TasteofHome.com

DONNA-MARIE RYAN, TOPSFIELD, MASSACHUSETTS

Whip up a quick batch of these savory, biscuit-like squares to complement dinner or whenever you need a bite of comfort.

smoky onion biscuit squares

PREP: 20 MINUTES / **BAKE:** 20 MINUTES

- 1 small onion, chopped
- 2 tablespoons butter
- 1/4 teaspoon sugar
- 1 garlic clove, minced
- 1-1/2 cups biscuit/baking mix
- 1/2 cup milk
- 1 egg
- 1/4 pound smoked mozzarella cheese, shredded, *divided*
- 1 teaspoon salt-free Southwest chipotle seasoning blend

In a small skillet, cook onion in butter over medium heat until tender. Add sugar; cook 10-15 minutes longer or until golden brown. Add garlic; cook for 1 minute. Cool slightly.

In a small bowl, combine the biscuit mix, milk and egg. Fold in 1/2 cup cheese, seasoning blend and onion mixture. Transfer to an 8-in. square baking dish coated with cooking spray. Sprinkle with remaining cheese.

Bake at 400° for 18-22 minutes or until a toothpick inserted near the center comes out clean. Cut into squares; serve warm. **YIELD: 16 servings.**

CHRISTINE BURGER, GRAFTON, WISCONSIN
My family members have always been big on freshly baked bread. When I created this simple loaf, they asked for it time and again. If there is any left over, I like to enjoy a slice or two in the morning toasted and topped with jam.

basil garlic bread

PREP: 15 MINUTES / **BAKE:** 3-4 HOURS

2/3	cup warm milk (70° to 80°)
1/4	cup warm water (70° to 80°)
1/4	cup warm sour cream (70° to 80°)
1-1/2	teaspoons sugar
1	tablespoon butter, softened
1	tablespoon grated Parmesan cheese
1	teaspoon salt
1/2	teaspoon minced garlic
1/2	teaspoon dried basil
1/2	teaspoon garlic powder
3	cups bread flour
2-1/4	teaspoons active dry yeast

In bread machine pan, place all ingredients in order suggested by manufacturer. Select basic bread setting. Choose crust color and loaf size if available.

Bake according to bread machine directions (check dough after 5 minutes of mixing; add 1 to 2 tablespoons of water or flour if needed). **YIELD: 1 loaf (16 slices).**

EDITOR'S NOTE: We recommend you do not use a bread machine's time-delay feature for this recipe.

LISA RADELET, BOULDER, COLORADO
It's impossible to resist this cheesy casserole with its golden crumb topping that is sprinkled over colorful vegetables. My mom has relied on this favorite to round out many family meals since it's versatile enough to go with any entree. For more variety, try changing up the veggies.

colorful veggie bake

PREP: 25 MINUTES / **BAKE:** 20 MINUTES

2	packages (16 ounces each) frozen California-blend vegetables
8	ounces process cheese (Velveeta), cubed
6	tablespoons butter, *divided*
1/2	cup crushed butter-flavored crackers (about 13 crackers)

Prepare vegetables according to the package directions; drain. Place half in an ungreased 11-in. x 7-in. baking dish. In a small saucepan, combine the cheese and 4 tablespoons butter; cook and stir over low heat until melted. Pour half over the vegetables. Repeat layers.

Melt the remaining butter; toss with cracker crumbs. Sprinkle over the top. Bake, uncovered, at 325° for 20-25 minutes or until golden brown. **YIELD: 8-10 servings.**

TERESA MORANCIE, BREWER, MAINE

I added to a family recipe to create this bright and pretty wreath. Served with herb butter, it makes a special accompaniment to holiday meals.

sun-dried tomato 'n' basil wreath

PREP: 50 MINUTES + RISING / **BAKE:** 20 MINUTES

- 1/2 cup boiling water
- 1/4 cup sun-dried tomatoes (not packed in oil)
- 1/2 cup fat-free milk
- 1/4 cup grated Parmesan cheese
- 3 tablespoons butter
- 2 tablespoons sugar
- 4-1/2 teaspoons minced fresh basil
- 1/2 teaspoon salt
- 1 package (1/4 ounce) active dry yeast
- 2 tablespoons warm water (110° to 115°)
- 1 egg, beaten
- 2-1/4 to 2-1/2 cups all-purpose flour

HERB BUTTER:

- 1 tablespoon butter
- 2-1/4 teaspoons minced fresh basil
- 1-1/2 teaspoons grated Parmesan cheese
- 1-1/2 teaspoons olive oil

Pour boiling water over tomatoes; let stand 15 minutes. In a saucepan, combine the next six ingredients. Drain and chop tomatoes; add to pan. Cook and stir mixture over low heat until sugar is dissolved. Remove from heat; cool slightly.

In a large bowl, dissolve yeast in warm water. Add the tomato mixture, egg and 2 cups flour; beat until smooth. Stir in enough remaining flour to form a soft dough. Knead on a floured surface until smooth, about 6-8 minutes. Place in a bowl coated with cooking spray; turn once to coat top. Cover and let rise until doubled, about 1 hour.

In a small saucepan, melt butter; add the basil, Parmesan and oil. Keep warm. Punch dough down; divide into three portions. Shape each into an 18-in. rope.

Brush with half of herb butter. Place ropes on a baking sheet coated with cooking spray; braid and shape into a wreath. Pinch ends to seal. Cover and let rise until doubled, about 40 minutes. Brush with remaining herb butter. Bake at 350° for 20-25 minutes or until golden brown. Remove to a wire rack. **YIELD: 1 loaf (12 slices).**

ELISA LOCHRIDGE, TIGARD, OREGON

When I made a friend's scone recipe, I didn't have enough milk, so I substituted hazelnut-flavored nondairy creamer and added chocolate chips. The result was amazing!

hazelnut chip scones

PREP: 20 MINUTES / **BAKE:** 15 MINUTES

- 4 cups all-purpose flour
- 3 tablespoons sugar
- 4 teaspoons baking powder
- 1/2 teaspoon salt
- 1/2 teaspoon cream of tartar
- 3/4 cup cold butter
- 1 egg, *separated*
- 1-1/2 cups refrigerated hazelnut nondairy creamer *or* half-and-half cream
- 1-1/2 cups semisweet chocolate chips

Additional sugar

SPICED BUTTER:

- 1/2 cup butter, softened
- 3 tablespoons brown sugar
- 1/4 teaspoon ground cinnamon
- 1/4 teaspoon ground allspice
- 1/8 teaspoon ground nutmeg

In a bowl, combine the first five ingredients; cut in butter until crumbly. In a bowl, whisk the egg yolk and creamer; add to dry ingredients just until moistened. Stir in the chocolate chips.

Turn onto a floured surface; knead 10 times. Divide dough in half. Pat each portion into a 7-in. circle; cut into eight wedges. Separate wedges and place on greased baking sheets.

Beat egg white; brush over dough. Sprinkle with additional sugar. Bake at 425° for 15-18 minutes or until golden brown. Meanwhile, in a small bowl, combine spiced butter ingredients; beat until smooth. Serve with warm scones. **YIELD: 16 scones.**

main dishes

Whether you are scrambling to put a home-cooked meal on the table or planning an elegant dinner with friends, these tried-and-true mainstays are sure to satisfy. Home-style pot roasts...cheesy lasagnas...juicy baked chicken...you will find plenty of answers to the question, "What's for dinner?" in this chapter.

SMOTHERED CHICKEN BREASTS / PAGE 122

GINA HARRIS, SENECA, SOUTH CAROLINA

If you like meatball subs, you'll love this tangy casserole—it has all the rich flavor of the popular sandwiches with none of the mess. Italian bread is spread with a cream cheese mixture, then topped with meatballs, spaghetti sauce and cheese. Served with a green salad, it's a hearty meal the whole family enjoys.

meatball sub casserole

PREP: 15 MINUTES / **BAKE:** 45 MINUTES

1/3 cup chopped green onions	1/2 cup mayonnaise
1/4 cup seasoned bread crumbs	1 teaspoon Italian seasoning
3 tablespoons grated Parmesan cheese	1/4 teaspoon pepper
1 pound ground beef	2 cups (8 ounces) shredded part-skim mozzarella cheese, *divided*
1 loaf (1 pound) Italian bread, cut into 1-inch slices	1 jar (28 ounces) spaghetti sauce
1 package (8 ounces) cream cheese, softened	1 cup water
	2 garlic cloves, minced

In a bowl, combine the onions, crumbs and Parmesan cheese. Add beef and mix well. Shape into 1-in. balls; place on a greased rack in a shallow baking pan. Bake at 400° for 15-20 minutes or until no longer pink.

Meanwhile, arrange bread in a single layer in an ungreased 13-in. x 9-in. baking dish (all of the bread might not be used). Combine the cream cheese, mayonnaise, Italian seasoning and pepper; spread over the bread. Sprinkle with 1/2 cup mozzarella.

Combine the sauce, water and garlic; add meatballs. Pour over cheese mixture; sprinkle with remaining mozzarella. Bake, uncovered, at 350° for 30 minutes or until heated through. **YIELD: 6-8 servings.**

EDITOR'S NOTE: Reduced-fat or fat-free mayonnaise is not recommended for this recipe.

LESLIE ADAMS, SPRINGFIELD, MISSOURI

No one would guess that these moist chicken breasts and tender potatoes are seasoned with herb- and garlic-flavored soup mix. The meal-in-one is simple to assemble, and it all bakes in one dish so there is very little cleanup.

savory chicken dinner

PREP: 10 MINUTES / **BAKE:** 45 MINUTES

2	envelopes savory herb with garlic soup mix
6	tablespoons water
4	boneless skinless chicken breast halves (6 to 8 ounces *each*)
2	large red potatoes, cubed
1	large onion, halved and cut into small wedges

In a small bowl, combine the soup mix and water; pour half into a large resealable plastic bag. Add chicken. Seal bag and toss to coat. Pour the remaining soup mix in another large resealable plastic bag. Add potatoes and onion. Seal bag and toss to coat.

Drain and discard marinade from chicken. Transfer chicken to a greased 13-in. x 9-in. baking dish. Pour potato mixture with marinade over chicken.

Bake, uncovered, at 350° for 40-45 minutes or until vegetables are tender and a meat thermometer reads 170°, stirring vegetables occasionally. **YIELD: 4 servings.**

LANA MASKUS, WRIGHT, KANSAS

I found this in a local newspaper when I was a newlywed. My husband raved about it, and I have served it at least once a month ever since. My daughter took the recipe with her when she went off to college and used it frequently, too. During warmer weather, prepare them on the grill!

bacon-wrapped beef patties

PREP/TOTAL TIME: 25 MINUTES

6	bacon strips
2	eggs, lightly beaten
3/4	cup crushed saltines
2	tablespoons chopped onion
1-1/2	teaspoons salt
1/8	teaspoon pepper
1	pound ground beef
1/2	cup ketchup
2	tablespoons brown sugar
1/4	teaspoon ground mustard

Place bacon on a microwave-safe plate lined with microwave-safe paper towels. Cover with another paper towel; microwave on high for 2-3 minutes or until cooked but not crisp.

Meanwhile, in a large bowl, combine the eggs, saltines, onion, salt and pepper. Crumble beef over mixture and mix well. Shape into six patties. Wrap bacon strips around patties; secure with toothpicks. Broil 3-4 in. from the heat for 6 minutes.

Meanwhile, in a small bowl, combine the ketchup, brown sugar and mustard. Turn patties; top with ketchup mixture. Broil 6-7 minutes longer or until meat is no longer pink and a meat thermometer reads 160°. Discard toothpicks. **YIELD: 6 servings.**

LAURIE JENSEN, CADILLAC, MICHIGAN

With its golden-brown crust and scrumptious, creamy filling, these comforting potpies will warm you down to your toes. Because it makes two, you can eat one now and freeze the other for later. They bake and cut beautifully.

turkey potpies

PREP: 40 MINUTES / **BAKE:** 40 MINUTES + STANDING

2	medium potatoes, peeled and cut into 1-inch pieces
3	medium carrots, cut into 1-inch slices
1	medium onion, chopped
1	celery rib, diced
2	tablespoons butter
1	tablespoon olive oil
6	tablespoons all-purpose flour
3	cups chicken broth
4	cups cubed cooked turkey
2/3	cup frozen peas
1/2	cup plus 1 tablespoon heavy whipping cream, *divided*
1	tablespoon minced fresh parsley
1	teaspoon garlic salt
1/4	teaspoon pepper
1	package (15 ounces) refrigerated pie pastry
1	egg

In a Dutch oven, saute the potatoes, carrots, onion and celery in butter and oil until tender. Stir in flour until blended; gradually add broth. Bring to a boil; cook and stir for 2 minutes or until thickened. Stir in the turkey, peas, 1/2 cup cream, parsley, garlic salt and pepper.

Spoon into two ungreased 9-in. pie plates. Roll out pastry to fit top of each pie; place over filling. Trim, seal and flute edges. Cut out a decorative center or cut slits in pastry. In a small bowl, whisk egg and remaining cream; brush over pastry.

Cover and freeze one potpie for up to 3 months. Bake remaining potpie at 375° for 40-45 minutes or until golden brown. Let stand for 10 minutes before cutting. **YIELD: 2 pies (6 servings each).**

TO USE FROZEN POTPIE: Remove from the freezer 30 minutes before baking. Cover edges of crust loosely with foil; place on a baking sheet. Bake at 425° for 30 minutes. Reduce heat to 350°; remove foil. Bake 55-60 minutes longer or until golden brown.

ARLENE KAY BUTLER, OGDEN, UTAH

I use my slow cooker to prepare this tender pot roast. Convenient packages of dressing and gravy create the delicious sauce.

flavorful pot roast

PREP: 10 MINUTES / **COOK:** 7 HOURS

2	boneless beef chuck roasts (2-1/2 pounds *each*)
1	envelope ranch salad dressing mix
1	envelope Italian salad dressing mix
1	envelope brown gravy mix
1/2	cup water

Place the chuck roasts in a 5-qt. slow cooker. In a small bowl, combine the salad dressing and gravy mixes; stir in water. Pour over meat. Cover and cook on low for 7-8 hours or until tender. If desired, thicken cooking juices for gravy. **YIELD: 12-15 servings.**

EDITOR'S NOTE: For a filling meal-in-one, serve pot roast over mashed potatoes.

DONNA PATTERSON, DAVENPORT, IOWA

This traditional lasagna is a real crowd-pleaser. With ground beef, Italian sausage, a from-scratch tomato sauce and a rich cheese sauce, it's hearty and delicious. I get lots of compliments when I put together and share this satisfying pasta bake.

donna lasagna

PREP: 40 MINUTES / **BAKE:** 1 HOUR + STANDING

1	pound lean ground beef (90% lean)
8	ounces mild *or* hot Italian sausage
1	can (15 ounces) tomato puree
2	cans (6 ounces *each*) tomato paste
3	tablespoons dried parsley flakes, *divided*
2	tablespoons sugar
1	tablespoon dried basil
1-1/2	teaspoons salt, *divided*
1	garlic clove, minced
2	eggs, lightly beaten
3	cups (24 ounces) cream-style cottage cheese
1/2	cup grated Parmesan cheese
1/2	teaspoon pepper
9	lasagna noodles, cooked and drained
4	cups (16 ounces) shredded part-skim mozzarella cheese

In a Dutch oven, cook the beef and sausage over medium heat until no longer pink; drain. Add the tomato puree, tomato paste, 1 tablespoon parsley, sugar, basil, 1 teaspoon salt and garlic. Bring to a boil. Reduce heat; simmer, uncovered, for 30 minutes.

In a large bowl, combine the eggs, cottage cheese, Parmesan cheese, pepper, and remaining parsley and salt.

Spread 1/2 cup meat mixture in a greased 13-in. x 9-in. baking dish. Layer with three noodles, a third of the cheese mixture, 1-1/3 cups mozzarella cheese and a third of remaining meat sauce. Repeat layers twice.

Bake at 350° for 1 hour or until a thermometer reads 160°. Let stand for 15 minutes before cutting. **YIELD: 12 servings.**

DEBRA MARTIN, BELLEVILLE, MICHIGAN

I pop these protein-packed fillets in the oven before whipping up a sweet basting sauce. Made in moments, the tangy entree is perfect for busy nights and lazy weekends alike.

brown sugar-glazed salmon

PREP/TOTAL TIME: 25 MINUTES

1	salmon fillet (1 pound)
1/4	teaspoon salt
1/4	teaspoon pepper
3	tablespoons brown sugar
1	tablespoon reduced-sodium soy sauce
4	teaspoons Dijon mustard
1	teaspoon rice vinegar

Cut salmon widthwise into four pieces. Place in a foil-lined 15-in. x 10-in. baking pan; sprinkle with salt and pepper. Bake, uncovered, at 425° for 10 minutes.

Meanwhile, in a small saucepan, combine the brown sugar, soy sauce, mustard and vinegar. Bring to a boil. Brush evenly over salmon. Broil 6 in. from the heat for 1-2 minutes or until fish flakes easily with a fork. **YIELD: 4 servings.**

KITCHEN TIP

If you have any leftover salmon, turn it into tasty salmon cakes the next day. When making the cakes, applesauce is a pleasant substitution for the egg. The cakes must be turned carefully, but the taste is fantastic and the cakes stay so moist in the center. Plus, because the salmon was marinated for the original recipe, the cakes have more flavor than if they had been prepared with canned salmon.

—Maggie G., Atlantic Beach, Florida

MELANIE KENNEDY, BATTLE GROUND, WASHINGTON
Mushrooms, bacon strips and Monterey Jack cheese top these tender marinated chicken breasts that provide a flavorful dining experience with very little fuss.

bacon-cheese topped chicken

PREP: 40 MINUTES + MARINATING / **BAKE:** 20 MINUTES

1/2	cup Dijon mustard
1/2	cup honey
4-1/2	teaspoons canola oil, *divided*
1/2	teaspoon lemon juice
4	boneless skinless chicken breast halves
1/4	teaspoon salt
1/8	teaspoon pepper

Dash paprika

2	cups sliced fresh mushrooms
2	tablespoons butter
1	cup (4 ounces) shredded Monterey Jack cheese
1	cup (4 ounces) shredded cheddar cheese
8	bacon strips, partially cooked
2	teaspoons minced fresh parsley

In a small bowl, combine the mustard, honey, 1-1/2 teaspoons oil and lemon juice. Pour 1/2 cup into a large resealable plastic bag; add the chicken. Seal the bag and turn to coat; refrigerate for 2 hours. Cover and refrigerate the remaining marinade.

Drain and discard marinade from chicken. In a large skillet over medium heat, brown chicken in remaining oil on all sides. Sprinkle with salt, pepper and paprika. Transfer to a greased 11-in. x 7-in. baking dish.

In the same skillet, saute the mushrooms in butter until tender. Spoon the reserved marinade over chicken. Top with Monterey Jack and cheddar cheeses and mushrooms. Place bacon strips in a crisscross pattern over chicken.

Bake, uncovered, at 375° for 20-25 minutes or until a meat thermometer reads 170°. Sprinkle with parsley. **YIELD: 4 servings.**

IOLA EGLE, BELLA VISTA, ARKANSAS
The first time I served this meaty Southwestern dish, it was gone before I knew it! Everyone loved the barbecued ground beef, veggie and cheese combination.

barbecue beef taco plate

PREP: 20 MINUTES / **COOK:** 20 MINUTES

4	pounds ground beef
2	envelopes taco seasoning
1	cup water
4	packages (8 ounces *each*) cream cheese, softened
1	cup milk
2	envelopes ranch salad dressing mix
4	cans (4 ounces *each*) chopped green chilies, drained
1	cup chopped green onions
3	to 4 cups shredded romaine
2	cups (8 ounces) shredded cheddar cheese
4	medium tomatoes, seeded and chopped
2	to 3 cups honey barbecue sauce
2	to 3 packages (13-1/2 ounces *each*) tortilla chips

In a Dutch oven, cook beef over medium heat until no longer pink; drain. Stir in taco seasoning and water. Bring to a boil. Reduce heat; simmer, uncovered, for 15 minutes.

In a large bowl, beat the cream cheese, milk and dressing mixes until blended. Spread over two 14-in. plates. Layer with the beef mixture, chilies, onions, romaine, cheese and tomatoes. Drizzle with barbecue sauce.

Arrange some tortilla chips around the edge; serve with remaining chips. **YIELD: 40-50 servings.**

CAROLIN CATTOI-DEMKIW, LETHBRIDGE, ALBERTA
My husband and I enjoy serving this tasty chicken to company as well as family. It looks like we fussed, but it's really fast and easy to fix. I found the recipe years ago and have made this dish many times. You can bet on it to prompt recipe requests.

bruschetta chicken

PREP: 10 MINUTES / **BAKE:** 30 MINUTES

1/2	cup all-purpose flour
1/2	cup egg substitute
4	boneless skinless chicken breast halves (4 ounces *each*)
1/4	cup grated Parmesan cheese
1/4	cup dry bread crumbs
1	tablespoon butter, melted
2	large tomatoes, seeded and chopped
3	tablespoons minced fresh basil
2	garlic cloves, minced
1	tablespoon olive oil
1/2	teaspoon salt
1/4	teaspoon pepper

Place flour and egg substitute in separate shallow bowls. Dip chicken in flour, then in eggs; place in a greased 13-in. x 9-in. baking dish. Combine the Parmesan cheese, bread crumbs and butter; sprinkle over chicken.

Loosely cover baking dish with foil. Bake at 375° for 20 minutes. Uncover; bake 5-10 minutes longer or until a meat thermometer reads 170°.

Meanwhile, in a small bowl, combine the remaining ingredients. Spoon over the chicken. Return to the oven for 3-5 minutes or until tomato mixture is heated through. **YIELD: 4 servings.**

LAUNA SHOEMAKER, MIDLAND CITY, ALABAMA
A coating containing cornflakes, Parmesan cheese and ranch dressing mix adds delectable flavor to the tender chicken that's baked to a pretty golden color. It's a mainstay entree I can always count on.

breaded ranch chicken

PREP: 10 MINUTES / **BAKE:** 45 MINUTES

3/4	cup crushed cornflakes
3/4	cup grated Parmesan cheese
1	envelope ranch salad dressing mix
8	boneless skinless chicken breast halves (4 ounces *each*)
1/2	cup butter, melted

In a shallow bowl, combine the cornflakes, Parmesan cheese and salad dressing mix. Dip chicken in butter, then roll in cornflake mixture to coat.

Place in a greased 13-in. x 9-in. baking dish. Bake, uncovered, at 350° for 45 minutes or until chicken juices run clear. **YIELD: 8 servings.**

SCOTT SCHMIDTKE, CHICAGO, ILLINOIS
Dijon, Parmesan and a hint of horseradish give delicate tilapia fillets lots of flavor. The preparation is so simple, it takes just a few minutes to get four servings ready for the oven.

dijon-crusted fish

PREP/TOTAL TIME: 25 MINUTES

3	tablespoons reduced-fat mayonnaise
2	tablespoons grated Parmesan cheese, *divided*
1	tablespoon lemon juice
2	teaspoons Dijon mustard
1	teaspoon horseradish
4	tilapia fillets (5 ounces *each*)
1/4	cup dry bread crumbs
2	teaspoons butter, melted

In a small bowl, combine the mayonnaise, 1 tablespoon cheese, lemon juice, mustard and horseradish. Place fillets on a baking sheet coated with cooking spray. Spread mayonnaise mixture evenly over fillets.

In a small bowl, combine the bread crumbs, butter and remaining cheese; sprinkle over fillets. Bake at 425° for 13-18 minutes or until fish flakes easily with a fork. **YIELD: 4 servings.**

RUTH KOBERNA, BRECKSVILLE, OHIO
Every time that I make this cheesy dish, I get requests for the recipe. It puts a different spin on spaghetti and is great for potlucks and other large gatherings. The leftovers, if there are any, also freeze well for a quick meal later on in the week.

baked spaghetti

PREP: 20 MINUTES / **BAKE:** 30 MINUTES

1	cup chopped onion
1	cup chopped green pepper
1	tablespoon butter
1	can (28 ounces) diced tomatoes, undrained
1	can (4 ounces) mushroom stems and pieces, drained
1	can (2-1/4 ounces) sliced ripe olives, drained
2	teaspoons dried oregano
1	pound ground beef, browned and drained, optional
12	ounces spaghetti, cooked and drained
2	cups (8 ounces) shredded cheddar cheese
1	can (10-3/4 ounces) condensed cream of mushroom soup, undiluted
1/4	cup water
1/4	cup grated Parmesan cheese

In a large skillet, saute onion and green pepper in butter until tender. Add the tomatoes, mushrooms, olives and oregano. Add ground beef if desired. Simmer, uncovered, for 10 minutes.

Place half of the spaghetti in a greased 13-in. x 9-in. baking dish. Top with half of the vegetable mixture. Sprinkle with 1 cup of cheddar cheese. Repeat layers. Mix the soup and water until smooth; pour over casserole. Sprinkle with Parmesan cheese. Bake, uncovered, at 350° for 30-35 minutes or until heated through. **YIELD: 12 servings.**

BRENDA CARPENTER, WARRENSBURG, MISSOURI

After trying this delicious chicken dish in a restaurant, I decided to re-create it at home. Topped with bacon, caramelized onions and zippy shredded cheese, it comes together in no time with ingredients I usually have on hand. Plus, it cooks in one skillet, so it's a cinch to clean up!

smothered chicken breasts

PREP/TOTAL TIME: 30 MINUTES

4	boneless skinless chicken breast halves (6 ounces *each*)
1/4	teaspoon salt
1/4	teaspoon lemon-pepper seasoning
1	tablespoon canola oil
8	bacon strips
1	medium onion, sliced
1/4	cup packed brown sugar
1/2	cup shredded Colby-Monterey Jack cheese

Sprinkle chicken with salt and lemon-pepper. In a large skillet, cook chicken in oil for 6-7 minutes on each side or until a meat thermometer reads 170°; remove and keep warm.

In the same skillet, cook bacon over medium heat until crisp. Using a slotted spoon, remove to paper towels; drain, reserving 2 tablespoons drippings.

In the drippings, saute the onion and brown sugar until onion is tender and golden brown. Place two bacon strips on each chicken breast half; top with caramelized onions and cheese. **YIELD: 4 servings.**

SUZANNE CODNER, STARBUCK, MINNESOTA

When my husband and I were first married, he refused to eat meat loaf because he said it was bland and dry. Then I prepared this version, and it became his favorite meal.

melt-in-your-mouth meat loaf

PREP: 15 MINUTES / **COOK:** 5-1/4 HOURS + STANDING

2	eggs
3/4	cup milk
2/3	cup seasoned bread crumbs
2	teaspoons dried minced onion
1	teaspoon salt
1/2	teaspoon rubbed sage
1-1/2	pounds ground beef
1/4	cup ketchup
2	tablespoons brown sugar
1	teaspoon ground mustard
1/2	teaspoon Worcestershire sauce

In a large bowl, combine the first six ingredients. Crumble beef over mixture and mix well (mixture will be moist.) Shape into a round loaf; place in a 5-qt. slow cooker. Cover and cook on low for 5-6 hours or until a meat thermometer reads 160°.

In a small bowl, whisk the ketchup, brown sugar, mustard and Worcestershire sauce. Spoon sauce over meat loaf. Cook 15 minutes longer or until heated through. Let stand for 10-15 minutes before cutting. **YIELD: 6 servings.**

MAURA MCGEE, TALLAHASSEE, FLORIDA

Tender chicken is draped in a creamy sauce that gets fast flavor from a salad dressing mix. Served over rice or pasta, it's rich, delicious and elegant enough for special occasions.

creamy italian chicken

PREP: 5 MINUTES / **COOK:** 4 HOURS

4	boneless skinless chicken breast halves (4 ounces *each*)
1	envelope Italian salad dressing mix
1/4	cup water
1	package (8 ounces) cream cheese, softened
1	can (10-3/4 ounces) condensed cream of chicken soup, undiluted
1	can (4 ounces) mushroom stems and pieces, drained

Hot cooked pasta *or* rice

Fresh oregano leaves, optional

Place the chicken in a 3-qt. slow cooker. Combine salad dressing mix and water; pour over chicken. Cover and cook on low for 3 hours.

In a small bowl, beat the cream cheese and soup until blended. Stir in mushrooms. Pour over chicken. Cook 1 hour longer or until a meat thermometer reaches 170°. Serve with pasta or rice. Garnish with oregano if desired. **YIELD: 4 servings.**

KRISTA FRANK, RHODODENDRON, OREGON

There's a little story behind the name of my favorite salmon recipe: When my husband, Kevin, and I couldn't find a spicy teriyaki-style marinade to our liking, we created one in and named it Double K—for Krista and Kevin. Every time we serve this flavorful fish, we are asked how we make it.

double k grilled salmon

PREP: 10 MINUTES + MARINATING / **GRILL:** 20 MINUTES

1/4	cup packed brown sugar
1/4	cup soy sauce
3	tablespoons unsweetened pineapple juice
3	tablespoons red wine vinegar
3	garlic cloves, minced
1	tablespoon lemon juice
1	teaspoon ground ginger
1/2	teaspoon pepper
1/2	teaspoon hot pepper sauce
1	salmon fillet (2 pounds)

In a small bowl, combine the first nine ingredients. Pour 3/4 cup into a large resealable plastic bag; add salmon. Seal bag and turn to coat; refrigerate for 1 hour, turning occasionally. Set aside remaining marinade for basting.

Coat grill rack with cooking spray before starting the grill. Drain and discard marinade. Place salmon skin side down on rack. Grill, covered, over medium heat for 5 minutes. Brush with reserved marinade. Grill 15-20 minutes longer or until fish flakes easily with a fork. **YIELD: 8 servings.**

SUE MACKEY, GALESBURG, ILLINOIS

This savory casserole is one of my husband's favorites. He loves the fluffy dumplings with plenty of gravy poured over them. The basil adds just the right touch of flavor and makes the whole house smell so good while this dish cooks.

chicken and dumpling casserole

PREP: 30 MINUTES / **BAKE:** 40 MINUTES

1/2	cup chopped onion
1/2	cup chopped celery
2	garlic cloves, minced
1/4	cup butter, cubed
1/2	cup all-purpose flour
2	teaspoons sugar
1	teaspoon salt
1	teaspoon dried basil
1/2	teaspoon pepper
4	cups chicken broth
1	package (10 ounces) frozen green peas
4	cups cubed cooked chicken

DUMPLINGS:

2	cups biscuit/baking mix
2	teaspoons dried basil
2/3	cup milk

In a large saucepan, saute the onion, celery and garlic in butter until tender. Stir in the flour, sugar, salt, basil and pepper until blended. Gradually add broth; bring to a boil. Cook and stir for 1 minute; reduce heat. Add the peas and cook for 5 minutes, stirring constantly. Stir in chicken. Pour into a greased 13-in. x 9-in. baking dish.

For dumplings, in a small bowl, combine baking mix and basil. Stir in milk with a fork until moistened. Drop by tablespoonfuls into 12 mounds over chicken mixture.

Bake, uncovered, at 350° for 30 minutes. Cover and bake 10 minutes longer or until a toothpick inserted in a dumpling comes out clean. **YIELD: 6-8 servings.**

KAREN ANN BLAND, VICTORIA, KANSAS

Loaded with Mexican-style ingredients, this filling lasagna is sure to please the whole gang, whether you make it for your family or take it to a potluck. Every bite is mouthwatering!

fiesta lasagna

PREP: 25 MINUTES / **BAKE:** 70 MINUTES + STANDING

1	pound ground beef
1/4	cup chopped onion
1	can (16 ounces) refried beans
1	can (16 ounces) mild chili beans, undrained
1	can (14-1/2 ounces) Mexican stewed tomatoes, drained
1	cup salsa
1	can (4 ounces) chopped green chilies
1	envelope reduced-sodium taco seasoning
1	teaspoon dried oregano
1	teaspoon ground cumin
1/4	teaspoon garlic powder
1-1/4	cups shredded Monterey Jack cheese
1-1/4	cups shredded part-skim mozzarella cheese
3/4	cup 4% cottage cheese
1-1/4	cups sour cream, *divided*
9	lasagna noodles, cooked, rinsed and drained

In a Dutch oven, cook beef and onion over medium heat until meat is no longer pink; drain. Stir in the beans, tomatoes, salsa, chilies and seasonings.

In a large bowl, combine Monterey Jack and mozzarella cheeses; set aside 1 cup. Stir cottage cheese and 3/4 cup sour cream into remaining cheese mixture.

Spread 1 cup meat sauce into a greased 13-in. x 9-in. baking dish. Layer with three noodles, and a third of the cottage cheese mixture and meat sauce. Repeat layers twice (dish will be full).

Cover and bake at 350° for 1 hour. Uncover; spread with the remaining sour cream. Sprinkle with the reserved cheeses. Bake 10-12 minutes longer or until the cheese is melted. Let stand for 20 minutes before serving. **YIELD: 12 servings.**

KIMBERLY LAABS, HARTFORD, WISCONSIN

The combination of tender salmon, a fresh cucumber sauce and a crisp, flaky crust makes this impressive dish perfect for special occasions. My mom likes to decorate the pastry with a star or leaf design for the holidays.

puff pastry salmon bundles

PREP: 20 MINUTES / **BAKE:** 25 MINUTES

2	packages (17.3 ounces *each*) frozen puff pastry, thawed
8	salmon fillets (6 ounces *each*), skin removed
1	egg
1	tablespoon water
2	cups shredded cucumber
1	cup (8 ounces) sour cream
1	cup mayonnaise
1	teaspoon dill weed
1/2	teaspoon salt

On a lightly floured surface, roll each pastry sheet into a 12-in. x 10-in. rectangle. Cut each pastry sheet into two 10-in. x 6-in. rectangles. Place a salmon fillet in the center of each pastry rectangle.

Beat egg and water; lightly brush over pastry edges. Bring opposite corners of pastry over each fillet; pinch seams to seal tightly. Place seam side down in a greased 15-in. x 10-in. baking pan; brush with remaining egg mixture.

Bake at 400° for 25-30 minutes or until pastry is golden brown. In a small bowl, combine the cucumber, sour cream, mayonnaise, dill and salt. Serve with bundles. **YIELD: 8 servings.**

KIM WALLACE, DENNISON, OHIO

Cream of celery soup adds rich flavor to this family-favorite Stroganoff. Besides its delicious, home-style taste, I love the recipe's effortless preparation. Just put the ingredients in the slow cooker and forget about it. When you get home, dinner is ready.

creamy celery beef stroganoff

PREP: 20 MINUTES / **COOK:** 8 HOURS

2	pounds beef stew meat, cut into 1-inch cubes
1	can (10-3/4 ounces) condensed cream of celery soup, undiluted
1	can (10-3/4 ounces) condensed cream of mushroom soup, undiluted
1	medium onion, chopped
1	jar (6 ounces) sliced mushrooms, drained
1	envelope onion soup mix
1/2	teaspoon pepper
1	cup (8 ounces) sour cream

Hot cooked noodles

In a 3-qt. slow cooker, combine the first seven ingredients. Cover and cook on low for 8 hours or until beef is tender. Stir in the sour cream. Serve Stroganoff with noodles. **YIELD: 6 servings.**

AMY CORLEW-SHERLOCK, LAPEER, MICHIGAN

Precooked, frozen popcorn chicken simmered in a thick, home-made sweet-and-sour sauce is the secret to this fabulously fast entree. It's also a tasty way to dress up frozen chicken nuggets! This is one recipe you'll find yourself returning to again and again.

sweet-and-sour popcorn chicken

PREP/TOTAL TIME: 25 MINUTES

1	medium green pepper, cut into 1-inch pieces
1	small onion, thinly sliced
1	tablespoon canola oil
1	can (20 ounces) unsweetened pineapple chunks
3	tablespoons white vinegar
2	tablespoons soy sauce
2	tablespoons ketchup
1/3	cup packed brown sugar
2	tablespoons cornstarch
1	package (12 ounces) frozen popcorn chicken

In a large skillet or wok, stir-fry green pepper and onion in oil for 3-4 minutes or until crisp-tender. Drain pineapple, reserving the juice in a 2-cup measuring cup; set pineapple aside. Add enough water to the juice to measure 1-1/3 cups. Stir in vinegar, soy sauce and ketchup.

In a large bowl, combine the brown sugar and cornstarch. Stir in pineapple juice mixture until smooth. Gradually add to the skillet. Bring to a boil; cook and stir for 2 minutes or until thickened. Add the pineapple. Reduce heat; simmer, uncovered, for 4-5 minutes or until heated through.

Meanwhile, microwave chicken according to package directions. Stir into pineapple mixture. Serve immediately. **YIELD: 4 servings.**

LORAINE VAN BROECK, GENEVA, ILLINOIS

After driving my family crazy trying new recipes, I always return to this standby. These moist, comforting pork chops come out great every time. We love the luscious gravy draped over the tender chops and mashed potatoes.

chops with mushroom gravy

PREP: 25 MINUTES / **BAKE:** 50 MINUTES

1/2	cup all-purpose flour
1	to 2 teaspoons paprika
1-1/2	teaspoons salt
1/4	teaspoon pepper
6	to 8 boneless pork loin chops (1 inch thick *each*)
1/4	cup butter
1	medium onion, chopped
1/2	cup chopped green pepper
1	can (4 ounces) mushroom stems and pieces, drained
2	cups milk
2	tablespoons lemon juice

Hot mashed potatoes

In a large resealable plastic bag, combine first four ingredients, reserve 3 tablespoons. Add the pork chops, one at a time; toss to coat.

In a large skillet, saute the chops in butter until golden brown; transfer to a greased 13-in. x 9-in. baking dish. In the same skillet, saute the onion, green pepper and mushrooms until tender. Stir in reserved flour mixture; gradually add milk until blended. Bring to a boil; cook and stir for 2 minutes or until thickened. Remove from the heat; stir in lemon juice. Pour over chops.

Cover and bake at 350° for 50-60 minutes or until the meat is no longer pink. Serve with potatoes. **YIELD: 6-8 servings.**

LORI MECCA, GRANTS PASS, OREGON

When I was living in California, I tasted this rich and gooey pasta dish at a neighborhood Italian restaurant. I got the recipe and made a few changes to it in my own kitchen. I'm happy to share the mouthwatering results with you.

cheese-stuffed shells

PREP: 35 MINUTES / **BAKE:** 50 MINUTES

- 1 pound bulk Italian sausage
- 1 large onion, chopped
- 1 package (10 ounces) frozen chopped spinach, thawed and squeezed dry
- 1 package (8 ounces) cream cheese, cubed
- 1 egg, lightly beaten
- 2 cups (8 ounces) shredded part-skim mozzarella cheese, *divided*
- 2 cups (8 ounces) shredded cheddar cheese
- 1 cup 4% cottage cheese
- 1 cup grated Parmesan cheese
- 1/4 teaspoon salt
- 1/4 teaspoon pepper
- 1/8 teaspoon ground cinnamon, optional
- 24 jumbo pasta shells, cooked and drained
SAUCE:
- 1 can (29 ounces) tomato sauce
- 1 tablespoon dried minced onion
- 1-1/2 teaspoons dried basil
- 1-1/2 teaspoons dried parsley flakes
- 2 garlic cloves, minced
- 1 teaspoon sugar
- 1 teaspoon dried oregano
- 1/2 teaspoon salt
- 1/4 teaspoon pepper

In a large skillet, cook sausage and onion over medium heat until meat is no longer pink; drain. Transfer to a large bowl. Stir in the spinach, cream cheese and egg. Add 1 cup mozzarella, cheddar, cottage cheese, Parmesan, salt, pepper and cinnamon if desired; mix well.

Stuff pasta shells with sausage mixture. Arrange in two 11-in. x 7-in. baking dishes coated with cooking spray. Combine the sauce ingredients; spoon over shells.

Cover and bake at 350° for 45 minutes. Uncover; sprinkle with remaining mozzarella. Bake 5-10 minutes longer or until bubbly and cheese is melted. Let stand for 5 minutes before serving. **YIELD:** 12 servings.

YVONNE NAVE, LYONS, KANSAS

This recipe came from my home economics teacher in high school. I enjoy making the hearty meatballs because you can throw them in the oven and have plenty of time to do other things.

barbecued meatballs

PREP: 20 MINUTES / **BAKE:** 30 MINUTES

- 1 egg, lightly beaten
- 1 can (5 ounces) evaporated milk
- 1 cup quick-cooking oats
- 1/2 cup finely chopped onion
- 1 teaspoon salt
- 1 teaspoon chili powder
- 1/4 teaspoon garlic powder
- 1/4 teaspoon pepper
- 1-1/2 pounds ground beef
SAUCE:
- 1 cup ketchup
- 3/4 cup packed brown sugar
- 1/4 cup chopped onion
- 1/2 teaspoon Liquid Smoke, optional
- 1/4 teaspoon garlic powder

In a large bowl, combine the first eight ingredients. Crumble beef over mixture and mix well. Shape into 1-in. balls.

Place meatballs on a greased rack in a shallow baking pan. Bake, uncovered, at 350° for 18-20 minutes or until meat is no longer pink; drain.

Meanwhile, combine sauce ingredients in a saucepan. Bring to a boil. Reduce heat and simmer for 2 minutes, stirring frequently. Pour sauce over the meatballs. Bake 10-12 minutes longer. **YIELD:** about 4 dozen.

NELLA PARKER, HERSEY, MICHIGAN
An appetizing blend of herbs complements the mild flavor of these flaky fillets. Red pepper flakes give the entree its zip.

herb-crusted red snapper

PREP/TOTAL TIME: 25 MINUTES

1	tablespoon dry bread crumbs
1	teaspoon dried basil
1	teaspoon paprika
1/2	teaspoon salt
1/2	teaspoon fennel seeds
1/2	teaspoon dried thyme
1/2	teaspoon dried oregano
1/4	teaspoon pepper
1/4	teaspoon crushed red pepper flakes
2	red snapper fillets (5 ounces *each*), skin removed
2	teaspoons canola oil

In a food processor, combine the first nine ingredients; cover and process until fennel is finely ground. Transfer to a shallow bowl; dip fillets in herb mixture, coating both sides.

In a heavy skillet over medium-high heat, cook fillets in oil for 3-4 minutes on each side or until fish flakes easily with a fork. **YIELD: 2 servings.**

LORI THOMPSON, NEW LONDON, TEXAS
This simple dish has been very popular at family gatherings and potlucks because it combines great taste with easy preparation.

meaty manicotti

PREP: 20 MINUTES / **BAKE:** 45 MINUTES

14	uncooked manicotti shells
1	pound bulk Italian sausage
3/4	pound ground beef
2	garlic cloves, minced
2	cups (8 ounces) shredded part-skim mozzarella cheese
1	package (3 ounces) cream cheese, cubed
1/4	teaspoon salt
4	cups meatless spaghetti sauce, *divided*
1/4	cup grated Parmesan cheese

Cook the manicotti shells according to package directions. Meanwhile, in a large skillet, cook the sausage, beef and garlic over medium heat until meat is no longer pink; drain. Remove from the heat. Cool for 10 minutes.

Drain shells and rinse in cold water. Stir the mozzarella, cream cheese and salt into the meat mixture. Spread 2 cups spaghetti sauce in a greased 13-in. x 9-in. baking dish. Stuff each shell with about 1/4 cupful meat mixture; arrange over sauce. Pour remaining sauce over top. Sprinkle with Parmesan cheese.

Cover and bake stuffed shells at 350° for 40 minutes. Uncover; bake 5-10 minutes longer or until bubbly and heated through. **YIELD: 7 servings.**

ANGELA OELSCHLAEGER, TONGANOXIE, KANSAS
Usually chimichangas are deep-fried, so my popular baked version is healthy as well as delicious. You can omit the chilies for less heat—or add more for a spicier bite!

baked chimichangas

PREP/TOTAL TIME: 30 MINUTES

2-1/2	cups shredded cooked chicken breast
1	cup salsa
1	small onion, chopped
3/4	teaspoon ground cumin
1/2	teaspoon dried oregano
6	flour tortillas (10 inches), warmed
3/4	cup shredded reduced-fat cheddar cheese
1	cup reduced-sodium chicken broth
2	teaspoons chicken bouillon granules
1/8	teaspoon pepper
1/4	cup all-purpose flour
1	cup fat-free half-and-half
1	can (4 ounces) chopped green chilies

In a nonstick skillet, simmer the chicken, salsa, onion, ground cumin and dried oregano until heated through and most of the liquid has evaporated.

Place 1/2 cup chicken mixture down the center of each tortilla; top with 2 tablespoons cheese. Fold sides and ends over filling and roll up.

Place seam side down in a 13-in. x 9-in. baking dish coated with cooking spray. Bake, uncovered, at 425° for 15 minutes or until lightly browned.

Meanwhile, in a small saucepan, combine the broth, bouillon and pepper. Cook until the bouillon is dissolved. In a small bowl, combine flour and half-and-half until smooth; gradually stir into broth. Bring to a boil; cook and stir for 2 minutes or until thickened. Stir in chilies; cook until heated through. To serve, cut chimichangas in half; top with sauce. **YIELD: 6 servings.**

MARIAN MISIK, SHERWOOD PARK, ALBERTA
"More, please!" is what I hear when I serve these zippy, finger-licking ribs to family or guests. The first time my husband and I tried them, we pronounced them "the best ever." The recipe has its roots in the Calgary Stampede, an annual Western and agricultural fair and exhibition in our province.

calgary stampede ribs

PREP: 2-1/2 HOURS + MARINATING / **GRILL:** 15 MINUTES

4	pounds pork back ribs, cut into serving-size pieces
3	garlic cloves, minced
1	tablespoon sugar
1	tablespoon paprika
2	teaspoons *each* salt, pepper, chili powder and ground cumin

BARBECUE SAUCE:

1	small onion, finely chopped
2	tablespoons butter
1	cup ketchup
1/4	cup packed brown sugar
3	tablespoons lemon juice
3	tablespoons Worcestershire sauce
2	tablespoons cider vinegar
1-1/2	teaspoons ground mustard
1	teaspoon celery seed
1/8	teaspoon cayenne pepper

Rub ribs with garlic; place in a shallow roasting pan. Cover and bake at 325° for 2 hours. Cool slightly. Combine the seasonings and rub over ribs. Cover and refrigerate for 8 hours or overnight.

In a small saucepan, saute onion in butter until tender. Stir in the remaining ingredients. Bring to a boil. Reduce heat; cook and stir until thickened, about 10 minutes. Remove from the heat; set aside 3/4 cup. Brush ribs with some of the remaining sauce.

Grill, covered, over medium heat for 12 minutes, turning and basting with sauce. Serve the ribs with the reserved sauce. **YIELD: 4 servings.**

LORI PACKER, OMAHA, NEBRASKA
This special shrimp main dish looks like you fussed, but it's a snap to prepare. Lemon and herbs enhance the shrimp, and bread crumbs add a pleasing crunch. Served over pasta, this entree is attractive and scrumptious.

shrimp scampi

PREP/TOTAL TIME: 20 MINUTES

3	to 4 garlic cloves, minced
1/4	cup butter, cubed
1/4	cup olive oil
1	pound uncooked medium shrimp, peeled and deveined
1/4	cup lemon juice
1/2	teaspoon pepper
1/4	teaspoon dried oregano
1/2	cup grated Parmesan cheese
1/4	cup dry bread crumbs
1/4	cup minced fresh parsley

Hot cooked angel hair pasta

In a 10-in. ovenproof skillet, saute garlic in butter and oil until tender. Stir in the shrimp, lemon juice, pepper and oregano; cook and stir for 2-3 minutes or until shrimp turn pink. Sprinkle with the cheese, bread crumbs and parsley.

Broil 6 in. from the heat for 2-3 minutes or until topping is golden brown. Serve with pasta. **YIELD: 4 servings.**

KATHY BOWRON, COCOLALLA, IDAHO
I got this recipe from my aunt when I was a teen and have made these miniature loaves many times. My husband and three children count this satisfying meal among their favorites. The recipe is also great for company since it can easily be doubled or tripled.

li'l cheddar meat loaves

PREP: 15 MINUTES / **BAKE:** 25 MINUTES

1	egg
3/4	cup milk
1	cup (4 ounces) shredded cheddar cheese
1/2	cup quick-cooking oats
1/2	cup chopped onion
1/2	teaspoon salt
1	pound ground beef
2/3	cup ketchup
1/2	cup packed brown sugar
1-1/2	teaspoons prepared mustard

In a large bowl, whisk the egg and milk. Stir in the cheese, oats, onion and salt. Crumble beef over mixture and mix well. Shape into eight loaves; place in a greased 13-in. x 9-in. baking dish. In a small bowl, combine the ketchup, brown sugar and mustard; spoon over loaves.

Bake, uncovered, at 350° for 25-30 minutes or until no pink remains and a meat thermometer reads 160°. **YIELD: 8 servings.**

NANCY HOLLAND, MORGAN HILL, CALIFORNIA
Homemade yeast rolls are stuffed with ground beef, tomato sauce and cheese to make these tasty sandwiches. They're great leftovers, too. My son takes the savory pockets in his lunch the next day.

cheeseburger buns

PREP: 30 MINUTES + RISING / **BAKE:** 10 MINUTES

2	packages (1/4 ounce *each*) active dry yeast
1/2	cup warm water (110° to 115°)
3/4	cup warm milk (110° to 115°)
1/4	cup sugar
1/4	cup shortening
1	egg
1	teaspoon salt
3-1/2	to 4 cups all-purpose flour
1-1/2	pounds ground beef
1/4	cup chopped onion
1	can (8 ounces) tomato sauce
8	slices process American cheese, quartered

In a large bowl, dissolve yeast in warm water. Add the milk, sugar, shortening, egg, salt and 2 cups flour; beat until smooth. Stir in enough remaining flour to form a soft dough.

Turn onto a floured surface; knead until smooth and elastic, about 4-6 minutes. Place in a greased bowl, turning once to grease top. Cover and let rise in a warm place until doubled, about 30 minutes.

In a large skillet, cook beef and onion over medium heat until meat is no longer pink; drain. Stir in tomato sauce. Remove from the heat; set aside.

Punch the dough down; divide into 16 pieces. On a lightly floured surface, gently roll out and stretch each piece into a 5-in. circle. Top each circle with two pieces of cheese and about 3 tablespoons beef mixture. Bring dough over filling to center; pinch edges to seal.

Place seam side down on a greased baking sheet. Cover and let rise in a warm place until doubled, about 20 minutes. Bake at 400° for 8-12 minutes or until golden brown. Serve warm. Refrigerate leftovers. **YIELD: 16 sandwiches.**

ROCHELLE BROWNLEE, BIG TIMBER, MONTANA
As a cattle rancher, my husband's a big fan of beef. For him to comment on a poultry dish is rare. But he always tells me, "I love this casserole!" I first tasted it at a potluck, but now I fix it once or twice a month and take it to most every get-together.

four-cheese chicken fettuccine

PREP: 20 MINUTES / **BAKE:** 30 MINUTES

8	ounces uncooked fettuccine
1	can (10-3/4 ounces) condensed cream of mushroom soup, undiluted
1	package (8 ounces) cream cheese, cubed
1	jar (4-1/2 ounces) sliced mushrooms, drained
1	cup heavy whipping cream
1/2	cup butter
1/4	teaspoon garlic powder
3/4	cup grated Parmesan cheese
1/2	cup shredded part-skim mozzarella cheese
1/2	cup shredded Swiss cheese
2-1/2	cups cubed cooked chicken

TOPPING:

1/3	cup seasoned bread crumbs
2	tablespoons butter, melted
1	to 2 tablespoons grated Parmesan cheese

Cook fettuccine according to package directions. Meanwhile, in a large kettle, combine the soup, cream cheese, mushrooms, cream, butter and garlic powder. Stir in the cheeses; cook and stir until melted. Add the chicken; heat through. Drain fettuccine; add fettuccine to the cheese sauce.

Transfer to a shallow greased 2-1/2-qt. baking dish. Combine topping ingredients; sprinkle over chicken mixture. Cover and bake at 350° for 25 minutes. Uncover; bake 5-10 minutes longer or until golden brown. **YIELD: 6-8 servings.**

DANETTE FORBES, OVERLAND PARK, KANSAS
I first made this recipe when I was a nanny. It comes together quickly at dinnertime and is a true lifesaver when the kids are hungry and can't wait very long to eat.

chicken and bows

PREP/TOTAL TIME: 25 MINUTES

1	package (16 ounces) bow tie pasta
2	pounds boneless skinless chicken breasts, cut into strips
1	cup chopped sweet red pepper
1/4	cup butter, cubed
2	cans (10-3/4 ounces *each*) condensed cream of chicken soup, undiluted
2	cups frozen peas
1-1/2	cups milk
1	teaspoon garlic powder
1/4	to 1/2 teaspoon salt
1/4	teaspoon pepper
2/3	cup grated Parmesan cheese

Cook pasta according to package directions. Meanwhile, in a Dutch oven, cook chicken and red pepper in butter over medium heat for 5-6 minutes or until chicken is no longer pink.

Stir in the soup, peas, milk, garlic powder, salt and pepper. Bring to a boil. Reduce heat; simmer, uncovered, for 1-2 minutes or until heated through. Stir in Parmesan cheese. Drain pasta; add to chicken mixture and toss to coat.

Serve half of the mixture immediately. Cool remaining mixture; transfer to a freezer container. Cover and freeze for up to 3 months. **YIELD: 2 casseroles (6 servings each).**

TO USE FROZEN CASSEROLE: Thaw in the refrigerator overnight. Transfer to an ungreased shallow 3-qt. microwave-safe dish. Cover and microwave on high for 8-10 minutes or until heated through, stirring once.

EDITOR'S NOTE: This recipe was tested in a 1,100-watt microwave.

LISA KIVIRIST, BROWNTOWN, WISCONSIN
Mom proudly serves this tender, flaky fish to family and guests. A savory marinade that includes fresh dill gives the salmon mouthwatering flavor. Since it can be grilled or broiled, we are able to enjoy it year-round.

lemon grilled salmon

PREP: 10 MINUTES + MARINATING / **BAKE:** 15 MINUTES

2	teaspoons snipped fresh dill *or* 3/4 teaspoon dill weed
1/2	teaspoon lemon-pepper seasoning
1/2	teaspoon salt, optional
1/4	teaspoon garlic powder
1	salmon fillet (1-1/2 pounds)
1/4	cup packed brown sugar
3	tablespoons chicken broth
3	tablespoons canola oil
3	tablespoons soy sauce
3	tablespoons finely chopped green onions
1	small lemon, thinly sliced
2	onion slices, separated into rings

Sprinkle dill, lemon-pepper, salt if desired and garlic powder over salmon. In a large resealable plastic bag, combine the brown sugar, broth, oil, soy sauce and green onions; add salmon. Seal bag and turn to coat. Cover and refrigerate for 1 hour, turning once.

Drain and discard marinade. Grill salmon skin side down, over medium heat; arrange lemon and onion slices over the top. Cover and cook for 15-20 minutes or until fish flakes easily with a fork. **YIELD: 6 servings.**

EDITOR'S NOTE: Salmon can be broiled instead of grilled. Place the fillet on a greased broiler pan. Broil 3-4 in. from the heat for 6-8 min. or until fish flakes easily with a fork.

KATHLEEN GRANT, SWAN LAKE, MONTANA

This delicious recipe uses a packaged stuffing mix to create a perfectly seasoned topping to this baked favorite. A salad and bread of your choice are all you'll need for a filling lunch or dinner. It's so versatile, you can even serve it at brunch.

sausage spinach bake

PREP: 20 MINUTES / **BAKE:** 35 MINUTES

1	package (6 ounces) savory herb-flavored stuffing mix
1/2	pound bulk pork sausage
1/4	cup chopped green onions
1/2	teaspoon minced garlic
1	package (10 ounces) frozen chopped spinach, thawed and squeezed dry
1-1/2	cups (6 ounces) shredded Monterey Jack cheese
1-1/2	cups half-and-half cream
3	eggs
2	tablespoons grated Parmesan cheese

Prepare stuffing according to package directions. Meanwhile, crumble the sausage into a large skillet; add onions; cook over medium heat until the meat is no longer pink. Add garlic; cook 1 minute longer. Drain.

In a large bowl, combine the stuffing, sausage mixture and spinach. Transfer to a greased 13-in. x 9-in. baking dish; sprinkle with Monterey Jack cheese. In a small bowl, combine cream and eggs; pour over sausage mixture.

Bake at 400° for 30 minutes or until a thermometer reads 160°. Sprinkle with Parmesan cheese; bake 5 minutes longer or until bubbly. **YIELD: 12 servings.**

BARBARA MCCALLEY, ALLISON PARK, PENNSYLVANIA

Here's a way to dress up chicken breasts for a weeknight dinner or party main dish, using fresh mushrooms, green onions and two kinds of cheese. It's a recipe I can count on to yield tender and flavorful chicken every time.

baked mushroom chicken

PREP: 20 MINUTES / **BAKE:** 20 MINUTES

4	boneless skinless chicken breast halves (1 pound)
1/4	cup all-purpose flour
3	tablespoons butter, *divided*
1	cup sliced fresh mushrooms
1/2	cup chicken broth
1/4	teaspoon salt
1/8	teaspoon pepper
1/3	cup shredded part-skim mozzarella cheese
1/3	cup grated Parmesan cheese
1/4	cup sliced green onions

Flatten each chicken breast half to 1/4-in. thickness. Place flour in a resealable plastic bag; add chicken, a few pieces at a time. Seal and shake to coat.

In a large skillet, brown chicken in 2 tablespoons butter on both sides. Transfer to a greased 11-in. x 7-in. baking dish. In the same skillet, saute mushrooms in the remaining butter until tender. Add broth, salt and pepper. Bring to a boil; cook for 5 minutes or until liquid is reduced to 1/2 cup. Spoon over chicken.

Bake, uncovered, at 375° for 15 minutes. Sprinkle with cheeses and green onions. Bake 5 minutes longer or until the chicken juices run clear. **YIELD: 4 servings.**

JENNIFER STANDRIDGE, DALLAS, GEORGIA

Enchiladas are typically prepared with corn tortillas. However, my husband, Jeff, and I prefer flour tortillas so I use them in this saucy casserole that has an irresistible home-cooked flavor and a subtle Southwestern kick.

garlic beef enchiladas

PREP: 30 MINUTES / **BAKE:** 40 MINUTES

1	pound ground beef
1	medium onion, chopped
2	tablespoons all-purpose flour
1	tablespoon chili powder
1	teaspoon salt
1	teaspoon garlic powder
1/2	teaspoon ground cumin
1/4	teaspoon rubbed sage
1	can (14-1/2 ounces) stewed tomatoes

SAUCE:

4	to 6 garlic cloves, minced
1/3	cup butter
1/2	cup all-purpose flour
1	can (14-1/2 ounces) beef broth
1	can (15 ounces) tomato sauce
1	to 2 tablespoons chili powder
1	to 2 teaspoons ground cumin
1	to 2 teaspoons rubbed sage
1/2	teaspoon salt
10	flour tortillas (6 inches), warmed
2	cups (8 ounces) shredded Colby-Monterey Jack cheese

In a large saucepan, cook beef and onion over medium heat until meat is no longer pink; drain. Stir in flour and seasonings until blended. Stir in tomatoes; bring to a boil. Reduce heat; cover and simmer for 15 minutes.

Meanwhile, in another saucepan, saute the garlic in butter until tender. Stir in flour until blended. Gradually stir in broth; bring to a boil. Cook and stir for 2 minutes or until thickened. Stir in tomato sauce and seasonings; heat through.

Pour about 1-1/2 cups sauce into an ungreased 13-in. x 9-in. baking dish. Spread about 1/4 cup beef mixture down the center of each tortilla; top with 1-2 tablespoons cheese. Roll up tightly; place seam side down over sauce. Top enchiladas with remaining sauce.

Cover and bake at 350° for 30-35 minutes. Sprinkle with the remaining cheese. Bake, uncovered, 10-15 minutes longer or until the cheese is melted. **YIELD: 5 servings.**

PAM SHINOGLE, ARLINGTON, TEXAS

Whenever I serve this pleasing poultry dish to family and friends, which is quite often, I'm bound to be asked for the recipe. It's a fast and tasty meal that I'm happy to share with others.

15-minute marinated chicken

PREP: 15 MINUTES + MARINATING / **GRILL:** 15 MINUTES

1/4	cup Dijon mustard
2	tablespoons lemon juice
1-1/2	teaspoons Worcestershire sauce
1/2	teaspoon dried tarragon
1/4	teaspoon pepper
4	boneless skinless chicken breast halves

Combine the first five ingredients; spread on both sides of chicken. Place chicken on plate. Marinate at room temperature for 10-15 minutes or for several hours in the refrigerator.

Grill, uncovered, over medium heat, for 10-15 minutes or until juices run clear, turning once. **YIELD: 4 servings.**

READERS' RAVES

> This is a great chicken dish to go with salad. Tastier, better for you and more economical than those ready-to-eat chicken packages.
>
> —Jblt2002 from TasteofHome.com

> This recipe was so easy to make, and it was delicious! I broiled the chicken in the oven instead of grilling it—it turned out so juicy!
>
> —Scarlet286 from TasteofHome.com

GAIL GRAHAM, MAPLE RIDGE, BRITISH COLUMBIA
Topped with a subtly sweet sauce, this old-fashioned standby tastes so good that you might want to double the recipe so everyone can have seconds. This meat loaf freezes well, too, for make-ahead convenience.

traditional meat loaf

PREP: 15 MINUTES / **BAKE:** 1 HOUR + STANDING

1	egg, lightly beaten
2/3	cup milk
3	slices bread, crumbled
1	cup (4 ounces) shredded cheddar cheese
1	medium onion, chopped
1/2	cup finely shredded carrot
1	teaspoon salt
1/4	teaspoon pepper
1-1/2	pounds ground beef
1/4	cup packed brown sugar
1/4	cup ketchup
1	tablespoon prepared mustard

In a large bowl, combine the first eight ingredients. Crumble beef over mixture and mix well. Shape into a loaf. Place in a greased 9-in. x 5-in. loaf pan.

In a small bowl, combine the brown sugar, ketchup and mustard; spread over loaf. Bake at 350° for 60-75 minutes or until no pink remains and a meat thermometer reads 160°. Drain. Let stand for 10 minutes before slicing. **YIELD: 6 servings.**

MARILYN MCGEE, TULSA, OKLAHOMA
I recently began experimenting with pork and came up with this simple skillet dish, which has turned out to be a family staple. I like to vary the flavor occasionally by using lemon-pepper or garlic-seasoned tenderloin.

pork tenderloin with gravy

PREP/TOTAL TIME: 25 MINUTES

1	envelope brown gravy mix
1/2	cup water
3	tablespoons soy sauce
2	tablespoons balsamic vinegar
1	garlic clove, minced
1	pork tenderloin (about 3/4 pound), cut into 1/2-inch slices
1/4	cup olive oil
1/2	pound fresh mushrooms, sliced
1	medium onion, sliced and separated into rings

Hot cooked rice

In a small bowl, combine the first five ingredients until blended; set aside. In a large skillet, brown pork in oil on all sides. Stir in the gravy mixture, mushrooms and onion. Bring to a boil. Reduce heat; cover and simmer for 10-15 minutes or until meat juices run clear and vegetables are tender. Serve over rice. **YIELD: 2 servings.**

VICKI MELIES, ELKHORN, NEBRASKA
I altered a friend's recipe for crab-stuffed chicken to include one of my favorite vegetables—spinach. Now my husband requests this elegant entree all the time. Served over rice, it's even a nice choice for special dinners.

spinach crab chicken

PREP: 45 MINUTES / **COOK:** 40 MINUTES

1/2	cup finely chopped onion
1/4	cup chopped fresh mushrooms
1/4	cup finely chopped celery
3	tablespoons butter
3	tablespoons all-purpose flour
1/2	teaspoon salt, *divided*
1	cup chicken broth
1/2	cup milk
4	boneless skinless chicken breast halves (6 ounces *each*)
1/8	teaspoon white pepper
1/2	cup dry bread crumbs
1	can (6 ounces) crabmeat, drained, flaked and cartilage removed
12	fresh spinach leaves, chopped
1	tablespoon minced fresh parsley
1	cup (4 ounces) shredded Swiss cheese

Hot cooked rice

For sauce, in a large skillet, sauce the onion, mushrooms and celery in butter until tender. Stir in flour and 1/4 teaspoon salt until blended. Gradually add broth and milk. Bring to a boil; cook and stir for 1-2 minutes or until thickened. Remove from the heat.

Flatten chicken to 1/4-in. thickness; sprinkle with the pepper and remaining salt. In a large bowl, combine the bread crumbs, crab, spinach and parsley; stir in 1/2 cup sauce. Spoon 1/4 cup down the center of each chicken breast half. Roll up; secure with toothpicks. Place seam side down in a greased 13-in. x 9-in. baking dish. Top with remaining sauce.

Cover and bake at 375° for 35-45 minutes or until chicken is no longer pink. Sprinkle with cheese. Broil 4-6 in. from the heat for 5 minutes or until lightly browned. Discard toothpicks. Serve with rice. **YIELD: 4 servings.**

CHRISTEL MCKINLEY, EAST LIVERPOOL, OHIO
I prepare this delicious main dish several times a month. The herbs give the beef an excellent taste. Adding the onion, carrots and potatoes makes this a meal-in-one. My husband, Jack, a real meat-and-potatoes man, even enjoys the leftovers, which isn't always the case with other recipes.

herbed pot roast

PREP: 25 MINUTES / **BAKE:** 3 HOURS

1	boneless beef rump *or* chuck roast (3 to 3-1/2 pounds)
1	tablespoon canola oil
1	teaspoon salt
1	teaspoon dried marjoram
1	teaspoon dried thyme
1/2	teaspoon dried oregano
1/2	teaspoon garlic powder
1/2	teaspoon pepper
1	can (10-1/2 ounces) condensed beef broth, undiluted
8	medium carrots, cut into thirds
8	medium potatoes, peeled and quartered
1	large onion, quartered
1	cup water

In a Dutch oven, brown roast in oil over medium heat. Combine seasonings; sprinkle over meat. Add broth and bring to a boil.

Cover and bake at 325° for 2 hours, basting occasionally. Add the carrots, potatoes, onion and water.

Cover and bake for 1 hour or until vegetables are tender. Thicken pan juices for gravy if desired. **YIELD: 8 servings.**

LORRI FOOCKLE, GRANVILLE, ILLINOIS

My family first tasted this rich, classic lasagna at a friend's home on Christmas Eve. We were so impressed that it became our own holiday tradition as well. I also prepare it other times of the year. It is even requested often by my sister's Italian in-laws...I consider that the highest compliment!

traditional lasagna

PREP: 30 MINUTES PLUS SIMMERING
BAKE: 70 MINUTES + STANDING

1	pound ground beef
3/4	pound bulk pork sausage
3	cans (8 ounces *each*) tomato sauce
2	cans (6 ounces *each*) tomato paste
2	garlic cloves, minced
2	teaspoons sugar
1	teaspoon Italian seasoning
1	teaspoon salt
1/2	teaspoon pepper
3	eggs
3	tablespoons minced fresh parsley
3	cups (24 ounces) 4% small-curd cottage cheese
1	carton (8 ounces) ricotta cheese
1/2	cup grated Parmesan cheese
9	lasagna noodles, cooked and drained
6	slices provolone cheese
3	cups (12 ounces) shredded part-skim mozzarella cheese, *divided*

In a large skillet, cook beef and sausage over medium heat until no longer pink; drain. Add tomato sauce, tomato paste, garlic, sugar, seasoning, salt and pepper. Bring to a boil. Reduce heat; simmer, uncovered, for 1 hour, stirring occasionally.

In a large bowl, combine the eggs and parsley. Stir in the cottage cheese, ricotta and Parmesan.

Spread 1 cup of the meat sauce in an ungreased 13-in. x 9-in. baking dish. Layer with three noodles, provolone cheese, 2 cups cottage cheese mixture, 1 cup mozzarella, three noodles, 2 cups meat sauce, remaining cottage cheese mixture and 1 cup shredded mozzarella. Top with the remaining noodles, meat sauce and mozzarella (dish will be full).

Cover and bake at 375° for 50 minutes. Uncover; bake 20 minutes longer or until heated through. Let lasagna stand for 15 minutes before cutting. **YIELD: 12 servings.**

LINDA GAIDO, NEW BRIGHTON, PENNSYLVANIA

Everyone loves slices of this fork-tender roast beef and its savory gravy. This well-seasoned roast is my mom's specialty. People always ask what her secret ingredients are—now you have the delicious recipe for our favorite meat dish!

mom's roast beef

PREP: 20 MINUTES / **COOK:** 2-1/2 HOURS

1	beef eye round roast (about 2-1/2 pounds)
1	tablespoon canola oil
1	medium onion, chopped
1	cup brewed coffee
1	cup cold water, *divided*
1	teaspoon beef bouillon granules
2	teaspoons dried basil
1	teaspoon dried rosemary, crushed
1	garlic clove, minced
1	teaspoon salt
1/2	teaspoon pepper
1/4	cup all-purpose flour

In a Dutch oven, brown roast in oil on all sides. Add onion; cook and stir until tender. Add the coffee, 3/4 cup water and bouillon to the pan. Combine basil, rosemary, garlic, salt and pepper; sprinkle over the roast.

Bring to a boil. Reduce heat; cover and simmer for 2-1/2 hours or until meat is tender. Remove roast; let stand for 10 minutes before slicing. Combine the flour and remaining water until smooth; stir into pan juices. Bring to a boil. Cook and stir for 1-2 minutes or until thickened and bubbly. Serve gravy with roast. **YIELD: 8 servings.**

guilt-free fare

Who says "good-for-you" food is limited to carrot sticks? Here, you'll find dozens of comforting recipes that won't throw your healthy eating habits off-track. Big, hearty burgers...creamy mashed potatoes...even heavenly chocolate cake let you feel good about every bite.

ITALIAN VEGGIE SKILLET / PAGE 144

MARGUERITE SHAEFFER, SEWELL, NEW JERSEY

For a surefire meatless mainstay, I swear by these moist and delicious salsa-topped burgers. I first sampled them at an "Eating Right" session hosted by our local library. They definitely hold their own against any veggie burger you'd buy at the supermarket. They're a flavorful alternative to ground beef

grilled bean burgers

PREP: 25 MINUTES / **GRILL:** 10 MINUTES

1	large onion, finely chopped	1-1/2	cups quick-cooking oats
1	tablespoon olive oil	2	tablespoons Dijon mustard
4	garlic cloves, minced	2	tablespoons reduced-sodium soy sauce
1	medium carrot, shredded	1	tablespoon ketchup
1	to 2 teaspoons chili powder	1/4	teaspoon pepper
1	teaspoon ground cumin	8	whole wheat hamburger buns, split
1	can (15 ounces) pinto beans, rinsed and drained	8	lettuce leaves
1	can (15 ounces) black beans, rinsed and drained	8	tablespoons salsa

In a large nonstick skillet coated with cooking spray, saute onion in oil for 2 minutes. Add garlic; cook for 1 minute. Stir in the carrot, chili powder and cumin; cook 2 minutes longer or until carrot is tender. Remove from the heat; set aside.

In a large bowl, mash the pinto beans and black beans. Stir in oats. Add the mustard, soy sauce, ketchup, pepper and carrot mixture; mix well. Shape into eight 3-1/2-in. patties.

Coat grill rack with cooking spray before starting the grill. Grill the patties, covered, over medium heat for 4-5 minutes on each side or until heated through. Serve on buns with lettuce and salsa. **YIELD: 8 servings.**

NUTRITION FACTS: 1 burger equals 307 calories, 5 g fat (1 g saturated fat), 0 cholesterol, 723 mg sodium, 53 g carbohydrate, 10 g fiber, 12 g protein. **DIABETIC EXCHANGES:** 3-1/2 starch, 1 very lean meat.

EDITOR'S NOTE: Our recipes often give a range on certain herbs and spices to accommodate different tastes. If you like the heat of chili powder, use 2 teaspoons chili powder in your Grilled Bean Burgers; for a milder version, use 1 teaspoon.

SHERI ERICKSON, MONTROSE, IOWA

Not only is this is a refreshing dessert, but it's virtually fat-free and doesn't have any cholesterol. Best of all, this light and luscious treat comes together easily.

raspberry angel cake

PREP: 15 MINUTES / **BAKE:** 45 MINUTES + COOLING

1	package (16 ounces) angel food cake mix
1/2	teaspoon almond extract
1/2	teaspoon vanilla extract
1	package (.3 ounce) sugar-free raspberry gelatin
1	package (12 ounces) frozen unsweetened raspberries, thawed
1	tablespoon sugar

Prepare cake batter according to package directions. Fold in the extracts. Spoon two-thirds of the batter into an ungreased 10-in. tube pan. Add the gelatin powder to remaining batter; drop by tablespoonfuls over batter in pan. Cut through with a knife to swirl.

Bake according to package directions. Immediately invert pan onto a wire rack; cool completely, about 1 hour. Carefully run a knife around sides of pan to remove cake. Cut into slices.

Combine raspberries and sugar; serve over cake. **YIELD: 12 servings.**

NUTRITION FACTS: 1 slice with 2 tablespoons sauce equals 155 calories, trace fat (0 saturated fat), 0 cholesterol, 224 mg sodium, 35 g carbohydrate, 1 g fiber, 4 g protein. **DIABETIC EXCHANGE:** 2 starch.

MARY BERGFELD, EUGENE, OREGON

This is an excellent quick meal that can be made with convenient ingredients from the grocery store. Cooked shrimp and bagged coleslaw mix reduce the prep time and work required to get it on the table.

shrimp 'n' noodle bowls

PREP/TOTAL TIME: 25 MINUTES

8	ounces uncooked angel hair pasta
1	pound cooked small shrimp
2	cups broccoli coleslaw mix
6	green onions, thinly sliced
1/2	cup minced fresh cilantro
2/3	cup reduced-fat sesame ginger salad dressing

Cook pasta according to package directions; drain and rinse in cold water. Transfer to a large bowl. Add the shrimp, coleslaw mix, onions and cilantro. Drizzle with dressing; toss to coat. Cover and refrigerate until serving. **YIELD: 6 servings.**

NUTRITION FACTS: 1-1/3 cups equals 260 calories, 3 g fat (trace saturated fat), 147 mg cholesterol, 523 mg sodium, 36 g carbohydrate, 2 g fiber, 22 g protein. **DIABETIC EXCHANGES:** 2 starch, 2 very lean meat, 1/2 fat.

MOLLY CAPPONE, LEWIS CENTER, OHIO
My sister Amy came up with this recipe that does a great job of making boring old chicken breasts incredibly enticing. My husband and I just love the wonderful, spicy sauce!

chicken with creamy jalapeno sauce

PREP/TOTAL TIME: 25 MINUTES

4	boneless skinless chicken breast halves (4 ounces *each*)
1/4	teaspoon salt
1	tablespoon canola oil
2	medium onions, chopped
1/2	cup reduced-sodium chicken broth
2	jalapeno peppers, seeded and minced
2	teaspoons ground cumin
3	ounces reduced-fat cream cheese, cubed
1/4	cup reduced-fat sour cream
3	plum tomatoes, seeded and chopped
2	cups hot cooked rice

Sprinkle chicken with salt. In a large nonstick skillet over medium-high heat, brown chicken in oil on both sides.

Add the onions, broth, jalapenos and cumin. Bring to a boil. Reduce heat; cover and simmer for 5-7 minutes or until a meat thermometer reads 170°. Remove chicken and keep warm.

Stir cream cheese and sour cream into onion mixture until blended. Stir in tomatoes; heat through. Serve with chicken and rice. **YIELD: 4 servings (2 cups sauce).**

NUTRITION FACTS: 1 chicken breast half with 1/2 cup sauce and 1/2 cup rice equals 376 calories, 13 g fat (5 g saturated fat), 83 mg cholesterol, 389 mg sodium, 34 g carbohydrate, 3 g fiber, 30 g protein. **DIABETIC EXCHANGES:** 3 very lean meat, 2 vegetable, 2 fat, 1-1/2 starch.

EDITOR'S NOTE: When cutting hot peppers, disposable gloves are recommended. Avoid touching your face.

LADONNA REED, PONCA CITY, OKLAHOMA
My husband and I are trying to eat lighter but still crave sweets. This moist, chocolate cake really helps curb our cravings. With the rich frosting, it makes a decadent no-guilt treat!

yummy chocolate cake

PREP: 20 MINUTES / **BAKE:** 15 MINUTES + COOLING

1	package (18-1/4 ounces) chocolate cake mix
1	package (2.1 ounces) sugar-free instant chocolate pudding mix
1-3/4	cups water
3	egg whites

FROSTING:

1-1/4	cups cold fat-free milk
1/4	teaspoon almond extract
1	package (1.4 ounces) sugar-free instant chocolate pudding mix
1	carton (8 ounces) frozen reduced-fat whipped topping, thawed

Chocolate curls, optional

In a large bowl, combine the cake mix, pudding mix, water and egg whites. Beat on low speed for 1 minute; beat on medium for 2 minutes.

Pour batter into a 15-in. x 10-in. baking pan coated with cooking spray. Bake at 350° for 12-18 minutes or until a toothpick inserted near the center comes out clean. Cool on a wire rack.

For frosting, place milk and extract in a large bowl. Sprinkle with a third of the pudding mix; let stand for 1 minute. Whisk pudding into milk. Repeat twice with remaining pudding mix. Whisk pudding 2 minutes longer. Let stand for 15 minutes. Fold in whipped topping. Frost cake. Garnish with chocolate curls if desired. **YIELD: 16 servings.**

NUTRITION FACTS: 1 piece (calculated without chocolate curls) equals 197 calories, 5 g fat (3 g saturated fat), trace cholesterol, 409 mg sodium, 35 g carbohydrate, 1 g fiber, 3 g protein.

SHARON SPETHMAN, HUTCHINSON, MINNESOTA
Flavored with a little bit of wine, these moist patties taste like they came from a gourmet restaurant.

barbecued mushroom-turkey burgers

PREP: 25 MINUTES + CHILLING / **GRILL:** 20 MINUTES

3/4	cup chopped sweet onion
2	teaspoons butter
1	cup sliced fresh mushrooms
1	medium carrot, grated
1/4	cup dry red wine *or* chicken broth
1/2	teaspoon salt
1/4	teaspoon pepper
1	pound lean ground turkey
1/2	cup barbecue sauce, *divided*
4	hamburger buns, split
4	Bibb lettuce leaves
4	slices tomato

In a large nonstick skillet, saute onion in butter for 3 minutes. Add mushrooms and carrot; cook and stir for 3 minutes. Add the wine or broth, salt and pepper; simmer for 2-3 minutes or until liquid is evaporated. Transfer to a large bowl; cool slightly. Crumble turkey over mixture and mix well. Shape into four patties. Cover and refrigerate for at least 1 hour.

Coat grill rack with cooking spray before starting the grill. Grill patties, uncovered, over medium heat for 8-10 minutes on each side or until juices run clear, brushing occasionally with 1/4 cup barbecue sauce. Serve on buns with lettuce, tomato and remaining barbecue sauce. **YIELD: 4 servings.**

NUTRITION FACTS: 1 burger equals 371 calories, 14 g fat (4 g saturated fat), 95 mg cholesterol, 926 mg sodium, 32 g carbohydrate, 3 g fiber, 25 g protein. **DIABETIC EXCHANGES:** 3 lean meat, 2 starch, 1 fat.

BETTY RICHARDSON, SPRINGFIELD, ILLINOIS
Here's a dinner that takes up very little of your time. We like the tender steaks with mashed potatoes, rice or noodles.

swiss steak

PREP: 10 MINUTES / **COOK:** 1 HOUR 35 MINUTES

4	beef cube steaks (4 ounces *each*)
1	tablespoon canola oil
1	medium onion, chopped
1	celery rib with leaves, chopped
1	garlic clove, minced
1	can (14-1/2 ounces) stewed tomatoes, cut up
1	can (8 ounces) tomato sauce
1	teaspoon beef bouillon granules
1	tablespoon cornstarch
2	tablespoons cold water

In a large nonstick skillet, brown cube steaks on both sides in oil over medium-high heat; remove and set aside. In the same skillet, saute the onion, celery and garlic for 3-4 minutes or until tender. Add the tomatoes, tomato sauce and bouillon. Return steaks to the pan. Bring to a boil. Reduce heat; cover and simmer for 1-1/4 to 1-3/4 hours or until meat is tender.

Combine cornstarch and water until smooth; stir into tomato mixture. Bring to a boil; cook and stir for 2 minutes or until thickened. **YIELD: 4 servings.**

NUTRITION FACTS: 1 steak with 3/4 cup sauce equals 255 calories, 8 g fat (2 g saturated fat), 65 mg cholesterol, 746 mg sodium, 18 g carbohydrate, 3 g fiber, 28 g protein. **DIABETIC EXCHANGES:** 3 lean meat, 3 vegetable, 1/2 fat.

KAREN MCCABE, PROVO, UTAH
My husband and I both love this cheesy, filling Italian specialty. Not only is it easy, it's also low-fat and a real time-saver since you don't cook the noodles before baking.

weekday lasagna

PREP: 35 MINUTES / **BAKE:** 1 HOUR + STANDING

1	pound lean ground beef
1	small onion, chopped
1	can (28 ounces) crushed tomatoes
1-3/4	cups water
1	can (6 ounces) tomato paste
1	envelope spaghetti sauce mix
1	egg, lightly beaten
2	cups (16 ounces) fat-free cottage cheese
2	tablespoons grated Parmesan cheese
6	uncooked lasagna noodles
1	cup (4 ounces) shredded part-skim mozzarella cheese

In a large saucepan, cook beef and onion over medium heat until meat is no longer pink; drain. Stir in the tomatoes, water, tomato paste and spaghetti sauce mix. Bring to a boil. Reduce heat; cover and simmer for 15-20 minutes, stirring occasionally.

In a small bowl, combine egg, cottage cheese and Parmesan cheese. Spread 2 cups meat sauce in a 13-in. x 9-in. baking dish coated with cooking spray. Layer with three noodles, half of cottage cheese mixture and half of the remaining meat sauce. Repeat layers.

Cover and bake at 350° for 50 minutes. Uncover; sprinkle with mozzarella cheese. Bake 10-15 minutes longer or until bubbly and cheese is melted. Let stand for 15 minutes before cutting. **YIELD: 9 servings.**

NUTRITION FACTS: 1 piece equals 280 calories, 7 g fat (3 g saturated fat), 65 mg cholesterol, 804 mg sodium, 29 g carbohydrate, 4 g fiber, 25 g protein. **DIABETIC EXCHANGES:** 3 lean meat, 2 vegetable, 1 starch.

CONNIE ADAMS, MONAVILLE, WEST VIRGINIA
A convenient cake mix, a can of pumpkin and a little applesauce make this mouthwatering cake a delight to throw together. With its thick cinnamon glaze, it seems anything but low-fat.

cinnamon pumpkin cake

PREP: 15 MINUTES / **BAKE:** 65 MINUTES + COOLING

1	package (18-1/4 ounces) yellow cake mix
1	can (15 ounces) solid-pack pumpkin
2/3	cup sugar
2	eggs
1/2	cup egg substitute
1/3	cup water
1/4	cup unsweetened applesauce
2-1/2	teaspoons ground cinnamon, *divided*
1/4	teaspoon ground nutmeg
1-1/2	cups confectioners' sugar
1/2	teaspoon vanilla extract
1	to 2 tablespoons fat-free milk

In a large bowl, combine the cake mix, pumpkin, sugar, eggs, egg substitute, water, applesauce, 1 teaspoon cinnamon and nutmeg. Beat on low speed for 30 seconds. Beat on medium for 2 minutes. Pour into a 10-in. fluted tube pan coated with cooking spray.

Bake at 350° for 65-75 minutes or until a toothpick inserted near the center comes out clean. Cool for 10 minutes before removing from pan to a wire rack to cool completely.

In a small bowl, combine the confectioners' sugar, vanilla, remaining cinnamon and enough milk to achieve desired drizzling consistency. Drizzle over cake. **YIELD: 14 servings.**

NUTRITION FACTS: 1 piece of cake equals 271 calories, 4 g fat (2 g saturated fat), 30 mg cholesterol, 261 mg sodium, 55 g carbohydrate, 2 g fiber, 4 g protein.

JOSEPHINE PIRO, EASTON, PENNSYLVANIA
Although I'm retired, I like recipes that are on the table fast. This veggie-packed side dish is ready in no time and incorporates vegetables and herbs from our garden for a refreshing taste.

italian veggie skillet

PREP/TOTAL TIME: 25 MINUTES

1	medium yellow summer squash, cut into 1/4-inch slices
1/2	cup sliced fresh mushrooms
1	tablespoon olive oil
1	cup cherry tomatoes, halved
1/2	teaspoon salt
1/2	teaspoon minced garlic
2	tablespoons minced fresh parsley
1-1/2	teaspoons minced fresh rosemary *or* 1/2 teaspoon dried rosemary, crushed
1-1/2	teaspoons minced fresh thyme *or* 1/2 teaspoon dried thyme
1-1/2	teaspoons plus 2 tablespoons minced fresh basil, *divided*
2	tablespoons sliced green onion
2	tablespoons grated Parmesan cheese

In a large skillet, saute the squash and mushrooms in olive oil for 4-5 minutes or until tender. Add the tomatoes, salt and garlic. Reduce heat; simmer, uncovered, for 6-8 minutes.

Stir in the parsley, rosemary, thyme and 1-1/2 teaspoons basil; cook 1-2 minutes longer or until heated through. Transfer to a serving bowl. Sprinkle with onion and remaining basil; lightly toss. Sprinkle with Parmesan cheese. **YIELD: 2-3 servings.**

NUTRITION FACTS: 2/3 cup equals 86 calories, 6 g fat (1 g saturated fat), 3 mg cholesterol, 464 mg sodium, 7 g carbohydrate, 2 g fiber, 3 g protein.

VICKI RAATZ, WATERLOO, WISCONSIN
These soft cookies have a cake-like texture and lots of banana flavor that folks devour. Throw in some decadent chocolate chips and you've got one irresistible treat.

banana chocolate chip cookies

PREP: 20 MINUTES / **BAKE:** 10 MINUTES/BATCH

1/3	cup butter, softened
1/2	cup sugar
1	egg
1/2	cup mashed ripe banana
1/2	teaspoon vanilla extract
1	cup all-purpose flour
1	teaspoon baking powder
1/4	teaspoon salt
1/8	teaspoon baking soda
1	cup (6 ounces) semisweet chocolate chips

In a small bowl, cream butter and sugar until light and fluffy. Beat in the egg, banana and vanilla. Combine the flour, baking powder, salt and baking soda; gradually add to creamed mixture and mix well. Stir in chocolate chips.

Drop by tablespoonfuls 2 in. apart onto baking sheets coated with cooking spray. Bake at 350° for 9-11 minutes or until edges are lightly browned. Remove to wire racks to cool. **YIELD: 3 dozen.**

NUTRITION FACTS: 1 cookie equals 66 calories, 3 g fat (2 g saturated fat), 10 mg cholesterol, 51 mg sodium, 9 g carbohydrate, trace fiber, 1 g protein. **DIABETIC EXCHANGES:** 1/2 starch, 1/2 fat.

ANGELA HANKS, ST. ALBANS, WEST VIRGINIA
This fragrant side packs flavor in but keeps extra fat, calories and sodium out. Red pepper lends sweetness and color to the eye-catching dish that makes a wonderful accompaniment to grilled chicken.

corn & pepper orzo

PREP/TOTAL TIME: 30 MINUTES

3/4	cup uncooked orzo pasta
1	large sweet red pepper, chopped
1	medium onion, chopped
1	tablespoon olive oil
2	cups frozen corn, thawed
2	teaspoons Italian seasoning
1/8	teaspoon salt
1/8	teaspoon pepper

Cook pasta according to package directions. Meanwhile, in a large nonstick skillet coated with cooking spray, saute red pepper and onion in oil for 2 minutes. Add the corn, Italian seasoning, salt and pepper; cook and stir until vegetables are tender. Drain pasta; stir into the pan. **YIELD: 6 servings.**

NUTRITION FACTS: 3/4 cup equals 178 calories, 3 g fat (trace saturated fat), 0 cholesterol, 55 mg sodium, 34 g carbohydrate, 3 g fiber, 6 g protein. **DIABETIC EXCHANGES:** 2 starch, 1/2 fat.

KATHY GARRISON, FORT WORTH, TEXAS
My husband and friends love this crusty salmon, not only for its flavor, but because it's so rich in heart-healthy omega-3s.

sauteed spiced salmon

PREP/TOTAL TIME: 15 MINUTES

2	teaspoons dill weed
2	teaspoons chili powder
1	teaspoon salt-free lemon-pepper seasoning
1/2	teaspoon ground cumin
4	salmon fillets (4 ounces *each*), skin removed
1	tablespoon canola oil

Lemon wedges, optional

Combine the dill weed, chili powder, lemon-pepper seasoning and cumin; rub mixture over the salmon fillets. In a large nonstick skillet coated with cooking spray, cook salmon in oil over medium-high heat for 5-6 minutes on each side or until fish flakes easily with a fork. Serve with lemon if desired. **YIELD: 4 servings.**

NUTRITION FACTS: 1 fillet equals 246 calories, 16 g fat (3 g saturated fat), 67 mg cholesterol, 82 mg sodium, 2 g carbohydrate, 1 g fiber, 23 g protein. **DIABETIC EXCHANGES:** 3 lean meat, 1-1/2 fat.

THERESA SMITH, SHEBOYGAN, WISCONSIN
My husband had a poor perception of healthy food until he tried this beefy casserole. The combination of pasta, oregano, fresh mushrooms and green peppers makes it a favorite in our house.

italian hot dish

PREP: 30 MINUTES / **BAKE:** 40 MINUTES

1-1/2	cups uncooked small pasta shells
1	pound lean ground beef (90% lean)
1	cup sliced fresh mushrooms, *divided*
1/2	cup chopped onion
1/2	cup chopped green pepper
1	can (15 ounces) tomato sauce
1	teaspoon dried oregano
1/2	teaspoon garlic powder
1/4	teaspoon onion powder
1/8	teaspoon pepper
1/2	cup shredded part-skim mozzarella cheese, *divided*
4	teaspoons grated Parmesan cheese, *divided*

Cook pasta according to package directions. Meanwhile, in a large nonstick skillet coated with cooking spray, cook the beef, 1/2 cup mushrooms, onion and green pepper until meat is no longer pink; drain. Stir in the tomato sauce, oregano, garlic powder, onion powder and pepper. Bring to a boil. Reduce heat; cover and simmer for 15 minutes.

Drain pasta; place in an 8-in. square baking dish coated with cooking spray. Top with meat sauce and remaining mushrooms. Sprinkle with 1/4 cup mozzarella and 2 teaspoons Parmesan.

Cover and bake at 350° for 35 minutes. Uncover; sprinkle with remaining cheeses. Bake 5-10 minutes longer or until heated through and cheese is melted. **YIELD: 4 servings.**

NUTRITION FACTS: 1 serving equals 391 calories, 12 g fat (5 g saturated fat), 65 mg cholesterol, 663 mg sodium, 36 g carbohydrate, 3 g fiber, 33 g protein.

KARI JOHNSTON, MARWAYNE, ALBERTA
I came up with this simple stovetop entree as a way to use leftover turkey after Thanksgiving and Christmas dinners. All my children really enjoy the creamy, cheesy flavor.

turkey fettuccine skillet

PREP: 10 MINUTES / **COOK:** 30 MINUTES

8	ounces uncooked fettuccine
1/2	cup chopped onion
1/2	cup chopped celery
4	garlic cloves, minced
1	teaspoon canola oil
1	cup sliced fresh mushrooms
2	cups fat-free milk
1	teaspoon salt-free seasoning blend
1/4	teaspoon salt
2	tablespoons cornstarch
1/2	cup fat-free half-and-half
1/3	cup grated Parmesan cheese
3	cups cubed cooked turkey breast
3/4	cup shredded part-skim mozzarella cheese

Cook fettuccine according to package directions. Meanwhile, in a large ovenproof skillet coated with cooking spray, saute the onion, celery and garlic in oil for 3 minutes. Add mushrooms; cook and stir until vegetables are tender. Stir in the milk, seasoning blend and salt. Bring to a boil.

Combine cornstarch and half-and-half until smooth; stir into skillet. Cook and stir for 2 minutes or until thickened and bubbly. Stir in Parmesan cheese just until melted.

Stir in turkey. Drain fettuccine; add to turkey mixture. Heat through. Sprinkle with mozzarella cheese. Broil 4-6 in. from the heat for 2-3 minutes or until cheese is melted. **YIELD: 6 servings.**

NUTRITION FACTS: 1 cup equals 361 calories, 7 g fat (3 g saturated fat), 76 mg cholesterol, 343 mg sodium, 38 g carbohydrate, 2 g fiber, 34 g protein. **DIABETIC EXCHANGES:** 4 very lean meat, 2-1/2 starch, 1/2 fat.

TASTE OF HOME TEST KITCHEN

When creating this decadent indulgence, our Test Kitchen home economists used a combination of sugar and sugar substitute for the best taste and texture while still cutting calories and carbs. They also used prune baby food in place of some of the oil. This savings allowed them to use full-fat whipped topping in the frosting.

frosted mocha cake

PREP: 20 MINUTES / **BAKE:** 30 MINUTES + COOLING

3/4	cup sugar blend
1/2	cup sugar
2	eggs
1/4	cup canola oil
1	container (2-1/2 ounces) prune baby food
3	teaspoons white vinegar
1	teaspoon vanilla extract
1	cup fat-free milk
1	cup cold strong brewed coffee
3	cups all-purpose flour
1/3	cup baking cocoa
2	teaspoons baking soda
1	teaspoon salt

FROSTING:

1	teaspoon instant coffee granules
1	teaspoon hot water
1/2	teaspoon vanilla extract
2	cups whipped topping

In a large bowl, combine the first seven ingredients; beat until well blended. In a small bowl, combine milk and coffee. Combine the flour, cocoa, baking soda and salt; gradually beat into egg mixture alternately with milk mixture.

Pour into a 13-in. x 9-in. baking pan coated with cooking spray. Bake at 350° for 30-35 minutes or until a toothpick inserted near the center comes out clean. Cool on a wire rack.

In a small bowl, dissolve coffee granules in hot water. Stir in vanilla extract. Place whipped topping in a large bowl; gently fold in the coffee mixture. Frost cake. Store cake in the refrigerator. **YIELD: 24 servings.**

NUTRITION FACTS: 1 piece equals 151 calories, 4 g fat (1 g saturated fat), 18 mg cholesterol, 214 mg sodium, 25 g carbohydrate, 1 g fiber, 3 g protein. **DIABETIC EXCHANGES:** 1-1/2 starch, 1 fat.

EDITOR'S NOTE: This recipe was tested with Splenda sugar blend.

HEATHER RATIGAN, KAUFMAN, TEXAS
I don't usually create my own recipes, but this one passed my family's palate test. It offers a buttery flavor that those of us who are watching our weight miss at times.

rice with summer squash

PREP: 15 MINUTES / **COOK:** 25 MINUTES

1	cup chopped carrots
1/2	cup chopped onion
1	tablespoon butter
1	cup reduced-sodium chicken broth *or* vegetable broth
1/3	cup uncooked long grain rice
1/4	teaspoon salt
1/4	teaspoon pepper
1	medium yellow summer squash, chopped
1	medium zucchini, chopped

In a saucepan coated with cooking spray, cook the carrots and onion in butter until tender. Stir in the chicken broth, rice, salt and pepper. Bring to a boil. Reduce heat; cover and simmer for 13 minutes.

Stir in the yellow summer squash and zucchini. Cover and simmer 6-10 minutes longer or until the rice and vegetables are tender. **YIELD: 4 servings.**

NUTRITION FACTS: 3/4 cup equals 123 calories, 3 g fat (2 g saturated fat), 8 mg cholesterol, 346 mg sodium, 21 g carbohydrate, 3 g fiber, 4 g protein. **DIABETIC EXCHANGES:** 1 starch, 1 vegetable, 1/2 fat.

READERS' RAVES

> Two of our children who otherwise won't eat zucchini and squash love this dish. We prefer brown rice, and substitute it for the long-grain rice, with the following changes. I saute the onion in the butter and add the brown rice and water. After about 45 minutes, I add the carrot. I add the zucchini and squash during the last 5 minutes of cooking. It's delicious!
>
> —Koekkenchef
> from TasteofHome.com

ANGELA OELSCHLAEGER, TONGANOXIE, KANSAS
For a simple but sensational side dish, I throw together this refreshing medley that stars the unusual combination of broccoli and raisins. I adjusted a friend's recipe to cut a few calories. The raisins add sweetness, and the bacon gives it a nice crunch.

broccoli raisin salad

PREP: 10 MINUTES + CHILLING

4	cups fresh broccoli florets (1 medium bunch)
3/4	cup golden raisins
1	small red onion, chopped
1/2	cup Miracle Whip
1	tablespoon white vinegar
2	teaspoons sugar
3	bacon strips, cooked and crumbled

In a large bowl, combine the broccoli, raisins and onion. In a small bowl, combine Miracle Whip, vinegar and sugar. Pour over broccoli mixture; toss to coat. Sprinkle with bacon. Refrigerate for at least 2 hours before serving. **YIELD: 6 servings.**

NUTRITION FACTS: 3/4 cup equals 116 calories, 2 g fat (1 g saturated fat), 3 mg cholesterol, 226 mg sodium, 23 g carbohydrate, 2 g fiber, 3 g protein. **DIABETIC EXCHANGES:** 1 vegetable, 1 fruit, 1/2 fat.

KRISTI LINTON, BAY CITY, MICHIGAN
This creamy, lightened-up dessert makes an amazing after-dinner treat—especially when served in pretty stemmed glasses. Break out the spoons and make sure you get a bite, because it won't last long!

makeover dirt dessert

PREP: 30 MINUTES + CHILLING

1	package (8 ounces) fat-free cream cheese
1	package (3 ounces) cream cheese, softened
3/4	cup confectioners' sugar
3-1/2	cups cold fat-free milk
2	packages (1 ounce *each*) sugar-free instant vanilla pudding mix
1	carton (12 ounces) frozen reduced-fat whipped topping, thawed
1	package (18 ounces) reduced-fat cream-filled chocolate sandwich cookies, crushed

In a large bowl, beat cream cheeses and confectioners' sugar until smooth. In a large bowl, whisk milk and pudding mixes for 2 minutes; let stand for 2 minutes or until soft-set. Gradually stir into cream cheese mixture. Fold in whipped topping.

Spread 1-1/3 cups of crushed cookies into an ungreased 13-in. x 9-in. dish. Layer with half of the pudding mixture and half of the remaining cookies. Repeat layers. Refrigerate for at least 1 hour before serving. **YIELD: 20 servings.**

NUTRITION FACTS: 1/2 cup equals 208 calories, 6 g fat (4 g saturated fat), 6 mg cholesterol, 364 mg sodium, 33 g carbohydrate, 1 g fiber, 5 g protein. **DIABETIC EXCHANGES:** 2 starch, 1 fat.

AMY TRINKLE, MILWAUKEE, WISCONSIN
I can't remember when or where I found this recipe, but I've used it nearly every week since. We like the Southwestern favorite with hot sauce for added spice.

baked chicken fajitas

PREP/TOTAL TIME: 30 MINUTES

1	pound boneless skinless chicken breasts, cut into thin strips
1	can (14-1/2 ounces) diced tomatoes and green chilies, drained
1	medium onion, cut into thin strips
1	medium green pepper, cut into thin strips
1	medium sweet red pepper, cut into thin strips
2	tablespoons canola oil
2	teaspoons chili powder
2	teaspoons ground cumin
1/4	teaspoon salt
12	flour tortillas (6 inches), warmed

In a 13-in. x 9-in. baking dish coated with cooking spray, combine the chicken, tomatoes, onion and peppers. Combine the oil, chili powder, cumin and salt. Drizzle over chicken mixture; toss to coat.

Bake, uncovered, at 400° for 20-25 minutes or until chicken is no longer pink and vegetables are tender. Spoon onto tortillas; fold in sides. **YIELD: 6 servings.**

NUTRITION FACTS: 2 fajitas equals 340 calories, 8 g fat (1 g saturated fat), 44 mg cholesterol, 330 mg sodium, 41 g carbohydrate, 5 g fiber, 27 g protein. **DIABETIC EXCHANGES:** 2 starch, 2 lean meat, 2 vegetable, 1/2 fat.

JOANN DESMOND, MADISON HEIGHTS, VIRGINIA
I got this wonderful recipe from a cousin whose husband was Hawaiian. I've changed it some to reduce the fat and calories, but it still tastes as rich as the original. It's very simple to make...and everyone loves it!

hawaiian wedding cake

PREP: 20 MINUTES / **BAKE:** 25 MINUTES + COOLING

1	package (18-1/4 ounces) yellow cake mix
1-1/4	cups buttermilk
4	egg whites
1	egg
1	package (8 ounces) reduced-fat cream cheese, cubed
1	cup cold 2% milk
1	package (1 ounce) sugar-free instant vanilla pudding mix
2	cans (one 20 ounces, one 8 ounces) unsweetened crushed pineapple, drained
1	carton (8 ounces) frozen fat-free whipped topping, thawed
1/2	cup flaked coconut, toasted

In a large bowl, combine the cake mix, buttermilk, egg whites and egg; beat on low speed for 30 seconds. Beat on medium speed for 2 minutes.

Transfer to a 13-in. x 9-in. baking pan coated with cooking spray. Bake at 350° for 25-30 minutes or until a toothpick inserted near the center comes out clean. Cool on a wire rack.

In a small bowl, beat cream cheese until fluffy. Gradually beat in milk; add pudding mix until well blended. Spread over the cake. Top with pineapple and whipped topping. Sprinkle cake with coconut. Store in the refrigerator. **YIELD: 18 servings.**

NUTRITION FACTS: 1 piece equals 221 calories, 5 g fat (2 g saturated fat), 17 mg cholesterol, 378 mg sodium, 38 g carbohydrate, 1 g fiber, 6 g protein. **DIABETIC EXCHANGES:** 2 starch, 1 fat, 1/2 fruit.

Cook pasta according to package directions. Meanwhile, in a small bowl, beat cream cheese until smooth. Beat in milk. Stir in spinach and oregano; set aside.

In a nonstick skillet, cook beef and garlic over medium heat until meat is no longer pink; drain. Stir in the picante sauce, tomato sauce, tomato paste, chili powder and cumin; bring to a boil. Reduce heat; simmer, uncovered, for 5 minutes. Drain pasta; stir into meat mixture.

In a 13-in. x 9-in. baking dish coated with cooking spray, layer half of the meat mixture and all of the spinach mixture. Top with remaining meat mixture.

Cover and bake at 350° for 30 minutes. Uncover; sprinkle with cheddar cheese. Bake 5 minutes longer or until the cheese is melted. Sprinkle with the olives and onions. Let stand for 10 minutes before serving. **YIELD: 8 servings.**

NUTRITION FACTS: 1 serving equals 328 calories, 9 g fat (4 g saturated fat), 40 mg cholesterol, 855 mg sodium, 36 g carbohydrate, 4 g fiber, 25 g protein. **DIABETIC EXCHANGES:** 3 lean meat, 2 vegetable, 1-1/2 starch.

CAROL LEPAK, SHEBOYGAN, WISCONSIN
Fat-free cream cheese and reduced-fat cheddar make this creamy casserole lower in fat and calories. It's a good way to get our kids to eat spinach in "disguise."

southwest pasta bake

PREP: 15 MINUTES / **BAKE:** 30 MINUTES + STANDING

8	ounces uncooked penne pasta
1	package (8 ounces) fat-free cream cheese, cubed
1/2	cup fat-free milk
1	package (10 ounces) frozen chopped spinach, thawed and squeezed dry
1	teaspoon dried oregano
1	pound lean ground beef
2	garlic cloves, minced
1	jar (16 ounces) picante sauce
1	can (8 ounces) no-salt-added tomato sauce
1	can (6 ounces) no-salt-added tomato paste
2	teaspoons chili powder
1	teaspoon ground cumin
1	cup (4 ounces) shredded reduced-fat cheddar cheese
1	can (2-1/4 ounces) sliced ripe olives, drained
1/4	cup sliced green onions

BRENDA RUSE, TRURO, NOVA SCOTIA
You won't miss the fat when you taste this moist, fudgy dessert that lets you have your cake and eat it, too! To save calories and fat, I substituted yogurt for the oil called for in a reduced-fat box mix to create this delicious cake.

guilt-free chocolate cake

PREP: 10 MINUTES / **BAKE:** 35 MINUTES + COOLING

1	package (18-1/4 ounces) devil's food cake mix
1-1/3	cups water
1	cup reduced-fat plain yogurt
1/2	cup baking cocoa
2	egg whites
1	egg
1-1/2	teaspoons confectioners' sugar

In a large bowl, combine the cake mix, water, yogurt, cocoa, egg whites and egg; beat on low for 30 seconds. Beat on medium for 2 minutes.

Pour into a 10-in. fluted tube pan coated with cooking spray. Bake at 350° for 35-40 minutes or until a toothpick inserted near the center comes out clean. Let cool for 10 minutes before removing from pan to a wire rack to cool completely. Dust with confectioners' sugar. **YIELD: 12 servings.**

NUTRITION FACTS: 1 piece equals 191 calories, 3 g fat (1 g saturated fat), 19 mg cholesterol, 399 mg sodium, 40 g carbohydrate, 2 g fiber, 5 g protein. **DIABETIC EXCHANGE:** 2-1/2 starch.

MONICA SHIPLEY, TULARE, CALIFORNIA
Pork tenderloin meat is treated to a rich and tasty sauce with a slight red-pepper kick. It's simple to prepare and always tasty.

tenderloin with herb sauce

PREP/TOTAL TIME: 25 MINUTES

2	pork tenderloins (1 pound *each*)
1/2	teaspoon salt
4	teaspoons butter
2/3	cup half-and-half cream
2	tablespoons minced fresh parsley
2	teaspoons herbes de Provence
2	teaspoons reduced-sodium soy sauce
1	teaspoon beef bouillon granules
1/2	to 3/4 teaspoon crushed red pepper flakes

Cut each tenderloin into 12 slices; sprinkle with salt. In a large nonstick skillet coated with cooking spray, brown pork in butter in batches over medium heat for 3-4 minutes on each side or until no longer pink. Return all pork to the skillet.

Combine the remaining ingredients; pour over pork. Cook and stir over low heat for 2-3 minutes or until sauce is thickened. **YIELD: 6 servings.**

NUTRITION FACTS: 4 ounces cooked pork with 2 tablespoons sauce equals 238 calories, 10 g fat (5 g saturated fat), 104 mg cholesterol, 495 mg sodium, 2 g carbohydrate, trace fiber, 31 g protein. **DIABETIC EXCHANGES:** 4 lean meat, 1 fat.

EDITOR'S NOTE: Look for herbes de Provence in the spice aisle. It is also available from Penzeys Spices. Call 1-800/741-7787 or visit www.penzeys.com.

BETTY JO MORRIS, LITTLE ROCK, ARKANSAS
Whether set on appetizer trays or dessert buffets, these darling bites will surely disappear in no time. I created the recipe by combining two of my favorite treats.

wonton sundaes

PREP: 25 MINUTES / **BAKE:** 10 MINUTES + COOLING

24	wonton wrappers
	Refrigerated butter-flavored spray
1	tablespoon plus 1/4 cup sugar, *divided*
1	teaspoon ground cinnamon
1	package (8 ounces) reduced-fat cream cheese
1	teaspoon vanilla extract
1/4	cup semisweet chocolate chips
1/4	cup chopped pecans
24	maraschino cherries with stems

Place wonton wrappers on a work surface; spritz with butter-flavored spray. Combine 1 tablespoon sugar and cinnamon; sprinkle over wontons. Press into miniature muffin cups coated with cooking spray.

Bake at 350° for 4-5 minutes or until lightly browned. Immediately remove wonton cups to an ungreased baking sheet. Bake 2-3 minutes longer or until bottoms of cups are lightly browned. Remove to a wire rack to cool.

In a small bowl, beat the cream cheese, vanilla and remaining sugar until smooth. Stir in chocolate chips and pecans. Spoon into wonton cups. Top each with a cherry. **YIELD: 2 dozen.**

NUTRITION FACTS: 1 sundae equals 83 calories, 3 g fat (1 g saturated fat), 6 mg cholesterol, 74 mg sodium, 12 g carbohydrate, trace fiber, 2 g protein. **DIABETIC EXCHANGE:** 1 starch.

LINDA UTTER, SIDNEY, MONTANA
This recipe proves you don't have to fudge on chocolate to make a decadent delight. These moist cupcakes are chock-full of sweet flavor, but they're low in saturated fat.

double chocolate cupcakes

PREP: 20 MINUTES / **BAKE:** 15 MINUTES + COOLING

2	tablespoons butter, softened
3/4	cup sugar
1	egg
1	egg white
1/2	cup plus 2 tablespoons buttermilk
1/3	cup water
1	tablespoon white vinegar
1	teaspoon vanilla extract
1-1/2	cups all-purpose flour
1/4	cup baking cocoa
1	teaspoon baking soda
1/2	teaspoon salt
1/3	cup miniature semisweet chocolate chips

In a large bowl, cream butter and sugar until light and fluffy. Add egg and egg white, one at a time, beating well after each addition. Beat on high speed until light and fluffy. Stir in the buttermilk, water, vinegar and vanilla. Combine the flour, cocoa, baking soda and salt; add to batter just until moistened. Stir in chocolate chips.

Fill muffin cups coated with cooking spray three-fourths full. Bake at 375° for 15-18 minutes or until a toothpick comes out clean. Cool for 5 minutes before removing from pans to wire racks. **YIELD: 14 cupcakes.**

NUTRITION FACTS: 1 cupcake equals 139 calories, 2 g fat (1 g saturated fat), 1 mg cholesterol, 221 mg sodium, 29 g carbohydrate, 1 g fiber, 3 g protein. DIABETIC EXCHANGES: 1-1/2 starch, 1/2 fat.

VALERIE MITCHELL, OLATHE, KANSAS
These creamy garlic mashed potatoes are so good, you can serve them plain—no butter or gravy is needed. Now, this is the only way my family prepares mashed potatoes.

garlic mashed red potatoes

PREP/TOTAL TIME: 30 MINUTES

8	medium red potatoes, quartered
3	garlic cloves, peeled
2	tablespoons butter
1/2	cup fat-free milk, warmed
1/2	teaspoon salt
1/4	cup grated Parmesan cheese

Place potatoes and garlic in a large saucepan; cover with water. Bring to a boil. Reduce heat; cover and simmer for 20-25 minutes or until the potatoes are very tender. Drain well. Add the butter, milk and salt; mash. Stir in Parmesan cheese. **YIELD: 6 servings.**

NUTRITION FACTS: 1 cup equals 190 calories, 5 g fat (3 g saturated fat), 14 mg cholesterol, 275 mg sodium, 36 g carbohydrate, 4 g fiber, 8 g protein. DIABETIC EXCHANGES: 2 starch, 1/2 fat.

READERS' RAVES

> These garlic mashed potatoes have fantastic flavor and are easy to prepare. The recipe can be doubled or even halved with no change in texture or flavor. This recipe has replaced our regular mashed potato side dish.
>
> —Wlachef from TasteofHome.com

> These are awesome. My husband loves potatoes in pretty much any way, shape or form, but he particularly loves red potatoes. This has become his favorite red potato recipe.
>
> —Aquarelle from TasteofHome.com

HEATHER BYERS, PITTSBURGH, PENNSYLVANIA

For a tasty twist, I jazz up fries with paprika and garlic powder. Something about the combination of spices packs a hefty punch. Everyone loves them—we even enjoy them as cold leftovers.

oven fries

PREP: 10 MINUTES / **BAKE:** 40 MINUTES

4	medium potatoes
1	tablespoon olive oil
2-1/2	teaspoons paprika
3/4	teaspoon salt
3/4	teaspoon garlic powder

Cut each potato into 12 wedges. In a large bowl, combine the oil, paprika, salt and garlic powder. Add potatoes; toss to coat.

Transfer to a 15-in. x 10-in. baking pan coated with cooking spray. Bake at 400° for 40-45 minutes or until tender, turning once. **YIELD: 4 servings.**

NUTRITION FACTS: 12 potato wedges equals 204 calories, 4 g fat (1 g saturated fat), 0 cholesterol, 456 mg sodium, 39 g carbohydrate, 4 g fiber, 5 g protein.

DIANE MARTIN, BROWN DEER, WISCONSIN

There are no complicated steps to follow when preparing this roasted medley of tender pork and veggies. Just season with a flavorful blend of herbs, then pop it in the oven for less than an hour.

roasted pork tenderloin and vegetables

PREP: 10 MINUTES / **BAKE:** 30 MINUTES

2	pork tenderloins (3/4 pound *each*)
2	pounds red potatoes, quartered
1	pound carrots, halved and cut into 2-inch pieces
1	medium onion, cut into wedges
1	tablespoon olive oil
2	teaspoons dried rosemary, crushed
1	teaspoon rubbed sage
1/2	teaspoon salt
1/4	teaspoon pepper

Place the pork in a shallow roasting pan coated with cooking spray; arrange the potatoes, carrots and onion around pork. Drizzle with oil. Combine the seasonings; sprinkle over meat and vegetables.

Bake, uncovered, at 450° for 30-40 minutes or until a meat thermometer reads 160°, stirring vegetables occasionally. **YIELD: 6 servings.**

NUTRITION FACTS: 3 ounces cooked meat with 1 cup vegetables equals 331 calories, 7 g fat (2 g saturated fat), 67 mg cholesterol, 299 mg sodium, 40 g carbohydrate, 5 g fiber, 28 g protein. **DIABETIC EXCHANGES:** 3 lean meat, 2 starch, 1 vegetable.

TASTE OF HOME TEST KITCHEN
Decreasing the amount of butter and replacing the half-and-half with milk helped cut a whopping 658 calories and more than half the fat from a popular casserole. Even though the cholesterol was reduced by 75% and the sodium by 40%, this gooey and cheesy baked entree offers all the heartwarming flavor of the original version.

makeover sloppy joe mac and cheese

PREP: 1 HOUR / **BAKE:** 30 MINUTES

1	package (16 ounces) elbow macaroni
3/4	pound lean ground turkey
1/2	cup finely chopped celery
1/2	cup shredded carrot
1	can (14-1/2 ounces) diced tomatoes, undrained
1	can (6 ounces) tomato paste
1/2	cup water
1	envelope sloppy joe mix
1	small onion, finely chopped
1	tablespoon butter
1/3	cup all-purpose flour
1	teaspoon ground mustard
3/4	teaspoon salt
1/4	teaspoon pepper
4	cups 2% milk
1	tablespoon Worcestershire sauce
8	ounces reduced-fat process cheese (Velveeta), cubed
2	cups (8 ounces) shredded cheddar cheese, *divided*

Cook macaroni according to package directions. Meanwhile, in a large nonstick skillet, cook the turkey, celery and carrot over medium heat until meat is no longer pink and vegetables are tender; drain. Add the tomatoes, tomato paste, water and sloppy joe mix. Bring to a boil. Reduce heat; cover and simmer for 10 minutes, stirring occasionally.

Drain macaroni; set aside. In a large saucepan, saute onion in butter until tender. Stir in the flour, mustard, salt and pepper until smooth. Gradually add milk and Worcestershire sauce. Bring to a boil; cook and stir for 1-2 minutes or until thickened. Remove from the heat. Stir in the process cheese until melted. Add macaroni and 1 cup cheddar cheese; mix well.

Spread two-thirds of the macaroni mixture in a 13-in. x 9-in. baking dish coated with cooking spray. Spread turkey mixture to within 2 in. of edges. Spoon remaining macaroni mixture around edges of pan. Cover and bake at 375° for 30-35 minutes or until bubbly. Uncover; sprinkle with remaining cheddar cheese. Cover and let stand until cheese is melted. **YIELD: 10 servings.**

NUTRITION FACTS: 1 cup equals 353 calories, 12 g fat (7 g saturated fat), 54 mg cholesterol, 877 mg sodium, 42 g carbohydrate, 3 g fiber, 20 g protein. **DIABETIC EXCHANGES:** 2 starch, 1-1/2 fat, 1 reduced-fat milk.

CAROLYN TOMATZ, JACKSON, WISCONSIN
I can't believe how effortless this pretty salad is to make. The colorful blend of bananas, pineapple, pears, peaches and grapes is tossed with a creamy pudding mixture. People of all ages enjoy this dish.

grandma's fruit salad

PREP: 25 MINUTES + CHILLING

1	can (20 ounces) unsweetened pineapple chunks
1	can (15 ounces) reduced-sugar sliced pears, drained
1	can (15 ounces) sliced peaches in juice, drained
1-1/2	cups seedless red grapes
1	package (3 ounces) cook-and-serve vanilla pudding mix
2	medium firm bananas
3	tablespoons lemon juice
1	jar (10 ounces) maraschino cherries, well drained

Drain pineapple, reserving juice in a 1-cup measuring cup. In a large bowl, combine the pineapple, pears, peaches and grapes. Cover and chill.

Add enough water to pineapple juice to measure 1 cup. Pour into a small saucepan. Whisk in pudding mix. Bring to a boil over medium heat, stirring constantly. Remove from heat; set aside to cool to room temperature.

Slice the bananas into a small bowl. Drizzle with lemon juice; gently toss to coat. Let stand for 5 minutes; drain. Add the bananas and cherries to chilled fruit. Add cooled pudding; toss gently to combine. Refrigerate salad until serving. Refrigerate leftovers. **YIELD: 12 servings (1/2 cup per serving).**

NUTRITION FACTS: 1/2 cup equals 126 calories, trace fat (trace saturated fat), 0 cholesterol, 59 mg sodium, 33 g carbohydrate, 2 g fiber, 1 g protein. **DIABETIC EXCHANGE:** 2 fruit.

NANCY GRANAMAN, BURLINGTON, IOWA
This restaurant specialty is usually high in fat and calories. But in this version, the flavor really comes from deglazing the skillet with the broth and wine, so even though I eliminated extra oil, the taste isn't lost.

chicken marsala

PREP: 25 MINUTES + MARINATING / **BAKE:** 25 MINUTES

- 6   boneless skinless chicken breast halves (4 ounces *each*)
- 1   cup fat-free Italian salad dressing
- 1   tablespoon all-purpose flour
- 1   teaspoon Italian seasoning
- 1/2   teaspoon garlic powder
- 1/4   teaspoon paprika
- 1/4   teaspoon pepper
- 2   tablespoons olive oil, *divided*
- 1   tablespoon butter
- 1/2   cup reduced-sodium chicken broth
- 1/2   cup Marsala wine *or* 3 tablespoons unsweetened apple juice plus 5 tablespoons additional reduced-sodium chicken broth
- 1   pound sliced fresh mushrooms
- 1/2   cup minced fresh parsley

Flatten chicken to 1/2-in. thickness. Place in a large resealable plastic bag; add salad dressing. Seal bag and turn to coat; refrigerate for 8 hours or overnight.

Drain and discard marinade. Combine flour, Italian seasoning, garlic powder, paprika and pepper; sprinkle over both sides of chicken. In a large nonstick skillet coated with cooking spray, cook chicken in 1 tablespoon oil and butter for 2 minutes on each side or until browned. Transfer to a 13-in. x 9-in. baking dish coated with cooking spray.

Gradually add broth and wine to skillet, stirring to loosen browned bits. Bring to a boil; cook and stir for 2 minutes. Strain sauce; set aside. In the same skillet, cook mushrooms in remaining oil for 2 minutes; drain. Stir sauce into mushrooms; heat through. Pour over chicken; sprinkle with parsley. Bake, uncovered, at 350° for 25-30 minutes or until chicken juices run clear. **YIELD: 6 servings.**

NUTRITION FACTS: 1 chicken breast half with 1/3 cup mushroom mixture equals 247 calories, 9 g fat (3 g saturated fat), 68 mg cholesterol, 348 mg sodium, 9 g carbohydrate, 1 g fiber, 26 g protein. **DIABETIC EXCHANGES:** 3 very lean meat, 1-1/2 fat, 1/2 starch.

KIM BELCHER, KINGSTON MINES, ILLINOIS
I cut 90% of the fat and nearly half the calories from one of my favorite desserts for this must-try sensation. Taste it for yourself. Guests never suspect the fluffy, layered specialty topped with candy bars is on the light side.

light toffee crunch dessert

PREP: 20 MINUTES + CHILLING

- 1-1/2   cups cold fat-free milk
- 1   package (1 ounce) sugar-free instant vanilla pudding mix
- 2   cartons (8 ounces *each*) frozen fat-free whipped topping, thawed
- 1   prepared angel food cake (16 ounces), cubed
- 4   Butterfinger candy bars (2.1 ounces *each*), crushed

In a large bowl, whisk milk and pudding mix for 2 minutes. Let stand for 2 minutes or until soft-set. Stir in 2 cups whipped topping. Fold in the remaining whipped topping.

In a 13-in. x 9-in. dish coated with cooking spray, layer half of the cake cubes, pudding mixture and crushed candy bars. Repeat layers. Cover and refrigerate for at least 2 hours before serving. **YIELD: 15 servings.**

NUTRITION FACTS: 3/4 cup equals 219 calories, 3 g fat (2 g saturated fat), 1 mg cholesterol, 366 mg sodium, 41 g carbohydrate, 1 g fiber, 5 g protein. **DIABETIC EXCHANGES:** 2-1/2 starch, 1/2 fat.

ALICE REED, WEBSTER, NEW YORK
This light and refreshing dessert is a snap to make using prepared angel food cake and convenient canned peaches. I sometimes layer it in a glass trifle bowl and top it with fresh raspberries, sliced fresh peaches and a sprig of mint for a truly elegant presentation that really stands out on a dessert table.

raspberry peach delight

PREP: 20 MINUTES + CHILLING

1	prepared angel food cake (8 inches), cut into 1-inch cubes
1	package (.3 ounce) sugar-free raspberry gelatin
1	cup boiling water
1	cup cold water
1	can (15 ounces) sliced peaches in juice, well drained and halved
3	cups cold fat-free milk
1	package (1.5 ounces) sugar-free instant vanilla pudding mix
1	carton (8 ounces) frozen reduced-fat whipped topping, thawed

Arrange the angel food cake cubes in a 13-in. x 9-in. dish. In a small bowl, dissolve the raspberry gelatin in boiling water; stir in cold water. Pour over cake. Arrange the sliced peaches over the gelatin.

In a large bowl, whisk milk and pudding mix for 2 minutes. Let stand for 2 minutes or until soft-set. Spoon over the peaches. Top with whipped topping. Cover and refrigerate for at least 2 hours before cutting. **YIELD: 15 servings.**

NUTRITION FACTS: 1 piece equals 76 calories, 2 g fat (2 g saturated fat), 1 mg cholesterol, 171 mg sodium, 11 g carbohydrate, trace fiber, 2 g protein. DIABETIC EXCHANGES: 1 starch, 1 fruit.

SUSAN AUTEN, DALLAS, GEORGIA
People always go back for seconds when I serve these rich, creamy potatoes. The casserole is a snap to fix and ideal when you're craving comfort food, but watching your fat and calories.

hash brown casserole

PREP: 10 MINUTES / **BAKE:** 55 MINUTES

2	cans (10-3/4 ounces *each*) condensed cream of potato soup, undiluted
1	cup (8 ounces) sour cream
1/2	teaspoon garlic salt
1	package (2 pounds) frozen hash brown potatoes
2	cups (8 ounces) shredded cheddar cheese
1/2	cup grated Parmesan cheese

In a large bowl, combine the cream of potato soup, sour cream and garlic salt. Add the hash brown potatoes and cheddar cheese; mix well.

Pour mixture into a greased 13-in. x 9-in. baking dish. Top with the grated Parmesan cheese. Bake, uncovered, at 350° for 55-60 minutes or until the potatoes are tender. **YIELD: 12-16 servings.**

NUTRITION FACTS: 1 cup equals 157 calories, 8 g fat (6 g saturated fat), 30 mg cholesterol, 357 mg sodium, 13 g carbohydrate, 1 g fiber, 7 g protein.

JON CAROLE GILBREATH, TYLER, TEXAS
Chicken and rice are dressed up with a zippy sauce to create a complete meal that's ready in a dash. Garnished with fresh cilantro, it's a quick weeknight supper you can feel good about.

santa fe chicken

PREP/TOTAL TIME: 30 MINUTES

- 1 large onion, chopped
- 1 to 2 tablespoons chopped seeded jalapeno pepper
- 1 garlic clove, minced
- 1 tablespoon olive oil
- 1-1/4 cups reduced-sodium chicken broth
- 1 can (10 ounces) diced tomatoes and green chilies, undrained
- 1 cup uncooked long grain rice
- 4 boneless skinless chicken breast halves (4 ounces *each*)
- 1/2 teaspoon salt
- 1/4 teaspoon pepper
- 1/4 teaspoon ground cumin
- 3/4 cup shredded reduced-fat cheddar cheese

Minced fresh cilantro, optional

In a large skillet, saute the onion, jalapeno and garlic in oil until tender. Add broth and tomatoes; bring to a boil. Stir in rice.

Sprinkle chicken with salt, pepper and cumin; place over rice mixture. Cover and simmer for 10-15 minutes on each side or until chicken juices run clear.

Remove rice mixture and chicken from the heat. Sprinkle with cheese; cover and let stand for 5 minutes. Garnish with cilantro if desired. **YIELD: 4 servings.**

NUTRITION FACTS: 1 chicken breast half with 1 cup rice mixture equals 412 calories, 11 g fat (4 g saturated fat), 78 mg cholesterol, 966 mg sodium, 44 g carbohydrate, 2 g fiber, 33 g protein. **DIABETIC EXCHANGES:** 3 very lean meat, 2 starch, 2 fat, 1 vegetable.

EDITOR'S NOTE: When cutting hot peppers, disposable gloves are recommended. Avoid touching your face.

MILDRED KELLER, ROCKFORD, ILLINOIS
The recipe for these tangy bars comes from my cousin Bernice, a farmer's wife who is famous for cooking up feasts. Packed with loads of lemon flavor, this handheld treat is perfect year-round and a bestseller at bake sales.

bake-sale lemon bars

PREP: 10 MINUTES / **BAKE:** 40 MINUTES + COOLING

- 1-1/2 cups all-purpose flour
- 2/3 cup confectioners' sugar
- 3/4 cup butter, softened
- 3 eggs, lightly beaten
- 1-1/2 cups sugar
- 3 tablespoons all-purpose flour
- 1/4 cup lemon juice

Additional confectioners' sugar

In a small bowl, combine flour, sugar and butter until crumbly; pat crumb mixture into a greased 13-in. x 9-in. baking pan. Bake at 350° for 20 minutes.

Meanwhile, in a bowl, whisk the eggs, sugar, flour and lemon juice until frothy; pour mixture over the hot crust.

Bake at 350° for 20-25 minutes or until light golden brown. Cool on a wire rack. Dust with confectioners' sugar. Cut into squares. **YIELD: 3-4 dozen.**

NUTRITION FACTS: 2 bars equals 153 calories, 6 g fat (4 g saturated fat), 42 mg cholesterol, 66 mg sodium, 23 g carbohydrate, trace fiber, 2 g protein.

READERS' RAVES

" These are so good and easy to make! I like to substitute crushed 'Nilla Wafers for the flour and sugar used in the crust. Turned out great! "

—Meredith1975
from TasteofHome.com

quick & easy

Just because you're short on time doesn't mean you have to sacrifice a good home-cooked meal. In mere moments, you can have a family-pleasing casserole, pasta entree, chicken main dish—even dessert—baking in the oven, thanks to these effortless favorites that prep in 30 minutes or less.

ARTICHOKE CHICKEN FETTUCCINE / PAGE 170

JENN SCHLACHTER, BIG ROCK, ILLINOIS

All ages really seem to go for this comforting, scrumptious meal-in-one. It takes just a handful of ingredients and a few minutes to put together. I've found that adding dried cranberries to the stuffing mix boosts the flavor and color wonderfully!

broccoli chicken casserole

PREP: 15 MINUTES / **BAKE:** 30 MINUTES

1-1/2	cups water
1	package (6 ounces) chicken stuffing mix
2	cups cubed cooked chicken
1	cup frozen broccoli florets, thawed

1	can (10-3/4 ounces) condensed broccoli cheese soup, undiluted
1	cup (4 ounces) shredded cheddar cheese

In a small saucepan, bring water to a boil. Stir in stuffing mix. Remove from the heat; cover and let the stuffing stand for 5 minutes.

Meanwhile, layer the chicken and broccoli florets in a greased 11-in. x 7-in. baking dish. Top the chicken and broccoli with broccoli cheese soup. Fluff the stuffing with a fork; spoon stuffing over soup. Sprinkle with shredded cheddar cheese. Bake, uncovered, at 350° for 30-35 minutes or until heated through. **YIELD: 6 servings.**

TASTE OF HOME TEST KITCHEN
Smoky kielbasa steals the show in this home-style all-in-one meal that can be on the table in half an hour!

potato kielbasa skillet

PREP/TOTAL TIME: 30 MINUTES

1	pound red potatoes, cubed
3	tablespoons water
3/4	pound smoked kielbasa *or* Polish sausage, cut into 1/4-inch slices
1/2	cup chopped onion
1	tablespoon olive oil
2	tablespoons brown sugar
2	tablespoons cider vinegar
1	tablespoon Dijon mustard
1/2	teaspoon dried thyme
1/4	teaspoon pepper
4	cups fresh baby spinach
5	bacon strips, cooked and crumbled

Place potatoes and water in a microwave-safe dish. Cover and microwave on high for 4 minutes or until tender; drain.

In a large skillet, saute kielbasa and onion in oil until onion is tender. Add potatoes; saute 3-5 minutes longer or until kielbasa and potatoes are lightly browned.

Combine the brown sugar, vinegar, mustard, thyme and pepper; stir into skillet. Bring to a boil. Reduce heat; simmer, uncovered, for 2-3 minutes or until heated through. Add spinach and bacon; cook and stir until spinach is wilted. **YIELD: 4 servings.**

WANDA BORGEN, MINOT, NORTH DAKOTA
If your gang likes corn chips, they'll love the sweet and salty blend in these fast-fixing bars. They also make great take-along treats for picnics or tailgate parties. They are so easy to create, the kids just may want to make their own batch.

salty peanut squares

PREP: 15 MINUTES + COOLING

1	package (10 ounces) corn chips, lightly crushed, *divided*
1	cup unsalted peanuts, *divided*
1	cup light corn syrup
1	cup sugar
1	cup peanut butter
1/2	cup milk chocolate chips, melted

Place half of the corn chips and peanuts in a greased 13-in. x 9-in. pan; set aside. In a large saucepan, bring the corn syrup and sugar to a boil. Stir in peanut butter until blended. Drizzle half over corn chip mixture in pan.

Add remaining corn chips and peanuts to remaining syrup; stir until combined. Spoon over mixture in pan; press down lightly. Drizzle with melted chocolate. Cool before cutting. **YIELD: 2 dozen.**

LYNNE BARGAR, SAEGERTOWN, PENNSYLVANIA

I made a few alterations to a great recipe and ended up with an impressive dessert. Everyone loves its appearance, light texture and chocolaty flavor.

chocolate swirl delight

PREP: 20 MINUTES + CHILLING

1	package (13 ounces) Swiss cake rolls
2-3/4	cups cold milk
2	packages (3.9 ounces *each*) instant chocolate fudge pudding mix
2	cups whipped topping

Cut each cake roll into eight slices; set aside any chocolate coating that separates from rolls for garnish. Line a 9-in. springform pan with cake slices, completely covering the bottom and sides.

In a small bowl, whisk milk and pudding mixes for 2 minutes. Let stand for 2 minutes or until soft-set. Pour over cake. Spread with whipped topping; sprinkle with any reserved chocolate coating.

Cover and refrigerate for at least 2 hours before serving. **YIELD: 12 servings.**

KITCHEN TIP

To make the whipped topping used in Chocolate Swirl Delight extra special, try stirring in 2 to 3 drops of almond or vanilla extract. It livens up the flavor with a delicious richness. If there is any whipped topping remaining in the container, drop it by rounded spoonfuls onto a cookie sheet and freeze. Place the frozen dollops into small resealable plastic bags and return to the freezer. The next time you serve hot chocolate or coffee beverages, top each serving with a frozen dollop.

SUE MILLER, MARS, PENNSYLVANIA

Whenever we get together as a family for Thanksgiving or Christmas, my kids, nieces and nephews literally beg me to make this comforting side dish. It goes together in minutes thanks to canned sweet potatoes, which is ideal for the busy holiday season.

buttery sweet potato casserole

PREP: 15 MINUTES / **BAKE:** 20 MINUTES

2	cans (15-3/4 ounces *each*) sweet potatoes, drained and mashed
1/2	cup sugar
1	egg
1/4	cup butter, melted
1/2	teaspoon ground cinnamon

Dash salt

TOPPING:

1	cup coarsely crushed butter-flavored crackers (about 25 crackers)
1/2	cup packed brown sugar
1/4	cup butter, melted

In a large bowl, combine the first six ingredients. Transfer the mixture to a greased 8-in. square baking dish. Combine the crackers, brown sugar and butter; sprinkle over sweet potato mixture. Bake, uncovered, at 350° for 20-25 minutes or until a thermometer reads 160°. **YIELD: 6-8 servings.**

KATHY SHEPARD, SHEPHERD, MICHIGAN
The pastry part of this torte bakes into one big crust, which eliminates filling individual eclairs. The homemade pudding is replaced with a rich vanilla layer that's a snap to blend together using convenient instant pudding and cream cheese.

eclair torte

PREP: 20 MINUTES + CHILLING / **BAKE:** 30 MINUTES

1	cup water
1/2	cup butter
1/4	teaspoon salt
1	cup all-purpose flour
4	eggs
1	package (8 ounces) cream cheese, softened
3	cups cold milk
2	packages (3.4 ounces *each*) instant vanilla pudding mix
1	carton (12 ounces) frozen whipped topping, thawed
2	to 3 tablespoons chocolate syrup

In a small saucepan over medium heat, bring the water, butter and salt to a boil. Add flour all at once and stir until a smooth ball forms. Remove from the heat; let stand for 5 minutes. Add eggs, one at a time, beating well after each addition. Continue beating until mixture is smooth and shiny.

Spread into a greased 13-in. x 9-in. baking pan. Bake at 400° for 30-35 minutes or until puffed and golden brown. Cool completely on a wire rack. If desired, remove puff from pan and place on a serving platter.

In a large bowl, beat cream cheese until light. Add the milk and pudding mix; beat until smooth. Spread over puff; refrigerate for 20 minutes. Spread with the whipped topping; refrigerate. Drizzle with chocolate syrup just before serving. Refrigerate leftovers. **YIELD: 12 servings.**

DEBBIE PRICE, LARUE, OHIO
For me, the ideal dessert combines the flavors of chocolate and peanut butter. So when I came up with this rich treat, it quickly became my all-time favorite. It's a cinch to pull together because it doesn't require any baking.

peanut butter chocolate dessert

PREP: 20 MINUTES + CHILLING

20	chocolate cream-filled chocolate sandwich cookies, *divided*
2	tablespoons butter, softened
1	package (8 ounces) cream cheese, softened
1/2	cup peanut butter
1-1/2	cups confectioners' sugar, *divided*
1	carton (16 ounces) frozen whipped topping, thawed, *divided*
15	miniature peanut butter cups, chopped
1	cup cold milk
1	package (3.9 ounces) instant chocolate fudge pudding mix

Crush 16 cookies; toss with the butter. Press into an ungreased 9-in. square dish; set aside.

In a large bowl, beat the cream cheese, peanut butter and 1 cup confectioners' sugar until smooth. Fold in half of the whipped topping. Spread over crust. Sprinkle with peanut butter cups.

In another large bowl, beat the milk, pudding mix and remaining confectioners' sugar on low speed for 2 minutes Let stand for 2 minutes or until soft-set. Fold in remaining whipped topping. Spread the pudding mixture over the peanut butter cups. Crush the remaining cookies; sprinkle over the top. Cover and chill dessert for at least 3 hours. **YIELD: 12-16 servings.**

MARGE HODEL, ROANOKE, ILLINOIS

I've been stuffing pasta shells with different fillings for years, but my family enjoys this version with taco-seasoned meat the most. The frozen shells are so convenient, because you can take out only the number you need for a single-serving lunch or family dinner and save the rest for later.

taco-filled pasta shells

PREP: 20 MINUTES + CHILLING / **BAKE:** 45 MINUTES

- 2   pounds ground beef
- 2   envelopes taco seasoning
- 1   package (8 ounces) cream cheese, cubed
- 24   uncooked jumbo pasta shells
- 1/4   cup butter, melted

ADDITIONAL INGREDIENTS (FOR EACH CASSEROLE):

- 1   cup salsa
- 1   cup taco sauce
- 1   cup (4 ounces) shredded cheddar cheese
- 1   cup (4 ounces) shredded Monterey Jack cheese
- 1-1/2   cups crushed tortilla chips
- 1   cup (8 ounces) sour cream
- 3   green onions, chopped

In a Dutch oven, cook beef over medium heat until no longer pink; drain. Add taco seasoning; prepare according to package directions. Add cream cheese; cook and stir for 5-10 minutes or until melted. Transfer to a bowl; chill for 1 hour.

Cook pasta according to package directions; drain. Gently toss with butter. Fill each shell with about 3 tablespoons of meat mixture. Place 12 shells in a freezer container. Cover and freeze for up to 3 months.

To prepare remaining shells, spoon salsa into a greased 9-in. square baking dish. Top with stuffed shells and taco sauce. Cover and bake at 350° for 30 minutes. Uncover; sprinkle with cheeses and crushed tortilla chips. Bake 15 minutes longer or until heated through. Serve with sour cream and onions. **YIELD: 2 casseroles (6 servings each).**

TO USE FROZEN SHELLS: Thaw in the refrigerator for 24 hours (shells will be partially frozen). Spoon salsa into a greased 9-in. square baking dish; top with shells and taco sauce. Cover; bake at 350° for 40 minutes. Uncover and continue as directed above.

JUDY BAKER, CRAIG, COLORADO

When I first read this recipe, I thought it looked difficult. But because I had all the ingredients readily at hand, I gave it a try. Am I glad I did! Not only is it simple to prepare, it tastes great.

chicken in basil cream

PREP/TOTAL TIME: 25 MINUTES

- 1/4   cup milk
- 1/4   cup dry bread crumbs
- 4   boneless skinless chicken breast halves (4 ounces *each*)
- 3   tablespoons butter
- 1/2   cup chicken broth
- 1   cup heavy whipping cream
- 1   jar (4 ounces) sliced pimientos, drained
- 1/2   cup grated Parmesan cheese
- 1/4   cup minced fresh basil
- 1/8   teaspoon pepper

Place milk and bread crumbs in separate shallow bowls. Dip the chicken in milk, then coat with crumbs. In a skillet over medium-high heat, cook chicken in butter for about 5 minutes on each side or until a meat thermometer reads 170°. Remove and keep warm.

Add broth to the skillet. Bring to a boil over medium heat; stir to loosen browned bits. Stir in the cream and pimientos; boil and stir for 1 minute. Reduce heat. Add Parmesan cheese, basil and pepper; cook and stir until heated through. Serve with chicken. **YIELD: 4 servings.**

READERS' RAVES

"I added a can of drained artichoke quarters to the sauce for Chicken in Basil Cream, and it turned out amazing! It's worth giving a try if you like artichokes!

—Erinelaine87
from TasteofHome.com

JENNIFER HOEFT, THORNDALE, TEXAS

This is a no-fuss entree that's fast and flavorful. French-fried onions are the secret ingredient to the yummy coating that keeps the meat moist and juicy.

tasty onion chicken

PREP/TOTAL TIME: 30 MINUTES

1/2	cup butter, melted
1	tablespoon Worcestershire sauce
1	teaspoon ground mustard
1	can (2.8 ounces) French-fried onions, crushed
4	boneless skinless chicken breast halves (4 ounces *each*)

In a shallow bowl, combine the butter, Worcestershire sauce and mustard. Place the onions in another shallow bowl. Dip the chicken in butter mixture, then coat with onions.

Place in a greased 11-in. x 7-in. baking dish; drizzle with remaining butter mixture. Bake, uncovered, at 400° for 20-25 minutes or until a meat thermometer reads 170°. **YIELD: 4 servings.**

READERS' RAVES

“ Tasty Onion Chicken could hardly be any easier to put together. Fast and flavorful, it's a great combination.

—Seminoles from TasteofHome.com

This was fast, tender, juicy and delicious! I used prepared honey mustard and it was great! I will make this again! Thank you so much!

—Tbcknc from TasteofHome.com ”

The key to these pretty flank steak pinwheels lies in their butterfly treatment. Because the steaks are flattened, marinade isn't need. Instead, our home economists filled them with a colorful stuffing of red pepper and spinach and draped the slices with a rich, homemade blue cheese sauce.

flank steak pinwheels

PREP: 30 MINUTES / **GRILL:** 10 MINUTES

8	bacon strips
1	beef flank steak (1-1/2 pounds)
4	cups fresh baby spinach
1	jar (7 ounces) roasted sweet red peppers, drained

CREAM CHEESE SAUCE:

1	package (3 ounces) cream cheese, softened
1/4	cup milk
1	tablespoon butter
1/4	teaspoon pepper
1/2	cup crumbled blue cheese

Place bacon strips on a microwave-safe plate lined with microwave-safe paper towels. Cover with another paper towel; microwave on high for 2-3 minutes or until partially cooked.

Meanwhile, cut the steak horizontally from a long side to within 1/2 in. of opposite side. Open the meat so it lies flat; cover with plastic wrap. Flatten to 1/4-in. thickness. Remove plastic. Place the spinach over steak to within 1 in. of edges; top with red peppers. With the grain of the meat going from left to right, roll up jelly-roll style. Wrap bacon strips around beef; secure with toothpicks. Slice beef across the grain into eight slices.

Grill, covered, over medium heat for 5-7 minutes on each side or until meat reaches desired doneness (for medium-rare, a meat thermometer should read 145°; medium, 160°; well-done, 170°). Discard toothpicks.

In a small saucepan, combine the cream cheese, milk, butter and pepper. Cook and stir over low heat just until smooth (do not boil). Stir in blue cheese. Serve with pinwheels. **YIELD: 4 servings.**

EDITOR'S NOTE: This recipe was tested in a 1,100-watt microwave.

KARA COOK, ELK RIDGE, UTAH
These light and flaky salmon fillets are wonderful for company since they take only a few minutes to prepare, yet they taste like you fussed. I receive requests for the recipe every time I serve them—I'm almost embarrassed by how simple it is.

pecan-crusted salmon

PREP: 15 MINUTES + STANDING / **BAKE:** 10 MINUTES

4	salmon fillets (about 6 ounces *each*)
2	cups milk
1	cup finely chopped pecans
1/2	cup all-purpose flour
1/4	cup packed brown sugar
2	teaspoons seasoned salt
2	teaspoons pepper
3	tablespoons canola oil

Place salmon fillets in a large resealable plastic bag; add milk. Seal bag and turn to coat. Let stand for 10 minutes; drain.

Meanwhile, in a shallow bowl, combine the pecans, flour, brown sugar, seasoned salt and pepper. Coat fillets with pecan mixture, gently pressing into the fish.

In a large skillet, brown salmon over medium-high heat in oil. Transfer to a 15-in. x 10-in. baking pan coated with cooking spray. Bake at 400° for 8-10 minutes or until fish flakes easily with a fork. **YIELD: 4 servings.**

HANNAH THOMPSON, SCOTTS VALLEY, CALIFORNIA
Canned tomato soup replaces some of the oil in this spice cake. This little "trick" decreases the fat while boosting the color of the cake—all without sacrificing any of the flavor. Four ingredients makes it a snap!

surprise spice cake

PREP: 15 MINUTES / **BAKE:** 30 MINUTES + COOLING

1	package (18-1/4 ounces) spice cake mix
1	can (10-3/4 ounces) condensed tomato soup, undiluted
3	eggs
1/2	cup water
1	can (16 ounces) cream cheese frosting

In a large bowl, combine the cake mix, soup, eggs and water; beat on low speed for 30 seconds. Beat on medium for 2 minutes. Pour into a greased 13-in. x 9-in. baking dish.

Bake at 350° for 30-33 minutes or until a toothpick inserted near the center comes out clean. Cool on a wire rack. Frost with cream cheese frosting. **YIELD: 12 servings.**

BEVERLY MARSHALL, ORTING, WASHINGTON
A creamy lime topping turns angel food cake into delectable dessert squares that are perfect for potlucks or picnics. You can eat a piece of this light and airy treat without feeling one bit of guilt. I adapted this luscious treat from another recipe. It is super-easy to make.

luscious lime angel squares

PREP: 15 MINUTES + CHILLING

1	package (.3 ounces) sugar-free lime gelatin
1	cup boiling water
1	prepared angel food cake (8 inches), cut into 1-inch cubes
1	package (8 ounces) reduced-fat cream cheese, cubed
1/2	cup sugar
2	teaspoons lemon juice
1-1/2	teaspoons grated lemon peel
1	carton (8 ounces) reduced-fat whipped topping, thawed, *divided*

In a bowl, dissolve gelatin in boiling water. Refrigerate until mixture just begins to thicken, about 35 minutes. Place cake cubes in a 13-in. x 9-in. dish coated with cooking spray; set aside.

In a small bowl, beat cream cheese until smooth. Beat in the sugar, lemon juice and peel. Add gelatin mixture; beat until combined. Fold in 1-1/2 cups whipped topping.

Spread over top of cake, covering completely. Refrigerate for at least 2 hours or until firm. Cut into squares; top with remaining whipped topping. **YIELD: 15 servings.**

MARY ANN MARINO, WEST PITTSBURG, PENNSYLVANIA
These decadent candies disappear just as fast as I put them out. They're a breeze to assemble and make a beautiful presentation on any holiday cookie plate. I mound them high, then step back to watch them vanish in a flash!

chocolate coconut candies

PREP: 30 MINUTES + CHILLING

1-3/4	cups confectioners' sugar
1-3/4	cups flaked coconut
1	cup chopped almonds
1/2	cup sweetened condensed milk
2	cups (12 ounces) semisweet chocolate chips
2	tablespoons shortening

In a large bowl, combine the confectioners' sugar, coconut, almonds and milk. Shape into 1-in. balls. Refrigerate until firm, about 20 minutes.

In a microwave, melt semisweet chips and shortening on high for about 1 minute; stir. Microwave at additional 10- to 20-second intervals, stirring until smooth.

Dip the balls in melted chocolate; allow excess to drip off. Place chocolate-covered balls on waxed paper; let stand until set. Store the candies in an airtight container. **YIELD: 2-1/2 dozen.**

DAWN HUIZINGA, OWATONNA, MINNESOTA
Tender chops cook on a bed of scrumptious potatoes in this all-in-one meal. It comes together effortlessly thanks to frozen hash browns, canned soup, shredded cheese and French-fried onions.

pork chop potato dinner

PREP: 10 MINUTES / **COOK:** 2-1/2 HOURS

6	bone-in pork loin chops (1/2 inch thick and 8 ounces *each*)
1	tablespoon canola oil
1	package (30 ounces) frozen shredded hash brown potatoes, thawed
1-1/2	cups (6 ounces) shredded cheddar cheese, *divided*
1	can (10-3/4 ounces) condensed cream of celery soup, undiluted
1/2	cup milk
1/2	cup sour cream
1/2	teaspoon seasoned salt
1/8	teaspoon pepper
1	can (2.8 ounces) French-fried onions, *divided*

In a large skillet, brown chops in oil on both sides; set aside and keep warm. In a large bowl, combine the potatoes, 1 cup cheese, soup, milk, sour cream, seasoned salt and pepper. Stir in half of the onions.

Transfer to a greased 5-qt. slow cooker; top with pork chops. Cover and cook on high for 2-1/2 to 3 hours or until meat is tender. Sprinkle with remaining cheese and onions. Cover and cook 10 minutes longer or until cheese is melted. **YIELD: 6 servings.**

JENNIFER SMITH, COLONA, ILLINOIS
With a toddler in the house, I look for foods that are a snap to make. Loaded with beef, cheese and a flavorful rice mix, these enchiladas come together without any fuss. But they're so good that guests think I spent hours in the kitchen.

beef 'n' rice enchiladas

PREP: 30 MINUTES / **BAKE:** 10 MINUTES

1	package (6.8 ounces) Spanish rice and pasta mix
1	pound ground beef
2	cans (10 ounces *each*) enchilada sauce, *divided*
10	flour tortillas (8 inches), warmed
4	cups (16 ounces) shredded cheddar cheese, *divided*

Prepare rice mix according to package directions. Meanwhile, in a large skillet, cook beef over medium heat until no longer pink; drain. Stir in Spanish rice and 1-1/4 cups enchilada sauce. Spoon about 2/3 cup beef mixture down the center of each tortilla. Top beef mixture each with 1/3 cup shredded cheddar cheese; roll up.

Place in an ungreased 13-in. x 9-in. baking dish. Top with the remaining enchilada sauce and cheese. Bake, uncovered, at 350° for 8-10 minutes or until the cheese is melted. **YIELD: 10 enchiladas.**

PENNY WALTON, WESTERVILLE, OHIO

Refrigerated pie pastry is the key to fixing this sensational main course. It's a favorite when I entertain. Guests dining at my home will find a succulent steak topped with pesto and mushrooms in every flaky bundle.

beef wellington bundles

PREP: 30 MINUTES / **BAKE:** 20 MINUTES + STANDING

5	tablespoons olive oil, *divided*
1/2	cup loosely packed basil leaves and fresh parsley sprigs
1/4	cup grated Parmesan cheese
1/8	teaspoon salt
6	beef tenderloin steaks (6 ounces *each*)
4	tablespoons butter, *divided*
1/2	pound fresh mushrooms, chopped
6	sheets refrigerated pie pastry
1	egg, lightly beaten
3	tablespoons all-purpose flour
1-1/4	cups beef broth
1/4	cup dry red wine *or* additional beef broth
1/4	cup water
1/2	teaspoon browning sauce, optional

For pesto, in a food processor, combine 3 tablespoons oil, basil, parsley, Parmesan cheese and salt. Cover and process until smooth; set aside.

In a large skillet, brown the steaks in 2 tablespoons butter and remaining oil for 5-6 minutes on each side or until meat reaches desired doneness (for medium-rare, a meat thermometer should read 145°; medium, 160°; well-done, 170°). Remove and keep warm. In the same skillet, saute the mushrooms until the liquid is absorbed.

Cut each pastry sheet into an 8-in. square (discard scraps or save for another use). Place a steak on each square. Spread steak with about 1 tablespoon of pesto; top with mushrooms.

Bring opposite corners of pastry over steak and pinch seams to seal tightly. Place in a greased 15-in. x 10-in. baking pan; brush egg over pastry.

Bake at 450° for 18-20 minutes or until golden brown. Let stand for 10 minutes before serving.

For gravy, melt remaining butter in the same skillet; stir in flour until smooth. Gradually stir in the remaining ingredients. Bring to a boil; cook and stir for 2 minutes or until thickened. Serve with the beef bundles. **YIELD: 6 servings.**

DEE DAVIS, SUN CITY, ARIZONA

Things don't get much simpler than this take on a traditional baked treat. They're great for little ones and keep adults guessing as to how they can be made with only five ingredients.

peanut butter kiss cookies

PREP: 20 MINUTES / **BAKE:** 10 MINUTES + COOLING

1	cup peanut butter
1	cup sugar
1	egg
1	teaspoon vanilla extract
24	milk chocolate kisses

In a large bowl, cream peanut butter and sugar. Add the egg and vanilla; beat until blended.

Roll into 1-1/4-in. balls. Place 2 in. apart on ungreased baking sheets. Bake at 350° for 10-12 minutes or until tops are slightly cracked. Immediately press one chocolate kiss into the center of each cookie. Cool for 5 minutes before removing from pans to wire racks. **YIELD: 2 dozen.**

EDITOR'S NOTE: This recipe does not contain flour. Reduced-fat or generic brands of peanut butter are not recommended for this recipe.

VELMA BROWN, TURNER STATION, KENTUCKY
While coffee ice cream is great, I sometimes vary the flavor used in this treasured dessert. It's one dreamy summertime treat that's always high on requests.

coffee ice cream pie

PREP: 30 MINUTES + FREEZING

2	ounces unsweetened chocolate
1/4	cup butter, cubed
1	can (5 ounces) evaporated milk
1/2	cup sugar
1	pint coffee ice cream, softened
1	chocolate crumb crust (8 inches)
1	carton (8 ounces) frozen whipped topping, thawed
1/4	cup chopped pecans

In a heavy saucepan, melt chocolate and butter over low heat. Stir in milk and sugar. Bring to a boil over medium heat, stirring constantly. Cook and stir for 3-4 minutes or until thickened. Remove from the heat; cool completely.

Spoon ice cream into crust. Stir sauce; spread over ice cream. Top with whipped topping; sprinkle with pecans. Freeze until firm. Remove from the freezer 15 minutes before serving. **YIELD: 8 servings.**

TERRI KEENAN, TUSCALOOSA, ALABAMA
If you like foods with Southwestern flair, this just might become a new favorite. Loaded with cheese, meat and beans, the layered casserole comes together in minutes. There are never any leftovers when I take this dish to potlucks.

taco lasagna

PREP: 20 MINUTES / BAKE: 25 MINUTES

1	pound ground beef
1/2	cup chopped green pepper
1/2	cup chopped onion
2/3	cup water
1	envelope taco seasoning
1	can (15 ounces) black beans, rinsed and drained
1	can (14-1/2 ounces) Mexican diced tomatoes, undrained
6	flour tortillas (8 inches)
1	can (16 ounces) refried beans
3	cups (12 ounces) shredded Mexican cheese blend

In a large skillet, cook the beef, green pepper and onion over medium heat until the meat is no longer pink; drain. Add water and taco seasoning; bring to a boil. Reduce heat; simmer, uncovered, for 2 minutes. Stir in the black beans and tomatoes. Simmer, uncovered, for 10 minutes.

Place two tortillas in a greased 13-in. x 9-in. baking dish. Spread with half of the refried beans and beef mixture; sprinkle with 1 cup Mexican cheese blend. Repeat layers. Top with the remaining tortillas and cheese. Cover and bake at 350° for 25-30 minutes or until lasagna is heated through and the cheese is melted. **YIELD: 9 servings.**

WINNIE STRUSE, HEREFORD, ARIZONA
My mother-in-law created this recipe after enjoying a similar dish on vacation. A medley of artichokes, red pepper and chicken forms a lovely entree when paired with tender fettuccine pasta and a rich, homemade cream sauce.

artichoke chicken fettuccine

PREP/TOTAL TIME: 30 MINUTES

8	ounces uncooked fettuccine
1	pound boneless skinless chicken breasts, cut into 1-inch strips
4	bacon strips, diced
1/4	cup chopped onion
2	tablespoons chopped sweet red pepper
2	tablespoons butter
2	tablespoons all-purpose flour
1	cup chicken broth
1/2	cup whole milk
1	teaspoon Dijon mustard
2	tablespoons grated Parmesan cheese
1	can (14 ounces) water-packed artichoke hearts, rinsed, drained and quartered
2	tablespoons mayonnaise

Cook fettuccine according to package directions. Meanwhile, in a large skillet, saute the chicken, bacon, onion and red pepper until chicken juices run clear and vegetables are tender; drain and keep warm.

In a large saucepan, melt the butter; stir in flour until smooth. Gradually add the broth, milk and mustard. Bring to a boil; cook and stir for 2 minutes or until thickened. Stir in Parmesan cheese and artichokes. Remove from the heat; stir in mayonnaise and chicken mixture. Drain fettuccine; serve with chicken mixture. **YIELD: 4 servings.**

KIMBERLY BIEL, JAVA, SOUTH DAKOTA
Convenient cake mix hurries along the preparation of these tasty dessert bars. I bring these quick-and-easy treats to church meetings, potlucks and housewarming parties. I often make a double batch so we can enjoy some at home.

can't leave alone bars

PREP: 20 MINUTES / **BAKE:** 20 MINUTES + COOLING

1	package (18-1/4 ounces) white cake mix
2	eggs
1/3	cup canola oil
1	can (14 ounces) sweetened condensed milk
1	cup (6 ounces) semisweet chocolate chips
1/4	cup butter, cubed

In a large bowl, combine cake mix, eggs and oil. Press two-thirds of the mixture into a greased 13-in. x 9-in. baking pan. Set the remaining cake mixture aside.

In a microwave-safe bowl, combine the milk, chocolate chips and butter. Microwave, uncovered, until chips and butter are melted; stir until smooth. Pour over crust.

Drop teaspoonfuls of remaining cake mixture over top. Bake at 350° for 20-25 minutes or until lightly browned. Cool before cutting. **YIELD: 3 dozen.**

EDITOR'S NOTE: This recipe was tested in a 1,100-watt microwave.

READERS' RAVES

> 'Can't Leave Alone Bars' is a good name for these treats! Even when they're just cooled, they are already half gone. Delicious! Will be making these often.
>
> —Issrls from TasteofHome.com

> So good! I added pecans to the top of the chocolate and served the bars while still warm. They were the hit of our family reunion!
>
> —Ruesae from TasteofHome.com

DEBBIE DUNAWAY, KETTERING, OHIO
How good is this dish? Well, I'll just say it's the only kind of meat my kids will eat and enjoy other than hot dogs! It's also incredibly easy to make because it's prepared right in the slow cooker. Simply delicious!

teriyaki pork roast

PREP: 10 MINUTES / **COOK:** 6 HOURS + STANDING

1	boneless pork shoulder roast (3 to 4 pounds), trimmed
1	cup packed brown sugar
1/3	cup unsweetened apple juice
1/3	cup soy sauce
1/2	teaspoon salt
1/4	teaspoon pepper
2	tablespoons cornstarch
3	tablespoons cold water

Cut roast in half; rub with brown sugar. Place in a 5-qt. slow cooker. Pour apple juice and soy sauce over roast. Sprinkle with salt and pepper. Cover and cook on low for 6 to 6-1/2 hours or until meat is tender.

Remove roast; cover and let stand for 15 minutes. Meanwhile, strain cooking juices and return to slow cooker. Combine the cornstarch and cold water until smooth; gradually stir into juices. Cover and cook on high for 15 minutes or until thickened. Slice pork; serve with gravy. **YIELD: 6-8 servings.**

LINDA SAKAL, BILOXI, MISSISSIPPI
I often prepare this moist golden cake at Easter, but it's wonderful just about any time of year. Pineapple frosting provides the fast finishing touch.

pineapple layer cake

PREP: 15 MINUTES / **BAKE:** 25 MINUTES + COOLING

1	package (18-1/4 ounces) yellow cake mix
1	can (11 ounces) mandarin oranges, drained
1	can (20 ounces) unsweetened crushed pineapple, drained
1	package (3.4 ounces) instant vanilla pudding mix
1	package (12 ounces) frozen whipped topping, thawed

Prepare cake batter according to package directions. Beat in oranges until blended. Pour into two greased and floured 9-in. round baking pans.

Bake at 350° for 25-30 minutes or until a toothpick inserted near the center comes out clean. Cool for 10 minutes before removing from pans to wire racks to cool completely.

Combine pineapple and dry pudding mix; fold in whipped topping. Spread between layers and over top and sides of cake. Store in the refrigerator. **YIELD: 12 servings.**

STEPHANIE KENNEY, FALKVILLE, ALABAMA
This spicy standout packs a one-two punch of flavor. The grilled chicken is basted with a peppery white sauce. Plus there's plenty of extra sauce left over for dipping.

blackened chicken

PREP/TOTAL TIME: 25 MINUTES

1	tablespoon paprika
4	teaspoons sugar, *divided*
1-1/2	teaspoons salt
1	teaspoon garlic powder
1	teaspoon dried thyme
1	teaspoon lemon-pepper seasoning
1	teaspoon cayenne pepper
1-1/2	to 2 teaspoons pepper, *divided*
4	boneless skinless chicken breast halves (4 ounces *each*)
1-1/3	cups mayonnaise
2	tablespoons water
2	tablespoons cider vinegar

In a small bowl, combine paprika, 1 teaspoon sugar, 1 teaspoon salt, garlic powder, thyme, lemon-pepper, cayenne and 1/2 to 1 teaspoon pepper; sprinkle over both sides of the chicken. Set aside.

In another bowl, combine the mayonnaise, water, vinegar and remaining sugar, salt and pepper; cover and refrigerate 1 cup for serving. Save remaining sauce for basting.

Grill chicken, covered, over indirect medium heat for 4-6 minutes on each side or until a thermometer reads 170°, basting frequently with remaining sauce. Serve with reserved sauce. **YIELD: 4 servings.**

KRISTA COLLINS, CONCORD, NORTH CAROLINA
I've made this salad for years—it's a recipe from a high school friend's mom. Any time I serve a sandwich meal like hamburgers, hot dogs or sloppy joes, I have this flavorful salad alongside.

ranch pasta salad

PREP/TOTAL TIME: 25 MINUTES

3	cups uncooked tricolor spiral pasta
1	cup chopped fresh broccoli florets
3/4	cup chopped seeded peeled cucumber
1/2	cup seeded chopped tomato
1	bottle (8 ounces) ranch salad dressing
1/2	cup shredded Parmesan cheese

Cook pasta according to package directions; drain and rinse in cold water. In a large bowl, combine pasta, broccoli, cucumber and tomato. Drizzle with salad dressing; toss to coat. Sprinkle with Parmesan cheese. **YIELD: 8 servings.**

SHERRI DANIELS, CLARK, SOUTH DAKOTA
Convenience items such as store-bought angel food cake, frozen strawberries and instant pudding mix make preparing this refrigerated delight as simple as can be. I whip up this refreshing dessert all year-round. It's particularly attractive when served in a glass dish.

no-bake strawberry dessert

PREP: 20 MINUTES + CHILLING

1	loaf (10-1/2 ounces) angel food cake, cut into 1-inch cubes
2	packages (.3 ounce *each*) sugar-free strawberry gelatin
2	cups boiling water
1	package (20 ounces) frozen unsweetened whole strawberries, thawed
2	cups cold 1% milk
1	package (1 ounce) sugar-free instant vanilla pudding mix
1	carton (8 ounces) frozen reduced-fat whipped topping, thawed

Arrange cake cubes in a single layer in a 13-in. x 9-in. dish. In a bowl, dissolve gelatin in boiling water; stir in strawberries. Pour over cake and gently press cake down. Refrigerate until set, about 1 hour.

In a bowl, whisk milk and pudding mix for 2 minutes or until slightly thickened. Spoon over gelatin layer. Spread with whipped topping. Refrigerate until serving. **YIELD: 20 servings.**

RENEE ENDRESS, GALVA, ILLINOIS
I created this recipe when I had spur-of-the-moment guests. I needed something speedy and simple enough to make from pantry items I had on hand. The result was an instant hit and is now a family staple.

cookies 'n' cream fluff

PREP/TOTAL TIME: 10 MINUTES

- 2 cups cold milk
- 1 package (3.4 ounces) instant vanilla pudding mix
- 1 carton (8 ounces) frozen whipped topping, thawed
- 15 cream-filled chocolate sandwich cookies, broken into chunks

Additional broken cookies, optional

In a bowl, whisk milk and pudding mix for 2 minutes or until slightly thickened. fold in the whipped topping and cookies. spoon into dessert dishes. Top with additional cookies if desired. Refrigerate until serving. **YIELD: 6 servings.**

RUTH ANDREWSON, LEAVENWORTH, WASHINGTON
My husband and I have company over for dinner often. Keeping a supply of these frozen meatballs on hand means I can easily prepare a quick, satisfying meal. I start with a versatile meatball mix that makes about 12 dozen meatballs, then freeze them in batches for future use in spaghetti or other dishes.

make-ahead meatballs

PREP/TOTAL TIME: 25 MINUTES

- 4 eggs
- 2 cups dry bread crumbs
- 1/2 cup finely chopped onion
- 1 tablespoon salt
- 2 teaspoons Worcestershire sauce
- 1/2 teaspoon white pepper
- 4 pounds lean ground beef

In a large bowl, beat the eggs. Add the next five ingredients. Crumble beef over mixture and mix well. Shape into 1-in. balls, about 12 dozen.

Place meatballs on greased racks in shallow baking pans. Bake at 400° for 10-15 minutes or until no longer pink, turning often; drain. Cool.

Place about 30 meatballs into each freezer container. May be frozen for up to 3 months. **YIELD: 5 batches (about 30 meatballs per batch).**

KARA DE LA VEGA, SANTA ROSA, CALIFORNIA
I make sure I always have the ingredients for this tender, flavorful chicken entree. The cheese-stuffed rolls are nice with a green salad or plate of fresh vegetables and Spanish rice.

taco chicken rolls

PREP: 15 MINUTES / **BAKE:** 35 MINUTES

- 1 cup finely crushed cheese-flavored crackers
- 1 envelope taco seasoning
- 6 boneless skinless chicken breast halves (4 ounces *each*)
- 2 ounces Monterey Jack cheese, cut into six 2-inch x 1/2-inch sticks
- 1 can (4 ounces) chopped green chilies

In a shallow dish, combine cracker crumbs and taco seasoning; set aside. Flatten chicken between two sheets of waxed paper to 1/4-in. thickness. Place a cheese stick and about 1 tablespoon of chilies on each piece of chicken. Tuck ends of chicken in and roll up; secure with a toothpick.

Coat chicken with crumb mixture. Place in a greased 13-in. x 9-in. baking dish. Bake, uncovered, at 350° for 35-40 minutes or until the chicken is no longer pink. Remove toothpicks. **YIELD: 6 servings.**

KIM SPENCER, HICKMAN, NEBRASKA
My mom, who's well-known in our community for her cooking, shared the recipe for this yummy layered dessert. It's very popular with my husband. He made it in a baking pan for his men's Bible study group and ended up giving out the recipe!

peanut butter apple dessert

PREP: 15 MINUTES + CHILLING

1-1/2	cups graham cracker crumbs (about 24 squares)
1/2	cup packed brown sugar
1/2	cups plus 1/3 cup peanut butter, *divided*
1/4	cup butter, melted
1	package (8 ounces) cream cheese, softened
3/4	cup sugar
1	carton (16 ounces) frozen whipped topping, thawed
2	cans (21 ounces *each*) apple pie filling
3/4	cup confectioners' sugar
1	teaspoon ground cinnamon

In a large bowl, combine graham cracker crumbs, brown sugar, 1/2 cup peanut butter and butter; spoon half into a 3-qt. bowl.

In a large bowl, beat the cream cheese and sugar until smooth; fold in whipped topping. Spread half over crumb mixture in the bowl. Top with one can of apple pie filling.

Combine the confectioners' sugar, cinnamon and remaining peanut butter until crumbly; sprinkle half over pie filling. Repeat layers. Refrigerate until serving. **YIELD: about 20 servings.**

JULIE MOUTRAY, WICHITA, KANSAS
I use leftover chicken to create a rich and creamy meal-in-one. This colorful dish has zippy flavor and makes a nice change of pace from the usual beef enchiladas.

chicken enchiladas

PREP: 15 MINUTES / **BAKE:** 35 MINUTES

1	can (16 ounces) refried beans
10	flour tortillas (8 inches), warmed
1	can (10-3/4 ounces) condensed cream of chicken soup, undiluted
1	cup (8 ounces) sour cream
3	to 4 cups cubed cooked chicken
3	cups (12 ounces) shredded cheddar cheese, *divided*
1	can (15 ounces) enchilada sauce
1/4	cup sliced green onions
1/4	cup sliced ripe olives

Shredded lettuce, optional

Spread about 2 tablespoons of beans on each tortilla. Combine soup and sour cream; stir in chicken. Spoon 1/3 to 1/2 cup down the center of each tortilla; top with 1 tablespoon cheese.

Roll up and place the seam side down in a greased 9-in. x 13-in. baking dish. Pour enchilada sauce over top; sprinkle with the onions, olives and remaining cheese.

Bake, uncovered, at 350° for 35 minutes or until heated through. Just before serving, sprinkle lettuce around the enchiladas if desired. **YIELD: 10 servings.**

LINDA WAHLGREN, MOUNT HOREB, WISCONSIN
The recipe for this beautiful blend came from a local berry farm some years ago. We like to take the sweet and savory salad on picnics to accompany cold chicken and a loaf of crusty bread.

berry-mandarin tossed salad

PREP/TOTAL TIME: 30 MINUTES

1/4	cup sugar
2	tablespoons cider vinegar
2	tablespoons honey
1-1/2	teaspoons lemon juice
1/2	teaspoon paprika
1/2	teaspoon ground mustard
1/2	teaspoon grated onion
1/4	teaspoon celery seed

Dash salt

1/3	cup canola oil
8	cups torn mixed salad greens
2	cups sliced fresh strawberries
1	can (11 ounces) mandarin oranges, drained
1	medium sweet onion, sliced into rings
1/3	cup slivered almonds, toasted
4	bacon strips, cooked and crumbled

In a 2-cup microwave-safe bowl, combine first nine ingredients. Microwave, uncovered, on high for 1-2 minutes; stir until sugar is dissolved. Whisk in oil. Cover and refrigerate until serving.

In a salad bowl, combine the greens, strawberries, oranges, onion, almonds and bacon. Drizzle with dressing and gently toss to coat. **YIELD: 12-14 servings.**

EDITOR'S NOTE: This recipe was tested in a 1,100-watt microwave.

MARIE PRZEPIERSKI, ERIE, PENNSYLVANIA
This dinner finale is very easy to make. I have tried lemonade, mango and pineapple juice concentrates instead of orange, and my family loves every variety. It's nice to know that it's light, too.

arctic orange pie

PREP: 20 MINUTES + FREEZING

1	package (8 ounces) fat-free cream cheese
1	can (6 ounces) frozen orange juice concentrate, thawed
1	carton (8 ounces) frozen reduced-fat whipped topping, thawed
1	reduced-fat graham cracker crust (8 inches)
1	can (11 ounces) mandarin oranges, drained

In a large bowl, beat cream cheese and orange juice concentrate until smooth. Fold in whipped topping; pour into crust. Cover and freeze for 4 hours or until firm. Remove from the freezer about 10 minutes before cutting. Garnish with oranges. **YIELD: 8 servings.**

GLADYS SHAFFER, ELMA, WASHINGTON
This recipe is excellent for working parents because it's fast. Fresh veggies add color and crunch to a boxed dinner mix.

lasagna soup

PREP/TOTAL TIME: 30 MINUTES

1	pound ground beef
1/2	cup chopped onion
1	package (7-3/4 ounces) lasagna dinner mix
5	cups water
1	can (14-1/2 ounces) diced tomatoes, undrained
1	can (7 ounces) whole kernel corn, undrained
2	tablespoons grated Parmesan cheese
1	small zucchini, chopped

In a Dutch oven or soup kettle, cook beef and onion over medium heat until meat is no longer pink; drain. Add contents of the lasagna dinner sauce mix, water, tomatoes, corn and Parmesan cheese; bring to a boil. Reduce heat; cover and simmer for 10 minutes, stirring occasionally.

Add the lasagna noodles and zucchini. Cover and simmer for 10 minutes or until noodles are tender. Serve immediately. **YIELD: 10 servings (2-1/2 quarts).**

DIANE WILLEY, BOZMAN, MARYLAND

This quick fudge is always popular wherever it shows up and makes great gifts for loved ones and friends. People love the creaminess and sweet toffee bits. The recipe is so easy, even young children can help make it—with a little supervision!

pecan toffee fudge

PREP: 20 MINUTES + CHILLING

1	teaspoon butter
1	package (8 ounces) cream cheese, softened
3-3/4	cups confectioners' sugar
6	ounces unsweetened chocolate, melted and cooled
1/4	teaspoon almond extract

Dash salt

1/4	cup coarsely chopped pecans
1/4	cup English toffee bits

Line a 9-in. square pan with foil and grease the foil with butter; set aside. In a large bowl, beat cream cheese until fluffy. Gradually beat in confectioners' sugar. Add the melted chocolate, extract and salt; mix well. Stir in pecans and toffee bits.

Spread into prepared pan. Cover and refrigerate overnight or until firm. Using foil, lift fudge out of pan. Gently peel off foil; cut the fudge into 1-in. squares. Store in an airtight container in the refrigerator. **YIELD: 2-1/2 pounds.**

LISA BLACKWELL, HENDERSON, NORTH CAROLINA

My husband was given this super-simple recipe by a man who sold shrimp at the fish market. It's now become our family's absolute favorite. We have even served it to guests with great success. It's one entree you won't want to miss.

honey grilled shrimp

PREP: 10 MINUTES + MARINATING / **GRILL:** 10 MINUTES

1	bottle (8 ounces) Italian salad dressing
1	cup honey
1/2	teaspoon minced garlic
2	pounds uncooked medium shrimp, peeled and deveined

In a small bowl, combine the salad dressing, honey and garlic; set aside 1/2 cup. Pour remaining marinade into a large resealable plastic bag; add the shrimp. Seal bag and turn to coat; refrigerate for 30 minutes. Cover and refrigerate reserved marinade for basting.

Coat grill rack with cooking spray before starting the grill. Drain and discard the marinade. Thread the shrimp onto eight metal or soaked wooden skewers. Grill, uncovered, over medium heat for 1 to 1-1/2 minutes on each side. Baste with the reserved marinade. Grill 3-4 minutes longer or until shrimp turn pink, turning and basting frequently. **YIELD: 8 servings.**

AMBER ZURBRUGG, ALLIANCE, OHIO

This delectable cold pizza proves that you can eat well even when you're trying to eat healthy. A tube of refrigerated pizza crust is baked, spread with some seasoned cream cheese and topped with nicely dressed salad fixings and moist chicken.

chicken caesar salad pizza

PREP/TOTAL TIME: 30 MINUTES

1	tube (13.8 ounces) refrigerated pizza crust
3/4	pound boneless skinless chicken breasts, cut into strips
2	teaspoons canola oil
1/2	cup fat-free creamy Caesar salad dressing
1/2	cup shredded Parmesan cheese, *divided*
1	teaspoon salt-free lemon-pepper seasoning
1	garlic clove, minced
1	package (8 ounces) fat-free cream cheese, cubed
4	cups thinly sliced romaine
1/2	cup diced sweet red pepper
1	can (2-1/4 ounces) sliced ripe olives, drained

Unroll pizza crust onto a 12-in. pizza pan coated with cooking spray; flatten dough and build up edges slightly. Prick with a fork. Bake at 400° for 11 minutes or until lightly browned. Cool on a wire rack.

In a nonstick skillet, cook the chicken in oil over medium heat until no longer pink; cool slightly. Meanwhile, in a small bowl, combine the dressing, 1/4 cup Parmesan, lemon-pepper and garlic. Combine cream cheese and half of the dressing mixture until well blended.

Combine romaine, red pepper and olives. Add the remaining dressing mixture; toss. Spread cream cheese mixture over crust. Top with romaine mixture, chicken and remaining Parmesan. **YIELD: 6 servings.**

KIM ROCKER, LAGRANGE, GEORGIA

This is an easy dinner to prepare ahead of time, refrigerate and bake just before company arrives. Canned soup makes this casserole creamy but it still cuts well for serving.

spaghetti casserole

PREP: 20 MINUTES / **BAKE:** 55 MINUTES

1	package (16 ounces) angel hair pasta
1-1/2	pounds ground beef
1	jar (26 ounces) spaghetti sauce
2	cans (8 ounces *each*) tomato sauce
1	can (10-3/4 ounces) condensed cream of mushroom soup, undiluted
1	cup (8 ounces) sour cream
2	cups (8 ounces) shredded Colby-Monterey Jack cheese

Cook pasta according to package directions. Meanwhile, in a large skillet, cook beef over medium heat until no longer pink; drain. Stir in spaghetti sauce and tomato sauce. Remove from the heat.

Drain pasta. Combine soup and sour cream. In two 8-in. square baking dishes, layer half of the meat sauce, pasta, soup mixture and cheese. Repeat layers.

Cover and freeze one casserole for up to 3 months. Cover and bake the remaining casserole at 350° for 55-65 minutes or until cheese is melted. **YIELD: 2 casseroles (6 servings each).**

TO USE FROZEN CASSEROLE: Thaw in the refrigerator overnight. Remove from refrigerator 30 minutes before baking. Bake as directed.

seasonal selections

Comforting fall favorites...fresh springtime delights...Yuletide staples...we've collected the very best seasonal recipes and put them right at your fingertips. You can make every occasion even more meaningful with the homemade specialties featured here.

QUICK GHOST COOKIES / PAGE 193

JOY VAN METER, THORNTON, COLORADO
This elegant-looking dessert is surprisingly easy to assemble, especially because the cute wonton "cups" can be made in advance to save time the day of your event. They're a different way to present fresh strawberries when entertaining. If you're expecting a large group, you're in luck—this doubles well.

strawberry tartlets

PREP: 25 MINUTES / **BAKE:** 10 MINUTES + COOLING

12	wonton wrappers	2	tablespoons honey
3	tablespoons butter, melted	2	teaspoons orange juice
1/3	cup packed brown sugar	3	cups fresh strawberries, sliced
3/4	cup Mascarpone cheese		Whipped cream and fresh mint, optional

Brush one side of each wonton wrapper with butter. Place brown sugar in a shallow bowl; press buttered side of wontons into sugar to coat. Press wontons sugared side up into greased muffin cups. Bake at 325° for 7-9 minutes or until edges are lightly browned. Remove to a wire rack to cool.

In a small bowl, combine the Mascarpone cheese, honey and orange juice. Spoon about 1 tablespoon into each wonton cup. Top with strawberries. Garnish with whipped cream and mint if desired. **YIELD: 1 dozen.**

KATIE SLOAN, CHARLOTTE, NORTH CAROLINA
Whoever said biscuits were boring never tasted these. We love their rich flavor. These tender treats are great with a meal or as a snack with honey butter.

sweet potato biscuits

PREP: 25 MINUTES / **BAKE:** 10 MINUTES

2	cups self-rising flour
1/4	cup packed brown sugar
1	teaspoon ground cinnamon
1	teaspoon ground ginger
7	tablespoons cold butter, *divided*
3	tablespoons shortening
1	cup mashed sweet potatoes
6	tablespoons milk

In a large bowl, combine the flour, brown sugar, cinnamon and ginger. Cut in 4 tablespoons butter and shortening until mixture resembles coarse crumbs.

In a small bowl, combine sweet potatoes and milk; stir into crumb mixture just until moistened. Turn onto a lightly floured surface; knead 10 times.

Pat or roll out to 1/2-in. thickness; cut with a floured 2-1/2-in. biscuit cutter. Place 2 in. apart on ungreased baking sheets.

Melt remaining butter; brush over dough. Bake at 425° for 10-12 minutes or until golden brown. Remove from pans to wire racks. Serve warm. **YIELD: 1-1/2 dozen.**

EDITOR'S NOTE: As a substitute for each cup of self-rising flour, place 1-1/2 teaspoons baking powder and 1/2 teaspoon salt in a measuring cup. Add all-purpose flour to measure 1 cup.

PATRICIA SIDLOSKAS, ANNISTON, ALABAMA
Your guests will never guess a dessert as creamy and succulent as this butterscotch-pumpkin blend could be so very simple! With just the right amount of cinnamon, ginger and allspice, it's a true fall favorite. We enjoy it best with a dollop of whipped cream and a sprinkling of cinnamon.

pumpkin mousse

PREP/TOTAL TIME: 15 MINUTES

1-1/2	cups cold fat-free milk
1	package (1 ounce) sugar-free instant butterscotch pudding mix
1/2	cup canned pumpkin
1/2	teaspoon ground cinnamon
1/4	teaspoon ground ginger
1/4	teaspoon ground allspice
1	cup fat-free whipped topping, *divided*

In a large bowl, whisk milk and pudding mix for 2 minutes. Let stand for 2 minutes or until soft-set. Combine the pumpkin, cinnamon, ginger and allspice; fold into pudding. Fold in 1/2 cup whipped topping.

Transfer to individual serving dishes. Refrigerate until serving. Garnish with the remaining whipped topping. **YIELD: 4 servings.**

DEBBIE WILSON, SELLERSBURG, INDIANA
My most-often-requested dessert, this exquisite cheesecake with apples, caramel and pecans wins me more compliments than anything else I make. My husband's co-workers say it's too pretty to cut...but agree it's well worth it to do so.

apple-of-your-eye cheesecake

PREP: 30 MINUTES / **BAKE:** 55 MINUTES + CHILLING

- 1 cup graham cracker crumbs (about 16 squares)
- 3 tablespoons sugar
- 2 tablespoons finely chopped pecans
- 1/2 teaspoon ground cinnamon
- 1/4 cup butter, melted

FILLING:
- 3 packages (8 ounces *each*) cream cheese, softened
- 3/4 cup sugar
- 3 eggs, lightly beaten
- 3/4 teaspoon vanilla extract

TOPPING:
- 2-1/2 cups chopped peeled apples
- 1 tablespoon lemon juice
- 1/4 cup sugar
- 1/2 teaspoon ground cinnamon
- 6 tablespoons caramel ice cream topping, *divided*

Sweetened whipped cream
- 2 tablespoons chopped pecans

In a bowl, combine the cracker crumbs, sugar, pecans and cinnamon; stir in butter. Press onto the bottom of a lightly greased 9-in. springform pan. Place pan on a baking sheet. Bake at 350° for 10 minutes. Place pan on a wire rack (leave oven on).

In a large bowl, beat cream cheese and sugar until smooth. Add eggs; beat on low speed just until combined. Stir in vanilla. Pour over crust. Toss apples with lemon juice, sugar and cinnamon; spoon over filling. Return pan to baking sheet.

Bake at for 55-60 minutes or until center is almost set. Cool on a wire rack for 10 minutes. Carefully run a knife around edge of pan to loosen. Drizzle with 4 tablespoons caramel topping. Cool for 1 hour. Chill overnight.

Remove sides of pan. Just before serving, garnish with whipped cream. Drizzle with remaining caramel; sprinkle with pecans. Store in refrigerator. **YIELD: 12 servings.**

RUBY WILLIAMS, BOGALUSA, LOUISIANA
Like most people, I always serve turkey for our Thanksgiving meal. But instead of roasting a whole bird, I opt for a large, bone-in turkey breast since most of us prefer white meat. The herb butter basting sauce keeps it so moist, plus it's easy to carve.

herbed turkey breast

PREP: 10 MINUTES / **BAKE:** 1-1/2 HOURS

- 1/2 cup butter, cubed
- 1/4 cup lemon juice
- 2 tablespoons soy sauce
- 2 tablespoons finely chopped green onions
- 1 tablespoon rubbed sage
- 1 teaspoon dried thyme
- 1 teaspoon dried marjoram
- 1/4 teaspoon pepper
- 1 bone-in turkey breast (5-1/2 to 6 pounds)

In a small saucepan, combine the first eight ingredients; bring to a boil. Remove from the heat. Place turkey breast in a shallow roasting pan; baste with butter mixture.

Bake, uncovered, at 325° for 1-1/2 to 2 hours or until a meat thermometer reads 170°, basting turkey breast every 30 minutes. **YIELD: 10-12 servings.**

SHERYL GOODNOUGH, ELIOT, MAINE
I love zucchini, so this colorful main dish is one of my favorites. I make it often during the summer. It's especially good with tomatoes picked fresh from my vegetable garden.

baked chicken and zucchini

PREP: 20 MINUTES / **BAKE:** 35 MINUTES

1	egg
1	tablespoon water
3/4	teaspoon salt, *divided*
1/8	teaspoon pepper
1	cup dry bread crumbs
4	boneless skinless chicken breast halves (6 ounces *each*)
4	tablespoons olive oil, *divided*
5	medium zucchini, sliced
4	medium tomatoes, sliced
1	cup (4 ounces) part-skim shredded mozzarella cheese, *divided*
2	teaspoons minced fresh basil

In a shallow bowl, beat the egg, water, 1/2 teaspoon salt and pepper. Set aside 2 tablespoons bread crumbs. Place the remaining crumbs in a large resealable plastic bag. Dip chicken in egg mixture, then place in bag and shake to coat.

In a large skillet, cook chicken in 2 tablespoons oil for 2-3 minutes on each side or until golden brown; remove and set aside. In the same skillet, saute the zucchini in remaining oil until crisp-tender; drain. Transfer to a greased 13-in. x 9-in. baking dish.

Sprinkle the reserved bread crumbs over the zucchini. Top with tomato slices; sprinkle with 2/3 cup mozzarella cheese, basil and remaining salt. Top with chicken. Cover and bake at 400° for 25 minutes or until a meat thermometer reads 170°. Uncover; sprinkle with remaining cheese. Bake 10 minutes longer or until cheese is melted. **YIELD: 4 servings.**

SANDRA PICHON, SLIDELL, LOUISIANA
Mom loves sweet potatoes and fixed them often in this creamy, comforting casserole. With its nutty topping, this side dish could almost serve as a dessert. It's a yummy treat!

mom's sweet potato bake

PREP: 10 MINUTES / **BAKE:** 45 MINUTES

3	cups cold mashed sweet potatoes (prepared without milk *or* butter)
1	cup sugar
3	eggs
1/2	cup milk
1/4	cup butter, softened
1	teaspoon salt
1	teaspoon vanilla extract

TOPPING:

1/2	cup packed brown sugar
1/2	cup chopped pecans
1/4	cup all-purpose flour
2	tablespoons cold butter

In a large bowl, beat the sweet potatoes, sugar, eggs, milk, butter, salt and vanilla until smooth. Transfer to a greased 2-qt. baking dish.

In a small bowl, combine the brown sugar, pecans and flour; cut in butter until crumbly. Sprinkle over the potato mixture. Bake, uncovered, at 325° for 45-50 minutes or until a meat thermometer reads 160°. **YIELD: 8-10 servings.**

KIM HINKLE, WAUSEON, OHIO

We make these buttery cutouts every Christmas and give lots of them as gifts. Last year, we baked a batch a week all through December to be sure we'd have plenty for ourselves, too. The rich cookies melt in your mouth!

white velvet cutouts

PREP: 25 MINUTES + CHILLING / **BAKE:** 10 MINUTES

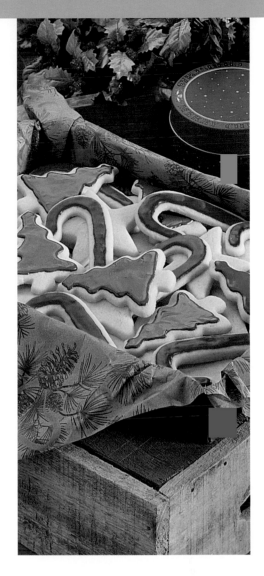

2	cups butter, softened
1	package (8 ounces) cream cheese, softened
2	cups sugar
2	egg yolks
1	teaspoon vanilla extract
4-1/2	cups all-purpose flour

BUTTER CREAM FROSTING:

3-1/2	cups confectioners' sugar, *divided*
3	tablespoons butter, softened
1	tablespoon shortening
1/2	teaspoon vanilla extract
3	to 4 tablespoons milk, *divided*

Red *and/or* green food coloring, optional

In a bowl, cream butter and cream cheese until light and fluffy. Add sugar, egg yolks and vanilla; mix well. Gradually add flour. Cover and chill 2 hours or until firm.

Roll out on a floured surface to 1/4-in. thickness. Cut into 3-in. shapes; place 1 in. apart on greased baking sheets. Bake at 350° for 10-12 minutes or until set (not browned). Cool 5 minutes; remove to wire racks to cool.

For frosting, combine 1-1/2 cups sugar, butter, shortening, vanilla and 3 tablespoons milk in a bowl; beat until smooth. Gradually add remaining sugar; beat until light and fluffy, about 3 minutes. Add enough remaining milk and food coloring until frosting reaches desired consistency. Frost cookies. **YIELD: about 7 dozen.**

SUE GRONHOLZ, BEAVER DAM, WISCONSIN

Folks will gobble up these sweet-tasting turkeys, whether the easy-to-assemble goodies are sold at bake sales or featured on holiday tables. Every Thanksgiving, my cousin makes the too-cute bites out of prepared cookies and candies much to the family's delight.

cookie turkeys

PREP: 20 MINUTES + STANDING

40	fudge-striped cookies
1/4	cup chocolate frosting
2	packages (5 ounces *each*) chocolate-covered cherries
20	pieces candy corn

Place 20 cookies on a flat surface, solid chocolate side down. With frosting attach a chocolate-covered cherry to the top of each base cookie. Position another cookie perpendicular to each base cookie; attach with frosting.

With a dab of frosting, attach one piece of candy corn to the front of each cherry for the head. Let stand until set. **YIELD: 20 servings.**

TASTE OF HOME TEST KITCHEN

With its toothy grin, lovely golden crust and tummy that's perfect for serving dip, this charming rabbit is sure to bring a smile to Easter guests of all ages.

easter bunny bread

PREP: 20 MINUTES + RISING / **BAKE:** 25 MINUTES + COOLING

2	loaves (1 pound *each*) frozen bread dough, thawed
2	raisins
2	sliced almonds
1	egg, lightly beaten

Lettuce leaves

Dip of your choice

Cut a fourth off of one loaf of dough; shape into a pear to form head. For body, flatten remaining portion into a 7-in. x 6-in. oval; place on a greased baking sheet. Place head above the body. Make narrow cuts, about 3/4 in. deep, on each side of the head for whiskers.

Cut second loaf into four equal portions. For ears, shape two portions into 16-in. ropes; fold ropes in half. Arrange ears with open ends touching head. Cut a third portion of dough in half; shape each into a 3-1/2-in. oval for back paws. Cut two 1-in. slits on top edge for toes. Position on each side of body.

Divide the fourth portion of dough into three pieces. Shape two pieces into 2-1/2-in. balls for front paws; shape the remaining piece into two 1-in. balls for cheeks and one 1/2-in. ball for nose. Place paws on each side of body; cut two 1-in. slits for toes. Place cheeks and nose on face. Add raisins for the eyes and almonds for teeth.

Brush dough with egg. Cover and let rise in a warm place until doubled, about 30-45 minutes. Bake at 350° for 25-30 minutes or until golden brown. Remove to a wire rack to cool.

Place bread on a lettuce-lined 16-in. x 13-in. serving tray. Cut a 5-in. x 4-in. oval in center of body. Hollow out bread, leaving a 1/2-in. shell (discard removed bread or save for another use). Line with lettuce and fill with dip. **YIELD: 1 loaf.**

BRENDA PAINE, NORTH SYRACUSE, NEW YORK

I usually serve this in summer when fresh berries are bountiful, but I recently prepared it with frozen cherries and light cherry pie filling instead. It was a delicious glimpse of summer-to-come!

angel berry trifle

PREP/TOTAL TIME: 15 MINUTES

1-1/2	cups cold fat-free milk
1	package (1 ounce) sugar-free instant vanilla pudding mix
1	cup (8 ounces) fat-free vanilla yogurt
6	ounces reduced-fat cream cheese, cubed
1/2	cup reduced-fat sour cream
2	teaspoons vanilla extract
1	carton (12 ounces) frozen reduced-fat whipped topping, thawed, *divided*
1	prepared angel food cake (18 inches), cut into 1-inch cubes
1	pint *each* blackberries, raspberries and blueberries

In a small bowl, whisk the milk and pudding mix for 2 minutes or until soft-set. In a large bowl, beat the yogurt, cream cheese, sour cream and vanilla until smooth. Fold in pudding mixture and 1 cup whipped topping.

Place a third of the cake cubes in a 4-qt. trifle bowl. Top with a third of the pudding mixture, a third of the berries and half of the remaining whipped topping. Repeat layers once. Top with the remaining cake, pudding and berries. Serve immediately or refrigerate. **YIELD: 14 servings.**

KELLY TOWNSEND, SYRACUSE, NEBRASKA
These Asian-inspired kabobs, served with a tasty dipping sauce, are special enough to make for guests at your next backyard get-together. Sometimes I substitute salmon for the chicken.

chicken and asparagus kabobs

PREP: 25 MINUTES + MARINATING / **GRILL:** 10 MINUTES

DIPPING SAUCE:

2	cups mayonnaise
1/4	cup sugar
1/4	cup soy sauce
2	tablespoons sesame seeds, toasted
1	tablespoon sesame oil
1/2	teaspoon white pepper

KABOBS:

1/4	cup soy sauce
2	tablespoons brown sugar
2	tablespoons water
1	tablespoon sesame oil
1	teaspoon crushed red pepper flakes
1	teaspoon minced fresh gingerroot
1-1/2	pounds boneless skinless chicken breasts, cut into 1-1/2-inch pieces
1	pound fresh asparagus, trimmed and cut into 2-inch pieces
2	tablespoons olive oil
1/2	teaspoon salt

In a small bowl, combine the dipping sauce ingredients. Cover the sauce and refrigerate for 2-4 hours.

In a large resealable plastic bag, combine soy sauce, brown sugar, water, sesame oil, pepper flakes and ginger. Add the chicken; seal the bag and turn to coat. Refrigerate for 2 hours, turning occasionally.

Drain and discard marinade. In a large bowl, toss the asparagus with olive oil and salt. On six metal or soaked wooden skewers, alternately thread one chicken piece and two asparagus pieces.

Grill, covered, over medium heat for 4-5 minutes on each side or until chicken is no longer pink and asparagus is crisp-tender. Serve with dipping sauce. **YIELD: 6 servings.**

LINDA GUYOT, FOUNTAIN VALLEY, CALIFORNIA
I rely on canned pumpkin and a yellow cake mix to fix this effortless alternative to pumpkin pie. It's a true symbol of fall that always elicits compliments and recipe requests.

great pumpkin dessert

PREP: 5 MINUTES / **BAKE:** 1 HOUR

1	can (15 ounces) solid-pack pumpkin
1	can (12 ounces) evaporated milk
3	eggs
1	cup sugar
4	teaspoons pumpkin pie spice
1	package (18-1/4 ounces) yellow cake mix
3/4	cup butter, melted
1-1/2	cups chopped walnuts

Vanilla ice cream *or* whipped cream

In a large bowl, beat pumpkin, milk, egg, sugar and pumpkin pie spice until smooth.

Transfer to a greased 13-in. x 9-in. baking dish. Sprinkle with dry cake mix and drizzle with butter. Top with walnuts. Bake at 350° for 1 hour or until a knife inserted near the center comes out clean. Serve with ice cream or whipped cream. **YIELD: 12-16 servings.**

DEBI BENSON, BAKERSFIELD, CALIFORNIA

This tender, moist cake is full of old-fashioned comfort. The golden butterscotch sauce makes it extra special. For a festive occasion, top each slice with a dollop of whipped cream.

chunky apple cake

PREP: 20 MINUTES / **BAKE:** 40 MINUTES + COOLING

1/2	cup butter, softened
2	cups sugar
2	eggs
1/2	teaspoon vanilla extract
2	cups all-purpose flour
1-1/2	teaspoons ground cinnamon
1	teaspoon ground nutmeg
1/2	teaspoon salt
1/2	teaspoon baking soda
6	cups chopped peeled tart apples

BUTTERSCOTCH SAUCE:

1/2	cup packed brown sugar
1/4	cup butter, cubed
1/2	cup heavy whipping cream

In a large bowl, cream butter and sugar until light and fluffy. Add eggs, one at a time, beating well after each addition. Beat in vanilla. Combine the flour, cinnamon, nutmeg, salt and baking soda; gradually add to creamed mixture and mix well (batter will be stiff). Stir in apples until well combined.

Spread into a greased 13-in. x 9-in. baking dish. Bake at 350° for 40-45 minutes or until top is lightly browned and springs back when lightly touched. Cool for 30 minutes before serving.

Meanwhile, in a small saucepan, combine the brown sugar and butter. Cook over medium heat until butter is melted. Gradually add the cream. Bring to a slow boil over medium heat, stirring constantly. Remove from the heat. Serve sauce with cake. **YIELD: 12-14 servings.**

MARY KAUFENBERG, SHAKOPEE, MINNESOTA

Just six ingredients are needed to create these cute Kris Kringle confections. Store-bought peanut butter sandwich cookies turn jolly with white chocolate, colored sugar, mini chips and red-hots.

santa claus cookies

PREP: 50 MINUTES / **COOK:** 5 MINUTES

12	ounces white baking chocolate, chopped
1	package (1 pound) Nutter Butter sandwich cookies

Red colored sugar

32	vanilla *or* white chips
64	miniature semisweet chocolate chips
32	red-hot candies

In a microwave, melt the white baking chocolate at 70% power for 1 minute; stir. Microwave at additional 10- to 20-second intervals, stirring until smooth.

Dip one end of each cookie into the melted chocolate, allowing excess to drip off. Place on wire racks. For Santa's hat, sprinkle red sugar on top part of the chocolate. Press one vanilla chip off-center on hat for pom-pom; let stand until set.

Dip other end of each cookie into the melted chocolate for beard, leaving center of cookie uncovered. Place on wire racks. With a dab of melted chocolate, attach semisweet chips for eyes and a red-hot for nose. Place on waxed paper until set. **YIELD: 32 cookies.**

READERS' RAVES

> I just love making the Santa Claus Cookies—they are so easy and look so nice on my cookie trays.
>
> —Glenpop1 from TasteofHome.com

CAROL STEVENS, MOUNT JACKSON, VIRGINIA
We're a meat-and-potatoes family, so this roast is a must at our holiday meals. It really is the highlight of an elegant dinner and provides fantastic leftovers for great sandwiches the next day.

herbed standing rib roast

PREP: 10 MINUTES / **BAKE:** 1-3/4 HOURS + STANDING

- 3 tablespoons grated onion
- 2 tablespoons olive oil
- 4 garlic cloves, minced
- 2 teaspoons celery seed
- 1 teaspoon coarsely ground pepper
- 1 teaspoon paprika
- 1/4 teaspoon dried thyme
- 1 bone-in beef rib roast (6 to 7 pounds)
- 2 large onions, cut into wedges
- 2 large carrots, cut into 2-inch pieces
- 2 celery ribs, cut into 2-inch pieces
- 1/4 cup red wine *or* beef broth

Assorted herbs and fruit, optional

In a small bowl, combine the first seven ingredients; rub over roast. Place the onions, carrots and celery in a large roasting pan; place roast over vegetables.

Bake, uncovered, at 325° for 1-3/4 to 2-1/2 hours or until the meat reaches the desired doneness (for medium-rare, a meat thermometer should read 145°; medium, 160°; well-done, 170°). Remove roast to a serving platter and keep warm; let stand for 15 minutes before slicing.

Meanwhile, for au jus, strain and discard the vegetables. Pour the drippings into a measuring cup; skim fat. Add red wine or beef broth to roasting pan, stirring to remove any browned bits. Stir in the drippings; heat through. Serve au jus with roast. Garnish serving platter with assorted herbs and fruit if desired. **YIELD: 12 servings.**

BERTHA JOHNSON, INDIANAPOLIS, INDIANA
For a side dish with harvesttime appeal, you can't go wrong with this savory squash bake. It's creamy, comforting and looks pretty, too, thanks to the rich yellow butternut squash and golden crumb topping.

butternut squash bake

PREP: 35 MINUTES / **BAKE:** 30 MINUTES

- 1 small butternut squash, peeled, seeded and cubed (about 2 cups)
- 1/2 cup mayonnaise
- 1/2 cup finely chopped onion
- 1 egg, lightly beaten
- 1 teaspoon sugar

Salt and pepper to taste

- 1/4 cup crushed saltines (about 8 crackers)
- 2 tablespoons grated Parmesan cheese
- 1 tablespoon butter, melted

Place squash in a saucepan and cover with water; bring to a boil. Reduce heat; cover and simmer for 20-25 minutes or until very tender. Drain well and place in a large bowl; mash squash.

In another bowl, combine the mayonnaise, onion, egg, sugar, salt and pepper; add to the squash and mix well.

Transfer to a greased 1-qt. baking dish. Combine the cracker crumbs, cheese and butter; sprinkle over top. Bake, uncovered, at 350° for 30-40 minutes or until heated through and top is golden brown. **YIELD: 6 servings.**

EDITOR'S NOTE: Reduced-fat or fat-free mayonnaise is not recommended for this recipe.

D. SMITH, FEATERVILLE-TREVOSE, PENNSYLVANIA
There's plenty of sweet berry flavor in this refreshing summer sensation. Made with sugar-free gelatin and a graham cracker crust, the ruby red pie is easy to fix and attractive enough to serve at special occasions. You can also make an equally delicious version using fresh peaches and peach gelatin.

strawberry pie

PREP: 20 MINUTES + CHILLING

2	pints fresh strawberries, hulled
2	tablespoons cornstarch
1-1/2	cups cold water
1	package (.3 ounce) sugar-free strawberry gelatin
3	tablespoons sugar
1	reduced-fat graham cracker crust (8 inches)
2	cups reduced-fat whipped topping

Set aside four whole strawberries for garnish. Slice the remaining strawberries and set aside. In a large saucepan, combine the cornstarch and water until smooth. Bring to a boil; cook and stir for 2 minutes or until thickened.

Remove cornstarch mixture from the heat; stir in gelatin and sugar until dissolved. Stir in sliced strawberries. Pour strawberry mixture into the crust. Cover and refrigerate for 2 hours or until firm. Cut the reserved strawberries in half. Garnish each serving with whipped topping and a berry half. **YIELD: 8 servings.**

JOAN HAMILTON, WORCESTER, MASSACHUSETTS
The heartwarming taste of cinnamon and apples is the perfect complement to these tender pork chops. This robust autumn favorite is always a winner with my family. With only four ingredients, it's a main course I can serve with little preparation.

pork chops with apples and stuffing

PREP: 15 MINUTES / **BAKE:** 45 MINUTES

6	boneless pork loin chops (1 inch thick and 4 ounces *each*)
1	tablespoon canola oil
1	package (6 ounces) crushed stuffing mix
1	can (21 ounces) apple pie filling with cinnamon

In a large skillet, brown the pork chops in oil over medium-high heat. Meanwhile, prepare stuffing according to package directions. Spread pie filling into a greased 13-in. x 9-in. baking dish. Place the pork chops on top; spoon stuffing over chops.

Cover and bake at 350° for 35 minutes. Uncover; bake 10 minutes longer or until a meat thermometer reads 160°. **YIELD: 6 servings.**

MARY ELLEN FRIEND, RAVENSWOOD, WEST VIRGINIA

This melt-in-your-mouth delight is doubly delicious, with two creamy layers...one strawberry, one vanilla. To prevent the cheesecake cracking, run the knife just through the very top when swirling the strawberry puree.

strawberry swirl cheesecake

PREP: 1 HOUR / **BAKE:** 1-1/4 HOURS + CHILLING

1-1/4	cups all-purpose flour
1	tablespoon sugar
1	teaspoon grated lemon peel
1/2	cup cold butter

FILLING:

4	packages (8 ounces *each*) cream cheese, softened
1-1/3	cups sugar
2	tablespoons all-purpose flour
2	tablespoons heavy whipping cream
4	eggs, lightly beaten
1	tablespoon lemon juice
2	teaspoons vanilla extract
1	cup pureed fresh strawberries, *divided*
8	to 10 drops red food coloring, optional

In a small bowl, combine the flour, sugar and lemon peel; cut in butter until crumbly. Pat dough onto the bottom and 1 in. up the sides of a greased 9-in. springform pan. Place on a baking sheet. Bake at 325° for 15-20 minutes or until lightly browned. Cool on a wire rack.

In a large bowl, beat cream cheese, sugar, flour and cream until smooth. Add eggs; beat on low speed just until combined. Beat in lemon juice and vanilla just until blended. Pour 2-1/2 cups batter into a bowl; set aside.

Stir 3/4 cup pureed strawberries and food coloring if desired into remaining batter. Pour into crust. Place pan on a double thickness of heavy-duty foil (about 16 in. square). Securely wrap foil around pan. Place in a large baking pan. Add 1 in. of hot water to larger pan. Bake for 35 minutes.

Carefully pour reserved batter over bottom layer. Spoon the remaining pureed berries over batter in three concentric circles. Carefully cut through top layer only with a knife to swirl. Bake 40-50 minutes longer or until center is almost set. Remove pan from water bath. Cool on a wire rack for 10 minutes. Carefully run a knife around edge of the pan to loosen; cool 1 hour longer. Refrigerate overnight. **YIELD: 12 servings.**

MARY LOU WAYMAN, SALT LAKE CITY, UTAH

Looking to liven up your same-old holiday ham? Try this tongue-tingling recipe, which features a sweet and spicy sauce infused with chipotle peppers and raspberry jam.

raspberry-chipotle glazed ham

PREP: 10 MINUTES / **BAKE:** 2 HOURS 20 MINUTES

1	bone-in fully cooked spiral-sliced ham (9 to 10 pounds)
2-1/4	cups seedless raspberry jam
3	tablespoons white vinegar
3	chipotle peppers in adobo sauce, drained, seeded and minced
3	to 4 garlic cloves, minced
1	tablespoon coarsely ground pepper

Place ham on a rack in a shallow roasting pan. Bake, uncovered, at 325° for 2 to 2-1/2 hours or until a meat thermometer reads 130°.

In a small saucepan, combine the raspberry jam, vinegar, chipotle peppers and garlic. Bring to a boil. Reduce heat; simmer, uncovered, for 5 minutes. Brush some of the raspberry-chipotle sauce over the ham. Bake 20 minutes longer or until a meat thermometer reads 140°, brushing twice with sauce. Sprinkle pepper over ham. Serve the ham with the remaining sauce. **YIELD: 16-20 servings.**

PHYLLIS SCHMALZ, KANSAS CITY, KANSAS
This luscious cheesecake belongs on a pedestal. Just pour the spiced pumpkin filling over the delectable gingersnap crust, bake and refrigerate overnight. The final touch is the delectable, crunchy almond topping.

white chocolate pumpkin cheesecake

PREP: 30 MINUTES / **BAKE:** 55 MINUTES + CHILLING

1-1/2	cups crushed gingersnap cookies (about 32 cookies)
1/4	cup butter, melted
3	packages (8 ounces *each*) cream cheese, softened
1	cup sugar
3	eggs, lightly beaten
1	teaspoon vanilla extract
5	ounces white baking chocolate, melted and cooled
3/4	cup canned pumpkin
1	teaspoon ground cinnamon
1/4	teaspoon ground nutmeg

ALMOND TOPPING:

1/2	cup chopped almonds
2	tablespoons butter, melted
1	teaspoon sugar

In a small bowl, combine gingersnap crumbs and butter. Press onto the bottom of a greased 9-in. springform pan; set aside.

In a large bowl, beat cream cheese and sugar until smooth. Add eggs and vanilla; beat on low speed just until combined. Stir in melted white chocolate. Combine pumpkin and spices; gently fold into cream cheese mixture. Pour over crust. Place pan on a baking sheet.

Bake at 350° for 55-60 minutes or until center is just set. Cool on a wire rack for 10 minutes. Meanwhile, combine the topping ingredients; spread in a shallow baking pan. Bake for 10 minutes or until golden brown, stirring twice. Cool.

Carefully run a knife around edge of springform pan to loosen; cool 1 hour longer. Refrigerate overnight. Transfer topping to an airtight container; store in the refrigerator.

Just before serving, remove sides of pan; sprinkle topping over cheesecake. Refrigerate leftovers. **YIELD: 12 servings.**

JOANNE FAZIO, CARBONDALE, PENNSYLVANIA
This is my surprise dessert! No one ever guesses that the "secret ingredient" is zucchini. Everyone says it tastes like apples. This sweet and comforting cobbler is a great dessert for potluck suppers or other large gatherings. It's been requested time and again in my house, and I'm always happy to make it.

zucchini cobbler

PREP: 35 MINUTES / **BAKE:** 35 MINUTES

8	cups chopped seeded peeled zucchini (about 3 pounds)
2/3	cup lemon juice
1	cup sugar
1	teaspoon ground cinnamon
1/2	teaspoon ground nutmeg

CRUST:

4	cups all-purpose flour
2	cups sugar
1-1/2	cups cold butter, cubed
1	teaspoon ground cinnamon

In a large saucepan over medium-low heat, cook and stir the zucchini and lemon juice for 15-20 minutes or until zucchini is tender. Add the sugar, cinnamon and nutmeg; simmer 1 minute longer. Remove from the heat; set aside.

For crust, combine the flour and sugar in a bowl; cut in butter until the mixture resembles coarse crumbs. Stir 1/2 cup into the zucchini mixture. Press half of remaining crust mixture into a greased 15-in. x 10-in. baking pan. Spread zucchini over top; crumble remaining crust mixture over zucchini. Sprinkle with cinnamon. Bake at 375° for 35-40 minutes or until golden and bubbly. **YIELD: 16-20 servings.**

MICHELE CORNISH, BLAIRSTOWN, NEW JERSEY
I found this recipe in an old community cookbook that I paid 50 cents for at a garage sale! My husband just loves the combination of delicate angel hair pasta, fresh asparagus and mellow Swiss cheese. I do, too!

swiss angel hair 'n' asparagus

PREP/TOTAL TIME: 30 MINUTES

12	ounces uncooked angel hair pasta
1	pound fresh asparagus, trimmed and cut into 2-inch pieces
1/2	pound sliced fresh mushrooms
1	teaspoon minced chives
3	tablespoons butter
2	tablespoons all-purpose flour
2-1/4	teaspoons salt-free seasoning blend
1/2	teaspoon salt
2-1/4	cups milk
1-1/2	cups (6 ounces) shredded Swiss cheese

Grated Parmesan cheese, optional

Cook pasta according to package directions. Meanwhile, place asparagus in a steamer basket; place in a large saucepan over 1 in. of water. Bring to a boil; cover and steam for 3-5 minutes or until crisp-tender.

In a large saucepan, saute mushrooms and chives in butter until tender. Stir in the flour, seasoning blend and salt; gradually add milk. Bring to a boil; cook and stir for 1-2 minutes or until thickened. Add the Swiss cheese; cook and stir until melted.

Drain pasta and place in a large bowl. Add asparagus and cheese sauce; toss to coat. Garnish with Parmesan cheese if desired. **YIELD: 10 servings.**

MARGARET MATSON, METAMORA, ILLINOIS
It's easy and convenient to prepare the base of this slushy punch ahead. Its rosy color makes it so pretty for Christmas. I've also made it with apricot gelatin for a bridal shower. This bubbly beverage makes any occasion a bit more special.

icy holiday punch

PREP: 10 MINUTES + FREEZING

1	package (6 ounces) cherry gelatin
3/4	cup sugar
2	cups boiling water
1	can (46 ounces) pineapple juice
6	cups cold water
2	liters ginger ale, chilled

In a 4-qt. freezer-proof container, dissolve gelatin and sugar in boiling water. Stir in pineapple juice and cold water. Cover and freeze overnight. Remove from the freezer 2 hours before serving. Place in a punch bowl; stir in the ginger ale just before serving. **YIELD: 32-36 servings (5-3/4 quarts).**

TRISHA KAMMERS, CLARKSTON, WASHINGTON

This moist, airy cake was my dad's favorite. My mom revamped the original recipe to include lemons. It takes some time, but every mouthwatering bite makes this luscious dessert well worth the effort.

lemon chiffon cake

PREP: 25 MINUTES / **BAKE:** 50 MINUTES + COOLING

7	eggs, *separated*
2	cups all-purpose flour
1-1/2	cups sugar
3	teaspoons baking powder
1	teaspoon salt
3/4	cup water
1/2	cup canola oil
4	teaspoons grated lemon peel
2	teaspoons vanilla extract
1/2	teaspoon cream of tartar

LEMON FROSTING:

1/3	cup butter, softened
3	cups confectioners' sugar
4-1/2	teaspoons grated lemon peel

Dash salt

1/4	cup lemon juice

Let eggs stand at room temperature for 30 minutes. In a large bowl, combine flour, sugar, baking powder and salt. In another bowl, whisk the egg yolks, water, oil, lemon peel and vanilla; add to dry ingredients. Beat until well blended.

In another large bowl, beat egg whites and cream of tartar on medium speed until soft peaks form; fold into batter. Gently spoon into an ungreased 10-in. tube pan. Cut through batter with a knife to remove air pockets.

Bake on the lowest oven rack at 325° for 50-55 minutes or until top springs back when lightly touched. Immediately invert the pan; cool completely, about 1 hour.

Run a knife around side and center tube of pan. Remove cake to a serving plate. In a small bowl, combine frosting ingredients; beat until smooth. Spread over top of cake. **YIELD: 12-16 servings.**

DEBORAH RANDALL, ABBEVILLE, LOUISIANA

As a pastor's wife and state auxiliary leader, I host many large gatherings. Whenever I make this "punch bowl cake," it makes a big impression—people love the combination of cake, pudding and apple pie flavor. Needless to say, I return home with an empty bowl.

colossal caramel apple trifle

PREP: 40 MINUTES

1	package (18-1/4 ounces) yellow cake mix
6	cups cold milk
3	packages (3.4 ounces *each*) instant vanilla pudding mix
1	teaspoon apple pie spice
1	jar (12-1/4 ounces) caramel ice cream topping
1-1/2	cups chopped pecans, toasted
2	cans (21 ounces *each*) apple pie filling
2	cartons (16 ounces *each*) frozen whipped topping, thawed

Prepare and bake cake according to package directions, using two greased 9-in. round baking pans. Cool for 10 minutes before removing to wire racks to cool completely.

In a large bowl, whisk milk, pudding mixes and apple pie spice for 2 minutes. Let stand for 2 minutes or until soft-set.

Cut one cake layer if necessary to fit evenly in an 8-qt. punch bowl. Poke holes in cake with a long wooden skewer; gradually pour a third of the caramel topping over cake. Sprinkle with 1/2 cup pecans and spread with half of the pudding mixture.

Spoon one can of pie filling over pudding; spread with one carton of whipped topping. Top with remaining cake and repeat layers. Drizzle with the remaining caramel topping and sprinkle with remaining pecans. Refrigerate until serving. **YIELD: 42 servings (3/4 cup each).**

LINDA BURNETT, PRESCOTT, ARIZONA
An enticing aroma drifts through my house when this tender cake-like bread is in the oven. I bake extra loaves to give as holiday gifts. My friends wait eagerly for it every year.

delicious pumpkin bread

PREP: 15 MINUTES / **BAKE:** 50 MINUTES + COOLING

5	eggs
1-1/4	cups canola oil
1	can (15 ounces) solid-pack pumpkin
2	cups all-purpose flour
2	cups sugar
2	packages (3 ounces *each*) cook-and-serve vanilla pudding mix
1	teaspoon baking soda
1	teaspoon ground cinnamon
1/2	teaspoon salt

In a large bowl, beat the eggs. Add oil and pumpkin; beat until smooth. Combine remaining ingredients; gradually beat into pumpkin mixture.

Pour batter into five greased 5-3/4-in. x 3-in. loaf pans. Bake at 325° for 50-55 minutes or until a toothpick inserted near the center comes out clean. Cool for 10 minutes before removing from pans to wire racks to cool completely. **YIELD: 5 mini loaves (8 slices each).**

EDITOR'S NOTE: Bread may also be baked in two greased 8-in. x 4-in. loaf pans for 75-80 minutes.

DENISE SMITH, LUSK, WYOMING
Here's a ghoulishly fun way to jazz up store-bought cookies for Halloween. The chocolate-covered peanut butter cookies are a real hit with "goblins" young and old.

quick ghost cookies

PREP/TOTAL TIME: 30 MINUTES

1	pound white candy coating, coarsely chopped
1	package (1 pound) Nutter Butter peanut butter cookies

Miniature semisweet chocolate chips

In a microwave-safe bowl, melt the candy coating, stirring occasionally. Dip cookies into coating, covering completely. Place on waxed paper.

Brush ends with a pastry brush dipped in coating where fingers touched cookies. While coating is still warm, place two chips on each cookie for eyes. Let stand until set. Store in an airtight container. **YIELD: about 3 dozen.**

READERS' RAVES

"
I found the easiest way to coat the ghost cookies is to stick a toothpick into the cookie's filling and dip it. That way there isn't so much on your fingers or tell-tale signs on the cookies where you had to patch the coating.

—Retherford from TasteofHome.com
"

VICKI SCHLECHTER, DAVIS, CALIFORNIA
You won't believe how delicious yet effortless this dish is. We tasted it for the first time when our son's godparents made it for us. Now the creamy dish is a standby for luncheons and special dinners alike.

saucy chicken and asparagus

PREP: 10 MINUTES / **BAKE:** 40 MINUTES

- 1-1/2   pounds fresh asparagus spears, halved
- 4   boneless skinless chicken breast halves
- 2   tablespoons canola oil
- 1/2   teaspoon salt
- 1/4   teaspoon pepper
- 1   can (10-3/4 ounces) condensed cream of chicken soup, undiluted
- 1/2   cup mayonnaise
- 1   teaspoon lemon juice
- 1/2   teaspoon curry powder
- 1   cup (4 ounces) shredded cheddar cheese

If desired, partially cook asparagus; drain. Place the asparagus in a greased 9-in. square baking dish. In a skillet over medium heat, brown the chicken in oil on both sides. Season with salt and pepper. Arrange chicken over asparagus.

In a bowl, mix soup, mayonnaise, lemon juice and curry powder; pour over chicken. Cover and bake at 375° for 40 minutes or until the chicken is tender and juices run clear. Sprinkle with cheese. Let stand 5 minutes before serving. **YIELD: 4 servings.**

MARYELLEN HAYS, WOLCOTTVILLE, INDIANA
After church services on Christmas morning, our family enjoys this cheesy, make-head casserole. But because it's so comforting, I'd also recommend it for a special breakfast or brunch any time of the year.

christmas breakfast casserole

PREP: 10 MINUTES + CHILLING / **BAKE:** 50 MINUTES + STANDING

- 7   slices white bread, crusts removed and cubed
- 2   cups (8 ounces) shredded cheddar cheese
- 6   eggs
- 3   cups milk
- 1   teaspoon ground mustard
- 1/2   teaspoon salt
- 1/4   teaspoon pepper
- 6   bacon strips, cooked and crumbled

In a greased 11-in. x 7-in. baking dish, combine the bread cubes and cheese. In a large bowl, whisk the eggs, milk, mustard, salt and pepper; pour over bread and cheese. Top with bacon. Cover and refrigerate overnight.

Remove from the refrigerator 30 minutes before baking. Bake, uncovered, at 350° for 50-55 minutes or until a knife inserted near the center comes out clean. Let stand 10 minutes before serving. **YIELD: 6-8 servings.**

TASTE OF HOME TEST KITCHEN

While the real bird is roasting, you can present your guests with this adorable Thanksgiving-themed cheese ball. Our very own flock of clever home economists dreamed up the recipe for this festive edible centerpiece.

turkey cheese ball

PREP: 45 MINUTES + CHILLING

- 2 packages (8 ounces *each*) cream cheese
- 6 ounces deli smoked turkey, finely chopped
- 1 cup (4 ounces) shredded cheddar cheese
- 1 tablespoon finely chopped onion
- 1 tablespoon Worcestershire sauce
- 1/2 teaspoon garlic powder

DECORATIONS:

- 3 packages (3 ounces *each*) cream cheese, softened
- 2 tablespoons milk

Brown, orange and yellow paste food coloring

- 6 large oval crackers
- 1 large sweet red pepper
- 1 small yellow summer squash
- 1 cup pecan halves

Assorted crackers

In a small bowl, beat the cream cheese, turkey, cheese, onion, Worcestershire and garlic powder until combined. Shape into a ball; wrap in plastic wrap. Refrigerate for 1 hour or until firm.

In another small bowl, beat the cream cheese and milk until smooth. Divide among four small bowls. With food coloring, tint one bowl brown, one dark orange and one light orange (using yellow and orange); leave one bowl plain.

Transfer each mixture to a heavy-duty resealable plastic bag; cut a small hole in a corner of each bag. For turkey tail feathers, decorate the top halves of the large oval crackers with tinted cream cheese.

Using the red pepper, form the turkey head, neck and snood. For beak, cut a small triangle from summer squash; attach with cream cheese. Add eyes, using brown and plain cream cheese. Insert pecan halves and decorated crackers into cheese ball. Serve with assorted crackers. **YIELD: 1 cheese ball (3 cups).**

EDITOR'S NOTE: This recipe was tested with Townhouse Oval Bistro crackers.

LAURA KIMBALL, WEST JORDAN, UTAH
I get a great deal of satisfaction making and giving time-tested Yuletide treats like these soft, chewy cookies. Dipping them in white chocolate makes great gingersnaps even better.

dipped gingersnaps

PREP: 20 MINUTES / **BAKE:** 10 MINUTES/BATCH + COOLING

- 2 cups sugar
- 1-1/2 cups canola oil
- 2 eggs
- 1/2 cup molasses
- 4 cups all-purpose flour
- 4 teaspoons baking soda
- 3 teaspoons ground ginger
- 2 teaspoons ground cinnamon
- 1 teaspoon salt

Additional sugar

- 2 packages (10 to 12 ounces *each*) vanilla *or* white chips
- 1/4 cup shortening

In a large bowl, combine sugar and oil. Beat in eggs. Stir in the molasses. Combine the flour, baking soda, ginger, cinnamon and salt; gradually add to creamed mixture and mix well.

Shape dough into 3/4-in. balls and roll in the sugar. Place 2 in. apart on ungreased baking sheets. Bake at 350° for 10-12 minutes or until cookie springs back when touched lightly. Remove to wire racks to cool.

In a small saucepan, melt chips with shortening over low heat, stirring until smooth. Dip the cookies halfway into the melted chips; shake off excess. Place on waxed paper-lined baking sheets until set. **YIELD: about 14-1/2 dozen.**

TASTE OF HOME TEST KITCHEN

Get ready for an assembly line because these marshmallow witches, dreamed up by our home economists, are just the sort of thing kids love helping with. The spooky treats are perfect for bewitching gatherings because a dozen can be put together in just 30 minutes.

marshmallow witches

PREP/TOTAL TIME: 30 MINUTES

1/2	cup vanilla frosting, *divided*
36	miniature semisweet chocolate chips
12	large marshmallows
1	drop *each* green, red and yellow food coloring, optional
1/4	cup flaked coconut
12	chocolate wafers
12	miniature peanut butter cups
12	milk chocolate kisses

For the face of each witch, place a dab of the frosting on the bottom of three chocolate chips; press two for eyes and one for nose onto each marshmallow.

For hair, combine green food coloring and a drop of water in a small resealable plastic bag; add coconut and shake well. Spread a small amount of frosting on sides of marshmallows; press coconut hair into frosting. Place 3 tablespoons of frosting in a small heavy-duty resealable plastic bag; tint orange with red and yellow food coloring. Set aside.

For hats, spread some of the remaining frosting in the center of chocolate wafers; press the peanut butter cups upside down into frosting. Lightly spread bottoms of chocolate kisses with frosting; place on the peanut butter cups. Cut a small hole in the corner of pastry or plastic bag; insert a small star tip. Fill the bag with frosting and pipe stars around the base of each peanut butter cup. Secure a hat to each witch with a dab of frosting. **YIELD: 1 dozen.**

EDITOR'S NOTE: Whip up an extra batch, put them in plastic wrap, and tie with curly orange or black ribbon for festive party favors.

DAWN LIET HARTMAN, MIFFLINBURG, PENNSYLVANIA
I first prepared this pie at Thanksgiving to share with my co-workers. It was such a success that now I freeze cranberries while they are in season so that I can make it year-round.

cranberry pecan pie

PREP: 25 MINUTES + CHILLING
BAKE: 45 MINUTES + COOLING

6	tablespoons shortening
1-1/2	teaspoons buttermilk
2	tablespoons hot water
1	cup all-purpose flour
1/2	teaspoon salt

FILLING:

3	eggs
1	cup corn syrup
2/3	cup sugar
1/4	cup butter, melted
1	teaspoon vanilla extract
2	cups fresh cranberries
1	cup chopped pecans

In a small bowl, cream the shortening and buttermilk until smooth. Gradually add the water, beating until light and fluffy. Beat in flour and salt. Wrap pastry in plastic wrap; refrigerate for 4 hours or overnight.

Roll out pastry to fit a 9-in. pie plate. Trim pastry to 1/2 in. beyond edge of plate; flute edges. In a large bowl, combine the eggs, corn syrup, sugar, butter and vanilla until blended. Stir in cranberries and pecans. Pour into crust.

Bake at 425° for 10 minutes. Reduce heat to 350°; bake 35-40 minutes longer or until filling is almost set. Cool completely on a wire rack. Cover pie and refrigerate overnight before slicing. **YIELD: 6-8 servings.**

CLAUDETTE BROWNLEE, KINGFISHER, OKLAHOMA
I love to have the dough for these muffins ready and waiting in the refrigerator when company comes. They bake up in just 20 minutes and taste delicious warm. Their cake-like texture makes them perfect for breakfast, dessert or snacking.

lemon crumb muffins

PREP: 25 MINUTES / **BAKE:** 20 MINUTES/BATCH

6	cups all-purpose flour
4	cups sugar
3/4	teaspoon baking soda
3/4	teaspoon salt
8	eggs
2	cups (16 ounces) sour cream
2	cups butter, melted
3	tablespoons grated lemon peel
2	tablespoons lemon juice

TOPPING:

3/4	cup all-purpose flour
3/4	cup sugar
1/4	cup cold butter, cubed

GLAZE:

1/2	cup sugar
1/3	cup lemon juice

In a large bowl, combine the flour, sugar, baking soda and salt. In another bowl, combine the eggs, sour cream, butter, lemon peel and juice. Stir into dry ingredients just until moistened. Fill greased or paper-lined muffin cups three-fourths full.

In a small bowl, combine flour and sugar; cut in the butter until mixture resembles coarse crumbs. Sprinkle over batter.

Bake at 350° for 20-25 minutes or until a toothpick inserted near the center comes out clean. Cool for 5 minutes before removing from pans to wire racks. In a small bowl, whisk glaze ingredients; drizzle over warm muffins. **YIELD: 40 muffins.**

RENDA DUFRESNE, MIDLAND, MICHIGAN
Everything about this dessert makes it the top request for family gatherings. The delightful crust cuts beautifully to reveal a filling with pieces of diced apple. At harvesttime or throughout the year, you cannot beat this delectable apple pie.

dutch apple pie

PREP: 20 MINUTES / **BAKE:** 40 MINUTES

2	cups all-purpose flour
1	cup packed brown sugar
1/2	cup quick-cooking oats
3/4	cup butter, melted

FILLING:

2/3	cup sugar
3	tablespoons cornstarch
1-1/4	cups cold water
3	cups diced peeled tart apples
1	teaspoon vanilla extract

In a large bowl, combine the flour, brown sugar, oats and butter; set aside 1 cup for topping. Press remaining crumb mixture into an ungreased 9-in. pie plate; set aside.

For filling, combine the sugar, cornstarch and water in a large saucepan until smooth; bring to a boil. Cook and stir for 2 minutes or until thickened. Remove the mixture from the heat; stir in diced apples and vanilla extract.

Pour into crust; top with reserved crumb mixture. Bake at 350° for 40-45 minutes or until crust is golden brown. Cool on a wire rack. **YIELD: 6-8 servings.**

VICKI MELIES, ELKHORN, NEBRASKA
A friend of mine shared this fun idea. She made the jolly loaf with purchased frozen dough, but I adapted it so I could use a family from-scratch recipe. The finished bread looks complicated, but it's actually very simple to create.

golden santa bread

PREP: 30 MINUTES + RISING / **BAKE:** 25 MINUTES + COOLING

4	to 4-1/2 cups bread flour
1/2	cup sugar
2	packages (1/4 ounce *each*) active dry yeast
1-1/2	teaspoons salt
1/2	cup milk
1/4	cup water
1/4	cup butter, cubed
2	eggs
2	raisins
2	egg yolks
2	to 3 drops red food coloring

In a large bowl, combine 2 cups flour, sugar, yeast and salt. In a small saucepan, heat the milk, water and butter to 120°-130°. Add to dry ingredients; beat just until moistened. Beat in the eggs until smooth. Stir in enough of the remaining flour to form a stiff dough.

Turn onto a floured surface; knead until smooth and elastic, about 6-8 minutes. Place in a greased bowl, turning once to grease top. Cover and let rise in a warm place until doubled, about 1 hour.

Punch the dough down. Turn the dough onto a lightly floured surface; divide dough into two portions, one slightly larger than the other. Shape the larger portion of dough into an elongated triangle with rounded corners for Santa's head and hat. Divide the smaller portion in half. Shape and flatten one half into a beard. Using scissors or a pizza cutter, cut into strips to within 1 in. of top. Position stips on Santa's face; twist and curl strips if desired.

Use the remaining dough for the mustache, nose, hat pom-pom and brim. Shape a portion of dough into a mustache; flatten and cut the ends into small strips with scissors. Place above beard. Place a small ball above mustache for nose. Fold tip of hat over and add another ball for pom-pom. Roll out a narrow piece of dough to create a hat brim; position under hat.

With a scissors, cut two slits for eyes; insert the raisins into slits. In separate small bowls, beat each egg yolk. Add the red food coloring to one yolk; carefully brush over hat, nose and cheeks. Brush plain yolk over remaining dough.

Cover loosely with foil. Bake at 350° for 15 minutes. Uncover; bake 10-12 minutes longer or until golden brown. Cool on a wire rack. **YIELD: 1 loaf.**

ROBERT & REBECCA LITTLEJOHN
MEADOW VISTA, CALIFORNIA
I got this deliciously different spin on a Thanksgiving staple from a friend. It's definitely worth the effort if you want to wow your gang. Leftovers are great with chicken, too.

mango cranberry sauce

PREP/TOTAL TIME: 25 MINUTES

1-1/2	cups whole-berry cranberry sauce
3	tangerines, peeled, seeded and chopped
1	medium mango, peeled and diced
1	cup diced fresh pineapple
1/4	cup finely chopped red onion
1/4	cup minced fresh cilantro
1	jalapeno pepper, seeded and finely chopped

In a large bowl, combine all the ingredients. Cover sauce and refrigerate until serving. **YIELD: 4-1/2 cups.**

EDITOR'S NOTE: When cutting hot peppers, disposable gloves are recommended. Avoid touching your face.

JEANNE MILLER, BIG SKY, MONTANA

This impressive ham makes an eye-fetching centerpiece for a holiday dinner. However, I've served it most often for brunch.

stuffed ham with raisin sauce

PREP: 30 MINUTES / **BAKE:** 1-3/4 HOURS

1	boneless fully cooked ham (6 to 7 pounds)
1	large onion, chopped
1/4	cup butter, cubed
2	cups corn bread stuffing mix
1-1/2	cups chopped pecans, toasted
1/2	cup minced fresh parsley
1/4	cup egg substitute
2	tablespoons prepared mustard
1/2	cup honey
2	tablespoons orange juice concentrate

RAISIN SAUCE:

1/2	cup packed brown sugar
2	tablespoons all-purpose flour
1/2	teaspoon ground mustard
1/2	cup raisins
1-1/2	cups water
1/4	cup cider vinegar

Using a sharp thin-bladed knife and beginning at one end of the ham, carefully cut a 2-1/2-in. circle about 6 in. deep; remove cutout. Cut a 1-1/2-in. slice from the end of removed piece; set aside.

Continue cutting a 2-1/2-in. tunnel halfway through ham, using a spoon to remove pieces of ham (save for another use). Repeat from opposite end of ham, cutting and removing ham until a tunnel has been cut through entire length of ham.

In a small skillet, saute onion in butter until tender. In a large bowl, combine the stuffing mix, pecans, parsley, egg substitute and mustard. Stir in onion. Stuff ham; cover end openings with reserved ham slices. Place in a shallow roasting pan.

Bake, uncovered, at 325° for 1-1/4 hours. In a small saucepan, combine honey and orange juice concentrate; cook and stir for 1-2 minutes or until blended. Brush over ham. Bake 30 minutes longer or until a meat thermometer reads 140°.

For sauce, combine the brown sugar, flour, mustard and raisins in a saucepan. Gradually add water and vinegar. Bring to a boil; cook and stir for 1-2 minutes or until thickened. Serve with ham. **YIELD: 12-14 servings.**

EDITOR'S NOTE: Two fully cooked boneless ham halves can be substituted for the whole ham. Simply hollow out each ham; loosely spoon stuffing into each half, then bake as directed.

CAROL JOHNSON, TYLER, TEXAS

Make the most of angel food cake, pie filling and whipped topping by creating this light and luscious dessert that doesn't keep you in the kitchen for hours. It's the perfect way to end a summer meal and makes use of fresh blueberries.

blueberry angel dessert

PREP: 10 MINUTES + CHILLING

1	package (8 ounces) cream cheese, softened
1	cup confectioners' sugar
1	carton (8 ounces) frozen whipped topping, thawed
1	prepared angel food cake (16 ounces), cut into 1-inch pieces
2	cans (21 ounces *each*) blueberry pie filling

In a large bowl, beat the cream cheese and sugar until smooth; fold in whipped topping and cake cubes. Spread evenly into an ungreased 13-in. x 9-in. dish; top with the pie filling. Cover and refrigerate for at least 2 hours before cutting into squares. **YIELD: 12-15 servings.**

RUTH SEITZ, COLUMBUS JUNCTION, IOWA
No store-bought Easter candy can compare to Mom's home-made chocolate-covered eggs. The heavenly centers have peanut butter, coconut and walnuts. These rich candies will simply melt in your mouth.

chocolate easter eggs

PREP: 25 MINUTES + CHILLING

1/4	cup butter, softened
3/4	cup chunky peanut butter
1-1/2	to 2 cups confectioners' sugar, *divided*
1	cup flaked coconut
1/2	cup finely chopped walnuts
2	cups (12 ounces) semisweet chocolate chips
2	tablespoons shortening

In a large bowl, cream the butter and peanut butter until fluffy. Gradually add 1 cup confectioners' sugar and mix well. Stir in coconut and nuts.

Turn peanut butter mixture onto a surface lightly dusted with some of the remaining confectioners' sugar; knead in enough of the remaining confectioners' sugar until mixture holds its shape when formed. Shape into small egg-shaped pieces. Cover and chill for 1 hour.

In a microwave, melt chocolate chips and shortening; stir until smooth. Dip egg into chocolate; allow excess to drip off. Place on waxed paper; let stand until set. Chill. **YIELD: 2 dozen.**

SHIRLEY PRIVRATSKY, DICKINSON, NORTH DAKOTA
I have lots of fun with this festive wreath. It's so colorful and pretty that when I serve it at Christmas gatherings, I often place a bowl of stuffed olives in the center.

appetizer wreath

PREP: 20 MINUTES / **BAKE:** 15 MINUTES + COOLING

2	tubes (8 ounces *each*) refrigerated crescent rolls
1	package (8 ounces) cream cheese, softened
1/2	cup sour cream
1	teaspoon dill weed
1/8	teaspoon garlic powder
1-1/2	cups chopped fresh broccoli florets
1	cup finely chopped celery
1/2	cup finely chopped sweet red pepper

Celery leaves

Remove the crescent dough from packaging (do not unroll). Cut each tube into eight slices. Arrange in an 11-in. circle on an ungreased 14-in. pizza pan.

Bake at 375° for 15-20 minutes or until golden brown. Cool for 5 minutes before carefully removing wreath to a serving platter; let cool completely.

In a small bowl, beat cream cheese, sour cream, dill and garlic powder until smooth. Spread over wreath; top with broccoli, celery and red pepper. Form a bow garnish with celery leaves. **YIELD: 16 servings.**

KITCHEN TIP

When a recipe, such as Appetizer Wreath, calls for fresh broccoli florets, save the stems for another use. Slice the stems into thin rounds, then place them into freezer bags and pop in the freezer. Add them to homemade vegetable soup or casseroles. You don't waste any of the broccoli and you give your recipes a boost of nutrition.

MARGENE PONS, WEST VALLEY CITY, UTAH

Assembling these merry mice is so much fun that the kids will definitely want to help. My daughter gave me the recipe, along with a warning...your guests just might think these treats are too cute to eat!

christmas eve mice

PREP: 25 MINUTES + CHILLING

24	double-stuffed cream-filled chocolate sandwich cookies
1	cup (6 ounces) semisweet chocolate chips
2	teaspoons shortening
24	red maraschino cherries with stems, well drained
24	milk chocolate kisses
48	sliced almonds
1	small tube green decorative icing gel
1	small tube red decorative icing gel

Carefully twist cookies apart; set aside the halves with cream filling. Save plain halves for another use. In a microwave, melt semisweet chocolate chips and shortening; stir until smooth. Holding each cherry by the stem, dip cherry in melted chocolate, then press onto the bottom of a chocolate kiss. Place on the cream filling of cookie, with cherry stem extending beyond cookie edge.

For ears, place slivered almonds between the cherry and kiss. Refrigerate until set. With green gel, pipe holly leaves on the cream. With red gel, pipe holly berries between leaves and pipe eyes on each chocolate kiss. Store in an airtight container at room temperature. **YIELD: 24 servings.**

EDNA HOFFMAN, HEBRON, INDIANA

My grandmother always served this sweet potato casserole at Thanksgiving. The puffy marshmallow topping gives the dish a festive look, while a blend of comforting spices enhance the sweet potato flavor.

mallow-topped sweet potatoes

PREP: 10 MINUTES / **BAKE:** 45 MINUTES

6	cups hot mashed sweet potatoes (prepared without milk and butter)
1	cup milk
6	tablespoons butter, softened
1/2	cup packed brown sugar
1	egg
1-1/2	teaspoons ground cinnamon
1-1/2	teaspoons vanilla extract
3/4	teaspoon ground allspice
1/2	teaspoon salt
1/4	teaspoon ground nutmeg
18	large marshmallows

In a large bowl, beat the sweet potatoes, milk, butter, brown sugar, egg, cinnamon, vanilla, allspice, salt and nutmeg until smooth. Transfer to a greased shallow 2-1/2-qt. baking dish. Bake, uncovered, at 325° for 40-45 minutes or until heated through. Top with marshmallows. Bake 5-10 minutes longer or until marshmallows just begin to puff and brown. **YIELD: 10-12 servings.**

desserts

A meal isn't complete without indulging your taste buds in some rich and decadent treat. From simple, freshly baked cookies and bars to elaborate and elegant cheesecakes and tortes, these most-requested recipes make every occasion a sweet success.

PEANUT BUTTER SANDWICH COOKIES / PAGE 210

ESTHER SHANK, HARRISONVILLE, VIRGINIA

I have to say that I've been asked to share this chocolaty layered recipe more than any other in my collection. It's a longtime favorite—I can't even count how many times I've made these.

deluxe chocolate marshmallow bars

PREP: 25 MINUTES / **BAKE:** 20 MINUTES + CHILLING

3/4	cup butter, softened		1/2	cup chopped nuts, optional
1-1/2	cups sugar		4	cups miniature marshmallows
3	eggs		**TOPPING:**	
1	teaspoon vanilla extract		1-1/3	cups semisweet chocolate chips
1-1/3	cups all-purpose flour		1	cup peanut butter
3	tablespoons baking cocoa		3	tablespoons butter
1/2	teaspoon baking powder		2	cups crisp rice cereal
1/2	teaspoon salt			

In a small bowl, cream butter and sugar until light and fluffy. Add eggs, one at a time, beating well after each addition. Beat in vanilla.

Combine the flour, cocoa, baking powder and salt; gradually add to creamed mixture. Stir in nuts if desired. Spread in a greased 15-in. x 10-in. baking pan.

Bake at 350° for 15-18 minutes. Sprinkle with marshmallows; bake 2-3 minutes longer. Remove to a wire rack. Using a knife dipped in water, spread the melted marshmallows evenly over top. Cool completely.

For topping, combine the chocolate chips, peanut butter and butter in a small saucepan. Cook and stir over low heat until blended. Remove from the heat; stir in rice cereal. Spread over bars immediately. Chill. **YIELD: about 3 dozen.**

MILDRED SHERRER, FORT WORTH, TEXAS
Raspberry jam adds fruity sweetness to these rich-tasting cookies. The buttery delights will absolutely melt in your mouth!

berry shortbread dreams

PREP: 20 MINUTES + CHILLING / **BAKE:** 15 MINUTES

1	cup butter, softened
2/3	cup sugar
1/2	teaspoon almond extract
2	cups all-purpose flour
1/3	to 1/2 cup seedless raspberry jam

GLAZE:

1	cup confectioners' sugar
1/2	teaspoon almond extract
2	to 3 teaspoons water

In a large bowl, cream butter and sugar until light and fluffy. Beat in the extract; gradually add flour until dough forms a ball. Cover and refrigerate for 1 hour or until dough is easy to handle.

Roll into 1-in. balls. Place 1 in. apart on ungreased baking sheets. Using the end of a wooden spoon handle, make an indentation in the center. Fill with jam.

Bake at 350° for 14-18 minutes or until edges are lightly browned. Remove to wire racks to cool. Spoon additional jam into cookies if desired. Combine confectioners' sugar, extract and enough water to achieve drizzling consistency; drizzle over cookies. **YIELD: about 3-1/2 dozen.**

DOROTHY ANDERSON, OTTAWA, KANSAS
Here's a family treasure that's guaranteed to get thumbs-up approval from your gang. Lime juice puts a tangy twist on these tantalizing bars, offering a burst of citrus flavor in every mouthwatering bite.

lime cooler bars

PREP: 15 MINUTES / **BAKE:** 40 MINUTES + COOLING

2-1/2	cups all-purpose flour, *divided*
1/2	cup confectioners' sugar
3/4	cup cold butter, cubed
4	eggs
2	cups sugar
1/3	cup lime juice
1/2	teaspoon grated lime peel
1/2	teaspoon baking powder

Additional confectioners' sugar

In a large bowl, combine 2 cups flour and confectioners' sugar; cut in butter until mixture resembles coarse crumbs. Pat into a greased 13-in. x 9-in. baking pan. Bake at 350° for 20 minutes or until lightly browned.

In a large bowl, whisk the eggs, sugar, lime juice and peel until frothy. Combine the baking powder and remaining flour; whisk in egg mixture. Pour over hot crust.

Bake for 20-25 minutes or until light golden brown. Cool on a wire rack. Dust with confectioners' sugar. Cut into squares. **YIELD: 3 dozen.**

MARY JONES, CUMBERLAND, MAINE

If you delight in the taste of chocolate, then this is the cheese-cake for you. Every creamy bite melts in your mouth. It is so impressive yet not difficult to prepare. I whip up this dessert each time I want a yummy treat for my family or friends.

chocolate truffle cheesecake

PREP: 30 MINUTES / **BAKE:** 45 MINUTES + CHILLING

1-1/2	cups chocolate wafer crumbs (about 27 wafers)
2	tablespoons sugar
1/4	cup butter, melted

FILLING:

1/4	cup semisweet chocolate chips
1/4	cup heavy whipping cream
3	packages (8 ounces *each*) cream cheese, softened
1	cup sugar
1/3	cup baking cocoa
3	eggs, lightly beaten
1	teaspoon vanilla extract

TOPPING:

1-1/2	cups (9 ounces) semisweet chocolate chips
1/4	cup heavy whipping cream
1	teaspoon vanilla extract

Whipped cream and miniature chocolate kisses, optional

In a small bowl, combine wafer crumbs and sugar; stir in butter. Press onto the bottom and 1-1/2 in. up the sides of a greased 9-in. springform pan. Bake at 350° for 10 minutes. Cool on a wire rack. Reduce heat to 325°.

For filling, melt chocolate chips in a small heavy saucepan or microwave; stir until smooth. Remove from the heat; add cream and mix well. Set aside. In a large bowl, beat cream cheese and sugar until smooth. Add cocoa and beat well. Add eggs; beat on low just until combined. Stir in vanilla and chocolate mixture just until blended. Pour mixture over the crust. Return the pan to baking sheet.

Bake for 45-50 minutes or until center is almost set. For the topping, melt the chocolate chips in a heavy saucepan or microwave, stir until smooth. Stir in cream and vanilla; mix well. Spread over the filling. Cool pan on a wire rack for 10 minutes. Carefully run a knife around edge of pan to loosen; cool 1 hour longer. Refrigerate overnight.

Remove sides of pan. Just before serving, garnish with whipped cream and miniature chocolate kisses if desired. Refrigerate any leftovers. **YIELD: 12 servings.**

MARLEEN ADKINS, PLACENTIA, CALIFORNIA

A cake baked in a slow cooker may seem unusual. But chocolaty smiles around the table prove how tasty it is. Sometimes for a change of pace, I substitute butterscotch chips for chocolate.

hot fudge cake

PREP: 20 MINUTES / **COOK:** 4 HOURS

1-3/4	cups packed brown sugar, *divided*
1	cup all-purpose flour
6	tablespoons baking cocoa, *divided*
2	teaspoons baking powder
1/2	teaspoon salt
1/2	cup milk
2	tablespoons butter, melted
1/2	teaspoon vanilla extract
1-1/2	cups semisweet chocolate chips
1-3/4	cups boiling water

Vanilla ice cream

In a bowl, combine 1 cup brown sugar, flour, 3 tablespoons cocoa, baking powder and salt. In another bowl, combine the milk, butter and vanilla; stir into the dry ingredients just until combined. Spread evenly into a 3-qt. slow cooker coated with cooking spray. Sprinkle with chocolate chips.

In a bowl, combine the remaining brown sugar and cocoa; stir in boiling water. Pour over batter (do not stir). Cover and cook on high for 4 to 4-1/2 hours or until a toothpick inserted near the center of cake comes out clean. Serve warm with ice cream. **Yield: 6-8 servings.**

EDITOR'S NOTE: This recipe does not use eggs.

REBECCA KAYS, KLAMATH FALLS, OREGON

These moist, fudgy brownies have a scrumptious topping that tastes just like chocolate chip cookie dough! My husband, sons and I enjoy them frequently at various potluck meals. Everyone loves these decadent bites, and there's enough to feed a crowd.

two-tone fudge brownies

PREP: 20 MINUTES / **BAKE:** 20 MINUTES

1	cup (6 ounces) semisweet chocolate chips
1/2	cup butter, softened
1	cup sugar
3	eggs
1	teaspoon vanilla extract
1-1/4	cups all-purpose flour
1/4	teaspoon baking soda
3/4	cup chopped walnuts

COOKIE DOUGH LAYER:

1/2	cup butter, softened
1/2	cup packed brown sugar
1/4	cup sugar
3	tablespoons milk
1	teaspoon vanilla extract
1	cup all-purpose flour
1	cup (6 ounces) semisweet chocolate chips

In a microwave, melt chocolate chips; stir until smooth. Cool slightly. In a large bowl, cream butter and sugar until light and fluffy. Beat in eggs and vanilla. Stir in melted chocolate. Combine flour and baking soda; gradually add to batter. Stir in walnuts.

Spread into a greased 13-in. x 9-in. baking pan. Bake at 350° for 16-22 minutes or until a toothpick inserted near the center comes out clean. Cool on a wire rack.

In a small bowl, cream butter and sugars until light and fluffy. Beat in milk and vanilla. Gradually add flour. Stir in chocolate chips. Drop by tablespoonfuls over cooled brownies; carefully spread over top. Cut into squares. Store in the refrigerator. **YIELD: 4 dozen.**

JEANNETTE NORD, SAN JUAN CAPISTRANO, CALIFORNIA

When I take this crowd-pleasing treat to a potluck, I come home with an empty pan every time. People gobble up the sweet and creamy bars that have just the right amount of pear flavor. Cooking and baking come naturally for me—as a farm girl, I helped my mother feed my 10 siblings.

pear custard bars

PREP: 20 MINUTES + CHILLING
BAKE: 50 MINUTES + COOLING

1/2	cup butter, softened
1/3	cup sugar
1/4	teaspoon vanilla extract
3/4	cup all-purpose flour
2/3	cup chopped macadamia nuts

FILLING/TOPPING:

1	package (8 ounces) cream cheese, softened
1/2	cup sugar
1	egg
1/2	teaspoon vanilla extract
1	can (15-1/4 ounces) pear halves, drained
1/2	teaspoon sugar
1/2	teaspoon ground cinnamon

In a large bowl, cream butter and sugar until light and fluffy. Beat in vanilla. Gradually add flour to creamed mixture. Stir in the nuts. Press into a greased 8-in. square baking pan. Bake at 350° for 20 minutes or until lightly browned. Cool on a wire rack.

In a small bowl, beat cream cheese until smooth. Beat in the sugar, egg and vanilla. Pour over crust. Cut pears into 1/8-in. slices; arrange in a single layer over filling. Combine sugar and cinnamon; sprinkle over pears. Bake at 375° for 28-30 minutes (center will be soft-set and will become firmer upon cooling). Cool on a wire rack for 45 minutes.

Cover and refrigerate for at least 2 hours before cutting. Store in the refrigerator. **YIELD: 16 bars.**

KIMBERLY LAABS, HARTFORD, WISCONSIN

Our family loves dessert, and this chocolaty, layered treat is one of my mom's most requested recipes. It's surprisingly simple to prepare.

ice cream cookie dessert

PREP: 15 MINUTES + FREEZING

1	package (18 ounces) cream-filled chocolate sandwich cookies, crushed, *divided*
1/4	cup butter, melted
1/2	gallon vanilla ice cream, softened
1	jar (16 ounces) hot fudge ice cream topping, warmed
1	carton (8 ounces) frozen whipped topping, thawed

In a large bowl, combine 3-3/4 cups cookie crumbs and butter. Press into a greased 13-in. x 9-in. dish. Spread with ice cream; cover and freeze until set.

Drizzle the fudge topping over ice cream; cover and freeze until set. Spread with whipped topping; sprinkle with remaining cookie crumbs. Cover and freeze for 2 hours or until firm. Remove from the freezer 10 minutes before serving. **YIELD: 12 servings.**

CLARA HINMAN, FLAGLER, COLORADO

I've served this highly anticipated dessert to family, friends and special guests many times. The buttery crumb topping melts in your mouth. I've used other fruits that are in season, but my gang likes peaches best.

colorado peach cobbler

PREP: 15 MINUTES / **BAKE:** 35 MINUTES

1	cup sugar
2	tablespoons all-purpose flour
1/4	teaspoon ground nutmeg
4	cups sliced peeled fresh peaches

TOPPING:

1	cup sugar
1	cup all-purpose flour
1	teaspoon baking powder
1	teaspoon salt
1/3	cup cold butter
1	egg, beaten

Ice cream, optional

In a large bowl, combine sugar, flour and nutmeg. Add peaches; stir to coat. Pour into a greased 11-in. x 7-in. baking pan.

For topping, in a small bowl, combine sugar, flour, baking powder and salt; cut in the butter until the mixture resembles fine crumbs. Stir in egg. Spoon over peaches. Bake at 375° for 35-40 minutes or until filling is bubbly and topping is golden. Serve hot or cold with ice cream if desired. **YIELD: 8-10 servings.**

ANN JANSEN, DEPERE, WISCONSIN
My father-in-law is diabetic, but this creamy pudding dessert is one treat he can eat. It has all the flavors of a true banana split, but without any of the guilt!

banana split dessert

PREP: 25 MINUTES + CHILLING

2	cups reduced-fat graham cracker crumbs (about 10 whole crackers)
5	tablespoons reduced-fat margarine, melted
1	can (12 ounces) cold reduced-fat evaporated milk
3/4	cup cold fat-free milk
2	packages (1 ounce *each*) sugar-free instant vanilla pudding mix
2	medium firm bananas, sliced
1	can (20 ounces) unsweetened crushed pineapple, drained
1	carton (8 ounces) frozen reduced-fat whipped topping, thawed
3	tablespoons chopped walnuts
2	tablespoons chocolate syrup
5	maraschino cherries, quartered

Combine cracker crumbs and margarine; press into a 13-in. x 9-in. dish coated with cooking spray.

In a bowl, whisk the evaporated milk, fat-free milk and pudding mixes for 2 minutes or until slightly thickened. Spread pudding evenly over crust. Layer with bananas, pineapple and whipped topping. Sprinkle with nuts; drizzle with chocolate syrup. Top with cherries. Refrigerate for at least 1 hour before cutting. **YIELD: 15 servings.**

EDITOR'S NOTE: This recipe was tested with Parkay Light stick margarine.

JOANNE SIMPSON, PORTLAND, OREGON
This is one of my most-asked-for recipes. It's sweet and buttery with plenty of crunch. You could use dark, milk or even white chocolate and substitute almonds for the hazelnuts if you wish.

hazelnut toffee

PREP: 45 MINUTES + COOLING

2	teaspoons plus 1 cup butter, *divided*
1	cup sugar
3	tablespoons water
1	tablespoon light corn syrup
1/3	cup chopped hazelnuts

TOPPING:

2	cups (12 ounces *each*) semisweet chocolate chips
1/2	cup finely chopped hazelnuts

Line a 13-in. x 9-in. pan with foil; coat with cooking spray and set aside. Butter sides of a large heavy saucepan with 2 teaspoons butter. Cube remaining butter; place in pan. Add sugar, water and corn syrup. Cook and stir until mixture turns golden brown and a candy thermometer reads 300° (hard crack stage).

Remove from the heat; stir in hazelnuts. Pour into prepared pan without scraping; spread evenly. Let stand at room temperature until cool, about 1 hour. In a microwave-safe bowl, melt the chocolate chips. Spread evenly over the toffee. Sprinkle with hazelnuts, pressing down gently. Let stand for 1 hour. Break into bite-sized pieces. Store in the refrigerator. **YIELD: 1-3/4 pounds.**

EDITOR'S NOTE: We recommend that you test your candy thermometer before each use by bringing water to a boil; the thermometer should read 212°. Adjust your recipe temperature up or down based on your test.

KATIE SLOAN, CHARLOTTE, NORTH CAROLINA
This ruby-red cake with its lovely cream cheese frosting has become my "signature dessert." I can't go to any family function without it. The cake is very moist with a buttery chocolate taste.

classic red velvet cake

PREP: 25 MINUTES / **BAKE:** 20 MINUTES + COOLING

1/2	cup shortening
1-1/2	cups sugar
2	eggs
1	bottle (1 ounce) red food coloring
3	teaspoons white vinegar
1	teaspoon butter flavoring
1	teaspoon vanilla extract
2-1/2	cups cake flour
1/4	cup baking cocoa
1	teaspoon baking soda
1	teaspoon salt
1	cup buttermilk

FROSTING:

1	package (8 ounces) cream cheese, softened
1/2	cup butter, softened
3-3/4	cups confectioners' sugar
3	teaspoons vanilla extract

In a large bowl, cream shortening and sugar until light fluffy. Add eggs, one at a time, beating well after each addition. Beat in the food coloring, vinegar, butter flavoring and vanilla. Combine the flour, cocoa, baking soda and salt; add to creamed mixture alternately with buttermilk.

Pour into three greased and floured 9-in. round baking pans. Bake at 350° for 20 25 minutes or until a toothpick inserted near the center comes out clean. Cool for 10 minutes before removing from pans to wire racks to cool completely.

In a large bowl, combine frosting ingredients; beat until smooth and creamy. Spread between layers and over top and sides of cake. **YIELD: 12 servings.**

CHRISTIE NELSON, TAYLORVILLE, ILLINOIS
I wasn't a big fan of tiramisu until I tried this recipe with its distinctive cheesecake- and coffee-flavored layers. It's one of my favorite desserts to make during the fall.

tiramisu cheesecake dessert

PREP: 20 MINUTES / **BAKE:** 40 MINUTES + CHILLING

1	package (12 ounces) vanilla wafers
5	teaspoons instant coffee granules, *divided*
3	tablespoons hot water, *divided*
4	packages (8 ounces *each*) cream cheese, softened
1	cup sugar
1	cup (8 ounces) sour cream
4	eggs, lightly beaten
1	cup whipped topping
1	tablespoon baking cocoa

Layer half of the wafers in a greased 13-in. x 9-in. baking dish. In a small bowl, dissolve 2 teaspoons coffee granules in 2 tablespoons hot water. Brush wafers with half of coffee; set remaining mixture aside.

In a large bowl, beat the cream cheese, sugar and sour cream until smooth. Add eggs; beat on low speed just until combined. Divide batter in half. Dissolve remaining coffee granules in remaining hot water; stir into one portion of batter. Spread over wafers. Layer with remaining wafers; brush with reserved coffee. Top with remaining batter.

Bake at 325° for 40-45 minutes or until center is almost set. Cool on a wire rack for 10 minutes. Carefully run a knife around edge of dish to loosen; cool 1 hour longer. Refrigerate overnight.

Spread with the whipped topping; dust with cocoa. Refrigerate leftovers. **YIELD: 12 servings.**

DEBBIE KOKES, TABOR, SOUTH DAKOTA
When I find time to bake a treat, I like it to be special. This creamy filling gives traditional peanut butter cookies a new twist.

peanut butter sandwich cookies

PREP: 20 MINUTES / **BAKE:** 10 MINUTES/BATCH + COOLING

1	cup butter-flavored shortening
1	cup creamy peanut butter
1	cup sugar
1	cup packed brown sugar
3	eggs
1	teaspoon vanilla extract
3	cups all-purpose flour
2	teaspoons baking soda
1/4	teaspoon salt

FILLING:

1/2	cup creamy peanut butter
3	cups confectioners' sugar
1	teaspoon vanilla extract
5	to 6 tablespoons milk

In a large bowl, cream the shortening, peanut butter and sugars until light and fluffy. Add eggs, one at a time, beating well after each addition after each addition. Add vanilla. Combine the flour, baking soda and salt; add to creamed mixture and mix well.

Shape into 1-in. balls and place 2 in. apart on ungreased baking sheets. Flatten to 3/8-in. thickness with fork. Bake at 375° for 7-8 minutes or until golden. Remove to wire racks to cool.

For filling, in a large bowl, beat the peanut butter, confectioners' sugar, vanilla and enough milk to achieve spreading consistency. Spread on half of the cookies and top each with another cookie. **YIELD: 44 sandwich cookies.**

MICHELLE TIEMSTRA, LACOMBE, ALBERTA
A friend gave me the recipe for these rich, cake-like brownies topped with a creamy, coffee-enhanced filling and a chocolate glaze. I like to garnish each square with a coffee bean.

coffee 'n' cream brownies

PREP: 25 MINUTES / **BAKE:** 25 MINUTES + COOLING

1/2	cup butter, cubed
3	ounces unsweetened chocolate, chopped
2	eggs
1	cup sugar
1	teaspoon vanilla extract
2/3	cup all-purpose flour
1/4	teaspoon baking soda

FILLING:

1	tablespoon heavy whipping cream
1	teaspoon instant coffee granules
2	tablespoons butter, softened
1	cup confectioners' sugar

GLAZE:

1	cup (6 ounces) semisweet chocolate chips
1/3	cup heavy whipping cream

In a microwave, melt butter and chocolate; stir until smooth. Cool slightly. In a small bowl, beat eggs, sugar and vanilla; stir in the chocolate mixture. Combine the flour and baking soda; gradually add to chocolate mixture.

Spread into a greased 8-in. square baking pan. Bake at 350° for 25-30 minutes or until a toothpick inserted near the center comes out clean (do not overbake). Cool on a wire rack.

For filling, combine cream and coffee granules in a small bowl; stir until coffee is dissolved. In a small bowl, cream butter and confectioners' sugar until light and fluffy. Beat in coffee mixture; Spread over brownies.

In a small saucepan, combine chips and cream. Cook and stir over low heat until chocolate is melted and mixture is thickened. Cool slightly. Carefully spread over the filling. Let stand for 30 minutes or until glaze is set. Cut into squares. Store in the refrigerator. **YIELD: 16 servings.**

MARY CHOATE, SPRING HILL, FLORIDA
The biggest sweet tooths are satisfied with just a small slice of this dense, decadent torte. A white-chocolate pattern on top gives it an elegant finish.

truffle torte

PREP: 35 MINUTES / **BAKE:** 30 MINUTES + CHILLING

3/4	cup butter, cubed
8	ounces semisweet chocolate, chopped
6	eggs
3/4	cup sugar
1	teaspoon vanilla extract
3/4	cup ground pecans
1/4	cup all-purpose flour

GANACHE:
4	ounces semisweet chocolate, chopped
1/2	cup heavy whipping cream
2	tablespoons butter

GARNISH:
2	ounces white baking chocolate
3/4	cup finely chopped pecans

Pecan halves, optional

Line the bottom of a greased 9-in. springform pan with waxed paper; grease the paper and set aside.

In a small saucepan, melt butter and chocolate over low heat. Cool. In a large bowl, beat eggs until frothy; gradually add sugar, beating for 4-5 minutes or until the mixture triples in volume. Gradually beat in chocolate mixture and vanilla. Combine pecans and flour; fold into batter. Pour into prepared pan.

Bake at 350° for 30-35 minutes or until cake springs back when lightly touched. Cool on a wire rack for 15 minutes. Run a knife around edge of pan; remove sides of pan. Invert cake onto wire rack; carefully remove pan bottom and waxed paper. Cool completely.

In a small saucepan, melt chocolate with cream over low heat; stir until blended. Remove from the heat. Stir in butter until melted.

Transfer to a small bowl; cover and refrigerate until mixture reaches spreading consistency, stirring occasionally. Place cake on a serving plate. Pour ganache over cake and quickly spread to edges.

In a microwave, melt the white chocolate; stir until smooth. Transfer to a heavy-duty resealable plastic bag; cut a small hole in a corner of bag. Pipe thin horizontal lines 1 in. apart over ganache. Use a sharp knife to draw right angles across the piped lines. Press pecans onto side of torte. Top with pecan halves if desired. Cover and refrigerate for 30 minutes or until set. **YIELD: 18 servings.**

TINA JACOBS, WANTAGE, NEW JERSEY
I like to make this dessert in June and early July so I can use fresh local strawberries. The fruit lightens up the intense chocolate flavor and pleases everyone.

banana-berry brownie pizza

PREP: 20 MINUTES / **BAKE:** 40 MINUTES

1	package fudge brownie mix (13-inch x 9-inch size)
1/3	cup boiling water
1/4	cup canola oil
1	egg

TOPPING:
1	package (8 ounces) cream cheese, softened
1/4	cup sugar
1	egg
1	teaspoon vanilla extract
2	cups sliced fresh strawberries
1	to 2 medium firm bananas, sliced
1	ounce semisweet chocolate, melted

In a large bowl, combine the brownie mix, water, oil and egg until well blended. Spread into a greased and floured 12-in. pizza pan. Bake at 350° for 25 minutes.

In a large bowl, beat the cream cheese, sugar, egg and vanilla until smooth. Spread over brownie crust. Bake 15 minutes longer or until topping is set. Cool on a wire rack.

Just before serving, arrange the strawberries and bananas over topping; drizzle with chocolate. Refrigerate leftovers. **YIELD: 10-12 servings.**

TASTE OF HOME TEST KITCHEN
These individual chocolate souffles dreamed up by our home economists are fudgy and delicious. They deliver an impressive presentation but are easy to make.

hot chocolate souffles

PREP: 20 MINUTES / BAKE: 15 MINUTES

1	cup butter, cubed
8	ounces bittersweet chocolate, chopped
4	eggs
4	egg yolks
1-1/2	cups plus 2 tablespoons sugar
2	tablespoons all-purpose flour
1/8	teaspoon baking powder
1	cup miniature marshmallows
4-1/2	teaspoons cinnamon-sugar

Grease the bottoms only of twelve 6-oz. ramekins or custard cups; set aside. In a large microwave-safe bowl, melt butter and chocolate; stir until smooth. Set aside.

In a large bowl, beat eggs and yolks on high speed for 3 minutes or until light and fluffy. Gradually add sugar, beating until thick and lemon-colored, about 5 minutes. Beat in chocolate mixture. Combine flour and baking powder; beat into the egg mixture just until combined.

Fill prepared ramekins half full; sprinkle with miniature marshmallows. Bake at 400° for 12-15 minutes or until a toothpick inserted near the center comes out with moist crumbs. Sprinkle tops with cinnamon-sugar; serve souffles immediately. Refrigerate leftovers. **YIELD: 12 servings.**

RHONDA KNIGHT, HECKER, ILLINOIS
Folks who love chocolate chip cookies will enjoy that same great flavor in these buttery, addicting bars. The golden snacks can be mixed up in a jiffy and taste wonderful. They're perfect for those times when company drops by unexpectedly or you need a treat in a hurry.

chocolate chip blondies

PREP: 10 MINUTES / BAKE: 20 MINUTES + COOLING

1-1/2	cups packed brown sugar
1/2	cup butter, melted
2	eggs, lightly beaten
1	teaspoon vanilla extract
1-1/2	cups all-purpose flour
1/2	teaspoon baking powder
1/2	teaspoon salt
1	cup (6 ounces) semisweet chocolate chips

In a large bowl, combine the brown sugar, butter, eggs and vanilla just until blended. Combine the flour, baking powder and salt; add to brown sugar mixture. Stir in chocolate chips.

Spread into a greased 13-in. x 9-in. baking pan. Bake at 350° for 18-20 minutes or until a toothpick inserted near the center comes out clean. Cool on a wire rack. Cut into bars. **YIELD: 3 dozen.**

DONNA GONDA, NORTH CANTON, OHIO

Tiramisu is Italian for "pick-me-up," and this version lives up to its name. It's worth every bit of effort to see my husband's eyes light up when I put a piece of this delectable torte in front of him.

tiramisu toffee torte

PREP: 25 MINUTES + CHILLING
BAKE: 25 MINUTES + COOLING

1	package (18-1/4 ounces) white cake mix
1	cup strong brewed coffee, room temperature
4	egg whites
4	Heath candy bars (1.4 ounces *each*), chopped

FROSTING:

4	ounces cream cheese, softened
2/3	cup sugar
1/3	cup chocolate syrup
2	teaspoons vanilla extract
2	cups heavy whipping cream
6	tablespoons strong brewed coffee, room temperature
1	Heath candy bar (1.4 ounces), chopped

Line two greased 9-in. round baking pans with waxed paper and grease the paper; set aside. In a large bowl, combine cake mix, coffee and egg whites; beat on low speed for 30 seconds. Beat on medium for 2 minutes. Fold in chopped candy bars. Pour into prepared pans.

Bake at 350° for 25-30 minutes or until a toothpick inserted near the center comes out clean. Cool for 10 minutes before removing to wire racks to cool.

For frosting, in a large bowl, beat cream cheese and sugar until smooth. Beat in chocolate syrup and vanilla. Add the whipping cream. Beat on high speed until light and fluffy, about 5 minutes.

Cut each cake horizontally into two layers. Place bottom layer on a serving plate; drizzle with 2 tablespoons of the coffee. Spread with 3/4 cup frosting. Repeat twice. Top with remaining cake layer. Frost top and sides of cake with remaining frosting. Refrigerate overnight. Garnish with chopped candy bar. Store in the refrigerator. **YIELD: 12-14 servings.**

DEBBIE KNIGHT, MARION, IOWA

I make these snackable, banana-flavored bars whenever I have ripe bananas on hand, then store them in the freezer to share later. With a rich cream cheese frosting and irresistible texture, this confection is a real crowd-pleaser.

frosted banana bars

PREP: 15 MINUTES / **BAKE:** 20 MINUTES + COOLING

1/2	cup butter, softened
1-1/2	cups sugar
2	eggs
1	cup (8 ounces) sour cream
1	teaspoon vanilla extract
2	cups all-purpose flour
1	teaspoon baking soda
1/4	teaspoon salt
2	medium ripe bananas, mashed (about 1 cup)

FROSTING:

1	package (8 ounces) cream cheese, softened
1/2	cup butter, softened
2	teaspoons vanilla extract
3-3/4	to 4 cups confectioners' sugar

In a bowl, cream butter and sugar. Add the eggs, sour cream and vanilla. Combine the flour, baking soda and salt; gradually add to the creamed mixture. Stir in bananas.

Spread into a greased 15-in. x 10-in. baking pan. Bake at 350° for 20-25 minutes or until a toothpick inserted near the center comes out clean. Cool.

For frosting, in a bowl, beat the cream cheese, butter and vanilla. Gradually beat in enough confectioners' sugar to achieve desired consistency. Frost bars. Store in the refrigerator. **YIELD: 3-4 dozen.**

DAWN LOWENSTEIN, HATBORO, PENNSYLVANIA
I said I'd bring dessert to a holiday party and tried this recipe. It was a winner. I'm sure you'll agree it tastes as luscious as it looks!

peanut butter cup cheesecake

PREP: 20 MINUTES / **BAKE:** 55 MINUTES + CHILLING

1-1/4	cups graham cracker crumbs
1/4	cup sugar
1/4	cup crushed cream-filled chocolate sandwich cookies
6	tablespoons butter, melted
3/4	cup creamy peanut butter

FILLING:

3	packages (8 ounces *each*) cream cheese, softened
1	cup sugar
1	cup (8 ounces) sour cream
3	eggs, lightly beaten
1-1/2	teaspoons vanilla extract
1	cup hot fudge ice cream topping, *divided*
6	peanut butter cups, cut into small wedges

In a bowl, combine the cracker crumbs, sugar, cookie crumbs and butter. Press onto the bottom and 1 in. up the sides of a greased 9-in. springform pan. Place on a baking sheet.

Bake at 350° for 7-9 minutes or until set. Cool on a wire rack. In a microwave-safe bowl, heat peanut butter on high for 30 seconds or until softened. Spread over crust to within 1 in. of edges.

In a large bowl, beat the cream cheese, sugar and sour cream until smooth. Add eggs; beat on low speed just until combined. Stir in vanilla. Pour 1 cup into a bowl; set aside. Pour remaining filling over peanut butter layer.

In a microwave-safe bowl, heat 1/4 cup fudge topping on high for 30 seconds or until thin; fold into reserved cream cheese mixture. Carefully pour over filling; cut through with a knife to swirl.

Place pan on a baking sheet. Bake at 350° for 55-65 minutes or until center is almost set. Let cool on a wire rack for 10 minutes. Carefully run a knife around edge of pan to loosen; cool 1 hour.

Microwave remaining fudge topping for 30 seconds or until warmed; spread over cheesecake. Garnish with peanut butter cups. Refrigerate overnight. Remove sides of pan. Refrigerate leftovers. **YIELD: 12-14 servings.**

EDITOR'S NOTE: Reduced-fat or generic brands of peanut butter are not recommended for this recipe.

DAWN BURNS, TROY, OHIO
My mom always made these dressy, sweet cookies for cookie exchanges when I was a little girl, letting me sprinkle on the almonds and coconut. They're so easy to fix that sometimes I can't wait till Christmas to make a batch.

caramel heavenlies

PREP: 20 MINUTES / **BAKE:** 15 MINUTES

12	whole graham crackers
2	cups miniature marshmallows
3/4	cup butter
3/4	cup packed brown sugar
1	teaspoon ground cinnamon
1	teaspoon vanilla extract
1	cup sliced almonds
1	cup flaked coconut

Line a 15-in. x 10-in. baking pan with foil. Place graham crackers in pan; cover with marshmallows. In a saucepan over medium heat, cook and stir butter, brown sugar and cinnamon until the butter is melted and sugar is dissolved. Remove from the heat; stir in vanilla.

Spoon over the marshmallows. Sprinkle with almonds and coconut. Bake at 350° for 14-16 minutes or until browned. Cool completely. Cut into 2-in. squares, then cut each square in half to form triangles. **YIELD: about 6 dozen.**

MARGERY BRYAN, MOSES LAKE, WASHINGTON
On occasion, I like to "fancy up" one of my favorite gelatin desserts with a buttery graham cracker crust and a layer of cream cheese filling. Mandarin oranges add color and pair well with the cranberry gelatin.

layered cranberry dessert

PREP: 25 MINUTES + CHILLING

2	packages (3 ounces *each*) cranberry gelatin
1-1/2	cups boiling water
1	can (14 ounces) whole-berry cranberry sauce
1-1/2	cups cold water
1-1/2	cups graham cracker crumbs
1/2	cup sugar, *divided*
1/2	cup butter, melted
1	package (8 ounces) cream cheese, softened
1	carton (16 ounces) frozen whipped topping, thawed, *divided*
1	can (15 ounces) mandarin oranges, drained

In a large bowl, dissolve gelatin in boiling water. Stir in cranberry sauce and cold water until blended. Refrigerate for 45 minutes or until partially set.

Meanwhile, in a bowl, combine the cracker crumbs, 1/4 cup sugar and butter. Press into an ungreased 13-in. x 9-in. dish. Refrigerate until set.

In a small bowl, beat cream cheese and remaining sugar until smooth. Fold in half of the whipped topping. Spread over crust. Fold oranges into gelatin mixture; spoon over cream cheese layer. Refrigerate for 4 hours or until firm. Cut into squares; dollop with remaining whipped topping. **YIELD: 12 servings.**

MERRILL POWERS, SPEARVILLE, KANSAS
Delight your family with these individual brownie-like cupcakes studded with pecan pieces. The crinkly tops of these chewy treats are so pretty that they don't even need frosting. Just enjoy as is!

brownie cups

PREP: 15 MINUTES / **BAKE:** 35 MINUTES

1	cup butter
1	cup (6 ounces) semisweet chocolate chips
1	cup chopped pecans
4	eggs
1-1/2	cups sugar
1	cup all-purpose flour
1	teaspoon vanilla extract

In a small saucepan over low heat, melt the butter and chocolate chips, stirring until smooth. Cool. Add pecans; stir until well-coated. In a large bowl, combine the eggs, sugar, flour and vanilla. Fold in chocolate mixture.

Fill paper-lined muffin cups two-thirds full. Bake at 325° for 35-38 minutes or until a toothpick inserted near the center comes out clean. Remove from pans to wire racks to cool. **YIELD: about 1-1/2 dozen.**

EDITOR'S NOTE: This recipe contains no leavening.

KATHY JOHNSON, LAKE CITY, SOUTH DAKOTA
My daughter requests this as her birthday cake every year. I also take it to potlucks, church dinners or any time the dessert is my responsibility. People can't get enough of the rich cheesecake flavor swirled into every chocolaty bite.

german chocolate cheesecake

PREP: 15 MINUTES / **BAKE:** 1-1/4 HOURS + COOLING

1	package (18-1/4 ounces) German Chocolate cake mix
2	packages (8 ounces *each*) cream cheese, softened
1-1/2	cups sugar
4	eggs, lightly beaten

FROSTING:

1	cup sugar
1	cup evaporated milk
1/2	cup butter, cubed
3	egg yolks, lightly beaten
1	teaspoon vanilla extract
1-1/2	cups flaked coconut
1	cup chopped pecans

Prepare cake batter according to package directions; set aside. In a small bowl, beat cream cheese and sugar until smooth. Add eggs; beat on low speed just until combined.

Pour half of the cake batter into a greased 13-in. x 9-in. baking dish. Gently pour cream cheese mixture over batter. Gently spoon remaining batter over top; spread to edge of pan. Bake at 325° for 70-75 minutes or until a toothpick inserted near the center comes out clean. Cool on a wire rack for 1 hour.

For frosting, in a heavy saucepan, combine sugar, milk, butter and egg yolks. Cook and stir over medium-low heat until thickened and a thermometer reads 160° or is thick enough to coat the back of a metal spoon.

Remove from the heat. Stir in vanilla; fold in coconut and pecans. Cool until frosting reaches spreading consistency. Frost cooled cake. Refrigerate leftovers. **YIELD: 16 servings.**

BARBARA DRISCOLL, WEST ALLIS, WISCONSIN
Everyone munches with joy when they bite into these chewy, gooey bars. They love the buttery shortbread-like crust and the wildly nutty topping.

rustic nut bars

PREP: 20 MINUTES / **BAKE:** 35 MINUTES + COOLING

1	tablespoon plus 3/4 cup cold butter, *divided*
2-1/3	cups all-purpose flour
1/2	cup sugar
1/2	teaspoon baking powder
1/2	teaspoon salt
1	egg, lightly beaten

TOPPING:

2/3	cup honey
1/2	cup packed brown sugar
1/4	teaspoon salt
6	tablespoons butter, cubed
2	tablespoons heavy whipping cream
1	cup chopped hazelnuts, toasted
1	cup roasted salted almonds
1	cup salted cashews, toasted
1	cup pistachios, toasted

Line a 13-in. x 9-in. baking pan with foil; grease foil with 1 tablespoon butter. Set aside.

In a large bowl, combine the flour, sugar, baking powder and salt; cut in remaining butter until mixture resembles coarse crumbs. Stir in egg until blended (mixture will be dry). Press mixture firmly onto the bottom of prepared pan. Bake at 375° for 18-20 minutes or until the edges are golden brown. Cool on a wire rack.

In a large heavy saucepan, bring the honey, brown sugar and salt to a boil over medium heat until sugar is smooth; stirring often. Boil without stirring for 2 minutes. Add butter and cream. Bring to a boil; cook and stir for 1 minute or until smooth. Remove from the heat; stir in the hazelnuts, almonds, cashews and pistachios. Spread over crust.

Bake at 375° for 15-20 minutes or until topping is bubbly. Cool completely on a wire rack. Using foil, lift bars out of pan. Discard foil; cut into squares. **YIELD: about 3 dozen.**

PATRICIA KREITZ, RICHLAND, PENNSYLVANIA
This old-fashioned cake always reminds me of my grandmother because it was one of her specialties. I bake it often for family parties and birthdays, and it brings back fond memories. The texture is light and airy with a delicious chocolate taste. It is definitely a keeper!

moist chocolate cake

PREP: 15 MINUTES / **BAKE:** 25 MINUTES

- 2 cups all-purpose flour
- 1 teaspoon salt
- 1 teaspoon baking powder
- 2 teaspoons baking soda
- 3/4 cup baking cocoa
- 2 cups sugar
- 1 cup canola oil
- 1 cup brewed coffee
- 1 cup milk
- 2 eggs
- 1 teaspoon vanilla extract

FAVORITE ICING:

- 1 cup milk
- 5 tablespoons all-purpose flour
- 1/2 cup butter, softened
- 1/2 cup shortening
- 1 cup sugar
- 1 teaspoon vanilla extract

Sift together dry ingredients in a bowl. Add oil, coffee and milk; mix at medium speed for 1 minute. Add eggs and vanilla; beat 2 more minutes. (Batter will be thin.) Pour into two greased and floured 9-in. round baking pans (or two 8-in. round baking pans and six muffin cups).

Bake at 325° for 25-30 minutes. Cool cakes for 10 minutes before removing from pans. Cool on wire racks.

Meanwhile, for icing, combine the milk and flour in a saucepan; cook until thick. Cover and refrigerate. In a bowl, beat butter, shortening, sugar and vanilla until creamy. Add chilled milk and flour mixture and beat for 10 minutes. Frost cooled cake. **YIELD: 12 servings.**

TERI LINDQUIST, GURNEE, ILLINOIS
This is my most requested dessert recipe. Everyone loves these yummy bars with their soft cream cheese filling. I love that they couldn't be easier to whip up.

chocolate chip cheese bars

PREP: 15 MINUTES / **BAKE:** 35 MINUTES

- 1 tube (18 ounces) refrigerated chocolate chip cookie dough
- 1 package (8 ounces) cream cheese, softened
- 1/2 cup sugar
- 1 egg

Cut cookie dough in half. For crust, press half of the dough onto the bottom of a greased 8-in. square baking pan.

In a large bowl, beat the cream cheese, sugar and egg until smooth. Spread over crust. Crumble remaining dough over top.

Bake at 350° for 35-40 minutes or until a toothpick inserted near the center comes out clean. Cool on a wire rack. Refrigerate leftovers. **YIELD: 12-16 servings.**

EDITOR'S NOTE: 2 cups of your favorite chocolate chip cookie dough can be substituted for the refrigerated dough.

READERS' RAVES

> I have made these bars several times, and they are a winner. When people ask for the recipe, they are so pleased to see how easy it is. I add a little almond extract to the cream cheese filling, and it pushes it over the top.
>
> —Hunkydoriest
> from TasteofHome.com

AMY THEIS, BILLINGS, MONTANA

My mother served this pretty pie for my birthday dinner one year, and now it's one of my favorites. Fudge sauce, chopped pecans and coffee ice cream top the chocolate crumb crust. Sometimes I garnish the pie with dollops of whipped cream.

fudgy nut coffee pie

PREP: 15 MINUTES + FREEZING

1-1/2	cups confectioners' sugar
1/2	cup heavy whipping cream
6	tablespoons butter, cubed
3	ounces unsweetened chocolate
3	tablespoons light corn syrup

Dash salt

1	teaspoon vanilla extract
1	chocolate crumb crust (9 inches)
3/4	cup coarsely chopped pecans, *divided*
3	pints coffee ice cream, softened

In a small saucepan, combine the confectioners' sugar, cream, butter, chocolate, corn syrup and salt. Cook and stir over low heat until smooth. Remove from the heat. Stir in vanilla. Cool completely.

Spread 1/2 cup fudge sauce over the crust. Sprinkle with 1/4 cup pecans. Freeze for 20 minutes or until set. Spread with half of the ice cream. Freeze for 1 hour or until firm. Repeat layers. Cover and freeze for 4 hours or until firm.

Just before serving, drizzle remaining fudge sauce over pie and sprinkle with remaining pecans. **YIELD: 8 servings.**

DIANE WINDLEY, GRACE, IDAHO

This is a simple recipe for any type of occasion where you're asked to bring a dish. A cookie dough crust layered with a cheesecake-like filling and creamy pudding means you'll come home with an empty pan.

chocolate chip cookie delight

PREP: 35 MINUTES + CHILLING

1	tube (16-1/2 ounces) refrigerated chocolate chip cookie dough
1	package (8 ounces) cream cheese, softened
1	cup confectioners' sugar
1	carton (12 ounces) frozen whipped topping, thawed, *divided*
3	cups cold milk
1	package (3.9 ounces) instant chocolate pudding mix
1	package (3.4 ounces) instant vanilla pudding mix

Chopped nuts and chocolate curls, optional

Let cookie dough stand at room temperature for 5-10 minutes to soften. Press into an ungreased 13-in. x 9-in. baking pan. Bake at 350° for 14-16 minutes or until golden brown. Cool on a wire rack.

In a large bowl, beat cream cheese and confectioners' sugar until smooth. Fold in 1-3/4 cups whipped topping. Spread over crust.

In a large bowl, whisk milk and pudding mixes for 2 minutes; let stand for 2 minutes or until soft-set. Spread over the cream cheese layer. Top with remaining whipped topping. Sprinkle with nuts and chocolate curls if desired. Cover and refrigerate for 8 hours or overnight until firm. **YIELD: 15 servings.**

MOLLY SEIDEL, EDGEWOOD, NEW MEXICO
This luscious concoction is the result of several attempts to duplicate a dessert I enjoyed while on vacation. It looks so beautiful on a buffet table that many folks are tempted to forgo the main course in favor of this chocolaty treat.

chocolate velvet dessert

PREP: 20 MINUTES + CHILLING
BAKE: 45 MINUTES + COOLING

1-1/2	cups chocolate wafer crumbs
2	tablespoons sugar
1/4	cup butter, melted
2	cups (12 ounces) semisweet chocolate chips
6	egg yolks
1-3/4	cups heavy whipping cream
1	teaspoon vanilla extract

CHOCOLATE BUTTERCREAM FROSTING:

1/2	cup butter, softened
3	cups confectioners' sugar
3	tablespoons baking cocoa
3	to 4 tablespoons milk

In a small bowl, combine wafer crumbs and sugar; stir in butter. Press onto the bottom and 1-1/2 in. up the sides of a greased 9-in. springform pan. Place on a baking sheet. Bake at 350° for 10 minutes. Cool on a wire rack.

In a microwave, melt chocolate chips; stir until smooth. Cool. In a small bowl, combine egg yolks, cream and vanilla. Gradually stir a third of the cream mixture into melted chocolate until blended. Fold in remaining cream mixture just until blended. Pour into crust.

Place pan on a baking sheet. Bake at 350° for 45-50 minutes or until center is almost set. Cool on a wire rack for 10 minutes. Carefully run a knife around edge of pan to loosen; cool 1 hour longer. Refrigerate overnight.

In a small bowl, combine the butter, confectioners' sugar, cocoa and enough milk to achieve a piping consistency. Using a large star tip, pipe frosting on dessert. **YIELD: 12-16 servings.**

DONNA HUITEMA, WHITBY, ONTARIO
Here's a dessert that's delicious, simple and inviting. You can vary the flavor by substituting strawberries or peaches (with preserves to match) for the raspberries.

raspberry cream trifle

PREP/TOTAL TIME: 30 MINUTES

1	can (14 ounces) sweetened condensed milk
1	cup cold water
1	teaspoon almond extract
1	package (3.4 ounces) instant vanilla pudding mix
2	cups heavy whipping cream, whipped
1	angel food cake (7 inches), cut into 1-inch cubes
2	tablespoons seedless raspberry jam
2	cups fresh raspberries

Chocolate curls and fresh mint

In a large bowl, beat the milk, water and extract until blended. Add pudding mix; whisk for 2 minutes. Let stand for 2 minutes or until soft-set. Cover and chill until mixture is partially set. Fold in the whipped cream.

Place half of the cake cubes in a 2-qt. glass serving bowl. Top with half of the cream mixture. Carefully spread with jam. Sprinkle with 1 cup raspberries. Layer with remaining cake cubes, cream mixture and raspberries. Garnish with chocolate curls and fresh mint. **YIELD: 14-16 servings.**

SHARI ROACH, SOUTH MILWAUKEE, WISCONSIN
Once I tried these refreshing bars, I just had to have the recipe so I could make them for my family and friends. The shortbread-like crust and rhubarb and custard layers inspire people to find rhubarb they can use to fix a batch for themselves.

rhubarb custard bars

PREP: 25 MINUTES + CHILLING
BAKE: 50 MINUTES + CHILLING

2	cups all-purpose flour
1/4	cup sugar
1	cup cold butter

FILLING:

2	cups sugar
7	tablespoons all-purpose flour
1	cup heavy whipping cream
3	eggs, beaten
5	cups finely chopped fresh *or* frozen rhubarb, thawed and drained

TOPPING:

2	packages (3 ounces *each*) cream cheese, softened
1/2	cup sugar
1/2	teaspoon vanilla extract
1	cup heavy whipping cream, whipped

In a bowl, combine the flour and sugar; cut in butter until the mixture resembles coarse crumbs. Press into a greased 13-in. x 9-in. baking pan. Bake at 350° for 10 minutes.

Meanwhile, for filling, combine sugar and flour in a bowl. Whisk in cream and eggs. Stir in the rhubarb. Pour over crust. Bake at 350° for 40-45 minutes or until custard is set. Cool.

For topping, beat cream cheese, sugar and vanilla until smooth; fold in whipped cream. Spread over top. Cover and chill. Cut into bars. Store in the refrigerator. **YIELD: 3 dozen.**

MICHELLE BORLAND, PEORIA, ILLINOIS
Tender, sweet pudding with delicious apple pieces, comforting spices and a luscious low-fat caramel topping make this an extremely tempting dessert without the guilt. Indulge!

caramel apple bread pudding

PREP: 15 MINUTES / **BAKE:** 35 MINUTES

1	cup unsweetened applesauce
1	cup fat-free milk
1/2	cup packed brown sugar
1/2	cup egg substitute
1	teaspoon vanilla extract
1/2	teaspoon ground cinnamon
5	cups cubed day-old bread
1/2	cup chopped peeled apple
1/2	cup fat-free whipped topping
1/2	cup fat-free caramel ice cream topping

In a large bowl, combine the applesauce, milk, brown sugar, egg substitute, vanilla and cinnamon. Fold in bread cubes and apple.

Pour into an 8-in. square baking dish coated with cooking spray. Bake, uncovered, at 325° for 35-40 minutes or until a knife inserted near the center comes out clean. Serve warm with whipped topping and caramel topping. Refrigerate leftovers. **YIELD: 8 servings.**

HAZEL BALDNER, AUSTIN, MINNESOTA

Most folk can't eat just one of these addictive, gooey bars. They taste just like chocolate pecan pie, but are much easier to prepare.

chunky pecan bars

PREP: 15 MINUTES / **BAKE:** 20 MINUTES + COOLING

1-1/2	cups all-purpose flour
1/2	cup packed brown sugar
1/2	cup cold butter, cubed

FILLING:

3	eggs
3/4	cup sugar
3/4	cup dark corn syrup
2	tablespoons butter, melted
1	teaspoon vanilla extract
1-3/4	cups semisweet chocolate chunks
1-1/2	cups coarsely chopped pecans

In a small bowl, combine the flour and brown sugar; cut in butter until crumbly. Press into a greased 13-in. x 9-in. baking pan. Bake at 350° for 10-15 minutes or until golden brown.

Meanwhile, in a large bowl, whisk the eggs, sugar, corn syrup, butter and vanilla until blended. Stir in chocolate chunks and pecans. Pour over crust.

Bake for 20-25 minutes or until set. Cool completely on a wire rack. Cut into bars. Store in an airtight container in the refrigerator. **YIELD: about 6 dozen.**

DIANE HEIER, HARWOOD, NORTH DAKOTA

Since you dump all the ingredients together for these brownies, a batch takes very little time to whip up. There's no mistaking the homemade goodness of a freshly baked batch of these rich and fudgy bites.

speedy brownies

PREP: 15 MINUTES / **BAKE:** 30 MINUTES

2	cups sugar
1-3/4	cups all-purpose flour
1/2	cup baking cocoa
1	teaspoon salt
5	eggs
1	cup canola oil
1	teaspoon vanilla extract
1	cup (6 ounces) semisweet chocolate chips

In a large bowl, beat the first seven ingredients. Pour into a greased 13-in. x 9-in. baking pan. Sprinkle with chocolate chips.

Bake at 350° for 30 minutes or until a toothpick inserted near the center comes out clean. Cool in pan on a wire rack. **YIELD: about 3 dozen.**

JULIE CRAIG, JACKSON, WISCONSIN

I created this recipe to combine two of my all-time favorite desserts, cheesecake for the grown-up in me and chocolate chip cookie dough for the little girl in me. Sour cream offsets the sweetness and adds a nice tang to the flavor. Everyone who tries this scrumptious treat loves it.

chocolate chip cookie dough cheesecake

PREP: 25 MINUTES / **BAKE:** 45 MINUTES + CHILLING

1-3/4	cups crushed chocolate chips cookies *or* chocolate wafer crumbs
1/4	cup sugar
1/3	cup butter, melted

FILLING:

3	packages (8 ounces *each*) cream cheese, softened
1	cup sugar
3	eggs, lightly beaten
1	cup (8 ounces) sour cream
1/2	teaspoon vanilla extract

COOKIE DOUGH:

1/4	cup butter, softened
1/4	cup sugar
1/4	cup packed brown sugar
1	tablespoon water
1	teaspoon vanilla extract
1/2	cup all-purpose flour
1-1/2	cups miniature semisweet chocolate chips, *divided*

In a small bowl, combine the cookie crumbs and sugar; stir in butter. Press onto the bottom and 1 in. up the sides of a greased 9-in. pan. Place pan on a baking sheet; set aside.

In a large bowl, beat cream cheese and sugar until smooth. Add eggs; beat on low just until combined. Add sour cream and vanilla; beat just until blended. Pour over crust; set aside.

In another bowl, cream butter and sugars on medium speed until light and fluffy. Add water and vanilla. Gradually add flour. Stir in 1 cup chocolate chips. Drop dough by teaspoonfuls over filling, gently pushing dough below surface (dough should be completely covered by filling). Place pan on a baking sheet.

Bake at 350° for 45-55 minutes or until center is almost set. Cool on a wire rack for 10 minutes. Carefully run a knife around edge of pan to loosen; cool 1 hour longer. Refrigerate overnight.

Remove sides of pan. Sprinkle with remaining chips. Refrigerate leftovers. **YIELD: 12-14 servings.**

TINA SAWCHUK, ARDMORE, ALBERTA

These soft chocolaty cookies can be easily altered to make several different varieties—I've added everything from mints to macadamia nuts to them. No matter how I've prepared them, people find it difficult to eat just one.

sour cream chocolate cookies

PREP/TOTAL TIME: 30 MINUTES

1/2	cup butter, softened
3/4	cup sugar
1/2	cup packed brown sugar
1	egg
1/2	cup sour cream
1	teaspoon vanilla extract
1-3/4	cups all-purpose flour
1/2	cup baking cocoa
1	teaspoon baking powder
1/2	teaspoon baking soda
1/4	teaspoon salt
1	cup (6 ounces) semisweet chocolate chips
1/2	cup vanilla *or* white chips

In a large bowl, cream butter and sugars until light and fluffy. Beat in egg, sour cream and vanilla. Combine dry ingredients; gradually add to the creamed mixture. Stir in chips.

Drop by rounded tablespoonfuls 2 in. apart onto greased baking sheets. Bake at 350° for 12-15 minutes or until set. Cool for 2 minutes before removing to wire racks to cool completely. **YIELD: about 3 dozen.**

CAROL WITCZAK, TINLEY PARK, ILLINOIS
I love cheesecake and my husband loves chocolate, so this blend of both is a favorite dessert of ours. The rhubarb adds a tartness that complements the sweet flavors so well.

rhubarb swirl cheesecake

PREP: 40 MINUTES / **BAKE:** 1 HOUR + CHILLING

2-1/2	cups thinly sliced fresh *or* frozen rhubarb
1/3	cup plus 1/2 cup sugar, *divided*
2	tablespoons orange juice
1-1/4	cups graham cracker crumbs
1/4	cup butter, melted
3	packages (8 ounces *each*) cream cheese, softened
2	cups (16 ounces) sour cream
1	tablespoon cornstarch
2	teaspoons vanilla extract
1/2	teaspoon salt
3	eggs, lightly beaten
8	ounces white baking chocolate, melted

In a large saucepan, bring rhubarb, 1/3 cup sugar and orange juice to a boil. Reduce heat; cook and stir until thickened and rhubarb is tender. Set aside.

In a small bowl, combine the cracker crumbs and butter. Press onto the bottom of a greased 9-in. springform pan. Place on a baking sheet. Bake at 350° for 7-9 minutes or until lightly browned. Cool on a wire rack.

In a large bowl, beat the cream cheese, sour cream, cornstarch, vanilla, salt and remaining sugar until smooth. Add eggs; beat just until combined. Fold in white chocolate.

Pour half of the filling into crust. Top with half of the rhubarb sauce; cut through batter with a knife to gently swirl rhubarb. Layer with remaining filling and rhubarb sauce; cut through top layers with a knife to gently swirl rhubarb.

Place pan on a double thickness of heavy-duty foil (about 16 in. square). Securely wrap foil around pan. Place in a large baking pan; add 1 in. of hot water to larger pan. Bake at 350° for 60-70 minutes or until center is almost set.

Cool on a wire rack for 10 minutes. Carefully run a knife around edge of pan to loosen; cool 1 hour longer. Cover and chill overnight. Refrigerate leftovers. **YIELD: 12-14 servings.**

EDITOR'S NOTE: If using frozen rhubarb, measure rhubarb while still frozen, then thaw completely. Drain in a colander, but do not press liquid out.

DIANE NETH, MENNO, SOUTH DAKOTA
Crazy about chocolate chips? These chewy cookies have plenty, not to mention lots of heart-healthy oatmeal. The gang will come back for more and more...so this big batch is perfect.

chocolate chip oatmeal cookies

PREP: 20 MINUTES / **BAKE:** 10 MINUTES/BATCH

1	cup butter, softened
3/4	cup sugar
3/4	cup packed brown sugar
2	eggs
1	teaspoon vanilla extract
3	cups quick-cooking oats
1-1/2	cups all-purpose flour
1	package (3.4 ounces) instant vanilla pudding mix
1	teaspoon baking soda
1	teaspoon salt
2	cups (12 ounces) semisweet chocolate chips
1	cup chopped nuts

In a large bowl, cream butter and sugars until light and fluffy. Beat in eggs and vanilla. Combine the oats, flour, pudding mix, baking soda and salt; gradually add to creamed mixture and mix well. Stir in chocolate chips and nuts.

Drop by rounded teaspoonfuls 2 in. apart onto ungreased baking sheets. Bake at 375° for 10-12 minutes or until lightly browned. Remove to wire racks. **YIELD: about 7 dozen.**

ANNMARIE SAVAGE, SKOWHEGAN, MAINE
With a creamy frosting and crunchy topping, these rich three-layer brownie bars are a decadent treat. They're a cinch to assemble, but completely irresistible. Whenever I make them for someone new, they always want the recipe.

triple-tier brownies

PREP: 15 MINUTES / **BAKE:** 30 MINUTES + CHILLING

1	package fudge brownie mix (13-inch x 9-inch pan size)
1	package (11-1/2 ounces) milk chocolate chips
1	cup peanut butter
3	cups crisp rice cereal
1	can (16 ounces) cream cheese frosting
1	cup salted peanuts, chopped

Prepare and bake brownie mix according to package directions, using a greased 13-in. x 9-in. baking pan. Cool on a wire rack.

In a large saucepan, combine chocolate chips and peanut butter. Cook over low heat for 4-5 minutes or until blended, stirring occasionally. Stir in cereal; set aside.

Spread frosting over brownies. Sprinkle with peanuts. Spread with peanut butter mixture. Chill for 30 minutes or until set before cutting. Store in the refrigerator. **YIELD: about 5 dozen.**

BARB HAUSEY, INDEPENDENCE, MISSOURI
A highlight of our annual family reunion is the dessert competition. The judges take their jobs very seriously! Last year's first-place winner was this divine and tasty trifle that showcases devil's food cake, caramel and toffee.

caramel chocolate trifle

PREP: 20 MINUTES / **BAKE:** 20 MINUTES + COOLING

1	package (9 ounces) devil's food cake mix
2	packages (3.9 ounces *each*) instant chocolate pudding mix
1	carton (12 ounces) frozen whipped topping, thawed
1	jar (12-1/4 ounces) caramel ice cream topping
1	package (7-1/2 *or* 8 ounces) English toffee bits *or* almond brickle chips

Prepare and bake cake according to package directions for an 8-in. square baking pan. Cool on a wire rack. Prepare pudding according to package directions.

Cut cake into 1-1/2-in. cubes. Place half of the cubes in a 3-qt. trifle bowl or large glass serving bowl; lightly press down to fill in gaps. Top with half of the whipped topping, pudding, caramel topping and toffee bits; repeat layers. Cover and refrigerate until serving. **YIELD: 16 servings.**

MARCIA ORLANDO, BOYERTOWN, PENNSYLVANIA
Holidays are a time to spend with family and friends...it's also a chance to enjoy every bite of scrumptious desserts like this luscious torte! It takes some time to prepare, but I assure you the lovely results make every minute worth the effort.

cappuccino torte

PREP: 65 MINUTES + CHILLING

1-1/4	cups graham cracker crumbs
1/4	cup sugar
1/3	cup butter, melted

GANACHE:

2-1/2	cups semisweet chocolate chips
2	cups heavy whipping cream
1/2	cup butter, cubed
2	tablespoons corn syrup

CAPPUCCINO BUTTERCREAM:

6	egg yolks
2-1/2	cups packed brown sugar
1/2	cup water
1-1/2	cups cold butter
1	tablespoon instant coffee granules
1	tablespoon hot water
4	ounces unsweetened chocolate, melted and cooled

COFFEE WHIPPED CREAM:

1-1/4	cups heavy whipping cream, *divided*
2	teaspoons instant coffee granules
2	tablespoons confectioners' sugar
1/2	teaspoon vanilla extract

Chocolate curls, optional

In a large bowl, combine the crumbs, sugar and butter; press onto the bottom of an ungreased 9-in. springform pan. Chill.

For ganache, place chocolate chips in a large bowl. In a small saucepan, bring cream just to a boil. Pour over chocolate; whisk until smooth. Add butter and corn syrup; stir until smooth. Cool slightly, stirring occasionally. Pour over crust. Chill until firm, about 2 hours.

For buttercream, place egg yolks in the bowl of a heavy-duty stand mixer; let stand for 30 minutes. In a large saucepan, combine brown sugar and water; cook and stir over medium-high heat until sugar is dissolved. Bring to a boil; cook and stir for 2 minutes. Beat egg yolks on high speed until thickened and lemon-colored. Reduce to low; with motor running, gradually add brown sugar syrup. Gradually increase mixer speed to medium; beat until thickened, about 15 minutes. Add butter, 1 tablespoon at a time, beating until well mixed.

Dissolve coffee granules in hot water; add to yolk mixture. Beat in cooled chocolate. Spread over the ganache layer. Cover and refrigerate for at least 4 hours or overnight. Several hours before serving, prepare coffee whipped cream. In a small bowl, combine 1 tablespoon cream and coffee; stir until dissolved. Beat in remaining cream until it begins to thicken. Gradually add confectioners' sugar and vanilla; beat until stiff peaks form.

Carefully run a knife around edge of springform pan to loosen; remove sides. Frost top with whipped cream; garnish with chocolate curls if desired. Refrigerate. **YIELD: 14 servings.**

CINDY LANG, HAYS, KANSAS
These cupcakes are just my style! The rich chocolate flavor is divine. They are delicious without frosting.

brownie cupcakes

PREP: 15 MINUTES / **BAKE:** 20 MINUTES + COOLING

1/4	cup semisweet chocolate chips
1/4	cup butter
1	egg
1/4	cup sugar
1/4	teaspoon vanilla extract
1/4	cup all-purpose flour
1/4	cup chopped pecans

In a microwave, melt chips and butter; stir until smooth. Cool slightly. In a small bowl, beat egg and sugar. Stir in vanilla and chocolate. Gradually add flour to chocolate; fold in pecans.

Fill paper-lined muffin cups two-thirds full. Bake at 325° for 20-25 minutes or until tops begin to crack. Cool for 10 minutes before removing from pan to a wire rack to cool completely. **YIELD: 4 servings.**

READERS' RAVES

Great for when you need a chocolate fix but don't want a ton of treats. Try adding 1/8 cup of chocolate chips.

—Irvandarn from TasteofHome.com

Easy to make. Not too sweet and I love the 'brownie' texture tops. Yummy!

—Stephanied1971 from TasteofHome.com

VIVIAN MORRIS, CLEBURNE, TEXAS

I got the recipe for these chewy, filled cupcakes from a friend several years ago. I have made them too many times to count for my family and for church functions. They're heavenly!

chocolate cream cheese cupcakes

PREP: 30 MINUTES / **BAKE:** 25 MINUTES + COOLING

1	package (8 ounces) cream cheese, softened
1-1/2	cups sugar, *divided*
1	egg
1	teaspoon salt, *divided*
1	cup (6 ounces) semisweet chocolate chips
1-1/2	cups all-purpose flour
1/4	cup baking cocoa
1	teaspoon baking soda
1	cup water
1/3	cup canola oil
1	tablespoon white vinegar

FROSTING:

3-3/4	cups confectioners' sugar
3	tablespoons baking cocoa
1/2	cup butter, melted
6	tablespoons milk
1	teaspoon vanilla extract
1/3	cup chopped pecans

For filling, in a small bowl, beat cream cheese and 1/2 cup sugar until smooth. Beat in egg and 1/2 teaspoon salt until combined. Fold in chocolate chips; set aside.

In a large bowl, combine the flour, cocoa, baking soda, remaining sugar and salt. In another bowl, whisk the water, oil and vinegar; stir into dry ingredients just until moistened.

Fill paper-lined muffin cups half full with batter. Drop filling by heaping tablespoonfuls into the center of each. Bake at 350° for 24-26 minutes or until a toothpick inserted in cupcake comes out clean. Cool for 10 minutes before removing from pans to wire racks to cool completely.

For frosting, in a large bowl, combine the confectioners' sugar, cocoa, butter, milk and vanilla; beat until blended. Frost the cupcakes; sprinkle with pecans. Store in the refrigerator. **YIELD: 20 cupcakes.**

PATRICIA SCHROEDL, JEFFERSON, WISCONSIN

A fantastic finale to any meal, this tantalizing trifle helped me finish first in a local competition. It took top prize in the low-fat category at the Wisconsin Strawberry Festival recipe contest.

strawberry raspberry trifle

PREP/TOTAL TIME: 20 MINUTES

3	cups cold fat-free milk
2	packages (1 ounce *each*) sugar-free instant white chocolate pudding mix
1	prepared angel food cake (14 ounces), cut into 1-inch cubes
3	cups sliced fresh strawberries
3	cups fresh raspberries
1	carton (8 ounces) frozen reduced-fat whipped topping, thawed
3	whole strawberries, quartered

In a large bowl, whisk milk and pudding mix for 2 minutes. Let stand for 2 minutes or until soft-set.

Place a third of the cake cubes in a trifle bowl or 3-1/2-qt. glass serving bowl. Top with a third of the pudding, 1 cup sliced strawberries, 1-1/2 cups raspberries and a third of the whipped topping. Layer with a third of the cake and pudding, 1 cup strawberries and a third of the whipped topping.

Top with remaining cake, pudding, strawberries, raspberries and whipped topping. Garnish with quartered strawberries. Serve immediately or cover and chill until serving. **YIELD: 14 servings.**

JUDI JANCZEWSKI, BERWYN, ILLINOIS

This decadent and creamy dessert with a tart raspberry sauce is deceptively fat-free! One bite and you'll be hooked!

sour cream bavarian

PREP: 15 MINUTES + CHILLING

1	envelope unflavored gelatin
3/4	cup cold water
2/3	cup sugar
1	cup (8 ounces) fat-free sour cream
1	teaspoon vanilla extract
2	cups fat-free whipped topping

RASPBERRY SAUCE:

1	package (10 ounces) frozen raspberries in syrup, thawed
1	tablespoon cornstarch
1	tablespoon sugar

In a small saucepan, sprinkle the gelatin over cold water; let stand for 1 minute. Add sugar; cook and stir over low heat until gelatin and sugar are completely dissolved. Remove from the heat. Whisk in the sour cream and vanilla. Refrigerate until slightly thickened.

Fold in the whipped topping. Pour into a 4-cup heart-shaped or other shape mold coated with cooking spray. Refrigerate until firm.

For sauce, drain raspberries, reserving syrup; set raspberries aside. Add enough water to the syrup to measure 3/4 cup. In a small saucepan, combine cornstarch and sugar. Stir in syrup mixture until smooth. Bring to a boil; cook and stir for 2 minutes or until thickened. Remove mixture from the heat; stir in raspberries. Refrigerate until serving

To serve, unmold the dessert onto a serving plate; top with raspberry sauce. **YIELD: 8 servings (1-1/4 cups sauce).**

CATHERINE DAWE, KENT, OHIO

You can't miss with this delightful old-fashioned dessert. The cake is moist and chocolaty, and its light, fluffy frosting stirs up in a jiffy. Use vanilla pudding instead of chocolate in the frosting if you wish.

best-ever chocolate cake

PREP: 15 MINUTES / **BAKE:** 40 MINUTES + COOLING

3	cups all-purpose flour
2	cups sugar
6	tablespoons baking cocoa
2	teaspoons baking soda
1	teaspoon salt
2	cups water
2/3	cup canola oil
2	teaspoons vinegar
2	teaspoons vanilla extract

FLUFFY CHOCOLATE FROSTING:

1	cup cold milk
1	package (3.9 ounces) instant chocolate pudding mix
1	carton (8 ounces) frozen whipped topping, thawed

In a bowl, combine the first five ingredients. Add the water, oil, vinegar and vanilla. Beat on low speed for 1 minute. Beat on medium for 1 minute.

Pour into a greased 13-in. x 9-in. baking pan. Bake at 350° for 40-45 minutes or until a toothpick inserted near the center comes out clean. Cool on a wire rack.

For frosting, in a bowl, beat milk and pudding mix for 2 minutes. Beat in the whipped topping. Spread over the cake. Refrigerate leftovers. **YIELD: 12-15 servings.**

general index

p. 58

p. 67

p. 132

p. 154

p. 212

p. 145

p. 71

p. 122

p. 51

p. 32

p. 96

p. 24

p. 69

alphabetical recipe index

p. 123

p. 75

p. 98

p. 189

get cooking with a well-stocked kitchen

In a perfect world you would plan out weekly or even monthly menus and have all the ingredients on hand to make each night's dinner. The reality, however, is you likely haven't thought about dinner until you've walked through the door.

With a reasonably stocked pantry, refrigerator and freezer, you'll still be able to serve a satisfying meal in short order. Consider these tips:

QUICK-COOKING MEATS like boneless chicken breasts, chicken thighs, pork tenderloin, pork chops, ground meats, Italian sausage, sirloin and flank steaks, fish fillets and shrimp should be stocked in the freezer. Wrap them individually (except shrimp), so you can remove only the amount you need. For the quickest defrosting, wrap meats for freezing in small, thin packages.

FROZEN VEGETABLES prepackaged in plastic bags are a real time-saver. Simply pour out the amount needed. No preparation is required!

PASTAS, RICE, RICE MIXES AND COUSCOUS are great staples to have in the pantry—and they generally have a long shelf life. Remember, thinner pastas, such as angel hair, cook faster than thicker pastas. Fresh (refrigerated) pasta cooks faster than dried.

DAIRY PRODUCTS like milk, sour cream, cheeses (shredded, cubed or crumbled), eggs, yogurt and butter or margarine are more perishable, so check the use-by date on the packages and replace as needed.

CONDIMENTS such as ketchup, mustard, mayonnaise, salad dressings, salsa, taco sauce, soy sauce, stir-fry sauce, lemon juice, etc. add flavor to many dishes. Personalize the list to suit your family's needs.

FRESH FRUIT AND VEGETABLES can make a satisfying predinner snack. Oranges and apples are not as perishable as bananas. Ready-to-use salad greens are great for an instant salad.

DRIED HERBS, SPICES, VINEGARS and seasoning mixes add lots of flavor and keep for months.

PASTA SAUCES, OLIVES, BEANS, broths, canned tomatoes, canned vegetables, and canned or dried soups are great to have on hand for a quick meal...and many of these items are common recipe ingredients.

GET YOUR FAMILY INTO THE HABIT of posting a grocery list. When an item is used up or is almost gone, just add it to list for next shopping trip. This way you won't completely run out of an item, and you'll also save time when writing your grocery list.

make the most of your time every night

With recipes in hand and your kitchen stocked, you're well on your way to a relaxing family meal. Here are some pointers to help you get dinner on the table fast:

WHEN USING AN OVEN OR GRILL, preheat it before starting on the recipe.

PULL OUT ALL THE INGREDIENTS, mixing tools and cooking tools before beginning any prep work.

WHENEVER POSSIBLE, use convenience items, such as pre-chopped garlic, onion and peppers, shredded or cubed cheese, seasoning mixes, jarred sauces, etc.

MULTI-TASK! While the meat is simmering for a main dish, toss a salad, cook a side dish or start on dessert.

ENCOURAGE HELPERS. Have younger children set the table. Older ones can help with ingredient preparation or even assemble simple recipes themselves.

TAKE CARE OF TWO MEALS IN ONE NIGHT by planning main dish leftovers or making a double batch of favorite sides.

tricks to tame hunger when it strikes

If rumbling tummies can't wait for dinner, calm the kids' appetites with some nutritious, yet not too filling presupper snacks.

START THEM WITH A SALAD tossed using their favorite dressing. Try a ready-to-serve salad mix and add a little protein like cubed cheese or julienned slices of deli meat.

CUT UP AN APPLE and smear a little peanut butter on each slice. Or offer other fruits such as seedless grapes, cantaloupe, oranges or bananas. For variety, give kids a vanilla yogurt or reduced-fat ranch dressing as a dipper for the fruit or combine a little reduced-fat sour cream with a sprinkling of brown sugar. Too tired to cut up the fruit? A fruit snack cup will do the trick, too.

DURING THE COLD MONTHS, a small mug of soup with a few oyster crackers will hit the spot.

RAW VEGGIES, such as carrots, cucumbers, mushrooms, broccoli and cauliflower, are tasty treats, especially when served with a little reduced-fat dressing for dipping. Plus, many of these vegetables can be purchased precut.

GIVE KIDS A SMALL SERVING of cheese and crackers. Look for presliced cheese and cut the slices into smaller squares to fit the crackers. Choose a cracker that is made from whole wheat, such as an all-natural, 7-grain cracker.

ingredient substitutions

WHEN YOU NEED:	IN THIS AMOUNT:	SUBSTITUTE:
Baking Powder	1 teaspoon	1/2 teaspoon cream of tartar plus 1/4 teaspoon baking soda
Broth	1 cup	1 cup hot water plus 1 teaspoon bouillon granules *or* 1 bouillon cube
Buttermilk	1 cup	1 tablespoon lemon juice *or* white vinegar plus enough milk to measure 1 cup; let stand 5 minutes. *Or* 1 cup plain yogurt.
Cajun Seasoning	1 teaspoon	1/4 teaspoon cayenne pepper, 1/2 teaspoon dried thyme, 1/4 teaspoon dried basil and 1 minced garlic clove
Chocolate, Semisweet	1 square (1 ounce)	1 square (1 ounce) unsweetened chocolate plus 1 tablespoon sugar *or* 3 tablespoons semisweet chocolate chips
Chocolate	1 square (1 ounce)	3 tablespoons baking cocoa plus 1 tablespoon shortening *or* canola oil
Cornstarch	1 tablespoon	2 tablespoons all-purpose flour (for thickening)
Corn Syrup, Dark	1 cup	3/4 cup light corn syrup plus 1/4 cup molasses
Corn Syrup, Light	1 cup	1 cup sugar plus 1/4 cup water
Cracker Crumbs	1 cup	1 cup dry bread crumbs
Cream, Half-and-Half	1 cup	1 tablespoon melted butter plus enough whole milk to measure 1 cup
Egg	1 whole	2 egg whites *or* 2 egg yolks *or* 1/4 cup egg substitute
Flour, Cake	1 cup	1 cup minus 2 tablespoons (7/8 cup) all-purpose flour
Flour, Self-Rising	1 cup	1-1/2 teaspoons baking powder, 1/2 teaspoon salt and enough all-purpose flour to measure 1 cup
Garlic, Fresh	1 clove	1/8 teaspoon garlic powder
Gingerroot, Fresh	1 teaspoon	1/4 teaspoon ground ginger
Honey	1 cup	1-1/4 cups sugar plus 1/4 cup water
Lemon Juice	1 teaspoon	1/4 teaspoon cider vinegar
Lemon Peel	1 teaspoon	1/2 teaspoon lemon extract
Milk, Whole	1 cup	1/2 cup evaporated milk plus 1/2 cup water *or* 1 cup water plus 1/3 cup nonfat dry milk powder
Molasses	1 cup	1 cup honey
Mustard, Prepared	1 tablespoon	1/2 teaspoon ground mustard plus 2 teaspoons cider *or* white vinegar
Onion	1 small onion	1 teaspoon onion powder *or* 1 tablespoon dried minced onion (1/3 cup chopped)
Poultry Seasoning	1 teaspoon	3/4 teaspoon rubbed sage plus 1/4 teaspoon dried thyme
Sour Cream	1 cup	1 cup plain yogurt
Sugar	1 cup	1 cup packed brown sugar *or* 2 cups sifted confectioners' sugar
Tomato Juice	1 cup	1/2 cup tomato sauce plus 1/2 cup water
Tomato Sauce	2 cups	3/4 cup tomato paste plus 1 cup water
Yeast	1 package (1/4 ounce) active dry	1 cake (5/8-ounce) compressed yeast